Capital Markets Union and Beyond

Capital Markets Union and Beyond

Franklin Allen, Ester Faia, Michael Haliassos,
and Katja Langenbucher

The MIT Press
Cambridge, Massachusetts
London, England

This book was set in Times New Roman by Westchester Publishing Services, Danbury, CT.

Library of Congress Cataloging-in-Publication Data

Names: Allen, Franklin, 1956- editor.
Title: Capital markets union and beyond / [edited by] Franklin Allen, Ester Faia, Michael
  Haliassos, and Katja Langenbucher
Description: Cambridge, MA : MIT Press, [2019] | Includes bibliographical references and
  index.
Identifiers: LCCN 2018056264 | ISBN 9780262042765 (hardcover : alk. paper)
ISBN 9780262551489 (paperback)
Subjects: LCSH: Capital market--Europe. | Finance--Europe. | Monetary unions--Europe. |
  Europe--Economic integration.
Classification: LCC HG5422 .C37 2019 | DDC 332/.0415094--dc23
LC record available at https://lccn.loc.gov/2018056264

Contents

Foreword

In June 2015 the European Commission issued a plan titled "Completing Europe's Economic and Monetary Integration." The steps devised for the future development of the union foretold the creation of a financial union that included both banking and a capital market union, followed by further integration in the labor market and in the social security system, leading toward a fiscal union. The document came after years of turbulence due to the worldwide financial crisis, the euro area sovereign debt crisis, and the political tensions fostering populist movements across Europe. This document, which came fifteen years after the creation of the euro, shows not only the determination in carrying through the integration process but perhaps also the desire to increase efficiency. The US monetary union began in 1788 with the ratification of the US Constitution. The first bank in the United States was chartered in 1791 as part of Alexander Hamilton's plan to reorganize the finances of the government. The development of the banking union in the United States occurred over several years and throughout various banking and financial crises. The creation of a capital market union started only at the beginning of the nineteenth century and developed faster in the second half of the century, hence taking several decades after the creation of the monetary union. The creation of the US monetary union suffered from several costs, including a civil war, but it's largely indicated as a successful example.

The need for a capital markets union (CMU) in Europe goes beyond the historical necessities of advancing the integration process. In Europe, and contrary to Anglo-Saxon countries, firms had largely relied on the banking system. In many cases regulation prevented markets from exerting the discipline needed to contain externalities and to advance in the growth process. The advent of the 2007–2008 crisis had shown the limits of this architecture as credit supply fell, spreading the consequences of unwise investment policies to the real sector. Moreover for several decades academics have been debating about the possible distortion created by banking systems with large monopoly power, mostly for their limitation to fund innovative enterprises. The joint need of granting access to funding to citizens and firms of all European countries and of improving the efficiency and risk-sharing opportunities of the financial system at large elevated the capital market union among the priorities in the agenda of the policy makers.

This book collects contributions from academics in economics, finance, and law, as well as from policy makers and practitioners, and is aimed at fostering public debate on the design and implementation of the CMU. The four parts of the book are devoted, respectively, to the overall design challenges and background of CMU; the main targets, namely households and firms; the markets that will be involved in or directly influenced by CMU; and the role of the institutional framework in the success of CMU.

Part I describes the background to the introduction of CMU and defines key overall challenges that the design of CMU needs to meet. There is evidence that consumption risk sharing is weaker in Europe than in other advanced economies, providing fertile ground for greater openness in financial markets. Financial and economic integration have increased considerably since the introduction of the European Union, but they have not made considerable leaps following introduction of the euro. This is clearly suggested by differences in industry earnings yields among European countries from 1990 to 2016, and they are now further challenged by the fiscal and other crises faced by the Eurozone. Substantial margins with respect to financial market integration can be exploited through CMU, but this will require design breakthroughs in the economic and legal framework, well beyond the sectorial single rule book. There are interesting lessons to be learned from the origins of CMU in the United States, and these are reviewed here.

Part II describes specific opportunities and challenges for CMU to reach its target of transforming the potential of households for economic well-being and of firms for viability and profitability. Among those, perhaps the largest is the informational burden posed by the sheer scale of developments arising from a capital markets union. On the side of households, informational requirements need to be met in the face of financial illiteracy, lack of trust, and conflicts of interest in providing financial advice. With respect to firms, informational problems arise for both sides of the financing arrangement. Differential obstacles faced by core and periphery households and firms coping with the informational and other challenges of CMU should not be allowed to widen gaps in access to financing and investment opportunities. Indeed, the promotion of small and medium-sized enterprises (SMEs) is already acting as a catalyst for European capital markets law, as discussed in this part.

The role that markets, old and new, can play in the future success of CMU are studied in Part III. Developments in fintech, such as crowd funding, peer-to-peer lending, virtual funding, and online investment platforms are described and critically discussed from both an economic and a legal framework. As these markets are novel, regulation should proceed with care: it needs to be permissive so as to learn from the operation of the markets while standing ready to intervene if markets fail to protect consumers adequately. Traditional equity markets will continue to be important, especially given the large role they have already played in promoting growth of SMEs. Adequate supervisory oversight needs to be exercised for activities that are both systemic and demonstrably prone to crises, such as housing finance.

Part IV takes a close look at the state and design of institutions and governance of CMU. The role that loss of confidence played in generating the recent long-lasting recession in the European economy points to the importance of further risk reduction and risk sharing. Shadow banking will also pose significant challenges in view of interconnectedness. While not formally part of CMU, the banking system will likely undergo a transformation with a view to operating seamlessly across international borders. The political system can find in CMU a much-needed instrument for strengthening the Eurozone architecture and regaining confidence after its failure in preventing Brexit. Yet, there are choices to be made—for example, between insisting on ever more complex harmonizing rules and removing obstacles to company mobility across international borders and pan-European transactions.

The set of contributors include authors with various backgrounds and various nationalities that provide a critical view on the list of issues with the goal of informing policy makers and fostering research agendas.

This book was initially planned to go into print almost one year ago. It was delayed to monitor the events following the Brexit vote. This was unfortunate, not so much for the delay that made us think even more carefully about the issues at stake but because of the risk that the union might lose a nation that has been crucial to the creation of Europe and that could bring valuable expertise precisely on the design of financial systems (among other things). However, we have no doubt that CMU can proceed regardless of the United Kingdom's participation.

I THE CHALLENGES IN DESIGN

1 Capital Markets Union: Key Challenges

Franklin Allen and Ľuboš Pástor

As of early 2018, capital markets union (CMU) is the likely next milestone in the ongoing process of European economic integration. The plan to develop CMU was first announced by the European Commission in November 2014 as part of the Commission's Investment Plan for Europe (the "Juncker plan"). While CMU is still work in progress, various details of the plan have already emerged. This chapter's objective is to discuss the rationale behind CMU, opine on the plan's strengths and weaknesses, and identify the key challenges to the development of capital markets in Europe.

To preview our main conclusions, CMU has the potential to bring large benefits to European firms, households, and the society as a whole. Firms would benefit from an alternative source of financing that would reduce their reliance on banks. Households would benefit from new investment opportunities with an attractive risk-return trade-off. The society as a whole would benefit from a financial system that is more resilient and more conducive to innovation. The CMU plan also has some drawbacks, such as a possible reduction in the intertemporal smoothing of risk resulting from a stronger emphasis on capital markets. But we believe the benefits of the CMU plan exceed the costs. The plan's first steps, as outlined in the Commission's action plan from September 2015, are small and unlikely to yield large direct benefits. However, future steps could potentially be larger, and so could the indirect benefits of the CMU plan due to its market-driven nature. The plan focuses on harmonization and consumer protection issues. We argue that it needs to focus more on the regulation of securities markets and the enforcement of these regulations at the European level. This could be done, for example, by expanding the powers of the European Securities and Markets Authority (ESMA).

The proposal to create CMU follows the launches of two other major financial unions in Europe, namely, the monetary union in 1999 and the banking union in 2014. While the two existing unions cover only the nineteen Eurozone countries, CMU is expected to encompass the whole European Union (EU).

Unlike the monetary and banking unions, CMU does not aim to centralize policymaking; instead, it is about development and integration. CMU is also more nebulous than the monetary and banking unions. While the two unions have been carved firmly into European law, the Commission does not foresee a similar legislative standing for CMU. At this point, CMU is best thought of as a vision accompanied by an evolving plan for how to achieve it.

In this chapter, we briefly outline the plan. The next section discusses the rationale behind the plan. We then consider the plan's strengths and weaknesses. Afterward we look at the challenges to European capital markets and then conclude the chapter. The discussion of CMU here is limited in length. For an excellent full evaluation, see Valiante (2016).

The Plan

The purpose of the CMU plan is to develop and integrate European capital markets with the aim of creating a single market for capital in Europe by 2019. The vision is for all European households and firms to have equal access to markets at equal cost and equal legal treatment regardless of where they are located. The single market should cover all the EU member states and be liquid, transparent, and well regulated. When the market was proposed, it was designed for the twenty-eight member states. Now with Brexit, this will be reduced to twenty-seven states in the long run. As Brexit negotiations are ongoing, the role of the United Kingdom is unclear at this stage.

The Commission plans to build CMU gradually, following the "bottom-up" approach. There is no intention to introduce any "big bang" legislation or new EU-level institutions, such as a single regulatory body or a listing authority. Instead, the Commission plans to work slowly and patiently, identifying the many existing obstacles to the single market and removing them one by one. The hope is that the cumulative effect of many small changes will be large. An important part of the Commission's plan is to harmonize rules and standards across member states to reduce the fragmentation of European capital markets along national lines. This process will inevitably take time.

Several steps have already taken place since the original announcement of the CMU plan in late 2014. On February 18, 2015, the Commission published a Green Paper (European Commission 2015c) that presents the Commission's view of the principles, objectives, and priorities for the development of CMU. On September 30, 2015, the Commission released its action plan for building CMU (European Commission 2015a). This plan describes the specific steps to be implemented in 2015–2018. Many of these steps have already been carried out, including changes to the Prospectus Directive and new rules for both securitization and infrastructure investments by insurance companies. Regarding the Prospectus Directive, the Commission has introduced a slimmed-down digital prospectus that should make it easier and less costly for businesses to raise funds publicly. As for securitization, the Commission has created a standard template that should make securitization simpler and more transparent. In addition, the Commission has eased the capital requirements for infrastructure investments by insurance companies in an effort to promote long-term investment in European infrastructure. A new European regulatory framework for insurers, Solvency II, came into effect in January 2016. By increasing capital charges, Solvency II made it more costly for insurance companies to undertake risky investments. Given the importance of infrastructure investments for growth, the Commission has acted to offset this disincentive by creating a distinct infrastructure asset class and reducing the capital charges for investments in that class. The Commission has also launched a number of other initiatives, such as a review of venture capital fund regulation. The Commission's "Capital Markets Union: First Status Report" (European Commission 2015e), released on April 25, 2016, summarized the progress achieved on all these fronts.

The Commission's *Mid-Term Review* (European Commission 2017), released on June 8, 2017, reports a successful delivery of twenty of the thirty-three measures announced in the 2015 CMU Action Plan. The Review also sets the timeline for new actions aimed at improving capital markets supervision, reviewing the prudential treatment of investment firms, and facilitating the cross-border distribution of investment funds, among other actions. The Commission is also committed to legislative proposals delivering pan-European personal pensions, an EU framework on covered bonds, and more legal certainty for cross-border security ownership. In September 2017, the Commission proposed strengthening the powers of the European supervisory authorities. In December 2017, the Commission announced new guidelines on withholding taxes in cross-border investing and new prudential rules for investment firms.

Another important regulatory change introduced by the Commission is the Markets in Financial Instruments Directive II, which partially came into effect in January 2018. This covers all asset classes from equities to fixed income, exchange traded funds, and foreign exchange. It is designed to strengthen investor protection and improve the functioning of financial markets by making them more competitive, efficient, resilient, and transparent. Its main components involve splitting payments for analyst research and trading commissions, more pricing transparency, volume caps for equity dark pools, and more stringent standards for investment products. As of the implementation date, January 3, 2018, only eleven out of the twenty-eight member states had added the legislation to their national laws.

The Rationale

The Underdevelopment of European Capital Markets

The starting point for understanding CMU efforts is the fact that European capital markets are underdeveloped. This fact emerges clearly from a comparison to the United States. While Europe's economy is about the same size as the US economy, Europe's equity markets are less than half the size of the US equity market. Europe's corporate debt market is one third, and its venture capital industry only one fifth of the size of its US counterpart.[1] One might argue that US capital markets are particularly well developed. But comparisons with other advanced industrial countries are not especially favorable, either. For example, the EU's ratio of stock market capitalization to gross domestic product (GDP), which stood at 65% as of 2013, is small not only compared to the United States, where the ratio was 138%, but also relative to Japan (94%), Australia (87%), and China (74%). The underdevelopment of European capital markets is due in part to the fragmentation of those markets, mostly along national lines. When restricted to domestic pools of capital, markets in some countries cannot reach a minimum critical size, hampering their development. As a result, some national markets have remained quite small; for example, as of 2013, Cyprus, Latvia, Lithuania, and Slovakia all had equity markets smaller than 10% of their GDP. In contrast, the equity markets of Great Britain and Netherlands were quite large at 121% and 98% of GDP, respectively. In both of these countries, markets have strong historical traditions; in fact, they had thrived long before the US markets were even born. In contrast, strong markets have been largely absent from the histories of many other European countries. Instead of raising funds directly in markets, European firms have relied primarily on indirect financing provided by banks. While total bank assets in the United States amount to 88% of GDP, those in the EU amount to 334% of GDP as of 2013 (Langfield and Pagano 2016).

Potential Benefits of More Developed Markets

More developed capital markets would bring benefits to European firms, households, and the society as a whole.

Benefits to Firms

Firms would benefit from having an alternative source of financing that would complement their traditional reliance on banks. Such an alternative source would be particularly beneficial during banking crises, such as the one that gripped Europe at the outset of the Eurozone debt crisis. During a banking crisis, bank credit tends to be constrained as banks repair their balance sheets, making it difficult for bank-dependent firms to raise financing. In such episodes, it is essential for firms to be able to raise funds elsewhere. Capital markets are a natural alternative source. Had European capital markets been more developed, the recent economic slump in Europe could very well have been shorter lived. In comparison with Europe, the United States rebounded from its 2007–2008 financial crisis much more quickly, with growth resuming in the second half of 2009.

Firms would benefit from more developed markets not only during banking crises. The presence of a strong capital markets alternative would put competitive pressure on banks to work more efficiently and provide higher-quality services at better terms. This competition would likely result in a lower cost of financing for European firms.

Capital markets tend to be the domain of larger and more mature firms. Smaller and younger firms are more likely to borrow from banks, even in the United States, in part because banks are in a better position than markets to screen and monitor such firms (see, e.g., Boot, Greenbaum, and Thakor 2015). Nonetheless, smaller and younger firms also have a lot to gain from more developed markets in at least two ways. First, capital markets can facilitate trading and therefore also the creation of securities backed by commercial loans. Promoting securitization is indeed a big part of the Commission's CMU plan, as noted earlier. Second, capital markets, and equity markets in particular, are critical to the development of the venture capital industry in Europe. Venture capitalists need a viable exit option for their early-stage investments, and equity markets offer such an option by enabling initial public offerings (IPOs).

The last point is particularly important. Allen and Gale (1999; 2000, chap. 13) show that capital markets are better suited to financing innovation and new technologies than banks because they deal with diversity of opinion better. One of the EU's main problems is a lack of innovative firms comparable to Apple, Google, or Facebook in the United States or Alibaba, Baidu, or Tencent in China. Developing capital markets that allow IPOs should help the development of new technologies in Europe. Currently the EU is lagging behind in this regard.

As the EU emerges from the recession associated with the crisis, firms in the European periphery, mostly in southern Europe, would benefit more from developed markets than northern European firms. The latter firms do not seem to face major financing constraints at present. Those firms, along with northern European banks, are awash in cash. There is an enormous amount of excess liquidity in the Eurosystem, which comes mostly from northern European banks. This excess liquidity is sitting idle in central banks, earning a negative rate of return. Given these large cash balances, many northern European firms do not need to borrow, and those that do can do it at unusually advantageous terms. In contrast, many firms in the southern European countries with weaker banks, such as Greece, Spain, and Italy, do face significant financing constraints. In a 2014 survey, 34% of small and medium enterprises in Greece identified access to finance as their most important problem, whereas only 7% of German and Austrian firms did the same (European Commission 2015b).

Benefits to Households

Households would benefit from having a more diverse set of investment opportunities. European households have traditionally preferred to keep their financial wealth deposited in banks. Over 96% of euro-area households have bank deposits, but only 11% of them own mutual funds, 10% have direct stock investments, and 5% have direct bond investments.[2] About 43% of the households' financial assets are held in currency and deposits. Mutual funds, stocks, and bonds each account for less than 10% of household financial assets, and their combined share is less than one quarter (European Central Bank 2013). In contrast, US households hold only 13% of their financial wealth in bank deposits, and their combined holdings of mutual funds, stocks, and bonds account for about half of their financial wealth (Véron and Wolff 2015).

Given the security of bank deposits and the cost of bank intermediation, the rate of return earned by deposit holders is on average significantly lower than the returns obtained by holders of corporate bonds and especially stocks. The historical equity risk premium, which approximates the difference between the average returns on stocks and bank deposits, in Europe has been 3.4% per year between 1900 and 2014 (Dimson et al. 2015). This figure is lower than the 4.3% worldwide equity premium over the same period, perhaps due to the destruction caused by the world wars, but it is substantial. By moving some of their savings into capital markets, households could expect to earn significantly higher rates of return. Of course, there is no free lunch—in exchange for the higher return, households would have to take on some risk. But given their high levels of wealth, job security, and social welfare, Europeans are in a relatively good position to bear this risk. Many more European households should find it desirable to take on the risk associated with capital market investments.

While European households bear too little risk in one way, they bear too much risk in another. Their limited investments in capital markets exhibit a strong "home bias." For example, 64% of EU equity holdings are of domestic origin (Véron and Wolff 2015).[3] The home bias likely in part results from people's preference for familiarity (e.g., Huberman 2001), but in part also results from various barriers to cross-border investments, such as the uncertainty about legal rules associated with such investments. As a result of this home bias, household portfolios are underdiversified and overexposed to local economic shocks. Since households are already exposed to local shocks though their labor income and real estate holdings, it would make sense for them to be biased away from home rather than toward home (Baxter and Jermann 1997). Given its objective to remove the fragmentation of the national markets, CMU aims to reduce home bias and thereby improve the risk-return position of European household portfolios.

Ensuring households have access to a unified capital market would allow better diversification and thus more cross-sectional risk sharing. The current segmentation of markets combined with home bias make holding equities very risky. This could be one reason behind the conservative investment behavior of European households.

Market segmentation combined with home bias also helps us understand why European mutual funds are more numerous and smaller on average than their US counterparts. Valiante (2016) reports 32,868 mutual funds in the EU compared to 7,673 funds in the United States in 2010–2014. He also reports the average size of European mutual funds to be €186 million, far below the €1.344 billion average size of US funds. The smaller sizes of European mutual funds translate into higher average management fees paid by European households. The trade-off between fund size and fee emerges from the equilibrium setting of Pástor, Stambaugh, and Taylor (2017), in which the product of fund size and fee—fee revenue—is determined by the fund's investment skill. The same study finds strong evidence of a negative relation between fund size and fee in US data on active equity mutual funds. A transition from segmentation to a unified European capital market would benefit households by enabling funds to get larger and thus less expensive.

Benefits to Society as a Whole

The society as a whole would benefit from having a more resilient financial system. History shows that financial crises tend to be banking crises (e.g., Reinhart and Rogoff 2009). By reducing firms' and households' reliance on banks, more developed capital markets would make the economy more resilient to banking crises. With more developed markets, the European financial system would essentially be flying on two engines instead of one, resulting in more financial stability.

More developed and less fragmented capital markets could significantly increase the shock absorption capacity in Europe. Capital markets are excellent shock absorbers because they encourage broad ownership of securities, thereby improving risk sharing in the economy.[4] The impact of any given shock is spread out across many different security holders, mitigating its negative effect on the economy. This is another example of the benefits of cross-sectional risk sharing.

This simple idea applies not only to corporate securities, such as stocks and bonds, but also to sovereign debt. The debt of European sovereigns is held to a large extent by local banks—with French banks holding French government bonds, Greek banks holding Greek government bonds, and so on—creating the infamous "doom loop" between banks and sovereigns. Given the concentrated debt holdings, a potential default by a sovereign threatens to take down the country's banking system, which cannot be bailed out by the bankrupt sovereign. If sovereign debt were held more broadly by a large disperse group of market participants, the impact of a potential sovereign default would be diversified and thus smaller. A poignant example is Greece, which has teetered on the brink of default several times, most recently in 2015. European finance ministers and heads of state spent long weekends negotiating to prevent a Greek default that would have bankrupted the Greek banking system (and also caused losses to public creditors who acquired a large amount of Greek sovereign debt in the earlier stages of the crisis). Those working weekends could have been avoided if Greek debt had been held more broadly because the impact of Greek sovereign default would then have been much smaller. In the presence of developed capital markets and broad ownership of sovereign debt, sovereign default is simply less of an issue.

An efficient single capital market would improve the allocation of capital in Europe. A removal of constraints would bring the economy closer to the first-best solution that would be favored by the social planner. In an unconstrained efficient market, price signals guide the movement of capital in real time. Capital migrates from less efficient to more efficient users, resulting in faster economic growth.

Last but not least, CMU has the potential to encourage innovation in Europe, as noted earlier. Innovation is often conducted by startup companies that cannot easily borrow from a bank due to their significant risk and the lack of tangible collateral. A more natural financing vehicle for start-ups is a venture capital fund. However, the European venture capital industry is quite underdeveloped. By promoting its development, the CMU plan promotes the most effective financial backers of innovation. Unlike various government-sponsored initiatives, such as subsidies and research and development tax credits, this market-based support for innovation should not cost European taxpayers a single cent.

The Plan's Strengths and Weaknesses

The purpose of the CMU plan is to develop and integrate capital markets in Europe. The plan has many strengths. As explained in the previous section, the CMU plan is likely to bring numerous benefits to firms, households, and the society as a whole. However, the plan is not without its drawbacks. These include a possible reduction of intertemporal risk sharing and limited ambition in the supervision and enforcement of securities regulations.

The Dark Side of Capital Markets

As discussed earlier, compared to US households, European households hold a significantly smaller share of their portfolios in equities. As a result, US households' wealth is more exposed to stock market fluctuations. For example, the 1970s oil shock, which was associated with roughly a halving of stock markets in real terms, greatly affected US households but not European ones whose equity exposures were much smaller. The reverse was true in the 1980s when stock markets boomed: US households did much better than European ones. Since financial markets are supposed to provide risk-sharing benefits, this observation is something of a paradox. How can it be understood?

Traditional financial theory has little to say about hedging nondiversifiable risks. It assumes that the set of assets is given and focuses on the efficient sharing of the associated risks through exchange. For example, the standard diversification argument requires individuals to exchange assets until each individual holds a relatively small amount of any one risk. Risks are also traded so that more risk-averse people bear less risk, and vice versa. Such trading does not eliminate macroeconomic shocks, which affect all assets in a similar way. This kind of risk sharing is *cross-sectional*, because it is achieved through exchanges of risk across individuals at a given point in time.

A different type of risk sharing is based on *intertemporal smoothing* of risk. Risks that cannot be diversified at a given point in time can nevertheless be averaged over time in a way that reduces their impact on individual welfare. One hedging strategy for nondiversifiable risks is *intergenerational risk sharing*, which spreads the risks associated with a given stock of assets across generations with heterogeneous experiences. Another strategy involves *asset accumulation* to reduce fluctuations in consumption over time. Both strategies are examples of the intertemporal smoothing of asset returns.

In standard financial models with fixed asset supplies and a single time period, nondiversifiable risk is unavoidable, and someone has to bear it. Such models implicitly overlook the possibilities for intertemporal smoothing. At the other extreme, in an ideal, Arrow-Debreu-McKenzie (ADM) world, cross-sectional risk sharing and intertemporal smoothing are undertaken automatically because markets are complete and there is complete participation in them. Neither the standard financial models, which assume a fixed set of assets, nor the idealized ADM model, which does not explicitly deal with institutions, provide much insight into the relationship between the structure of a country's financial system and the stock of assets accumulated. In particular, they do not tell us how a country's reliance on financial markets or intermediaries affects its ability to smooth asset returns by changing its dynamic accumulation path. The opportunities for engaging in intertemporal smoothing may be very different in market-based and bank-based financial systems. Allen and Gale (1997; 2000, chap. 6) argue that incomplete markets do not provide for effective intertemporal smoothing but that long-lived financial institutions such as banks and insurance companies can do so, *as long as they are not subject to competition from financial markets*. Competition from financial markets can lead to the unraveling of intertemporal smoothing provided by long-lived institutions: in good times individuals would rather opt out of the banking system and invest in the market. Therefore, in the long run, intertemporal smoothing by banks is not viable in the presence of competition from markets. This is the dark side of capital markets and an argument against them.

How does intertemporal smoothing operate? In practice, markets may not be complete in the ADM sense for a variety of reasons, including moral hazard, adverse selection, transaction costs, and incomplete participation. For simplicity, Allen and Gale consider an economy with an overlapping-generation structure that results in incomplete participation by future generations. This is a tractable paradigm for the analysis of intertemporal smoothing and captures many of the features common to a wide range of models of market incompleteness. In the Allen and Gale model there are two assets: a risky asset in fixed supply and a safe asset that can be accumulated over time. Under certain conditions, the safe asset is never held in the market equilibrium as it is dominated by the risky asset. It is next shown that intertemporal smoothing can lead to a higher level of average expected utility than is possible in the market equilibrium because the safe asset is accumulated to hedge against fluctuations in the returns of the risky asset. The market equilibrium is not ex ante Pareto efficient: allocations with intertemporal smoothing that make all generations better off ex ante compared to the market equilibrium exist. This inefficiency is used to suggest that intertemporal smoothing could be implemented by long-lived intermediaries. One interpretation of the bank-dominated financial system in most of the EU is that it has the advantages of intertemporal smoothing. These will be lost when CMU is implemented.

The Enforcement of Securities Regulations

The second major issue with the CMU plan is that it does not properly address the important issue of securities regulations and their enforcement. In the 1930s the United States passed a series of securities regulation acts that set up the Securities and Exchange Commission (SEC) and prohibited many market abuses. These include insider trading, market manipulation, the provision of misleading accounting statements, and so forth. These changes in the law underlay the significant expansion in the securities markets that occurred after World War II. Much of Europe only adopted these kinds of regulations in the 1980s and 1990s, and their enforcement remains limited. This is one possible reason why capital markets are smaller than in the United States.

An interesting example is Germany. The EU's largest economy, it is very much a bank-based economy whose securities markets are much smaller than in the United States. Allen et al. (2018) document the development of securities law in Germany and point to the Volkswagen (VW) short squeeze in 2008 as an example of the problems that lack of enforcement can lead to.

US-style securities law to protect investors did not exist in Germany until the mid-1990s. Before then, the rules and regulations concerning the issuance and trading of securities were scattered across various parts of the law, particularly in stock corporation law, securities exchange law, and banking law. Market manipulation is now part of the Securities Trading Act, the Market Manipulation Definition Regulation (or WertpapierHandelsGesetz), and MakonV (or Verordnung zur Konkretisierung des Verbotes der Marktmanipulation). According to Section 20a of German securities law, an intentional false statement about a fact significant to the valuation of a security, as well as any other deliberate deceptive measure that influences the valuation, is punishable as a criminal act.

La Porta et al. (1997) (LLSV) gave Germany a score of only one out of five possible points on an aggregated index of shareholder protection. This was less than the score for the United States (5.0) and the United Kingdom (5.0); less than the average score of the forty-nine countries considered (3.0); and less even than the scores for Thailand (2.0), Greece (2.0), or Ecuador (2.0). In 2015, the World Bank's International Finance Corporation's *Doing Business* report that follows the revised LLSV methodology of Djankov et al. (2008) ranked Germany as 103rd of 189 countries for investor protection between the Dominican Republic and Kenya (World Bank Group 2018). So the level of investor protection has been poor and does not seem to have improved much in the last twenty years.

Enforcement of securities laws is carried out by the German equivalent of the SEC, known as the Bundesanstalt für Finanzdienstleistungsaufsicht (BaFin). BaFin is a federal institution governed by public law and is affiliated with Germany's Federal Ministry of Finance. Under the Securities Trading Act, BaFin investigates all possible cases of market manipulation and monitors the collection and evaluation of all securities and derivatives transactions. If a case of market abuse or manipulation is suspected, BaFin has to pass the case on to a public prosecutor, who may (or may not) conduct further investigations and criminal prosecution. The lack of enforcement powers on the part of BaFin has long been criticized, and it is cited by Nowak (2004) as the reason why there have been so few insider trading prosecutions to date. For market manipulation cases from 2013 to 2015, BaFin started 698 investigations and passed 458 cases to public prosecutors (*BaFin Annual Report* 2015). Of those, only fourteen final judgments were made with a conviction following a full public trial. The prosecutors turned all the other cases down or settled them with down payments or administrative fines, so the risk of being convicted of market manipulation in Germany—conditional on having been investigated by BaFin—is only 2%. BaFin does not mention any incidents of short squeezes or corners as special cases of market abuse in their annual reports.

On Friday, October 24, 2008, VW's stock price closed at €210 per share. On Sunday, October 26, Porsche issued a press release concerning their holdings of VW stock. That Monday, the share price for VW rose dramatically. This continued on Tuesday, October 28, when the price rose above €1,005 per share. As a result, VW briefly became the most valuable company in the world by market capitalization. Allen et al. (2018) argue that Porsche had an incentive to create a short squeeze to drive up the price and save Porsche from bankruptcy because they were attempting to take over VW, and the financial crisis had caused prices to move against them. Moreover, Allen et al. argue that the release did in fact lead to a short squeeze that benefited Porsche. The evidence consists of the movement of the price and its volatility in the two trading days following the announcement. Also, the fact that a Porsche press release issued on Wednesday, October 29, stating that they would increase liquidity in the market by making available 5% of Volkswagen shares, was followed by a fall in the price is evidence of a short squeeze in the previous two days. In the case of the Porsche announcement of October 26, 2008, BaFin first started investigations of market manipulation and then dropped those charges, only to later pass the case to the public prosecution office in Stuttgart where Porsche is headquartered. The chief executive officer and chief financial officer were acquitted in this criminal trial as the standard of proof required in these cases is very high. A civil suit is still under way.

The overall effect of the short squeeze was that Porsche benefited by several billion euros while arbitrageurs lost much more. The long-term impact of incidents of this kind is to make potential market participants wary of entering markets that may be manipulated when there is little chance of the manipulators being punished.

This example is only one illustration. Christiansen, Hail, and Leuz (2016) examine the enforcement of securities regulations in EU countries. They find that stricter implementation leads to larger increases in market liquidity. However, countries with initially weaker regulation do not converge to stronger countries. The effect of harmonizing regulation is that weak and strong countries diverge.

All this suggests that securities regulation enforcement needs to be done at the EU level if an effective CMU is to be implemented.

A closely related issue is fragmented supervision. The original CMU plan does not envision an EU-level supervisory body for the single capital market. This intention is in marked contrast to the recent developments on the banking side of the financial sector. As a part of the creation of the banking union, the Single Supervisory Mechanism was launched in November 2014 to supervise all large banks in the euro area. Without a similar arrangement on the capital market side, the single market will never be truly single. Even if all rules were perfectly harmonized across member states, national supervisors could take different attitudes toward enforcement. For example, some local supervisors could face political pressure to take a relaxed approach in an effort to promote national champions. The resulting non-level playing field could undermine the future of the single market.

To mitigate concerns about regulatory arbitrage and political entrenchment, some policy centralization would be useful. Such centralization would also facilitate policy integration with the highly centralized banking union in areas of common interest such as accounting and auditing (Véron 2014). The simplest way to achieve more centralization would be to expand the powers of ESMA. In September 2017, in a significant step along these lines, the Commission proposed extending ESMA's modest supervisory powers to several additional areas of capital markets, such as capital market data and market abuse cases. A more ambitious approach would establish ESMA as the single supervisor enforcing a single rule book that covers all areas of capital markets. Among other potential advantages, a single rule book would be able to respond to financial innovation faster than twenty-eight national regulators. The absence of a single supervisor from the CMU plan seems motivated by the Commission's desire to find the path of least political resistance. It remains to be seen whether this issue will be addressed in the future.

Bottom-Up versus Top-Down Approach

The institution of a single supervisor would be an example of top-down policy centralization that is not envisioned by the Commission in its original plan. As noted earlier, the Commission plans to follow a bottom-up approach by working patiently to identify and remove obstacles to the single market. The implementation of this approach is likely to take a long time. Moreover, the first steps of this approach, as revealed in the Commission's 2015 action plan, were not very ambitious. Those steps included simplifying the prospectus, standardizing securitization, and reversing a small part of new restrictive regulations (Solvency II). These are three steps in the right direction, but they are quite small. For comparison, imagine North Korea trying to promote tourism by simplifying the tourist visa application, standardizing tourist visits, and canceling future plans to double the visa fee. While these steps would be helpful, they would make little difference if few people wanted to visit North Korea in the first place. We believe that the Commission's approach would benefit from adding some top-down elements.

The strong preference for a bottom-up approach in the Commission's plan is a legacy of the British influence. Until the Brexit vote in June 2016, Britain had been the driving force behind the CMU project. But the day after the vote, Jonathan Hill, Britain's EU commissioner in charge of the financial services portfolio, resigned. While the British departure is a major loss for the CMU project, there is also a silver lining in the form of an opportunity to make the project more ambitious by adding some top-down elements.

Pan-European Private Pensions

A top-down approach will certainly be necessary to push through one of the Commission's ideas that we find particularly valuable—that of pan-European portable private pensions. The introduction of such pensions would have at least four major benefits. First, it would promote the growth of private pension funds and pension savings more generally. Since pension funds are key players in capital markets, their growth would contribute to the development of European capital markets. Scharfstein (2018), for example, argues that policies that promote pension savings also promote the development of capital markets. Second, a pan-European portable private pension scheme would educate Europeans about capital markets. There is no better way of educating people about markets than by giving them choices and letting their pension balances fluctuate as a result of their choices and market movements. A population well versed in markets is a prerequisite for CMU.

We list these two benefits of private pensions first because they contribute to the achievement of CMU. While the third and fourth benefits are unrelated to CMU, they are arguably even more important for Europe's future. Third, pan-European private pensions would help facilitate labor mobility in Europe. The relative rigidity of labor within Europe is one of the main reasons why Europe does not constitute an optimal currency area (Mundell 1961). Free labor movement across EU countries would help smooth out asymmetric shocks hitting these countries. In theory, people are free to move, yet in practice they move little. This rigidity has many reasons that are beyond the control of policymakers, such as family ties, cultural differences, and language barriers. But another reason, which is under the policymakers' control, is that pension systems in Europe continue to operate on a national basis, complicating the lives of cross-border migrants. With pan-European portable private pensions, any EU citizen would retain the same pension account with the same rules for access and contributions after moving from one European country to another. Fourth, private pensions would help solve the demographic problem in Europe. Given the well-known demographic trends, the pay-as-you-go systems of most European countries are not sustainable in the present form. Since pensions are a national competence, the creation of pan-European portable pensions would require top-down legislation at the European level.

Harmonizing Rules and Standards

The Commission plans to eliminate the fragmentation of European capital markets by harmonizing rules and standards across EU member states. The national rules concerning insolvency, accounting, and taxes vary significantly across countries. This variation hinders cross-border investment by making it hard for investors to fully assess the risks they are taking on. The creation of a single rulebook would in principle solve the problem, but its implementation will be difficult because it involves areas in which national governments tenaciously guard their own policymaking powers. Harmonizing the rules of twenty-eight countries (twenty-seven after Brexit)—rules that may have complex connections and interactions with other national rules—could take a long time and potentially even prove infeasible. After all, discussions of rule harmonization have been going on for years with limited success.

While the harmonization of national rules is a worthwhile long-term goal, a useful intermediate step would be to clarify and to clearly publicize which country's rules apply in what situation. If a German buys shares in a Dutch company that is listed in London, and the company goes bankrupt, which country's rules govern the insolvency proceedings? If investors are uncertain about the answer, they will be reluctant to invest outside their home country. Removing this uncertainty by publishing simple and clear guidelines could achieve a significant part of the benefits of full harmonization in a much shorter period of time. Alternatively, one could create a special Europe-level regime (the "29th regime") for rules that are particularly difficult to harmonize, such as corporate insolvency. The 29th regime could be optional, irrevocably chosen at the time of issuance (Brühl et al. 2015).

Unequal Levels of Market Development

The discussion of CMU often highlights the unequal levels of development of capital markets across EU member states. While countries such as Great Britain, Luxembourg, the Netherlands, and Sweden are among the world's leaders in capital market development, others such as Latvia and Slovakia have markets of negligible size, even relative to the size of their economies. However, it is not clear that this unequal development presents a major problem.

Once a true single capital market in Europe is created, it will not matter that capital market institutions in, say, Slovakia are underdeveloped. A Slovakian firm looking to raise funds will be able to list on any European exchange, and a Slovakian household looking to invest will be able to do so via any European investment fund. Such cross-border access has been possible to some extent for years—after all, free flow of capital is one of the fundamental principles of the EU—but local firms tend to enjoy a cost advantage. Once the single market is built, there will be no a priori reason for capital market institutions to be located in each member state, although there will remain some role for local firms to provide local advice in the local language about how to access the pan-European market.

Taking Stock

To summarize, while the CMU plan has both strengths and weaknesses, we believe its strengths prevail. The benefits related to cross-sectional risk sharing and particularly innovation seem very valuable. The possible reduction in intertemporal smoothing is a drawback that is mitigated to some extent by pay-as-you-go pension schemes. The lack of implementation and enforcement of securities regulation at the EU level can be addressed in the coming years.

The plan's first steps, as outlined in the Commission's action plan from September 2015, are relatively modest. As a result, the direct benefits from implementing those steps are likely to be modest as well. But future steps, such as the creation of pan-European private pensions, might be more ambitious.

In addition to its direct benefits, the CMU plan could also potentially yield a large indirect benefit. By launching CMU, the Commission is sending a clear pro-market signal, effectively announcing "we are open for business." This is a welcome change of tone in the public discourse. Ever since the eruption of the financial crisis in 2007–2008, the public debate has focused on additional regulation needed to prevent future financial crises. While new regulation may prevent crises, it will not boost growth; in fact, it often has the opposite effect. To restart growth in Europe, we need market-driven solutions. In that sense, CMU is one of the most enlightened goals of the current European policy.

Challenges to European Capital Markets

The CMU plan represents a strong boost to the development of European capital markets. However, these markets currently face several major headwinds whose combined negative effect could potentially outweigh the positive effect of CMU. These headwinds include, but are not limited to, the proposed financial transactions tax, the low-interest-rate environment, cultural reasons, and potential political opposition.

The Financial Transactions Tax

A major threat to the development of European capital markets is the financial transactions tax (FTT) proposed by the European Commission in September 2011. The Commission's proposal calls for a 0.1% tax on transactions in stocks and bonds and a 0.01% tax on derivatives transactions, excluding activities such as raising capital, restructuring operations, and European Central Bank refinancing transactions. According to the Commission, the objectives of the FTT are to make the financial sector pay for the cost of the crisis, disincentivize excessive trading, and avoid the development of an uncoordinated patchwork of national FTTs. The FTT is not yet in place as of this writing. Its introduction, originally planned for January 2014, has been postponed several times due to continuing negotiations on fundamental issues such as what instruments to cover, how to collect the tax revenue, and whether to tax market-making activities. As of January 2018, the FTT is supported in principle by ten of the twenty-eight EU countries, including Germany, France, Italy, Spain, and six smaller countries. But the progress stalled recently due to the ongoing Brexit negotiations. The big players seem reluctant to move forward with the tax while they are trying to attract financial institutions looking to leave London. The imposition of the tax could undermine these efforts to the benefit of countries such as Ireland and Luxembourg, which are also courting UK-located banks but are not among the ten countries pursuing the FTT.

The FTT has always been popular among some politicians. The idea of having the financial sector pay appeals to many voters, making the FTT a "perennial populist favorite" (Geithner 2014). While the broader merits of the FTT are debatable, its effects on market liquidity seem clear. Imposing the FTT in some European countries would make trading in those countries less attractive. Some trading would inevitably migrate elsewhere, reducing the liquidity of what are already fairly illiquid markets. The lower liquidity would weaken capital markets and raise the cost of capital for European firms.

The FTT proposal highlights an apparent ambivalence of the Commission toward capital markets. On the one hand, the Commission is promoting the CMU whose introduction would clearly strengthen capital markets. On the other hand, it is promoting the FTT whose introduction would weaken the same markets. This approach is akin to saying, "We want to promote [European] football. We also want a new rule that says every time you kick the ball, you pay one euro." This ambivalence is likely to be driven by political considerations.

Low Interest Rates

The European economic landscape in early 2018 is characterized by exception-ally low interest rates. Since 2015, the sovereign debt of many European countries has been trading at negative yields, especially at short maturities. The potential reasons behind the low rates, such as demographic forces and monetary policy, are the subject of ongoing debates among economists. Whatever the reasons, the ultralow interest rates have unfavorable implications for European capital markets. They create problems for pension funds and mutual funds—institutions that are central to the development of capital markets.

Defined-benefit pension funds tend to have long-term liabilities with bond-like features. Many pension funds find it prudent to hedge those liabilities by purchasing long-term bonds. Given the ultralow bond yields, the future returns of pension fund portfolios are likely to be low. Defined-contribution pension funds also hold substantial bond positions so they, too, are likely to deliver low returns going forward. The poor performance of funded pension schemes can make those schemes look unappealing, leading to further entrenchment of the pay-as-you-go pension schemes that are so popular in continental Europe. The low returns of private pension funds make it easy for myopic politicians to tell their voters: "Look, private pensions are not working. We need to stick to pay-as-you-go." The absence of a robust private pension fund sector is a major impediment to the development of European capital markets.

Mutual funds, especially those investing in fixed-income securities, face the same problem. Therefore, European deposit-hoarding households might be reluctant to migrate to mutual funds or other capital market vehicles. Those households can be forgiven for asking: "If I can earn zero return on my insured bank deposit and zero return in a mutual fund, why should I switch to a mutual fund?"

Knowledge and Culture

Financial knowledge among Europeans is imperfect, in part due to the lack of experience with financial markets.[5] This fact might play a role in explaining the reluctance of European firms to access capital markets as well as the preference of European households for insured bank deposits over uninsured stock and bond investments. Europeans' suspicion toward markets could also reflect fundamental values and traditions. For example, the competitive nature of markets could be perceived by some as being at odds with the widely cherished European social model. The strong home bias observed in Europe could have a component related to the continent's troubled history. Culture and the lack of financial knowledge are likely to represent "soft" barriers to the development of European capital markets. Overcoming these deep-rooted barriers will take years of patient education and trust building. For example, to build up households' appetite for equity investments, it will be necessary to ingrain in the public mind the idea of the equity risk premium. To overcome home bias, it will be necessary to popularize the benefits of international diversification.

Home bias is found not only among the general public but also among relatively sophisticated investors, including institutions.[6] Some of these investors might be discouraged from investing abroad because they are unsure about which country's insolvency, tax, and accounting rules apply to such investments. Clearly publicizing the rules of the game in cross-border investment could help reduce home bias in Europe.[7]

Political Support

Ever since its launch in early 2015, the CMU project has enjoyed solid political support. This support is most likely due to the inherent quality of the project and perhaps also due to the nonconfrontational, bottom-up approach chosen by the Commission. At some point, though, political opposition might emerge.

This opposition could very well come from institutions with vested interests, such as banks or organizations providing local market infrastructure. Like any other reform, CMU will produce not only winners but also losers, especially in the short run. Even if there are many more winners, the losers tend to organize and speak with a loud voice.

Who will lose from CMU in the longer term? The creation of a true single capital market, if successful, will result in a more efficient allocation of capital across Europe. The losers will thus be inefficient users of both public and private capital. These users will lose a long-standing comfortable source of domestic capital that will now be able to flow elsewhere in pursuit of better investment opportunities. To identify the losers more precisely, we only need to wait and see where the future opposition to CMU comes from.

Political opposition could also come from other directions. For example, it could arise from national squabbles about supervision. Another important threat is the recent rise of populism in Europe, which questions the whole idea of European integration. If Europe manages to overcome these challenges, it will take another major step forward in its economic development.

Concluding Remarks

In this chapter, we have argued that while CMU features significant trade-offs, overall it is a good policy that deserves to be pursued vigorously. There are large potential benefits from cross-sectional risk sharing and innovation as well as benefits from diversifying funding sources beyond banks. There are also drawbacks, however. Intertemporal risk sharing may be reduced. This problem can be countered to some extent with appropriate government policies. In addition, the current proposals focus too much on the investor side and too little on effective securities regulation. This drawback can be solved by expanding the powers of ESMA. Finally, a number of other factors, such as the FTT, act as headwinds to CMU. The Commission and member governments need to think carefully about how to counteract these factors.

Notes

The authors' views are their own and not of the institutions they are affiliated with. Pástor is grateful to the Brevan Howard Center at Imperial College London for its hospitality during his visit when the first draft of this chapter was written. For helpful comments, we thank Christian Leuz, Martin Šuster, Diego Valiante (our discussant), and participants at the first and second conferences on CMU at Imperial College in 2016 and 2018.

1. See, for example, European Commission (2015b, 2015d); Véron and Wolff (2015).

2. See European Central Bank (2013). In Greece, Portugal, and Slovakia, more than 90% of households report no holdings of mutual funds, stocks, or bonds.

3. For early empirical evidence of home bias, see French and Poterba (1991). For an optimal portfolio choice perspective on home bias, see Pástor (2000). For recent evidence on home bias in European portfolios, see Schoenmaker and Soeter (2014).

4. For recent evidence on imperfect risk sharing in Europe, see Furceri and Zdzienicka (2015). The authors show that risk sharing in the euro area is significantly less effective than in the United States and that its effectiveness falls sharply during severe downturns. For a broader discussion of the implications of CMU for financial stability, see Anderson et al. (2015).

5. For examples of evidence, see the surveys cited by European Commission (2015b), 44–45.

6. For example, as of 2014, euro-area equity mutual funds hold about 13% of their assets in domestic stocks (Kaya 2015). This fraction may not seem large, but it is much larger than any euro-area country's share of the global stock market capitalization, often by an order of magnitude. The home bias among European institutional investors has declined since 2000 when the same fraction was 29%, perhaps due to the elimination of the exchange rate risk within the euro area after the introduction of the euro.

7. Uncertainty about the rules of the game has real effects that include discouraging investment. See, for example, Julio and Yook (2012); Fernández-Villaverde et al. (2015). This uncertainty also has financial effects, such as higher risk premiums (Pástor and Veronesi 2012, 2013).

References

Allen, Franklin, and Douglas Gale. 1997. "Financial Markets, Intermediaries, and Intertemporal Smoothing." *Journal of Political Economy* 105: 523–546.

Allen, Franklin, and Douglas Gale. 1999. "Diversity of Opinion and the Financing of New Technologies." *Journal of Financial Intermediation* 8: 68–89.

Allen, Franklin, and Douglas Gale. 2000. *Comparing Financial Systems.* Cambridge, MA: MIT Press.

Allen, Franklin, Marlene Haas, Eric Nowak, and Angel Tengulov. 2018. "Market Efficiency and Limits to Arbitrage: Evidence from the Volkswagen Short Squeeze." Working paper, Imperial College London and SSRN.

Anderson, Niki, Martin Brooke, Michael Hume, and Miriam Kürtösiová. 2015. "A European Capital Markets Union: Implications for Growth and Stability." Bank of England Financial Stability Paper 33, February.

BaFin Annual Report. 2015. Bonn: German Federal Financial Supervisory Authority.

Baxter, Marianne, and Urban J. Jermann. 1997. "The International Diversification Puzzle Is Worse than You Think." *American Economic Review* 87: 170–180.

Boot, Arnoud, Stuart Greenbaum, and Anjan Thakor. 2015. *Contemporary Financial Intermediation.* Waltham, MA: Academic Press.

Brühl, Volker, Helmut Gründl, Andreas Hackethal, Hans-Helmut Kotz, Jan Pieter Krahnen, and Tobias Tröger. 2015. "Comments on the EU Commission's Capital Markets Union Project." SAFE White Paper 27, Universitätsbibliothek Johann Christian Senckenberg.

Christiansen, Hans B., Luzi Hail, and Christian Leuz. 2016. "Capital-Market Effects of Securities Regulation: Prior Conditions, Implementation, and Enforcement." Working paper, University of Chicago.

Dimson, Elroy, Paul Marsh, Mike Staunton, David Holland, Bryant Matthews, and Pratyasha Rath. 2015. *Credit Suisse Global Investment Returns Yearbook.* Zurich: Credit Suisse AG.

Djankov, S., F. Lopez de Silanes, R. La Porta, and A. Shleifer. 2008. "The Law and Economics of Self-Dealing." *Journal of Financial Economics* 88, no. 3: 430–465.

European Central Bank (ECB). 2013. "The Eurosystem Household Finance and Consumption Survey: Results for the First Wave." Frankfurt am Main: ECB, April.

European Commission. 2015a. "Action Plan on Building a Capital Markets Union." Communication from the Commission to the European Parliament, the Council, the European Economic and Social Committee, and the Committee of the Regions, COM (2015) 468, September 30.

European Commission. 2015b. "Feedback Statement on the Green Paper 'Building a Capital Markets Union.'" Staff Working Document SWD (2015) 184 accompanying the Action Plan, September 30.

European Commission. 2015c. "Green Paper: Building a Capital Markets Union." Green paper, COM (2015) 63, February 18.

European Commission. 2015d. "Staff Working Document SWD (2015) 13 accompanying the Green Paper," February 18.

European Commission. 2015e. "Capital Markets Union: First Status Report." Staff Working Document SWD (2016) 147, April 25.

European Commission. 2017. *Mid-Term Review of the Capital Markets Union Action Plan.* Brussels: European Union, COM (2017) 292 final, June. https://ec.europa.eu/info/publications/mid-term -review-capital-markets-union-action-plan_en.

Fernández-Villaverde, Jesús, Pablo Guerrón-Quintana, Keith Kuester, and Juan Rubio-Ramírez. 2015. "Fiscal Volatility Shocks and Economic Activity." *American Economic Review* 105: 3352–3384.

French, Kenneth R., and James M. Poterba. 1991. "Investor Diversification and International Equity Markets." *American Economic Review* 81: 222–226.

Furceri, Davide, and Aleksandra Zdzienicka. 2015. "The Euro Area Crisis: Need for a Supranational Fiscal Risk Sharing Mechanism?" *Open Economies Review* 26: 683–710.

Geithner, Timothy. 2014. *Stress Test: Reflections on Financial Crises.* New York: Random House.

Huberman, Gur. 2001. "Familiarity Breeds Investment." *Review of Financial Studies* 14: 659–680.

Julio, Brandon, and Youngsuk Yook. 2012. "Corporate Financial Policy under Political Uncertainty: International Evidence from National Elections." *Journal of Finance* 67: 45–83.

Kaya, Orcun. 2015. "Capital Markets Union." Deutsche Bank Research, November 2.

Langfield, Sam, and Marco Pagano. 2016. "Bank Bias in Europe: Effects on Systemic Risk and Growth." *Economic Policy* 31, no. 85: 51–106.

La Porta, R., F. Lopez-de Silanes, A. Shleifer, and R. W. Vishny. 1997. "Legal Determinants of External Finance." *Journal of Finance* 52: 1131–1150.

Mundell, Robert A. 1961. "A Theory of Optimum Currency Areas." *American Economic Review* 51: 657–665.

Nowak, E. 2004. *"Investor Protection and Capital Market Regulation in Germany."* In *The German Financial System,* edited by J. Krahnen and R. Schmidt, 425–449. Oxford: Oxford University Press.

Pástor, Luboš. 2000. "Portfolio Selection and Asset Pricing Models." *Journal of Finance* 55: 179–223.

Pástor, Luboš, Robert F. Stambaugh, and Lucian A. Taylor. 2017. "Fund Tradeoffs." NBER Working Paper 23670, National Bureau of Economic Research.

Pástor, Luboš, and Pietro Veronesi. 2012. "Uncertainty about Government Policy and Stock Prices." *Journal of Finance* 67: 1219–1264.

Pástor, Luboš, and Pietro Veronesi. 2013. "Political Uncertainty and Risk Premia." *Journal of Financial Economics* 110: 520–545.

Reinhart, Carmen, and Kenneth Rogoff. 2009. *This Time Is Different: Eight Centuries of Financial Folly*. Princeton, NJ: Princeton University Press.

Scharfstein, David S. 2018. "Presidential Address: Pension Policy and the Financial System." *Journal of Finance* 73: 1463–1512.

Schoenmaker, Dirk, and Chiel Soeter. 2014. "New Evidence on the Home Bias in European Investment." DSF Policy Brief 34, Duisenberg School of Finance, September.

Valiante, Diego. 2016. *Europe's Untapped Capital Market: Rethinking Financial Integration after the Crisis*. Brussels: CEPS; London: Rowman and Littlefield. www.ceps.eu/system/files/Capital%20 Markets%20Union_1.pdf.

Véron, Nicolas. 2014. "Defining Europe's Capital Markets Union." Policy Contribution 2014/12, Bruegel.

Véron, Nicolas, and Guntram B. Wolff. 2015. "Capital Markets Union: A Vision for the Long Term." Policy Contribution 2015/5, Bruegel.

World Bank Group. 2018. *Doing Business 2018: Reforming to Create Jobs*. Washington, DC: International Bank for Reconstruction and Development/The World Bank. http://www.doingbusiness .org/content/dam/doingBusiness/media/Annual-Reports/English/DB2018-Full-Report.pdf.

Discussion: Capital Markets Union and Europe's Financial Structure

Diego Valiante

Franklin Allen and Ľuboš Pástor's chapter offers an interesting summary of the lights and shadows of a capital markets union (CMU) in the European context. I would like to dwell more on the risk-sharing nature of capital markets and the challenge posed by its very nature for European policies, according to Allen and Pástor.

The 2008 financial crisis caused a significant drop in gross domestic product in many European countries, along with a massive increase of unemployment rates and widespread losses in the financial system. Due to recapitalizations and additional losses caused by foregone growth potentials, the ensuing banking crisis left many parts of Europe's economy, especially small and medium-sized enterprises, with limited access to finance. Disorderly government interventions, in turn, came at a cost of a massive capital flow retrenchment in the banking groups' original countries after the unfettered expansion via interbank financial flows in the years before.

The lack of capital flow diversification was therefore (and still is) a core reason of financial instability and, at the same time, a big constraint on Europe's economic recovery. Europe faced poor intertemporal risk sharing via traditional institution-based credit markets and an even scarcer cross-sectional risk sharing that capital markets' risk dispersion can offer. Capital markets union came about to complement the pan-European intertemporal risk-sharing component (developed via the banking union project) with the cross-sectional risk sharing offered by capital markets.

Allen and Pástor's argument about crowding out risks that capital markets' cross-sectional risk sharing might have on intertemporal risk sharing and its safe asset accumulation in good times is a valid one, but the role of frictions in the intermediation channel (such as the limited supply of safe assets or cognitive biases in investors' behaviors) may actually be underestimated when expressing their preference for intertemporal risk sharing. Some important developments in the empirical literature on financial integration of recent years also show the complementarity of both risk-sharing mechanisms.

But let us go step by step.

The risk-sharing role of financial markets is an old debate (Arrow 1964), but the relationship between cross-sectional and intertemporal risk sharing in determining the optimal financial structure of a given economy is a more recent discussion (Allen and Gale 1995, 2000). Levine (2002) argues for a "neutrality view"—in other words, that neither banks nor markets are individually superior to achieve growth. More specifically, the balance among institution and market-based funding (financial structure) is intrinsically related to the level of economic development (Boot and Thakor 1997). A bank-based system would provide a more important contribution in less developed economies and vice versa. However, as for the fallacy in the Modigliani-Miller theorem about the irrelevance of the capital structure, the financial structure of an economy does also depend on the right balance among its different components. The claim that one would de facto crowd out the other assumes away the frictions that make the two types of risk sharing work better in some kind of combination.

In the post-crisis period, several studies have suggested that the pendulum in Europe is by far leaning on the side of the intertemporal risk sharing (among others, ESRB 2014). It is also easy to argue that the form of intertemporal risk sharing is very poor. The absence of a truly European safe asset, combined with a banking integration led by interbank market activities, makes Europe's financial system even more vulnerable. There is a parabolic relationship between credit (intertemporal risk sharing) and growth (Cecchetti and Karrhoubi 2012, 2015) that can also be seen by using a rough ratio of intertemporal over cross-sectional risk sharing (as Langfield and Pagano 2016 did). Cross-sectional risk sharing is therefore in great need in Europe. It is a better tool to fund innovation as it spreads the high risk across multiple agents and scores better in funding illiquid projects that can have long-lasting positive effects on total factor productivity (Giordano and Guagliano 2016).

As a result, CMU could be a formidable tool to rebalance Europe's financial structure with stronger private risk-sharing mechanisms. Capital market instruments, such as equity and debt instruments, are legal structures that operate with smaller cost structure for intermediaries (agent models) than intertemporal risk-sharing instruments (like traditional loans). Therefore, policies to develop the necessary economies of scale for such risk-sharing channels have to remove most of the transaction costs that are not foreseeable ex ante and thus cannot be priced in market prices or internalized by a heavy cost structure. Nonprice barriers can take different forms, but they mostly affect three areas in a pan-

European context: cross-border comparability and availability of information flows; costs of access to the execution infrastructure (competition); and enforcement of contracts and rules. A successful CMU would be one that is able to deliver on these three fronts. Therefore, it should be expected that policy actions be subject to constant reviews to adapt the level of ambition to the evolving circumstances.

Note

The views expressed here are personal and do not necessarily reflect those of the European Commission. The author wishes to thank Franklin Allen and Ľuboš Pástor for the interesting discussions and comments that led to this commentary on their work.

References

Allen, F., and D. Gale. 1995. "A Welfare Comparison of Intermediaries and Financial Markets in Germany and the US." *European Economic Review* 39: 179–209.

Allen, F., and D. Gale. 2000. *Comparing Financial Systems*. Cambridge, MA: MIT Press.

Arrow, K. 1964. "The Role of Securities in the Optimal Allocation of Risk Bearing." *Review of Economic Studies* 31: 91–96.

Boot, W. A. A., and A. Thakor. 1997. "Financial System Architecture." *Review of Financial Studies* 10, no. 3: 693–733.

Cecchetti, S. G., and E. Kharroubi. 2012. "Reassessing the Impact of Finance on Growth." BIS Working Papers No. 381, July.

Cecchetti, S. G., and E. Kharroubi. 2015. "Why Does Financial Sector Growth Crowd out Real Economic Growth?" BIS Working Papers No. 490, February.

European Systemic Risk Board (ESRB). 2014. "Is Europe Overbanked?" Report of the Advisory Scientific Committee no. 4, June.

Giordano, L., and C. Guagliano. 2016. "The Impact of Financial Architecture on Technical Innovation." *Applied Economics and Finance* 3, no. 3 (August). https://www.researchgate.net/publication/303974584_The_Impact_of_Financial_Architecture_on_Technical_Innovation.

Langfield, S., and M. Pagano. 2016. "Bank Bias in Europe: Effects on Systemic Risk and Growth." *Economic Policy* 31, no. 85: 51–106.

Levine, R. 2002. "Bank-Based or Market-Based Financial Systems: Which Is Better?" *Journal of Financial Intermediation* 11: 398–428.

Valiante, D. 2016. *Europe's Untapped Capital Market: Rethinking Financial Integration after the Crisis*. Brussels: CEPS; London: Rowman & Littlefield.

2 Capital Markets Union and Cross-Border Risk Sharing

Claudia M. Buch and Franziska Bremus

Financial crises have many things in common and yet hold their specific lessons. Levels of debt that become inconsistent with underlying fundamentals are a common trigger of financial crises. Economic history is rich with examples, not least of which is the Asian financial crisis of the late 1990s. As a result of a new mix of policies that focus on realigning macroeconomic policies and correct misaligned incentives in banking systems, growth has resumed in the countries affected by the Asian crisis. The structure of cross-border capital flows has shifted from short-term debt flows toward equity and foreign direct investment (FDI).[1]

Only a decade later, the perils of overborrowing occurred in a different disguise in the advanced economies. Europe has been one of the epicenters. Domestic credit growth has often been excessive, and banks rapidly increased lending across borders prior to the crisis. The complexity of financial transactions increased due to the use of derivatives, and the international allocation of risks was distorted, thus eventually leading to a repricing of assets and a meltdown of markets.

Many important lessons have been learned. At the international level, reforms of the financial sector focus on increased resilience—in particular, through higher levels of capital and reduced risk-taking incentives—on reforming derivatives markets and on a better surveillance of shadow banking activities. Progress to date is monitored by the Financial Stability Board (FSB), and first reform elements are undergoing a structured evaluation (FSB 2018).

At the European level, two major reform projects have been started. The Banking Union focuses on banks. It aims at reducing incentives for risk taking and risk shifting through centralizing supervision of banks, at ensuring common supervisory standards, and at establishing mechanisms of dealing with banks under distress. The capital markets union (CMU) goes one step further and addresses the overall structure of European financial systems. In a nutshell, the CMU project starts from the observation that many important channels for growth and risk sharing remain unexploited. It thus aims to remove frictions for the development and integration of resilient financial markets. This chapter focuses on the main motivation of the CMU to rebalance financing through debt and equity and to improve risk sharing.

First, we compare financial structures for the pre- and the post-crisis period, and we examine how these are related to changes in institutions and regulations. The goal is to get an idea about how the potential of institutional adjustments, as envisaged in the realm of the CMU, affects financial development. We find that, with regard to the composition of external positions, equity finance has tended to gain in importance relative to debt. Notwithstanding heterogeneous changes across countries, key structural features of financial markets and institutions have changed only gradually. Generally, the correlation between institutional factors and changes in financial structures varies considerably across indicators. This suggests that, under the CMU, focused policy measures are needed to tilt financial structures toward those conducive to improved risk sharing.

Second, we provide new evidence on the determinants of risk sharing through financial markets as one core objective of the CMU. We follow the risk-sharing literature by analyzing how country-specific consumption co-moves with country-specific income and how this co-movement relates to financial structures and openness. In European countries with deeper financial markets and a larger share of equity in external positions, consumption risk sharing tends to be stronger. Both are parameters which are at the center of the CMU discussion.

Capital Markets Union: The Main Policy Objectives

Equity Finance and the "Double Dividend"

One key motivation behind the plan for a CMU has been the observation that equity finance plays a special role in the overall mix of finance. A well-designed CMU has thus the potential to yield a "double dividend" in terms of growth and stability.[2]

First, firms' demand for external equity increases with their need to finance research and development. Start-ups that do not have an established track record typically receive funding from informal sources, such as family, friends, or their employees. When firms leave the seed stage, they start using venture capital or bank finance to finance growth and investments. Bond finance and external equity are used primarily by large and more established companies. Hence, there is a pecking order of financing sources.

Second, equity capital provides a buffer against unexpected shocks and thus an ex ante insurance mechanism. Investments and innovations are drivers of growth. But they are also, by their very nature, risky. Whenever risks materialize, the value of equity adjusts, and dividend payments can be suspended. Equity investors thus bear upside and downside risks. Standard debt contracts, in contrast, are insensitive to the borrower's situation. Risks are not shared unless the debtor enters insolvency proceedings and unless risk sharing occurs through haircuts. Insolvency proceedings, however, are often ineffective and not only may create distortions if investments are postponed but also may lead to the liquidation of viable parts of businesses.

Third, higher cross-border equity positions can contribute to improved risk sharing across countries. If a certain region or country is hit by a (local) macroeconomic shock, cross-border equity liabilities induce an immediate sharing of losses among investors. Conversely, by holding equity assets abroad, income (and consumption) of domestic residents is affected by the foreign business cycle. Two-way asset holdings can thus smoothen the impact of shocks on income and consumption. Empirical evidence shows that, in advanced economies, cross-border holdings of equity in particular have contributed to risk sharing (Artis and Hoffmann 2012; Kose, Prasad, and Terrones 2009).

In this sense, cross-border equity finance can play a particularly beneficial role in the context of the Banking Union (Buch, Körner, and Weigert 2015). Cross-border bank ownership can reduce the impact of local shocks affecting the banking sector. This mitigates pressure on resolution authorities to invoke formal mechanisms of burden sharing. For this channel to be effective, there should be no incentives to ring-fence foreign affiliates.

Financial Structures in Europe

One objective of the CMU is to enhance risk sharing by removing obstacles for an adequate mix of funding and, in particular, equity funding. Currently, financial systems across European countries differ, reflecting differences in institutions and preferences and in the structures of the real economy. Some banking systems, for example, are highly concentrated while others are highly competitive. Also, the role of private- and public-sector banks and patterns of securitization differ. One common feature of European financial markets is that bank finance provides a higher share to the financing of firms as compared to the Anglo-Saxon financial systems. In terms of the stocks of finance in Europe, loans account for 52% of euro area gross domestic product (GDP), listed shares for 13%, and securities for 9% (ECB 2017b, 11).

These numbers do not provide information on the welfare effects of finance, though. Financial systems should be judged by their performance in terms of higher growth and stability over longer time horizons. Ultimately, intermediaries fulfill different functions in an economy and bear different types of risks.[3] Complementarities between finance provided via banks or markets play an important role.[4] At the same time, excessive borrowing, fueled by misaligned incentives and risk-taking behavior, can destabilize entire financial systems.

It is difficult to integrate the different dimensions of finance and financial systems into a single indicator. As we are interested in the role of finance for risk sharing, we use indexes that account for the multidimensional nature of financial markets and institutions. We use a number of indicators compiled by Svirydzenka (2016) which fall into two main groups: indexes for financial market development as measured by market depth (stock and bond market capitalization, turnover ratios), access and efficiency, and indicators for the development of financial institutions (comprising banks, insurance companies, mutual funds, and pension funds).[5] These indexes provide a useful starting point for our discussion.

Overall, financial market development is quite heterogeneous across European countries (figure 2.1). Figure 2.1 also indicates changes in financial structures across the pre- and the post-crisis period (2000–2007 versus 2009–2014). Both the overall index of financial markets and financial institutions development were rather stable. If anything, financial market efficiency (measured by stocks traded to GDP) has declined. Overall, there is no clear trend of an increase or a decrease in financial market indicators.

What drives changes in financial structures? To get an idea how institutional and regulatory changes could affect financial markets, we have correlated changes in financial development and institutional factors pre- and post-crisis.[6] Generally, the correlation of institutional variables with the development or depth of financial markets is higher than the correlation with the overall development of financial institutions. In countries with tightened capital controls or larger increases in the stringency of banking regulation, the index of financial market development and depth decreased. Rising regulatory quality and government effectiveness have been related to an increasing depth of financial markets. Among the institutional variables considered here, capital controls have a relatively strong correlation with indicators of financial market depth.

Overall, the explanatory power of the institutional variables considered for financial structures differs. The focus of the CMU project should thus be on targeting policy measures to relevant frictions that impede improvement of the trade-off between growth and stability. Without such a clear focus, it may run the risk of focusing on measures that are less effective or that are driven by other motives. Historically, changes in financial regulations have often been driven by interests of incumbent firms and the political impact of "insiders" (Rajan and Ramcharan 2016; Rajan and Zingales 2003).

Figure 2.1
Changes in the financial development indexes, pre- and post-crisis. "Pre" denotes pre-crisis averages (2000–2007); "post" denotes post-crisis averages (2009–2014). *Sources*: Svirydzenka 2016; authors' own calculations.

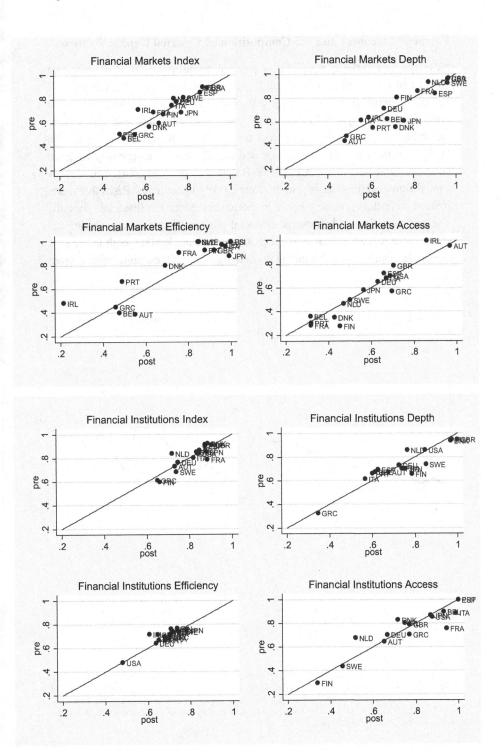

Financial Openness and the Composition of External Capital Positions

Next, we turn to the composition of external capital positions as an important channel of consumption risk sharing across countries. Generally, the share of equity in external positions is lower in the euro area compared to other advanced economies (see figure 2.2). Yet, there have been noticeable shifts over time. Regarding the volume of cross-border capital flows, the integration of financial markets in the euro area had progressed rapidly, but it has partially reversed since the financial crisis (ECB 2015). Before the financial crisis, cross-border capital flows occurred largely in the form of debt instruments. Risks that materialized were thus primarily borne by borrowers. Since the financial crisis, the share of debt finance in external financial positions has declined. During the crisis, there was a "sudden stop" in cross-border bank lending, both in the euro area and globally. Notwithstanding the heterogeneity of these adjustments across

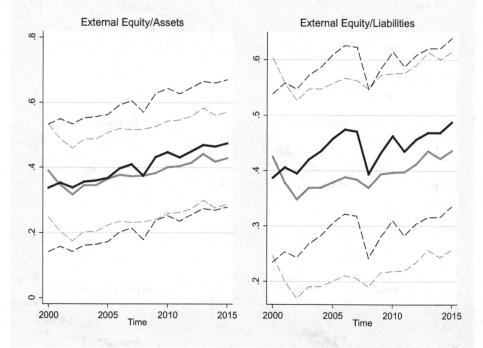

Figure 2.2
Share of equity in external assets and liabilities. Gray = Sample mean of euro area countries, Black = Non–euro area OECD countries. Dashed lines are sample means +/– one standard deviation. Equity is defined as portfolio equity assets plus FDI here. Assets (liabilities) are total external assets (liabilities). *Sources*: External wealth of nations dataset by Lane and Milesi-Ferretti (2017); authors' own calculations.

banks and countries (Darvas et al. 2017), the retrenchment of banks from foreign markets reflects a reassessment of risks and the response to regulatory changes.[7]

Likewise, cross-border investments into bond markets within the euro area increased until 2007–2008 but receded in the aftermath of the crisis. In contrast, cross-border equity investments in stock markets within the euro area grew steadily over the past fifteen years and remained stable even during the crisis. Yet, while intra–euro area cross-border holdings of equity gain ground, they remain smaller than cross-border debt holdings (ECB 2016, 52).[8]

At the same time, there are market segments such as the European market for venture capital that remain highly fragmented. Also, cross-border investments such as mergers and acquisitions are often impeded by institutional barriers and specificities of national corporate governance structures.

Financial Structures and Consumption Risk Sharing

How do financial structures affect consumption risk sharing as a key measure of welfare? Empirical work for the euro area shows that there are unexploited gains from risk sharing. The bulk of shocks to output in the euro area is not smoothened through financial markets, fiscal policy, or price adjustments, thus affecting the volatility—and hence the risk—of consumption (ECB 2017a). Previous research on risk sharing shows that financial markets in the United States contribute more to risk sharing than in Europe and that a larger fraction of shocks to GDP was smoothed in the United States compared to the European countries considered (Sørensen and Yosha 1998).[9] While euro area countries increasingly relied on private capital markets as a risk-sharing device until 2007 (Balli, Kalemli-Ozcan, and Sørensen 2012), Kalemli-Ozcan, Luttini, and Sørensen (2014) find that risk sharing nearly entirely dried up in 2010 in countries most severely affected by the European sovereign debt crisis.

In the remainder of this section, we update previous empirical work on consumption risk sharing. The aim is to show (1) how the level of consumption risk sharing in Europe compares to levels of other world regions and (2) whether the level of consumption risk sharing is related to the indicators of financial market structures and openness that the CMU will impact. Within Europe, we distinguish between the EU countries (for which the CMU is discussed) from the euro area (for which there is a discussion about fiscal risk sharing).

Following previous literature (Kose, Prasad, and Terrones 2009; Sørensen et al. 2007), we measure risk sharing based on the correlation between country-specific per capita consumption growth and country-specific GDP per capita growth. We estimate the following equation that accounts for country- and time-specific trends and for the presence of global shocks:

$$\Delta \log c_{it} - \Delta \log C_t = \alpha_i + \beta_t + \kappa \left(\Delta \log y_{it} - \Delta \log Y_t \right) + \epsilon_{it} \tag{1}$$

where i denotes the country, and t denotes time (1987–2014).[10] $\Delta \log c_{it}$ denotes the growth in per capita consumption in country i and year t. Because aggregate shocks cannot be insured against, the growth rate of global consumption, $\Delta \log C_t$, is subtracted from consumption growth in country i. This difference yields a measure of country-specific consumption growth.[11] Country-specific output growth is computed accordingly.

The parameter κ captures the link between country-specific consumption and output growth. The smaller the coefficient κ (the weaker the link between consumption and output growth), the higher is the degree of risk sharing, $1 - \kappa$. As laid out (e.g., by Sørensen et al. 2007), consumption smoothing captures risk sharing through different channels like fiscal income stabilization or procyclical savings.

In order to study how financial structures influence the degree of consumption smoothing, we follow Sørensen et al. (2007) and impose a structure on κ, such that $\kappa = \kappa_0 + \kappa_1 \gamma_{it}$, where γ_{it} captures indicators of financial structures (*FS*) and financial openness (*FO*). $1 - \kappa_0 - \kappa_1 \gamma_{it}$ then yields the average degree of risk sharing as a function of financial structure or the degree of financial openness.

FS includes the indexes of the development of financial markets and institutions provided by Svirydzenka (2016). *FO* includes measures of financial openness such as the share of cross-border assets and liabilities to GDP and different combinations of equity and debt assets and liabilities, both relative to total assets plus liabilities and relative to GDP. Both sets of variables do not change at business cycle frequency and are thus to some extent predetermined. Yet our aim is not to establish causal patterns in the data, as this would require a more sophisticated identification strategy.

The parameter κ_1 measures whether more financially open or more financially developed economies experience a higher degree of consumption risk sharing. A negative estimate of the value of κ_1 implies that the link between idiosyncratic consumption and output growth weakens as the degree of financial openness (development) increases and, hence, as risk sharing improves.

Table 2.1 presents the estimation results for the link between financial structures and risk sharing. Column 1 shows the results for a simple model relating country-specific consumption to output growth only. In this setup, the degree of overall risk sharing is given by $(1 - \kappa)$.[12] The estimations reveal that risk sharing is stronger in the advanced economies than in emerging markets. In the EU and the euro area (EA), the link between country-specific consumption and output growth is stronger than in other regions. Hence, risk sharing is weaker in Europe than both the advanced economies and in the full sample that contains emerging economies as well. This confirms prior evidence suggesting that there is room for better risk sharing in Europe (ECB 2017a).

Table 2.1
Risk sharing and financial structures.

	(1)	(2)	(3)	(4)	(5)	(6)	(7)	(8)	(9)
		Financial Market Indexes				Financial Institutions Indexes			
		FM	FMD	FME	FMA	FI	FID	FIE	FIA
Full sample									
Output	0.496***	0.543***	0.575***	0.482***	0.546***	0.655***	0.512***	1.001***	0.545***
	(0.015)	(0.022)	(0.020)	(0.019)	(0.021)	(0.034)	(0.022)	(0.043)	(0.025)
Output×FS		−0.194***	−0.372***	0.057	−0.190***	−0.438***	−0.074	−0.897***	−0.163**
		(0.070)	(0.067)	(0.047)	(0.059)	(0.084)	(0.078)	(0.073)	(0.068)
Observations	1,921	1,921	1,921	1,921	1,921	1,921	1,921	1,921	1,921
R-squared	0.454	0.456	0.463	0.454	0.457	0.462	0.454	0.496	0.456
Number of countries	71	71	71	71	71	71	71	71	71
Advanced economies									
Output	0.351***	0.604***	0.428***	0.592***	0.571***	−0.127	0.187**	0.467**	−0.003
	(0.025)	(0.064)	(0.053)	(0.054)	(0.058)	(0.099)	(0.073)	(0.204)	(0.062)
Output×FS		−0.444***	−0.152	−0.411***	−0.360***	0.704***	0.281**	−0.170	0.576***
		(0.103)	(0.092)	(0.082)	(0.086)	(0.142)	(0.116)	(0.298)	(0.094)
Observations	621	621	621	621	621	621	621	621	621
R-squared	0.374	0.393	0.377	0.400	0.392	0.400	0.380	0.374	0.413
Number of countries	23	23	23	23	23	23	23	23	23
EU countries									
Output	0.674***	0.839***	0.812***	0.769***	0.796***	0.947***	0.893***	1.946***	0.536***
	(0.033)	(0.058)	(0.053)	(0.052)	(0.051)	(0.133)	(0.068)	(0.357)	(0.109)
Output×FS		−0.394***	−0.347***	−0.223**	−0.291***	−0.398**	−0.419***	−1.849***	0.202
		(0.114)	(0.105)	(0.096)	(0.094)	(0.188)	(0.113)	(0.516)	(0.152)

(continued)

Table 2.1 (continued)

	(1)	(2)	(3)	(4)	(5)	(6)	(7)	(8)	(9)
		Financial Market Indexes				Financial Institutions Indexes			
		FM	FMD	FME	FMA	FI	FID	FIE	FIA
Observations	474	474	474	474	474	474	474	474	474
R-squared	0.631	0.641	0.640	0.636	0.639	0.635	0.643	0.642	0.632
Number of countries	25	25	25	25	25	25	25	25	25
EA countries									
Output	0.567***	0.695***	0.736***	0.538***	0.651***	1.060***	0.828***	2.019***	0.496**
	(0.046)	(0.157)	(0.129)	(0.096)	(0.115)	(0.291)	(0.129)	(0.675)	(0.208)
Output×FS		−0.219	−0.295	0.055	−0.132	−0.639*	−0.412**	−2.055**	0.091
		(0.256)	(0.211)	(0.156)	(0.165)	(0.372)	(0.191)	(0.953)	(0.262)
Observations	193	193	193	193	193	193	193	193	193
R-squared	0.631	0.632	0.635	0.631	0.632	0.637	0.641	0.641	0.631
Number of countries	15	15	15	15	15	15	15	15	15

Notes: The dependent variable is country-specific consumption growth, "Output" is country-specific output growth, and FS stands for the different measures of financial structures listed in each column, where FM = financial markets index, FI = financial institutions index, FMD(FID), FME(FIE), FMA(FIA) = subindexes for markets (institutions) depth, efficiency, and access. All regressions include country fixed effects and year dummies. The full sample contains all countries listed in the online appendix to this chapter at https://www.diw.de/sixcms/detail.php?id=diw_01.c.669860.de. Standard errors in parentheses. *** $p < 0.01$, ** $p < 0.05$, * $p < 0.1$.

Regarding financial structures, financial *market* development is conducive to risk sharing for advanced economies (table 2.1). In contrast, higher levels of financial *institutions* development come along with weaker risk sharing. For the EU economies, development of financial markets and financial institutions are positively related to the degree of risk sharing.[13] One possible explanation is that the EU countries comprise Eastern European economies that have a high presence of foreign banks. Hence, the results may indirectly account for the fact that there are cross-border equity holdings of banks that affect risk sharing.[14] By contrast, financial development indexes tend to matter less for risk sharing in the euro area.

Some of the results reported so far may be related to the fact that measures of financial structure are correlated with the degree of financial openness. Table 2.2 thus turns to the relationship between financial openness and risk sharing. Our results confirm the positive link between equity or FDI openness and risk sharing for advanced economies (Kose, Prasad, and Terrones 2009; Levy-Yeyati and Williams 2014), while debt positions tend to be less favorable for consumption risk sharing. This finding is in line with table 2.1's result that the depth of financial institutions can mitigate risk sharing while advanced countries with more developed financial markets experience more risk sharing. Depending on whether debt positions are expressed in relation to total external positions (A + L) or in relation to GDP, larger shares of debt positions can even be detrimental for risk sharing (column 10). The results for the EU and EA countries are qualitatively similar.

In unreported regressions, we further decompose the financial openness measures and consider the relation of risk sharing with asset and liability positions separately. For the advanced economies, equity assets are conducive for risk sharing while equity liabilities mostly do not matter. In the EU countries, however, both equity assets and liabilities are related to more risk sharing.

Summing Up

The CMU is an ambitious project. The Banking Union basically took the existing regulatory framework as given and focused on moving the supervision of banks to the European level. The main focus of the CMU differs; its focus is on removing obstacles to a more efficient allocation of capital across borders and to a better sharing of risks across European economies through markets. The institutional framework of surveillance and supervision remains unchanged. This is a challenging project because it requires changing the structure of the financial system.

The structure of financial systems is closely related to deep-rooted preferences and institutions. These change only slowly. Seen this way, the potential for the CMU project to increase the capacity of the financial system to

Table 2.2
Risk sharing and financial openness.

	(1)	(2)	(3)	(4)	(5)	(6)	(7)	(8)	(9)	(10)
		(A+L)/GDP	(E+FDI)/GDP	(E+FDI)/(A+L)	E/GDP	E/(A+L)	FDI/GDP	FDI/(A+L)	Debt/GDP	Debt/(A+L)
Full sample										
Output	0.496***	0.585***	0.547***	0.501***	0.565***	0.621***	0.547***	0.443***	0.563***	0.405***
	(0.015)	(0.020)	(0.018)	(0.029)	(0.018)	(0.021)	(0.018)	(0.025)	(0.019)	(0.055)
Output×FO		-0.049***	-0.121***	-0.099	-0.206***	-1.435***	-0.121***	0.279**	-0.063***	0.134
		(0.005)	(0.016)	(0.097)	(0.020)	(0.148)	(0.016)	(0.113)	(0.007)	(0.084)
Observations	1,921	1,849	1,849	1,855	1,717	1,717	1,849	1,850	1,850	1,851
R-squared	0.454	0.453	0.449	0.441	0.466	0.465	0.449	0.454	0.455	0.448
Number of countries	71	71	71	71	71	71	71	71	71	71
Advanced economies										
Output	0.351***	0.372***	0.340***	0.595***	0.341***	0.488***	0.340***	0.490***	0.384***	-0.199*
	(0.025)	(0.035)	(0.032)	(0.064)	(0.030)	(0.048)	(0.032)	(0.060)	(0.035)	(0.117)
Output×FO		-0.006	-0.007	-0.808***	-0.020	-1.285***	-0.007	-0.763***	-0.017	0.869***
		(0.007)	(0.013)	(0.185)	(0.026)	(0.340)	(0.013)	(0.280)	(0.011)	(0.183)
Observations	621	607	606	618	608	615	606	616	609	619
R-squared	0.374	0.374	0.366	0.388	0.367	0.381	0.366	0.378	0.373	0.393
Number of countries	23	23	23	23	23	23	23	23	23	23

EU countries

Output	0.674***	0.760***	0.762***	0.891***	0.748***	0.826***	0.762***	0.654***	0.766***	0.523***
	(0.033)	(0.046)	(0.041)	(0.083)	(0.037)	(0.047)	(0.041)	(0.072)	(0.048)	(0.122)
Output×FO		−0.011	−0.045***	−0.645***	−0.102***	−1.775***	−0.045***	0.125	−0.028*	0.252
		(0.008)	(0.014)	(0.227)	(0.026)	(0.394)	(0.014)	(0.268)	(0.015)	(0.198)
Observations	474	460	463	470	465	472	463	463	462	474
R-squared	0.631	0.647	0.642	0.638	0.647	0.650	0.642	0.636	0.641	0.632
Number of countries	25	25	25	25	25	25	25	25	25	25

EA countries

Output	0.567***	0.696***	0.675***	0.845***	0.659***	0.683***	0.675***	0.667***	0.792***	0.096
	(0.046)	(0.075)	(0.061)	(0.105)	(0.056)	(0.078)	(0.061)	(0.091)	(0.094)	(0.188)
Output×FO		−0.014	−0.037**	−0.860***	−0.073***	−1.002*	−0.037**	−0.410	−0.064**	0.726**
		(0.012)	(0.015)	(0.293)	(0.028)	(0.546)	(0.015)	(0.403)	(0.027)	(0.281)
Observations	193	179	182	193	184	191	182	191	181	193
R-squared	0.631	0.671	0.665	0.650	0.670	0.648	0.665	0.644	0.666	0.645
Number of countries	15	15	15	15	15	15	15	15	15	15

Notes: The dependent variable is country-specific consumption growth, "Output" is country-specific output growth, and FO stands for the different measures of financial openness listed in each column where A=total foreign assets, L=total foreign liabilities, E=equity assets and liabilities, FDI=FDI assets and liabilities, and Debt=Debt assets and liabilities. All regressions include country fixed effects and year dummies. The full sample contains all countries listed in the online appendix to this chapter at https://www.diw.de/sixcms/detail.php?id=diw_01.c.669860.de. Standard errors in parentheses. *** $p < 0.01$, ** $p < 0.05$, * $p < 0$.

contribute to risk sharing may be limited. It is thus important to remain realistic and to focus on relevant frictions that prevail and that limit financial market integration and risk sharing. Identification of frictions that are relevant for the real economy, ultimately, requires using identification methods and disaggregated data that are beyond the scope of this chapter.

We have, instead, focused on factors at an aggregate level that affect consumption risk sharing. We have argued that the share of equity in the overall mix of finance plays an important role for risk sharing and for the financing of innovation. This can lead to a double dividend in terms of growth and stability. First, we have thus described the evolution of financial structures focusing in particular on the importance of equity finance. While the structure of financial markets changes only gradually, the share of cross-border equity positions in external positions has increased. Second we have provided new evidence on consumption risk sharing. We find consumption risk sharing to be weaker in Europe compared to other advanced economies. More open financial markets tend to come along with better risk sharing, and this is particularly the case for countries with a higher share of equity in their external positions.

Taken together, our results suggest that targeted measures under the CMU project are needed. This, in turn, requires a prioritization of which institutional features of financial markets constrain investment (in particular, cross-border investment) the most. Generally, removing obstacles to the cross-border movement of capital can contribute to better risk sharing. Priority should be given to financial instruments (and, most importantly, equity instruments) that have clear rules for the allocation of potential losses. At the domestic level, improved access to equity finance such as venture capital can also promote an improved allocation of financial resources and the financing of innovations. At the same time, given the nature of European financial systems, bank finance will continue to remain important. For banks to perform their role in the financing of the economy, strong equity buffers and effective mechanisms to deal with emerging risks and overcapacities in the financial systems are thus needed.

To draw more specific policy implications, more granular cross-country data should be used to identify relevant frictions that impede the evolution of financial markets that are conducive to growth and stability. Also, at a very practical level, improved information on regulations and institutional features of financial markets would be an important input for analytical work and policy discussions alike.

Notes

This chapter was prepared for the conference "Capital Markets Union and Beyond," London, January 26–27, 2018. Franziska Bremus acknowledges funding under the project "European Capital Markets and Macroeconomic Stability" by the Leibniz Competition. The chapter has benefited from comments by Manuel Buchholz and Zsolt Darvas. All errors and inconsistencies are our own.

1. In emerging markets, the share of portfolio equity and FDI in gross stocks of foreign assets and liabilities has risen from 13% (1980–1984) to 37% (2000–2004) (Kose et al. 2006).

2. This section draws on Buch (2017).

3. Hellwig (1998), for example, stresses the comparative advantage of banks to manage and to bear idiosyncratic credit risk while financial markets play a role in the allocation of macroeconomic aggregate risk.

4. See Heinrich (2002), Saillard and Url (2012), Schmidt and Spindler (2000), or Song and Thakor (2010).

5. For more detailed information see Svirydzenka (2016, table 1).

6. See table A1 in the online appendix to this chapter at https://www.diw.de/sixcms/detail.php?id=diw_01.c.669860.de.

7. Higher capital requirements tend to reduce international bank lending, and unconventional monetary policy can amplify this effect (Forbes, Reinhard, and Wieladek 2017).

8. A similar shift from debt to equity could be observed at the global level (Bussière, Schmidt, and Valla 2016).

9. For a recent review of the literature, see Bremus and Stelten (2017).

10. Note that for the EA countries, the sample period starts in 1999 only.

11. Following Levy-Yeyati and Williams (2014), global per capita consumption (output) growth is computed as the weighted average of advanced countries' consumption (output) growth rates, the weights being defined as advanced countries' share of consumption (output) in total consumption (output) of advanced economies.

12. Note that overall consumption smoothing is the result of risk sharing through different channels (e.g., transfers, credit and capital markets, or precautionary saving). Cross-country risk sharing is just one of those channels.

13. We exclude the financial centers Cyprus, Luxembourg, and Malta from the set of EU and EA countries.

14. Indeed, when leaving out the Eastern European countries from the regressions for the EU countries (not reported), the links between most financial development indexes and risk sharing turn statistically insignificant.

References

Artis, M. J., and M. Hoffmann. 2012. "The Home Bias, Capital Income Flows and Improved Long-Term Consumption Risk Sharing between Industrialized Countries." *International Finance* 14, no. 3: 481–505.

Balli, Faruk, Sebnem Kalemli-Ozcan, and Bent E. Sørensen. 2012. "Risk Sharing through Capital Gains." *Canadian Journal of Economics* 45, no. 2: 472–492.

Barth, James R., Gerard Caprio Jr., and Ross Levine. 2013. "Bank Regulation and Supervision in 180 Countries from 1999 to 2011." *Journal of Financial Economic Policy* 5, no. 2: 111—219.

Bremus, Franziska, and Ruth Stelten. 2017. "Capital Market Integration and Macroeconomic Stability." Deutsches Institut für Wirtschaftsforschung (DIW) Berlin Roundup, Politik im Fokus No. 116.

Buch, Claudia M. 2017. "The Capital Markets Union Project: Policy Priorities." Speech at the 7th Annual ECMI Conference "Moving Europe's Capital Markets to the Next Level," Centre for European Policy Studies, Brussels, November 23.

Buch, Claudia M., Tobias Körner, and Benjamin Weigert. 2015. "Towards Deeper Financial Integration in Europe: What the Banking Union Can Contribute." *Credit and Capital Markets—Kredit und Kapital* 48, no. 1: 11–49.

Bussière, Matthieu, Julia Schmidt, and Natacha Valla. 2016. "International Financial Flows in the New Normal: Key Patterns (and Why We Should Care)." CEPII Policy Brief No 10, Paris.

Darvas, Z., K. Efstathiou, P. Huttl, and D. Schoenmaker. 2017. *Analysis of Developments in EU Capital Flows in the Global Context*. 3rd annual report. Brussels: Bruegel.

European Central Bank (ECB). 2015. *Financial Integration in Europe 2015*. Frankfurt am Main: ECB, April.

European Central Bank (ECB). 2016. "Dealing with Large and Volatile Capital Flows and the Role of the IMF." IRC Task Force on IMF Issues, Occasional Paper Series 180, Frankfurt am Main.

European Central Bank (ECB). 2017a. *Financial Integration in Europe 2017*. Frankfurt am Main: ECB, May.

European Central Bank (ECB). 2017b. *Report on Financial Structures*. Frankfurt am Main: ECB, October.

Fernandez, Andres, Michael W. Klein, Alessandro Rebucci, Martin Schindler, and Martin Uribe. 2016. "Capital Control Measures: A New Dataset." *IMF Economic Review* 64, no. 3: 548–574.

Financial Stability Board (FSB). 2018. *Implementation and Effects of the G20 Financial Regulatory Reforms: Fourth Annual Report*. Basel: FSB.

Forbes, Kristin J., Dennis Reinhardt, and Tomasz Wieladek. 2017. "The Spillovers, Interactions, and (Un)intended Consequences of Monetary and Regulatory Policies." *Journal of Monetary Economics* 85 (January): 1–22.

Heinrich, Ralph P. 2002. *Complementarities in Corporate Governance*. Berlin: Springer.

Hellwig, Martin. 1998. "Banks, Markets, and the Allocation of Risks in an Economy." *Journal of Institutional and Theoretical Economics* 154: 328–345.

Kalemli-Ozcan, Sebnem Luttini, and Bent E. Sørensen. 2014. "Debt Crises and Risk Sharing: The Role of Markets versus Sovereigns." *Scandinavian Journal of Economics* 116, no. 1: 253–276.

Kose, M. Ayhan, Eswar S. Prasad, Kenneth Rogoff, and Shang-Jin Wei. 2006. "Financial Globalization: A Reappraisal." IMF Working Paper 06/189, International Monetary Fund, Washington, DC.

Kose, M. Ayhan, Eswar S. Prasad, and Marco E. Terrones. 2009. "Does Financial Globalization Promote Risk Sharing?" *Journal of Development Economics* 89, no. 2: 258–270.

Lane, Philip R., and Gian Maria Milesi-Ferretti. 2017. "International Financial Integration in the Aftermath of the Global Financial Crisis." IMF Working Paper No. 17/115, International Monetary Fund, Washington, DC.

Levy-Yeyati, Eduardo, and Tomas Williams. 2014. "Financial Globalization in Emerging Economies: Much Ado about Nothing?" *Economia* 14, no. 2: 91–131.

Rajan, Raghuram G., and Rodney Ramcharan. 2016. "Constituencies and Legislation: The Fight over the McFadden Act of 1927." *Management Science* 62, no. 7: 1843–1859.

Rajan, Raghuram G., and Luigi Zingales. 2003. "The Great Reversals: The Politics of Financial Development in the Twentieth Century." *Journal of Financial Economics* 69: 5–50.

Saillard, Adeline, and Thomas Url. 2012. "Measuring Complementarity in Financial Systems." CES Working Paper No. 2012.39, Université Paris Pantheon-Sorbonne.

Schmidt, Reinhard H., and Gerald Spindler. 2000. "Path Dependence, Corporate Governance and Complementarity." Working Paper Series: Finance and Accounting 27, Department of Finance, Johann Wolfgang Goethe-Universität, Frankfurt am Main.

Song, Fenghua, and Anjan V. Thakor. 2010. "Financial System Architecture and the Co-Evolution of Banks and Capital Markets." *Economic Journal* 120, no. 547: 1021–1055.

Sørensen, Bent E., Yi-Tsung Wu, Oved Yosha, and Yu Zhu. 2007. "Home Bias and International Risk Sharing: Twin Puzzles Separated at Birth." *Journal of International Money and Finance* 26, no. 4: 587–605.

Sørensen, Bent E., and Oved Yosha. 1998. "International Risk Sharing and European Monetary Unification." *Journal of International Economics* 45, no. 29: 211–238.

Svirydzenka, Katsiaryna. 2016. "Introducing a New Broad-Based Index of Financial Development." IMF Working Papers 16/5, International Monetary Fund, Washington, DC.

3 A Legal Framework for Financial Market Integration: Resetting the Agenda beyond the Sectoral Single Rulebook

Eilis Ferran

More European Union (EU) financial integration in both banking and capital markets has the potential to improve the efficient allocation of savings and to enhance stability through better risk sharing, greater resilience, and more diversity of funding sources.[1] Financial integration is positively associated with greater financial development, which can boost the real economy and overall prosperity.[2] On the downside, the greater interconnectedness between systems that comes with financial integration may also facilitate the cross-border transmission of shocks. Hence the need for a robust legal framework that simultaneously facilitates the benefits of integration and contains the risk of harms. It was ever thus, but there are powerful reasons to consider the issues afresh in the context of the push for more developed EU capital markets and in the aftermath of the seismic UK referendum decision to leave the EU.

Brexit presents the EU with opportunities and threats. Despite doing well in the realm of financial regulation from its membership of the EU—in effect exporting many of its financial market regulatory preferences to the EU as a whole and in turn reinforcing the preeminence of London as the entry point to the European single market and as the location where professional expertise in navigating the regulatory framework was most concentrated—the United Kingdom was a somewhat troublesome member state. The collapse of Lehman Brothers in 2008 and the ensuing market turmoil, seen by some as an indictment of free-wheeling Anglo-American capitalism, revealed the strength of discomfort in other European capitals with the British so-called "light touch" approach to the regulation of financial markets. During this difficult period, policy preferences at the EU level switched sharply from wanting to emulate London's success to blaming the United Kingdom for having infected the EU with risky practices.[3] Later, the growing anti-EU sentiment in the United Kingdom and the resulting need for British politicians and officials to be seen to be acting tough in resisting "power grabs" by Brussels were unhelpful complicating factors at a time when severe problems arising from deep structural issues within the euro area became the predominant concern for the EU.

Brexit then provides an opportunity to reset various agendas. Shaping EU financial regulation around the needs of a deepening economic and monetary union may become less contentious without the UK's troublesome close scrutiny of every step. This is not to say that the remaining twenty-seven member states, both in the euro area and outside it, will simply coalesce around a single shared vision of EU financial regulatory policy, but none has quite the same incentives as the United Kingdom to act as the veto player. Vítor Constâncio, vice president of the European Central Bank (ECB), has acknowledged that "the departure of the largest non-banking union Member State is an opportunity to explore the interlinkages between capital markets union and banking union."[4] The EU can now shape a version of financial regulation that is not dominated by the needs and preferences of a mature, outsized capital market, although the loss of the city of London—dubbed Europe's "investment bank" by the Governor of the Bank of England[5] and acknowledged also by senior ECB officials as an important provider of financial services to EU firms[6]—is as much a threat as it is an opportunity. Brexit sharpens the focus for the EU in financial regulation because it faces the prospect of not only losing its most developed national capital market but also having that market on its doorstep as a direct regional competitor. So the capital markets union (CMU) project—once plausibly described as little more than a political gesture by the European Commission to placate the United Kingdom[7]—assumes a different and far more politically salient character. It has become the vehicle through which the EU can begin to demonstrate its level of post-Brexit ambitions for regulation that seeks to catalyze cross-border private sector capital market activity to complement bank-based sources of finance for the real economy, mitigate systemic risk, and deepen financial integration.

A report published in 2015 by the president of the European Commission (Jean-Claude Juncker), together with the presidents of the European Council (Donald Tusk), Eurogroup (Jeroen Dijsselbloem), the ECB (Mario Draghi), and Martin Schultz (European Parliament) gives a sense of what an ambitious vision for the integration of European capital markets could look like.[8] It would include regulation to create incentives for risk pooling and risk sharing, and to ensure that all financial institutions had sufficient risk management structures in place and were prudentially sound. It would be supported by a taxation system that provides for a neutral treatment for different but comparable activities and investments across jurisdictions. Detailed aspects of capital market regulation would be improved, but crucially in the context of this chapter, the reform agenda would also extend beyond core capital markets regulatory issues and the "most important bottlenecks preventing the integration of capital markets"[9] would also be tackled. For the five presidents (and also for the Commission itself), these bottlenecks lay in areas like insolvency law, company law, and property rights as well as the legal enforceability of cross-border claims. Institutional arrangements would also be strengthened, with the establishment of a single European capital markets supervisor identified as the ultimate step.

The functional interrelationship among capital markets law and substantive company, insolvency, and property laws and how they influence and drive each other are issues that have attracted significant scholarly attention over many years. Worth singling out is *Capital Markets and Company Law*, a major volume edited by Klaus Hopt and Eddy Wymeersch and published in 2003, that considered whether market developments were putting pressure for change on the more traditional legal regimes that were perceived to be resistant to harmonization because of their deep embeddedness within still-divergent member state economic, social, and cultural settings.[10] Christiaan Timmermans concluded that the internal market had been completed without completion of the harmonization of company law; the coexistence of different company law systems with the daily practice of the financial markets had "apparently not been really painful or caused real problems."[11] Paul Davies was also relatively sanguine about the ability of the markets to move forward in spite of unchanging company law.[12] Yet for Jaap Winter, close analysis of the suboptimal operation of the system for shareholder cross-border voting led to the conclusion that there was a need for harmonization of company law as well as capital markets laws.[13] In his chapter Eddy Wymeersch called for a law on groups of companies in Europe,[14] and elsewhere in the volume Friedrich Kübler enumerated the ways that market innovations such as securitization were in effect eroding underpinning assumptions on which creditor protection within company law had been developed.[15]

The recent prominence given to the inclusion of company, insolvency, and property law on the agenda to improve EU capital markets makes this an opportune moment to revisit the debate about the interrelationship between sectoral regulation and general laws. This chapter will examine with particular reference to company law and corporate governance the potential implications of allowing the needs of the capital markets to drive reform of general laws. It will develop the argument that there are potential dangers in going too far down the route of thinking about company law and corporate governance as handmaidens to the needs of the capital markets. As such, this chapter will build on Klaus Hopt's cautionary words about "an exclusive emphasis on the support and further promotion of the internal market through harmonized corporate law" and his call instead to focus "on the necessary minimum rules for the functioning of the core areas of management and supervision that will cause the least interruption and distortion to the economy, investors, employees, and creditors in the internal market."[16]

To place this discussion in context it is helpful to begin with a short over-view of key features of the CMU project. Detailed coverage of the scope of the CMU project can be omitted because this is covered extensively in other chapters.

What Is the CMU? Origins and Evolution

The CMU is a plan put forward by the European Commission to mobilize capital in Europe.[17] The overarching objective is to develop deeper capital markets to complement bank financing and thereby diversify sources of finance. By further removing barriers to cross-border investment, the CMU is intended to unlock investment capital, giving savers more investment choices and businesses a greater choice of funding at lower costs. These are not new aims for the EU. Indeed it is possible, as Niamh Moloney has noted, to see a golden thread going right back to the 1960s of policy references to the importance of capital markets to the EU project.[18] The Commission, which has remained steadfast in its belief that legal harmonization is constitutive of financial market development, has consistently demonstrated its willingness to play a long and patient game; the overall vision remains more or less the same, notwithstanding the multiplicity of endogenous and exogenous factors that keep financial regulation in a state of "continual adaptation"[19] and around which pragmatic compromises and (temporary) concessions must be made. Step-by-step incrementalism is the Commission's tried-and-tested way of doing business in a complex policy setting and in a legal order where EU-level competences are subject to Treaty on the Functioning of the European Union (TFEU) constraints.

The first version of the CMU Action Plan, adopted in 2015, contained a list of over thirty actions and measures to establish what were described by the Commission as the "building blocks of an integrated EU capital market" by 2019.[20] After a midterm review in 2017, other measures were added to the agenda, including the proposed introduction of more proportionate rules for small and medium-sized enterprises (SMEs), investment firms and fintech, and a revision of the European Supervisory Authorities to foster more effective and consistent supervision. In introducing the new proposals resulting from the midterm review, the Commission openly acknowledged the influence of Brexit: "the future departure of the largest financial centre from the EU makes it neces-sary to re-assess how CMU can ensure that EU businesses and investors have access to strong, dynamic and more integrated capital markets, while risks to financial stability are properly managed. This calls for stronger action, more effective supervision and measures to ensure the full benefits of CMU are felt across the entire EU."[21] Furthermore, progress has already been made on delivery of CMU legislative measures within time frames that would have been unthinkable in earlier decades. Along with the CMU agenda, there has also been a substantial amount of concrete regulatory policy activity in adjacent areas, including changes to the EU prudential and resolution frameworks.[22] The speed of delivery on CMU and related measures is, of course, in part a consequence of substantial past investment by the EU in the development of a sophisticated law and rule-making apparatus for the financial sector.

The Rise of the Sectoral Single Rulebook and Its Intersection with General Laws

Another way in which the CMU has benefited by building on what has gone before is that the need for a "single rulebook" for EU-wide financial regulation had become axiomatic by the time it was launched. The single rulebook is to be understood as a shorthand phrase that denotes an increasingly dense thicket of harmonized legislative requirements (Level 1), delegated rules (Level 2), and guidance and associated measures (Level 3) covering financial institutions, markets, and infrastructures as well as the relevant institutional framework. The single rulebook advances financial integration in a fundamental way because, within the EU, integration is characterized by a single set of rules, equal access for market participants, and equal treatment of market actors.[23]

The idea of a single rulebook for EU financial regulation was first mooted in the early 2000s but really took hold after the publication of the influential de Larosière Report in 2009, which put in train a sequence of events that led to the adoption of the creation of a single European rulebook applicable to all financial institutions in the single market as an agreed policy goal. The articulation of the single rulebook as a distinct policy objective signified a change that was driven by the crisis-related realization of the vulnerabilities created by a single market without common rules. As the crisis deepened and morphed from banks to sovereigns, the need for a single rulebook to spread beyond the revamp of bank prudential requirements that were triggered by the financial crisis to other areas of the EU regulatory framework for financial services secured broad acceptance. Thus by the time of launch of the CMU, it was uncontroversial for the Commission to treat a single rulebook for capital markets as both a natural and essential complement to the single rulebook in banking.

Under the banner of the single rulebook, regulations have increasingly usurped directives as the preferred form of legal instrument for financial regulation—quite literally, then, a "single," definitive source rather than a large compendium of national laws giving effect to an EU directive. An important driver of the continued use of directives in particular areas is the need for alignment with aspects of member states' national legal regimes that are not harmonized. This was the case, for example, for the EU-wide bank resolution framework where a directive was the legal instrument of choice because of close links with nonharmonized areas of national law, such as insolvency and property law;[24] the EU legal framework needed to work within the specificities of relevant national law, and transposition, rather than direct effect, was required to achieve that effect.[25] This was also the thinking behind the post-crisis reform of EU prudential regulation where uniform and directly applicable requirements are now set by regulation,[26] but this is complemented by a directive[27] that sets out provisions in a range of areas, including corporate governance requirements and remuneration restrictions. The Commission noted with regard to the corporate governance requirements that a regulation would not have been appropriate because the diversity of corporate governance structures and company laws in member states would not allow for a directly applicable "one size fits all" approach.[28] There is a similar pattern in the financial markets context where a regulation[29] sets out uniform rules in areas such as trading data disclosure, mandatory trading of derivatives on organized venues, and the removal of barriers between trading venues and clearing houses and a directive[30] containing provisions on other matters such as requirements regarding investor protection.

The fact that unharmonized company, insolvency, or property laws may make it necessary to choose directives rather than regulations does not, in itself, constitute a compelling argument for greater harmonization of those laws. However, the frictions that arise at points of intersection between very harmonized sectoral regulation and less harmonized general laws could point at something more fundamental that does, on closer examination, turn out to be a real barrier to the deepening of financial integration. This is the question to which we can now turn. The next section explores this issue with particular reference to company law and, where appropriate, its close associate corporate governance regulation. There are also references to developments with respect to the advancement of insolvency law at the EU level.

Company Law as a Bottleneck to a True Capital Markets Union, and What Can or Should Be Done about It

Despite being a "cornerstone of the internal market,"[31] the attention given by EU policymakers to the link between industrial policy and company law has fluctuated over the years.[32] During the early 2000s there was a resurgence of interest in this link, and during this period it was recognized that the primary purpose of company law should be to facilitate the running of efficient and competitive business enterprises.[33] Dynamic and flexible company law and corporate governance were found to be essential for a modern, dynamic, inter-connected industrialized society for millions of investors and for deepening the internal market and building an integrated European capital market.[34] Whereas older EU policy interventions in the field of company law had been driven by the perceived need to protect shareholders and creditors, the more modern think-ing saw proper mechanisms for the protection of those who dealt with companies as adding to the efficiency of company law regulation rather than an end in themselves. The Treaty base for company law regulation (TFEU, article 50) was wide enough to accommodate this shift in philosophical approach.[35]

However, the interest in a new approach to company law that began during this period translated less into a momentum for a new dynamic in the EU-wide harmonization agenda and rather more into looking at other ways in which barriers arising from divergent national company laws could be dismantled. This preference reflected the political-legal environment of the period, the impact of the subsidiarity and proportionality principles on EU policy setting, the economic context of globalization, a certain fear of "petrification" within the existing EU company law harmonization program, rising interest in alter-native regulatory techniques including optional "model laws," nonbinding best practice codes, recommendations, and self-regulation, and also the extent to which the positive view of regulatory competition as a force for good had gained ground in epistemic communities.[36] Extensive further formal harmoni-zation of company law was seen by many to be a question of rather low prior-ity.[37] Arguably the most significant developments in European company law during the 2000s were driven not by the legislative institutions but by the European Court of Justice, which in the famous *Centros* line of cases[38] dis-mantled barriers in national company laws to cross-border corporate mobil-ity.[39] The position today can be viewed as one in which member states' national systems of company law rub along quite well with each other despite differ-ences in their detail—a state of affairs that owes much to the "negative har-monization" catalyzed by the court.[40] Collaborative working with the member states to address national barriers to capital flows is now deeply embedded in how the Commission does its business.[41] Top-down convergence in EU com-pany law may remain largely "formal and superficial" even if it is "not entirely irrelevant,"[42] and it may be true that "even after multi-year efforts to move on with the company law harmonization programme, little progress has been made in the direction of company law uniformity within the EU,"[43] but these are not necessarily pessimistic assessments.

The difficult passage of the Takeover Bids Directive[44] highlighted the for-midable challenges that in the 2000s stood in the way of ambitious plans for top-down company law making at the EU level. This experience is still worth revisiting today because while the Commission, in a more recent Action Plan for company law and corporate governance,[45] continued to extol the need for a modern and efficient framework, translating that aspiration into concrete legislative action of the top-down, single rulebook variety that has become the norm in the financial sector remains difficult.

Ideas for an EU law on takeovers had been around since at least the 1970s and a plan for harmonization of the rules governing takeovers was mentioned by the Commission in its 1985 White Paper on completing the internal market, but it was not until 2004 that the directive was finally adopted. Over the years, various draft versions of the directive had run into serious opposition from member states and failed to make progress. Member states' concerns, fed by vigorous lobbying from business and employee bodies and other special interest groups, reflected national priorities ranging from a preference for nonstatutory self-regulation of takeovers through to different views on the appropriate protections for employees of companies involved in bids and on the legitimacy of defensive measures by target companies. The version finally adopted was weakened by expedient compromises needed to secure its passage. The directive was in minimum harmonization form and allowed member states to derogate from some important provisions, including the mandatory bid rule. In addition, key provisions on board neutrality that prohibit defensive measures without shareholder approval and on allowing bidders to break through multiple voting rights and restrictions on voting rights were subject to various degrees of optionality at both member state and company levels.

The extent of the watering down led some to query whether the directive was even worth the paper it was written on,[46] although others saw more merit in it as a flexible directive that was pragmatic and workable.[47] In terms of practical impact, a European Commission review of the Takeovers Directive in 2012 gave a rather muted evaluation.[48] The report noted that economically it was difficult to calculate the impact of the directive because there had been few European takeovers due to economic conditions resulting from the financial crisis. So, in the absence of market data, the measurement of impact therefore had to rest more on the extent to which it had driven change in national laws. Here, the Commission found that the minimum harmonization character of the directive had allowed a wide variety of national rules in the field of takeover bids to continue to persist. On the other hand, the Commission found that the board neutrality rule had been relatively successful in the sense that it had been transposed by nineteen member states, but not so the breakthrough rule, which had been transposed by only three member states. The Commission also found that about half of the member states allowed companies that were subject to the board neutrality rule and/or breakthrough rule to not apply the rule when they were confronted with a takeover bid or by an offer that was not subject to the same rule. Academic commentary suggested, first, that in some respects the directive had had the directly opposite effect to that intended in that some member states ended up with less board neutrality than before,[49] and second, that a significantly changed economic and regulatory environment—including the proliferation of trading venues and trading techniques, the creative use of equity derivatives as a takeover instrument, the post-crisis revaluation of once-totemic concepts such as the efficient markets theory and of the merits of long-term stable shareholders, and the emergence of the European Securities and Markets Authority as an authority capable of assuming an expanded role—could justify revisiting fundamental concepts in the directive.[50] In spite of this, the Commission showed little interest in reopening old battles and confined its recommendations to largely technical changes. This stance was backed by the European Parliament, and so for now serious revision of the directive remains on hold.[51]

While there was notable success in regulating cross-border mergers at the EU level during the period,[52] another failure originating in the 2000s that reinforces the impression of company law as an area where it is especially difficult to reach agreement at the EU level was the failure of the proposed statute on the European private company, which had the aim of creating a new legal form with a view to enabling smaller businesses to operate more cost-effectively on an EU-wide basis. This proposal was announced in 2008 but withdrawn in 2013.[53] The Commission then introduced an alternative proposal for a directive on single-member private limited liability companies that would establish a new national company law form (SUP) governed by the same rules in all member states.[54] However, the alternative SUP proposal also ran into political opposition, and in its 2018 work program the Commission indicated it intended to withdraw the proposal and would instead table new proposals on company law.[55] The European company thus remains a rare success for the EU in creating a new supranational corporate legal form, but it too had a difficult passage and the final structure[56] draws on member states' national company laws to such an extent that it has been said it "fails to deliver on its promises" and "cannot be called a genuinely European company."[57]

But the 2000s was also the decade that marked the start of a significant intensification of EU harmonization relating to matters sitting at or near the boundary between company law and capital markets law. Historically issuer disclosure requirements would typically have been regarded as an aspect of company law, but prospectus and periodic/episodic disclosure requirements are now indisputably part of capital markets law and regulation, and in the EU context the relevant requirements are within the scope of the single rulebook. Since the 2000s there has also been rapid acceleration in the area of financial disclosure requirements for listed companies with the adoption by regulation of the International Financial Reporting Standards. This, too, can be seen as an outcome of the reorientation of an area of regulation that had historically been strongly associated with shareholder and creditor protection to a more modern capital market and investor protection purpose. However, outside the listed company context the older philosophies that underpin financial disclosure requirements in company law have proved to be stickier,[58] and progress on the modernization of EU-wide company financial disclosure requirements has been more mixed, as evidenced by the 2013 Accounting Directive,[59] which contains so many options at member state level for the treatment of medium-sized and large companies that the European Federation of Accountants and Auditors for SMEs has described it as "illogical" because it means "that the smallest of companies in Europe and the largest of companies in Europe are harmonised to the fullest extent and the medium-sized and large companies are not."[60]

Another striking example of the increasingly indistinct boundary between capital markets law and company law over the past two decades has been in the area of shareholder rights. Shareholder rights are an intrinsic part of core company law and corporate governance, but where the exercise of those rights is affected by the way in which equity investment is conducted it becomes a capital markets law issue as well. Hence the 2007 Shareholder Rights Directive, which, in its original form, sought to address the rather narrow (but important) matter of problems encountered by shareholders in listed companies in exercising shareholder voting rights cross-border that had been exacerbated by modern forms of intermediated holdings of investments.[61] This directive is in minimum harmonization form and expressly preserves the right of member states to impose further obligations or to take further measures.[62] In the original 2007 version of the directive, the importance of financial intermediaries in facilitating the exercise of voting rights was acknowledged,[63] but the directive itself did not extend regulation into that area. The financial crisis, however, triggered a reconsideration of the appropriate reach of EU-level intervention. The financial crisis was not primarily about failures in company law or general corporate governance, but it became received wisdom that it did expose weaknesses in those areas,[64] including excessive shareholder short-termism, insufficient engagement by institutional investors and asset managers, and the failure of regulatory policy to keep pace with the growing importance of proxy advisers as well as continuing difficulties with the exercise of cross-border voting rights that the 2007 directive had not solved. There was much discussion not only of inadequacies in disclosure and transparency requirements, which are issues that sit both in company law (where the purpose is to enable shareholders to make informed governance decisions) and in capital markets law (where the purpose is to improve the informational efficiency of the market) but also of whether shareholders should have enhanced voting rights in the key areas of remuneration and related-party transactions. This is going deeply into questions that we would traditionally regard as being squarely in the realm of substantive company law and corporate governance.[65] Much of this thinking was then channeled into the Shareholders Rights Directive 2017, which amends and extends the scope of the 2007 version.[66] Given the focus in this chapter on company law as a bottleneck to further financial integration, the revisions with respect to remuneration and related-party transactions are of particular interest.

With regard to remuneration, the revised position is that member states must ensure that companies establish a remuneration policy regarding directors and that shareholders have the right to cast a vote on that policy at every material change and at least every four years.[67] There are prescriptive requirements relating to the content of the remuneration policy, including that it must contribute to the company's business strategy, long-term interests, and sustainability, and that when a company awards variable remuneration, the nonfinancial criteria for its award shall "where appropriate" include criteria relating to corporate social responsibility.[68] But member states have the option to provide for the vote to be advisory rather than binding,[69] and there is also provision for member states to allow companies to temporarily derogate from the remuneration policy in certain circumstances.[70] There is also now an obligation on member states to give shareholders an annual nonbinding advisory vote on the remuneration report, although for SMEs, member states may soften this to a requirement for discussion at the annual general meeting as a separate agenda item.[71]

Regarding related-party transactions as well as transparency-enhancing changes, there are now new requirements on the approval of material related-party transactions.[72] It is left to member states themselves to define "material transactions." Different materiality definitions may be adopted for different purposes, and definitions may also be differentiated according to company size.[73] There is also member state optionality with regard to the approving body, which may be the shareholders or the administrative or supervisory body[74] with a further option for member states to provide for the shareholders to have the right to vote on material transactions with related parties that have been approved by the administrative or supervisory body.[75] There are carve-outs for certain categories of transaction.

The final version of the directive is less interventionist than the first draft proposed by the Commission,[76] and it is also less far-reaching than proposals that emerged in the European Parliament that would have gone further than the Commission draft with respect to the types of company within scope and on employee participation.[77] Luca Enriques has cited the watering down of the Commission's proposal as an example of the extent to which national interest groups still have the upper hand "whenever meaningful harmonized rules are proposed."[78] Certainly looking through the CMU lens with the idea of company law as a bottleneck to the realization of a genuine CMU in mind, it could be argued that the Shareholder Rights Directive falls very far short of what is needed because it fails to impose the required degree of regulatory uniformity. However, this is a troubling argument that takes us to the heart of the discussion in this chapter—namely, the existence of potential dangers in going too far down the route of thinking about company law and corporate governance as handmaidens to the needs of the capital markets.

Practically speaking this danger may not be great at present because, as Enriques has argued, member states' political preferences that are usually fed by influential interest groups can be relied on to block the ideology of the single rulebook from reaching too far into core company law. These preferences, which have legal ballast in the form of the subsidiarity and proportionality principles, reflect the ground conditions in national economies, and Brexit is unlikely to be an immediate game changer in this area because different flavors of market capitalism will continue to be prevalent across the remaining EU27. Despite that there is no immediate risk of it happening, we should not become complacent about the danger of a new emerging dynamic in favor of it being desirable, in principle, for company law and corporate governance to follow the same pathway of EU-level regulatory intensification that has occurred in the financial sectoral context. Leaving everything to be shaped by what Klaus Hopt has dubbed "the forces or deadlocks of political compromise"[79] would be both intellectually impoverished and potentially naïve with regard to the way that the EU works. After all, the history of EU financial regulation history tells us that seemingly small but incremental steps lay down roots that can, over time, develop into something transformative and that the crises in the markets that are inevitable from time to time can provide windows of opportunities to do things at the EU level that would once have been considered unthinkable. It also tells us that the EU is functional in its approach; that capital markets law has an imperialist, invasive tendency; and that in receptive conditions, it is capable of encroaching into areas that would have once been considered to be core company law. We should not be blind to the fact that once a matter is seen to be part of capital markets law, it could thereafter be carried along by the dynamic of the single rulebook and by associated institutional developments at the EU level that seek to foster uniformity in action as well as on paper. To quote Klaus Hopt once again, we should pay attention to the potential "bandwagon effect" of the CMU in this respect.[80] In the US context it has come to be seen that federal lawmakers can, and do, put aside state corporate laws on issues of true economic significance and that there is in fact no hard limit on federal lawmaking, notwithstanding the apparent sharp divide whereby states govern internal corporate affairs while the external trading of securities is a federal matter.[81] This insight is also relevant to the EU notwithstanding the many differences in constitutional frameworks and institutional structures. It is also true that the trend for securities law actions—based on misleading disclosures to displace orthodox corporate actions for breach of directors' duties as the means by which directors of listed companies are held accountable—is spreading from the United States across the Atlantic.[82]

Shaping a Response to the Invasive Capital Markets Regulatory Agenda

What is the vision for company law and corporate governance at the EU level? What is the underpinning philosophy? What is the principled, and not simply politically pragmatic, case for action at the EU level on corporate law matters? Where there is a case for EU-level action, what form should it take, and how intensive should it be? Should it apply to entire population of EU companies or just a subset? These questions are not new, and there is no shortage of views on possible responses, but there is rather less of a developed consensus on the answers than now exists in the adjacent field of financial regulation. To an extent this has not mattered greatly thus far, at least not if your preferences are for diversity and selective harmonization, because EU policy ambition has been hemmed in by political constraints in any event. However, the inclusion of company law in the broader CMU agenda—an agenda that embraces the single rulebook ideology—is a new force against those whose preference is for diversity, and selectivity may need to sharpen their arguments.

There are three issues to highlight. The first is that, while we may assume that the diversity of corporate governance models is safe because this is a matter on which member states, and their interest groups, hold strong views that the Commission has no option but to accept,[83] we should not ignore the risk of finding that, over time, a particular version of corporate organization has crept into the ascendancy at the EU level under the cover of capital markets law. There may be hints of this already. One charge that has been laid against the Shareholder Rights Directive, for instance, is that it has a "myopic" focus on shareholders and, as a result, falls far short of addressing the underlying causes of short-termism so as to prevent future crises, which would, it is suggested, call for more sweeping reforms to effect a shift toward a model that prioritizes the long-term interests of the company while respecting the interests of shareholders and other stakeholders.[84] Many would probably quite quickly conclude that the shareholder/stakeholder debate is contentious enough within national settings without trying to grapple with the multiplicity of diverse views that would undoubtedly emerge at supranational level and so might applaud the Commission for not going there at least on pragmatic grounds and perhaps also from a more principled perspective on what it is appropriate to do at the EU level. We can see a similar reticence about opening up a debate on fundamental questions when the Commission reviewed corporate governance in the aftermath of the financial crisis—an exercise that referred to shareholder/stakeholder considerations but was essentially about "how to improve the effectiveness of the current rules."[85] The unwillingness of the Commission to go beyond technical matters in its review of the Takeover Directive is another example. However, further discussion at the EU level of the question whether the shareholder-oriented underlying purpose of company law and corporate governance that gained ground in EU policy thinking around the turn of the millennium is still convincing as a vision and philosophy or whether, in the light of the shortcomings in the tenets of good corporate governance as understood in the late 1990s and early 2000s that were exposed by the financial crisis, it requires reevaluation cannot be deferred indefinitely.

The second is that momentum could build for EU-level intervention with respect to company law to become less selective in scope. One potential pressure point arising from the CMU agenda relates to the population of companies that are addressed by EU measures. In the past two decades the view among many corporate scholars has been that, broadly speaking, the EU should concern itself with companies that access the capital markets (with the proviso that this should be done carefully so as not to put listed companies at an unwarranted disadvantage to other firms)[86] and leave the rest to be regulated at national level with intervention only to remove national barriers to cross-border mobility. However, EU public markets for smaller companies are weak, and so a strategy of focusing on listed companies reaches only a small proportion of the total population.[87] The CMU is for all companies; new start-ups are seen to be critical to driving economic growth, and many of the initiatives under the CMU banner are about improving and expanding the financing choices for start-ups and scale-ups as well as for more established companies. Admittedly, the emphasis for now is mostly on improving the finance supply side, but there are already relevant developments on the demand side too. This takes us briefly into the realm of insolvency law.

Under the CMU agenda, the Commission has tabled proposed EU legislation applicable to all companies[88] to address problems arising from substantive differences in national insolvency regimes[89] (replacing a nonbinding Commission recommendation[90] that failed to drive consistent changes across all member states). The Commission's case for the proposed minimum harmonization of substantive insolvency law through the draft directive has many elements,[91] but part of the rationale is that a supranational approach is justified because very few companies are purely national these days. This is a rationale that could easily be applied to company law too. Advances in insolvency law at the EU level could set the stage for more extensive substantive company law changes than has seemed practically and politically possible until now. The boundaries between company law and insolvency law are themselves somewhat indistinct. For example, the question of directors' personal liability for corporate failure that the proposed Restructuring Directive proposes to address[92] straddles both, and the intersection is a source of frictions and can lead to undesirable legal arbitrage.[93] The European Court has now given a clear (if controversial)[94] answer to the conflict of laws question of which national substantive liability rules apply on the insolvency of a company that is incorporated in one member state but has its center of main interests in another.[95] However, it is possible to envisage that in the longer term the arguments for dealing with such frictions through an integrated package of harmonized and increasingly prescriptive company and insolvency laws could gain traction as a simplifying, certainty-enhancing approach that would better encourage cross-border investment and corporate mobility and hence deepen financial regulation. In this regard, it is relevant to note that the Commission's Informal Company Law Expert Group has already suggested that introducing a rule to harmonize directors' creditor facing obligations, as now provided for in the draft directive, would greatly facilitate the recognition of the interests of the corporate group—an issue that has been debated in EU corporate law circles for many years.[96] For insolvency law to take the lead at European level would be a reversal of fortune given that there was substantial activity to harmonize company law until it stalled in the 1990s, whereas it took the EU some forty years even to harmonize aspects of insolvency process.[97] But there is a palpable sense that, helped by the CMU agenda, the moment for at least baby steps[98] toward substantive harmonization of insolvency law has finally arrived and, notwithstanding the "suspicion that the political imperatives of the Capital Markets Union project pushed the Commission into legislative mode and such action is perhaps premature,"[99] will it be welcomed by market participants who have identified insolvency regime diversity as negatively impacting confidence in cross-border investment?[100]

The obvious rejoinder to the vision of a coordinated and broad program of harmonized insolvency and company law envisaged here is that it is so divorced from contemporary reality that it is not worth spending time on. After all, even if the proposed Restructuring Directive is adopted intact—unlikely given the controversy it has generated[101]—its main impact will be the introduction of a minimally harmonized pre-insolvency preventative restructuring framework, and it will still leave many core aspects of insolvency law unharmonized because the current diversity in member states' legal systems is too great to be bridged. Meanwhile on the corporate side, current Commission priorities such as updating company law for the digital age and codification of the existing body of EU law[102] are worthy but hardly transformative, so it is not as if we can credibly view the CMU agenda as having opened the door to truly radical change. The added dimension of Brexit does not change the position because wide diversity in legal systems will still remain among the EU27 after the United Kingdom leaves. And even if we did entertain significant expansion of EU insolvency and company law as a serious possibility, there would still be the matter of all the other laws and regulations that impinge on the functioning of the financial markets. Also, to imagine all-encompassing harmonization really would strain credulity too far, not least because there is no Treaty competence that would allow for harmonization of private law in its entirety. However, in response to these indisputably powerful points, it can also be said that significant milestones are not always obvious at the time, that political preferences are not immutable, and that as we have seen in financial regulation, a strategy of long-term patient policymaking can deliver dramatic change over the longer term.

The third issue, which is related to the second, is that the form and style of EU regulation of companies could come under pressure to change as a result of the CMU agenda. In "core" financial regulation, options and discretions that are left to member states are now often perceived to be a problem because they have the potential to undermine the quest for uniformity that is signified by the single rulebook. In EU company law, on the other hand, there is a more evenly balanced debate about the benefits and downsides of optionality at the member state level and about intensive prescriptiveness more generally. As mentioned earlier, aspirations for comprehensive harmonization were effectively abandoned around the turn of the century, and since then, alternative approaches to designing corporate regulation that meets the needs of the internal market have come more into favor. Formal harmonization is more the exception than the rule and is usually by directives in minimum harmonization form. The orthodoxy is to favor flexibility and freedom of choice.[103] Yet the underlying reasons for this are rooted in pragmatism as much as principle with the result that conceptually, it can be hard to see a clear vision. There is actually a lot to be said in favor of a flexible stance that welcomes optionality in some circumstances and decries it in others because the basic philosophy of company law is that it is enabling, and so the solution should fit the problem rather than being rigid and unbending. However, we now need to ask whether this nuanced approach is sufficiently robust to resist the bandwagon of the strong uniforming force of the single rulebook ideology. The point that needs to be made clearly is that while a single rulebook is good for integration because it represents an advance toward the conditions in which the law of one price can obtain, legal and regulatory uniformity also has downsides. Uniform but poor-quality rules could be worse for society than a more diverse system in which legal and regulatory approaches that successfully foster sustainable innovation and growth compete with less suitable models. The EU corporate law harmonization agenda should remain driven by distinct corporate law objectives, which are rooted in facilitation of socially worthwhile business activity, and should not be completely overtaken by the capital and financial markets agenda and its prescriptive single rulebook ideology.

All of this being said, the final point is that this chapter should not be read as seeing nothing positive in the attempt to use the CMU agenda to go beyond sectoral regulation and to address bottlenecks in company law and related areas as well. There are dangers in treating company law simply as the handmaiden of the CMU project to be sure, but the new push to deepen financial integration also presents an opportunity for beneficial change. For instance, more receptive ground conditions for rethinking how to protect shareholders and creditors and relaxing old-style EU company laws on shareholder and creditor protection that have not kept pace with modern realities would be welcome. Sectoral legislation has led the way on this,[104] and the proposed Restructuring Directive follows that lead.[105] Sectoral developments[106] are also serving as an important catalyst for closer engagement with proposals for an intervention at the EU level that would better align the general law with the economic realities of the functioning of corporate groups.[107] Some ways in which recent financial sectoral regulation has resolved tensions between the sectoral situation and general company and insolvency laws are by insulating certain financial market transactions from the general law[108] or by displacing the general law and applying a bespoke regime for financial institutions.[109] How such special arrangements work merits close study. When or to what extent it is appropriate for financial regulation to modify how the general law applies in relation to financial institutions is an important question.[110] Also worth monitoring are sectoral regulatory requirements that add to what is required by the general law. Much has been written, for example, about why the special corporate governance requirements that are now imposed on banks by EU prudential regulation should not be adopted for nonfinancial companies.[111] However, we should remain open to the possibility of approaches that were developed first in the sectoral context becoming models for wider reforms. Being wary of the danger of the general law being refashioned just to suit the regulatory agenda does not mean shutting down the possibility that an innovation within the sectoral context may prove to be suitable for wider application. Lastly, as the EU harmonization agenda continues to operate at intersections and to exploit functional substitutionality, we can expect a deepening of learning on the materiality or triviality of individual legal rules and the interrelationship between that and the distribution of legislative competences between Brussels and the member states.

Notes

1. Véron and Wolff 2016.
2. Valiante 2016.
3. Ferran 2012.
4. Constâncio 2017.
5. Quoted in Khan (2016).
6. Constâncio 2017.
7. Ringe 2015.
8. Juncker et al. 2015.
9. Juncker et al. 2015, 12.
10. Hopt and Wymeersch 2003.
11. Timmermans 2003, 629.
12. Davies 2003.
13. Winter 2003.
14. Wymeersch 2003.
15. Kübler 2003.
16. Hopt 2015, 194.
17. European Commission 2015.
18. Moloney 2016.
19. European Parliament 2015, para C.
20. European Commission 2015.
21. European Commission 2017d, 2–3.
22. European Commission 2017b.
23. European Central Bank 2017, 2.
24. Directive 2014/59/EU of 15 May 2014 establishing a framework for the recovery and resolution of credit institutions and investment firms, [2014] OJ L173/190 (BRRD).
25. Proposal for a Directive establishing a framework for the recovery and resolution of credit institutions and investment firms, COM (2012) 280, 8.
26. Regulation (EU) No. 575/2013 of 26 June 2013 on prudential requirements for credit institutions and investment firms, [2013] OJ L176/3 (CRR).
27. Directive 2013/36/EU on access to the activity of credit institutions and the prudential supervision of credit institutions and investment firms, [2013] OJ L176/338 (CRDIV).
28. Commission Staff Working Paper: Impact Assessment Accompanying the document Proposal for a Directive on the access to the activity of credit institutions and the prudential supervision of credit institutions and investment firms, SEC (2011) 952, 131.

29. Regulation (EU) No 600/2014 of the European Parliament and of the Council of 15 May 2014 on markets in financial instruments, [2014] OJ L 173/84 (MiFIR).

30. Directive 2014/65/EU of 15 May 2014 on markets in financial instruments, [2014] OJ L 173/349 (MiFID II).

31. European Commission 2012a, 4.

32. Wouters 2000.

33. Winter 2003.

34. European Commission 2003.

35. Edwards 1999, 7.

36. Wouters 2000.

37. Wymeersch 2004, 182.

38. *Centros*, March 9, 1999, C-212/97; *Überseering*, November 5, 2002, C-208/00; *Inspire Art*, September 30, 2003, C-167/01; *Cartesio*, December 16, 2008, C-210/06; *National Grid Indus*, November 29, 2011, C-371/10; *Vale*, July 12, 2012, C-378/10; *Polbud*, October 22, 2017, C-106/16.

39. Böckli et al. 2017; Gelter 2018.

40. Enriques 2017.

41. European Commission 2017a.

42. Gelter 2018.

43. Enriques 2017, 763.

44. Directive 2004/25/EC of 21 April 2004 on takeover bids, [2004] OJ L142/12.

45. European Commission 2012a.

46. Edwards 2004.

47. McCahery and Vermeulen 2011.

48. European Commission 2012b.

49. Davies et al. 2010.

50. Wymeersch 2012.

51. Mukwiri 2015.

52. Directive 2005/56/EC of 26 October 2005 on cross-border mergers of limited liability companies, [2005] OJ L310/1 (now consolidated into Directive [EU] 2017/1132 of 14 June 2017 relating to certain aspects of company law, [2017] OJ L 169/46).

53. European Commission 2013.

54. Proposal for a directive on single-member private limited liability companies, COM (2014) 212, 2.

55. European Commission 2017e.

56. Regulation (EC) No. 2157/2002 of 8 October 2001 on the Statute for a European Company, [2001] OJ L294/1; Directive 2001/86/EC of 8 October 2001 supplementing the Statute for a European company with regard to the involvement of employees, [2001] OJ L294/22.

57. Ghetti 2016.

58. Panetsos 2016.

59. Directive 2013/34/EU of 26 June 2013, [2013] OJ L182/19.

60. European Federation of Accountants and Auditors for SMES 2013.

61. Directive 2007/36/EC of 11 July 2007 on the exercise of certain rights of shareholders in listed companies, [2007] OJ L184/17.

62. Article 3.

63. Recital 11.

64. European Commission 2012a, 3.

65. The history of EU company law does include an attempt (the proposed Fifth Company Law Directive) to harmonize the distribution of powers between directors and shareholders but it was finally abandoned in 2001 after around thirty years of trying (Gelter 2018).

66. Directive (EU) 2017/828 of 17 May 2017 amending Directive 2007/36/EC as regards the encouragement of long-term shareholder engagement, [2017] OJ L132/1.

67. Article 9a.

68. Article 9a(6).

69. Article 9a(3).

70. Article 9a(4).

71. Article 9b.

72. Article 9c.

73. Article 9c(1).

74. Article 9c(2).

75. Article 9c(4).

76. Gelter 2018.

77. Hopt 2015.

78. Enriques 2017, 770.

79. Hopt 2015.

80. Hopt 2015.

81. Roe 2003.

82. Moore 2017.

83. See, e.g., Commission Recommendation of 9 April 2014 on the quality of corporate governance reporting ("comply or explain"), [2014] OJ L109/43, which provides nonbinding guidance to member states in this sensitive area. The Recommendation stresses that good corporate governance is first and foremost an internal corporate responsibility (recital 1) and it expressly noted that "given the diversity of legal traditions and approaches, these recommendations offer a general framework, which can be further developed and adapted to the specific national context" (recital 12).

84. Johnston and Morrow 2015.

85. European Commission 2012a, 3.

86. Reflection Group 2011, 10.

87. European Commission 2017c.

88. Save for banks and other financial sector actors to which special regimes apply.

89. Proposal for a Directive on preventive restructuring frameworks, second chance and measures to increase the efficiency of restructuring, and discharge procedures and amending Directive 2012/30/EU, COM (2016) 723 (Restructuring Directive).

90. Commission Recommendation of 12 March 2014 on a new approach to business failure and insolvency, [2014] OJ L74/65.

91. McCormack 2017.

92. Restructuring Directive, art. 18. Note also art. 7 (suspending the obligation of the debtor to file for insolvency during the period of a stay on individual enforcement actions).

93. Gerner-Beuerle and Schuster 2014.

94. Ringe 2017; Informal Company Law Expert Group 2016.

95. *Kornhaas v. Dithmar*, December 10, 2015, C-594/14, [2016] BCC 116.

96. Informal Company Law Expert Group 2016, 27.

97. Rajak 2016.

98. Ghio 2017.

99. McCormack 2017, 538–539.

100. European Commission 2015, 59–60.

101. Eidenmüller 2017.

102. Directive (EU) 2017/1132 of 14 June 2017 relating to certain aspects of company law, [2017] OJ L 169/46.

103. Reflection Group 2011.

104. E.g., BRRD, art. 123 (amendments to Directive 2012/30/EU (now Directive [EU] 2017/2399).

105. By requiring member states to derogate from shareholders' rights derived from (now) Directive 2017/2399 on capital increases and reductions and pre-emption rights to ensure that shareholders do not frustrate restructuring efforts by abusing those rights. Restructuring Directive, art. 32.

106. E.g., BRRD, art. 19(4) (removal of legal impediments in national law to intra-group financial support transactions).

107. Informal Company Law Expert Group 2016.

108. E.g., Directive 98/26/EC of 19 May 1998 on settlement finality in payment and securities settlement systems, [1998] OJ L166/45.

109. E.g., Directive 2017/2399 on amending Directive 2014/59/EU of the European Parliament and of the Council as regards the ranking of unsecured debt instruments in insolvency hierarchy, [2017] OJ L 345/96.

110. Ferrarini 2017.

111. Hopt 2013; Mülbert 2010.

References

Böckli, P. et al. 2017. "The Consequences of Brexit for Companies and Company Law." University of Cambridge Faculty of Law Research Paper No 22/2017, Cambridge, UK.

Constâncio, V. 2017. "Synergies between Banking Union and Capital Markets Union." Keynote speech at the joint conference of the European Commission and European Central Bank on European Financial Integration, Brussels, May 19.

Davies, P. 2003. "Shareholder Value, Company Law, and Securities Market Law: A British View." In *Capital Markets and Company Law*, edited by K. Hopt and E. Wymeersch, 261–288. Oxford: Oxford University Press.

Davies, P. L., E. Schuster, and E. Walle de Ghelcke. 2010. "The Takeover Directive as a Protectionist Tool?" In *Company Law and Economic Protectionism: New Challenges to European Integration*, edited by U. Bernitz and W.-G. Ringe, 105–160. Oxford: Oxford University Press.

Edwards, V. 1999. *EC Company Law*. Oxford: Oxford University Press.

Edwards, V. 2004. "The Directive on Takeover Bids—Not Worth the Paper It's Written On?" *European Company and Financial Law Review* 4: 416–439.

Eidenmüller, H. 2017. "Contracting for a European Insolvency Regime." *European Business Organization Law Review* 18: 273–304.

Enriques, L. 2017. "A Harmonized European Company Law: Are We There Already?" *International and Comparative Law Quarterly* 66, no. 3: 763–777.

European Central Bank (ECB). 2017. *Financial Integration in Europe*. Frankfurt am Main, May 2017.

European Commission. 2003. *Modernising Company Law and Enhancing Corporate Governance in the European Union—A Plan to Move Forward*. Luxembourg: Publications Office of the European Union, COM (2003) 284.

European Commission. 2012a. *Action Plan: European Company Law and Corporate Governance—A Modern Legal Framework for More Engaged Shareholders and Sustainable Companies*. Luxembourg: Publications Office of the European Union, COM (2012) 740.

European Commission. 2012b. *Application of Directive 2004/25/EC on Takeover Bids.* Luxembourg: Publications Office of the European Union, COM (2012) 347.

European Commission. 2013. *Regulatory Fitness and Performance (REFIT): Results and Next Steps.* Luxembourg: Publications Office of the European Union, COM (2013) 685.

European Commission. 2015. *Action Plan on Building a Capital Markets Union.* Luxembourg: Publications Office of the European Union, COM (2015) 468.

European Commission. 2017a. *Accelerating the Capital Markets Union: Addressing National Barriers to Capital Flows.* Luxembourg: Publications Office of the European Union, COM (2017) 147.

European Commission. 2017b. "Banking Reform: EU Reaches Agreement on First Key Measures." Press release, October 25, Brussels.

European Commission. 2017c. "Building a Proportionate Regulatory Environment to Support SME Listing." Consultation document.

European Commission. 2017d. *Mid-Term Review of the Capital Markets Union Action Plan.* Brussels: European Union, COM (2017) 292 final, June. https://ec.europa.eu/info/publications /mid-term-review-capital-markets-union-action-plan_en.

European Commission. 2017e. "Work Programme 2018: An Agenda for a More United, Stronger and More Democratic Europe." Luxembourg: Publications Office of the European Union, COM (2017) 650.

European Federation of Accountants and Auditors for SMES. 2013. "The Revision of the Accounting Directives—Missed Opportunity?" Position paper.

European Parliament. 2015. *Report on Stocktaking and Challenges of the EU Financial Services Regulation.* Brussels: European Parliament.

Ferran, E. 2012. "Crisis-Driven Regulatory Reform: Where in the World Is the EU Going?" In *The Regulatory Aftermath of the Global Financial Crisis,* edited by E. Ferran et al., 1–110. Cambridge: Cambridge University Press.

Ferrarini, G. 2017. "Understanding the Role of Corporate Governance in Financial Institutions: A Research Agenda." ECGI Law Working Paper No 347/2017, European Corporate Governance Institute.

Gelter, M. 2018. "EU Company Law Harmonization between Convergence and Varieties of Capitalism." In *Research Handbook on the History of Corporate Law,* edited by H. Wells, 323–352. Cheltenham, UK: Edward Elgar.

Gerner-Beuerle, C., and E. Schuster. 2014. "The Costs of Separation: Friction between Company and Insolvency Law in the Single Market." *Journal of Corporate Law Studies* 14, no. 2: 287–332.

Ghetti, R. 2016. "Unification, Harmonisation and Competition in European Company Forms." *European Business Law Review,* 29, no. 5: 813–842.

Ghio, E. 2017. "The EU Incremental Approach to Cross-Border Insolvency Regulation: A Critical Analysis." *International Company and Commercial Law Review* 28, no. 10: 369–376.

Hopt, K. J. 2013. "Corporate Governance of Banks and Other Financial Institutions after the Financial Crisis." *Journal of Corporate Law Studies* 13: 219–253.

Hopt, K. J. 2015. "Corporate Governance in Europe, A Critical Review of the European Commission's Initiatives on Corporate Law and Corporate Governance." *NYU Journal of Law & Business* 12: 139–213.

Hopt, K. J., and F. Wymeersch. 2003. *Capital Markets and Company Law.* Oxford: Oxford University Press.

Informal Company Law Expert Group. 2016. *Report on the Recognition of the Interest of the Group.* A report for the European Commission.

Johnston, A., and P. Morrow. 2015. "Towards Long-Termism in Corporate Governance: The Shareholder Rights Directive and Beyond." In *Long-Term Investment and the Sustainable Company,* edited by S. Vitols, 19–45. Brussels: ETUI.

Juncker, J.-C. et al. 2015. *The Five Presidents' Report: Completing Europe's Economic and Monetary Union*. Brussels: European Commission.

Khan, M. 2016. "Carney: UK Is 'Investment Banker for Europe.'" *Financial Times*, November 30.

Kübler, F. 2003. "The Rules of Capital under Pressure of the Securities Markets." In *Capital Markets and Company Law*, edited by K. Hopt and E. Wymeersch, 95–114. Oxford: Oxford University Press.

McCahery, J. A., and E. P. Vermeulen. 2011. "The Case against Reform of the Takeover Bids Directive." *European Business Law Review* 22: 541–557.

McCormack, G. 2017. "Corporate Restructuring Law—A Second Chance for Europe?" *European Law Review* 42, no. 4: 532–561.

Moloney, N. 2016. "Capital Markets Union: 'Ever Closer Union' for the EU Financial System?" *European Law Review* 41, no. 3: 307–337.

Moore, M. T. 2017. "Redressing Risk Oversight Failure in UK and US Listed Companies: Lessons from the RBS and Citigroup Litigation." *European Business Organization Law Review* 18: 733–759.

Mukwiri, J. 2015. "Reforming EU Takeover Law Remains on Hold." *European Company Law* 4: 186–187.

Mülbert, P. O. 2010. "Corporate Governance of Banks after the Financial Crisis—Theory, Evidence, Reforms." ECGI Law Working Paper No 130/2009, European Corporate Governance Institute.

Panetsos, L. 2016. "Accounting Standards and Legal Capital in EU Law." *Utrecht Law Review* 12, no. 1: 139–158.

Rajak, H. 2016. "Insolvency Law v Company Law—EU Style." *Company Law Newsletter* 381: 1–3.

Reflection Group. 2011. *Report of the Reflection Group on the Future of EU Company Law*. Brussels: European Commission.

Ringe, W.-G. 2015. "Capital Markets Union for Europe—A Political Message to the UK." *Law and Financial Markets Review* 9: 5.

Ringe, W.-G. 2017. "Kornhaas and the Challenge of Applying Keck in Establishment." *European Law Review* 42, no. 2: 270–279.

Roe, M. J. 2003. "Delaware's Competition." *Harvard Law Review* 117: 588–646.

Timmermans, C. 2003. "Harmonization in the Future of Company Law in Europe." In *Capital Markets and Company Law*, edited by K. Hopt and E. Wymeersch, 623–637. Oxford: Oxford University Press.

Valiante, D. 2016. *Europe's Untapped Capital Market: Rethinking Financial Integration after the Crisis*. London: Rowman and Littlefield International.

Véron, N., and G. B. Wolff. 2016. "Capital Markets Union: A Vision for the Long Term." *Journal of Financial Regulation* 2: 130–153.

Winter, J. 2003. "Cross-Border Voting in Europe." In *Capital Markets and Company Law*, edited by K. Hopt and E. Wymeersch, 387–426. Oxford: Oxford University Press.

Wouters, J. 2000. "European Company Law: Quo vadis?" *Common Market Law Review* 37: 257–307.

Wymeersch, E. 2003. "Do We Need a Law on Groups of Companies?" In *Capital Markets and Company Law*, edited by K. Hopt and E. Wymeersch, 573–600. Oxford: Oxford University Press.

Wymeersch, E. 2004. "Modern Company Law-Making." In *Reforming Company and Takeover Law in Europe*, edited by G. Ferrarini et al., 145–182. Oxford: Oxford University Press.

Wymeersch, E. 2012. "A New Look at the Debate about the Takeover Directive." Financial Law Institute Working Paper No. 2012-05, Ghent University. https://ssrn.com/abstract=1988927.

4 Economic and Financial Integration in Europe

Geert Bekaert, Campbell R. Harvey, Christian T. Lundblad, and Stephan Siegel

For a long time, ever-larger flows of goods, capital, and labor across national borders were seen as a welcome consequence of increased globalization. Indeed, financial economists have documented how policy changes such as capital market liberalization have reduced market segmentation, improved the allocation of capital, and ultimately spurred economic growth. However, the benefits of economic openness as well as the institutions built around it are increasingly questioned by politicians and voters alike. In June 2016, the unthinkable happened when UK citizens voted to exit the European Union ("Brexit"). It is therefore timely to assess the historical contribution of specific institutions whose policies and even existence are in doubt. In this article, we perform such an assessment for Europe; in particular, we examine the role that the European Union (EU) and the common currency euro have played in the financial and economic integration of Europe.

After World War II, the EU set out to free the movement of goods, services, capital, and labor among its member countries. With more and more countries joining the EU, barriers among member countries disappearing, and the introduction of a common currency, the EU and, later, the euro have been perceived as the driving forces behind the integration of European economies. However, European integration happened against the backdrop of an integration process across the world (Bekaert et al. 2011). Differentiating between a global trend and the effects of EU membership and euro adoption is, of course, critical when evaluating the consequences of the United Kingdom leaving the EU or Greece reintroducing its own currency in place of the euro.

In contrast to existing studies on European equity market integration, which have focused on equity returns (see, e.g., Adjaouté and Danthine 2004; Baele 2005; Fratzscher 2002; Hardouvelis, Malliaropulos, and Priestley 2006), we use equity market valuations. Specifically, we evaluate financial *and* economic integration in Europe through the lens of stock market valuations of industry portfolios in different countries. Stock market valuations reflect financial integration through its impact on discount rates as well as economic integration through its impact on capitalized growth opportunities. Integration should lead to "valuation convergence" of similar firms across different countries. Hence, we assess the degree of bilateral integration in Europe and the impact of the EU and the euro by determining whether in a given country-pair, similar assets are valued similarly across both countries.

Most of our study focuses on the pre-crisis period from 1990 to 2007; this covers the expansion of the EU across many countries and the completion of the "single market," as well as the introduction of the euro. We initially examine the effect of EU membership on bilateral valuation differentials as well as its components, discount rates, and growth opportunities. We then consider the adoption of the euro in addition to EU membership on valuation differences between countries. Finally, accounting for EU membership and euro adoption, we also confront the recent crisis years by extending our sample period through August 2016.

Measuring Integration

We assess financial and economic integration in Europe by measuring the extent of equity market segmentation in Europe. Our measure of market segmentation was first introduced by Bekaert et al. (2011) and has since been used by a number of researchers (see, e.g., Beck et al. 2016; Goyenko and Sarkissian 2014). It is based on the simple intuition that two markets are integrated if similar assets are valued similarly.

As a starting point, consider the Gordon growth model, which assumes that the discount rate, r, is constant and expected earnings grow at a constant rate, g. If a firm pays out all earnings every year, its earnings yield simply is $r-g$. Hence, in this simple model, discount rates and growth opportunities are linearly related to earnings yields. Assume further that systematic risk is industry-specific rather than firm-specific, and that the industry structure is sufficiently granular so that industries are comparable across countries.[1] Financial market integration then equalizes industry betas as well as industry risk premia across countries. Further, assume that in economically integrated countries, persistent growth opportunities are mostly industry-specific rather than country-specific, or at least rapidly transmitted across countries. This is plausible as firms in the same industries face similar production processes and market conditions (again, under the null of free competition and lack of trade barriers). It then follows that the process of market integration should cause valuation differentials between industries in different countries to converge. We build on this intuition to create bilateral valuation differentials that serve as our segmentation measure.

Specifically, let $EY_{i,k,t}$ denote industry k's earnings yield in country i at time t and $EY_{j,k,t}$ the corresponding value for the same industry k in country j. Our main variable of analysis is the absolute value of the difference between the two industry valuations, $|EY_{i,k,t} - EY_{j,k,t}|$. The weighted sum of these bilateral industry valuation differentials is our measure of the degree of equity market segmentation between these two countries:

$$SEG_{i,j,t} = \sum_{k=1}^{N_{i,j,t}} IW_{i,j,k,t} \left| EY_{i,k,t} - EY_{j,k,t} \right|.$$

where $IW_{i,j,k,t}$ is the relative market capitalization of industry k and $N_{i,j,t}$ is the number of industries for country-pair (i,j) at time t.[2]

Bekaert et al. (2011) discuss several biases in this segmentation measure, such as country-specific differences in financial leverage and in the volatility of earnings growth rates and discount rates. In addition, the number of firms in a particular industry should affect the accuracy of the measure. However, it is straightforward to control for these biases in a regression analysis, and this is what we do.

Differently from the standard approach in the international finance literature that relies on historical return correlations or systematic risk exposures to *estimate* measures of segmentation (see Bekaert, Hodrick, and Zhang 2009 and the references therein), our measure requires nothing more than industry-level valuation ratios that are observed at every point in time.

European Integration over Time

We construct our measure of annual bilateral valuation differentials, *SEG*, for a sample of thirty-three European countries using firm-level data from Datastream from 1990 to 2007. Using the Industry Classification Benchmark framework, we form thirty-eight value-weighted industry portfolios for all countries. For each country-pair, we compute *SEG* as described above. The number of country-pairs with non-missing data is growing over time, from 120 country-pairs in 1990 to a maximum of 528 country-pairs.

During our main sample period from 1990 to 2007, the average segmentation level between European countries is 5.1%. However, for country-pairs for which both countries are EU members, the average segmentation is only 3.8%. While substantially lower than the level of non-EU country-pairs (6.0%), it is not clear whether this level is "close" to integration or not. Because the segmentation measure uses absolute differences in earnings yields, it need not be zero even under full financial and economic integration. Therefore, we use US equity market data to measure the average level of segmentation for fictitious, randomly created country-pairs that mimic our European pairs but exclusively reflect US valuations.[3] To the extent that the United States is financially and economically integrated, this exercise provides a meaningful benchmark to judge whether European country-pairs are segmented or not.

Figure 4.1 shows the average segmentation level for all EU and for all non-EU European country-pairs between 1990 and 2007. EU country-pairs are country-pairs where both countries are EU members; all other country-pairs are non-EU country-pairs. At all times, EU country-pairs are less segmented than non-EU country-pairs. Figure 4.1 also shows the average, randomly created US benchmark segmentation level corresponding to the set of all European country-pairs, together with a 90% confidence interval. Note that, even though the United States is an integrated market, the level of measured segmentation was mostly in the 2% to 4% range. With the exception of 2005, the valuation differentials of non-EU country-pairs were above the 90% confidence interval of valuation differences in the United States. In contrast, the measured segmentation levels across EU countries were similar to those in the United States by 2000. After 2000, segmentation was again larger across EU members than in the United States but still lower than for non-EU pairs. Importantly, this does not necessarily mean that EU membership was the cause of integration. For example, a plausible alternative hypothesis is that the general movement toward global market integration led to narrower valuation differentials across equity markets in the EU. We next use a regression framework to address this question.

The EU and Integration

One potential problem with our full sample underlying figure 4.1 is that the sample is unbalanced. Moreover, with the emergence of Eastern European countries in the 1990s, the sample composition changes substantially over time. We therefore focus our analysis on a balanced sample of the 120 country-pairs for which we have data since 1990. This sample excludes all Eastern European countries. For this balanced sample of 2,160 observations, the average overall level of bilateral segmentation is 4.0%—3.4% for EU country-pairs and 4.6% for non-EU country-pairs.

We investigate the effect of EU membership on bilateral equity valuation differentials using a linear regression model and controlling for several potentially confounding factors:

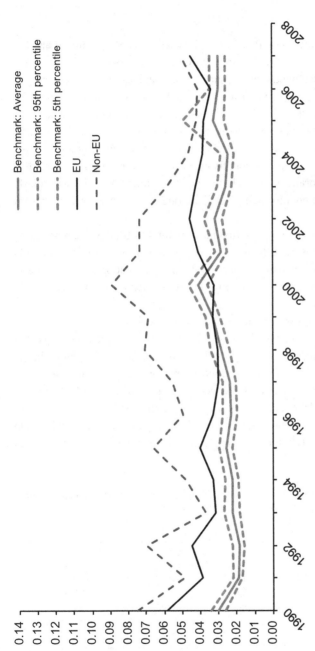

This figure presents average bilateral segmentation between 1990 and 2007 for all EU and Non-EU country-pairs. For comparison, the figure shows the average US benchmark segmentations level (constructed for the set of all European countries) together with a 90% confidence interval.

Figure 4.1
Benchmarking segmentation: full sample, 1990–2007 (annual frequency). *Note*: This figure presents average bilateral segmentation between 1990 and 2007 for all EU and non-EU country-pairs. For comparison, the figure shows the average US benchmark segmentations level (constructed for the set of all European countries) together with a 90% confidence interval.

$$SEG_{i,j,t} = a + b_{EU} \, EU_{i,j,t} + b_X \, X_{i,j,t} + c_{i,j} + d_t + \varepsilon_{i,j,t},$$

where $EU_{i,j,t}$ is an indicator that is one in year t if both countries are EU members and zero otherwise, $X_{i,j,t}$ represents a set of controls related to the construction of the segmentation measure,[4] and $c_{i,j}$ and d_t represent country-pair and year fixed effects. Their inclusion yields a difference-in-differences (DID) estimation, in which the EU effect is identified by country-pairs' changes in EU membership status while year fixed effects capture potential global integration trends. All standard errors are robust to arbitrary correlation over time within country-pairs and across country-pairs within years. Adjusting standard errors for contemporaneous correlation across country-pairs is particularly important given that country-pairs that share one country are not independent of one another.

Table 4.1, column 1 reports the first main result. For brevity, we report only the coefficient estimate and the associated standard error for the effect of EU membership.[5] EU membership reduces bilateral segmentation by 1.43 percentage points (pp) or by about 31% relative to the segmentation level of non-EU country-pairs.

From the Gordon growth model, we know that such a convergence in earnings yields represents a convergence in the cost of equity capital (i.e., expected returns) and/or expected earnings growth. While we measure absolute differences, EU membership typically reduced earnings yields toward the levels observed for existing EU members. Hence, our results indicate that EU membership is accompanied by a reduction in the cost of capital and/or an improvement in growth opportunities. Measuring these effects separately is of considerable interest, because the EU's impact on financial market integration likely operates

Table 4.1
The impact of the European Union on financial and economic segmentation in Europe: balanced sample, 1990–2007 (annual frequency).

	SEG	SEG^{DR}	SEG^{GO}
	1	2	3
EU indicator	**−0.0143**	**−0.0434**	**−0.0398**
	(0.0045)	(0.0105)	(0.0114)
Number of observations	2,160	1,962	1,962
Adj. R^2	0.47	0.49	0.27

Note: This table reports coefficient estimates and standard errors for linear regression models of pairwise segmentation. All standard errors are robust to heteroscedasticity and to arbitrary correlation across country-pairs in a given year as well as across years for a given country-pair. All specifications contain additional control variables as well as year and country-pair fixed effects. Coefficient estimates with absolute t-statistics larger than 1.96 appear in bold.

through changes in the cost of capital, whereas changes in expected earnings may have been associated with a variety of EU-induced measures to promote trade, labor mobility, and competition.

Using an empirical three-equation model of annual returns, earnings growth rates, and earnings yields at the country-industry portfolio level, we estimate country-industry discount rates ($DR_{i,k,t}$) and growth opportunity ($GO_{i,k,t}$). We then form two measures of segmentation between countries i and j, reflecting differences in cost of capital and in growth opportunities between these countries:

$$SEG_{i,j,t}^{DR} = \sum_{k=1}^{N_{i,j,t}} IW_{i,j,k,t} \left| DR_{i,k,t} - DR_{j,k,t} \right|$$

$$SEG_{i,j,t}^{GO} = \sum_{k=1}^{N_{i,j,t}} IW_{i,j,k,t} \left| GO_{i,k,t} - GO_{j,k,t} \right|,$$

where $IW_{i,j,k,t}$ is the relative market capitalization of industry k and N is the number of industries.

The first measure, SEG^{DR}, captures the degree to which industry-level discount rates differ between two countries—that is, the degree to which markets are not financially integrated. However, the second measure, SEG^{GO}, highlights the degree to which industry-level expected growth rates differ for a country-pair, which could reflect economic integration. As above, we focus on segmentation measured in December of each year, starting, if available, in 1990 and ending in 2007.

Table 4.1, columns 2 and 3 report the results for the same DID estimation as for the aggregate segmentation measure (SEG). These results suggest that joint EU membership was associated with significantly lower cross-country differences in discount rates (-4.34 pp). The financial integration effect was sizable and consistent with the evidence in Hardouvelis, Malliaropulos, and Priestley (2007), who show that the cross-country dispersion of industry-level cost of equity dropped in Europe in the 1990s. However, the integration effects associated with EU membership went beyond the discount rate channel and also implied lower cross-country differences in earnings growth rates (-3.98 pp).

The EU or the Euro?

The introduction of the euro in 1999 constituted another momentous change in Europe. Most but not all EU countries adopted the euro, with some joining later and others, such as the United Kingdom, Sweden, and Denmark, declining to join the currency union. Given that euro adoption was often viewed as the culmination of the process toward economic and monetary integration within the EU, it is conceivable regarding our finding that the EU significantly contributed to equity market integration is in fact due to the adoption of the euro rather than to EU membership per se.

While it is possible that our results are related to the introduction of the euro, it is also conceivable that EU membership and the move toward global market integration already integrated EU equity markets before the advent of the euro. By 1999, regional and global market integration may have moved far enough along for the euro to have only small effects. In addition, ex ante we would expect the process of financial market integration to be more important for equity valuations than the adoption of a single currency, as currency movements account for only a small part of the total variation in equity returns.

In table 4.2, column 1, we report results from our baseline model when adding a euro indicator variable to the specification from column 1 of table 4.1. The euro indicator equals one if both countries in a country-pair are part of the euro area in a given year and zero otherwise. Maybe surprisingly, we find a positive although statistically insignificant effect of the euro on market segmentation. These results suggest it is hard to make a case for a strong euro effect on market integration within Europe during our sample period. Importantly, the EU effect is not significantly impacted by the introduction of the euro indicator.

Table 4.2
The European Union and the euro: balanced sample, 1990–2007 ($N=2$, annual frequency).

	Dependent Variable: *SEG*	
	1	2
EU indicator	**−0.0145**	**−0.0142**
	(0.0045)	**(0.0045)**
Euro indicator	0.0028	
	(0.0030)	
Exchange rate stability indicator		−0.0008
		(0.0045)
Adj. R²	0.47	0.47

Note: This table reports coefficient estimates and standard errors for linear regression models of pairwise segmentation. All standard errors are robust to heteroscedasticity and to arbitrary correlation across country-pairs in a given year as well as across years for a given country-pair. All specifications contain additional control variables as well as year and country-pair fixed effects. Coefficient estimates with absolute *t*-statistics larger than 1.96 appear in bold. *N* denotes the number of observations.

It is quite conceivable that some of the effects ascribed to the introduction of the euro in the literature are simply induced by EU membership. For example, Hardouvelis, Malliaropulos, and Priestley (2006) find that several euro-adopting countries experienced increased equity market integration during the 1990s, while the United Kingdom did not, but they do not formally compare the effects of EU membership and euro adoption. Moreover, Engel and Rogers (2004) find no tendency for goods prices to converge after January 1999 but find a significant reduction in price dispersion throughout the decade of the 1990s. Goldberg and Verboven (2005) similarly document substantial price convergence in the EU's car market throughout the 1990s, although absolute price differentials persisted until the end of their sample in 2000. Hence, the EU, not the euro, led to the integration of consumer markets.

However, there may have been strong *indirect* effects of the euro related to the original mission of the EU. After all, the Maastricht Treaty, drafted in 1991 and officially adopted in November 1993, set out a path to harmonize national regulation that would culminate in economic and monetary union and the eventual adoption of the euro. It is possible that some of the EU effects we detect are related to changes only occurring in the 1990s with the adoption of the Maastricht Treaty. However, in our opinion, the euro effect should measure the actual effect of the single currency, not the capital, trade, and labor market integration that may have preceded it.

Nevertheless, we test an additional specification that changes the timing of the euro effect. We recognize that preparations for the euro may have been long underway and countries may have undertaken measures to limit exchange rate volatility some time before the euro was actually adopted.

We test the anticipation effect directly by replacing the euro indicator by an exchange rate stability indicator, which is inversely related to exchange rate volatility. Using daily exchange rates for all of our countries relative to the deutsche mark before 1999 and relative to the euro thereafter, we assign the value of one to a country with zero exchange rate volatility (i.e., to all euro countries once they adopt the euro) and a value of zero to a country with 12% annual volatility (roughly that of a major floating currency).[6] For a country-pair, we employ the average value of the two countries in a pair. In column 2 of table 4.2, we show that the effect associated with this alternative measure based on exchange rate volatility is similar to the effect of the euro indicator. While the stability variable indeed moves up prior to the introduction of the euro as exchange rate volatility decreases, the estimated euro effect is essentially zero. Further, the introduction of this alternative indicator has little impact on the coefficient on the EU indicator.

Robustness

So far we have documented a significantly lower earnings yield differential associated with EU membership but not with euro adoption. In table 4.3, we report three robustness checks.

First, in column 1 of table 4.3, we consider a segmentation measure that only includes those industries that contain at least five firms in a country and year. This should improve the precision of our segmentation measure. Implementing this rule, we lose fifteen observations as no common industries are left to construct the segmentation measure. The EU effect increases by 1.00 *pp*, suggesting that measurement error may have reduced our estimate. The coefficient on euro adoption is again not significantly different from zero.

Above, we have defined our segmentation measure as the *value*-weighted average industry valuation differential. An industry's value is the sum of the industry's equity market capitalization across both countries in a country-pair. In column 2 of table 4.3, we report results when measuring bilateral segmentation as the *equally* weighted average across industries.[7] The estimated EU effect is again quite similar to the one for the value-weighted segmentation measure, at −1.25 *pp*. The euro effect is once again insignificant.

Finally, in column 3 of table 4.3, we investigate whether our results hold in the full but unbalanced sample that uses all of our data, including many Eastern European countries whose data became available throughout the 1990s.

Table 4.3
Robustness, 1990–2007 (annual frequency).

	At Least 5 Firms	Equal Weights	Full Sample
	1	2	3
EU indicator	**−0.0250**	**−0.0125**	**−0.0134**
	(0.0083)	(0.0041)	(0.0054)
Euro indicator	0.0037	0.0013	**0.0096**
	(0.0035)	(0.0029)	(0.0044)
Number of observations	2,145	2,145	3,918
Adj. R²	0.36	0.37	0.36

Note: This table reports coefficient estimates and standard errors for linear regression models of pairwise segmentation. Column 1 includes only industry-country portfolios with at least five firms in a given year. The segmentation measure in column 2 uses equally weighted averages of industry valuation differentials. Column 3 uses data from the full, unbalanced sample. All standard errors are robust to heteroscedasticity and to arbitrary correlation across country-pairs in a given year as well as across years for a given country-pair. All specifications contain additional control variables as well as year and country-pair fixed effects. Coefficient estimates with absolute *t*-statistics larger than 1.96 appear in bold.

We again include only those industries that contain at least five firms in a country and year. We find a significantly negative EU effect ($-1.34\ pp$). The euro effect is positive, and, maybe surprisingly, statistically significant ($0.96\ pp$), providing further evidence that euro adoption did not increase integration in our framework.

In the results reported here, we identify the effect of the EU through changes in EU membership status. In untabulated results, again using the full, unbalanced sample, we explore an alternative identification by modeling EU membership as a function of a country's distance to Brussels—a distance that does not vary over time and addresses concerns that a country joins the EU as a function of time-varying economic conditions. We indeed find that the maximum distance to Brussels for a given country-pair is significantly negatively related to the pair's EU membership status. Using the distance to Brussels as an instrument, we find that EU membership retains its significantly negative effect on bilateral valuation differentials. Indeed, the effect is more prominent, suggesting that country-pairs with higher valuation differentials were more likely to become EU members, biasing the previous results against finding an EU effect. For details, see Bekaert et al. (2013).

Europe in Times of Crisis

Since the end of 2007, Europe has experienced a global financial crisis, several sovereign debt and banking crises, and most recently, the decision of the United Kingdom to leave the EU. Our results show that EU integration efforts led to significantly lower segmentation between EU member states than non-member states until 2007. This finding holds when explicitly controlling for the introduction of the euro, which by 2007 had not contributed to the increased equity market integration in Europe. Our results imply that policy makers should be particularly concerned with preserving "EU institutions" so that the current euro crisis does not endanger past accomplishments of economic and financial integration.

But have the recent crises already "undone" some of the integration benefits the EU countries experienced before 2007? To address this question, we extend our sample to include data through August 2016, covering the same country-pairs as the balanced sample above. Differently from our pre-crisis analysis, we employ monthly rather than annual data. This allows us to extend the sample through the Brexit referendum in the United Kingdom rather than ending the sample in 2015.[8]

In column 1 of table 4.4, we show the monthly results for the 1990–2007 sample period to compare with the annual results in table 4.2. The main results

Table 4.4
Market integration in times of crisis: monthly frequency, January 1990–August 2016.

	1990–2007	1990–2016	
	1	3	4
EU indicator	**−0.0209**	**−0.0214**	
	(0.0050)	(0.0047)	
Euro indicator	**0.0074**	**0.0092**	
	(0.0024)	(0.0024)	
EU indicator until 2007			**−0.0221**
			(0.0047)
EU indicator after 2007			**−0.0181**
			(0.0056)
Euro indicator until 2007			**0.0072**
			(0.0024)
Euro indicator after 2007			**0.0096**
			(0.0031)
Number of observations	25,402	37,882	37,882
Adj. R^2	0.42	0.38	0.38

Note: This table reports coefficient estimates and standard errors for linear regression models of pairwise segmentation (*SEG*). The segmentation measure is constructed for all country-pairs in the balanced sample, using Datastream industry index data at the monthly frequency. All standard errors are robust to heteroscedasticity and to arbitrary correlation across country-pairs in a given year as well as across years for a given country-pair. All specifications contain additional controls as well as time and country-pair fixed effects. Coefficient estimates with absolute t-statistics larger than 1.96 appear in bold.

remain intact, constituting another robustness check of our main results. The EU effect is a bit stronger than the result in table 4.2 and not too far from the finding in table 4.3 where we restricted the sample to industries with a least five firms to minimize measurement error. We do find a small but now significantly positive euro effect—not surprising given the positive euro effects shown before in tables 4.2 and 4.3.

Columns 2 and 3 of table 4.4 report results for the extended sample period through August 2016. Column 2 reveals that extending the sample and increasing the number of observations by about 50% does not substantially affect the overall estimates of the EU and euro effects. The EU effect remains essentially unchanged, while the euro effect increases slightly, likely reflecting the differential economic impact of the euro crisis within the eurozone. In column 3, we separately estimate the EU and the euro effect for 1990 to 2007 and 2008 to 2016. We find that the EU effect changed from −2.21 *pp* during the earlier period to −1.81 *pp* during the more recent period. On the other hand, the euro effect changed from 0.71 *pp* to 0.96 *pp*. The combined effect of EU membership and euro adoption changed from −1.49 *pp* during 1990 to 2007 to −0.85 *pp* during 2008 to 2016.

Conclusions

Using industry-level equity market valuations, we measure financial and economic integration among European countries and study the effects of joint EU membership and euro adoption on bilateral segmentation. Our measure is based on average differences in industry earnings yields and the assumption that in financially as well as economically integrated markets industry earnings yields converge.

Our main result reveals that between 1990 and 2007, bilateral earnings yield differences were about 1.50 *pp* lower if both countries were EU members. EU membership significantly lowered both discount rate differentials (financial integration) as well as expected earnings growth rate differentials (economic integration) across countries. Importantly, we do not find that euro adoption increased financial and economic integration between European countries.

Extending our sample period through August 2016 does not alter our main finding: EU membership increases integration, while there is no evidence in our analysis that the introduction of a common currency has had a positive impact on integration. However, the extended sample analysis reveals that integration benefits due to EU membership decreased somewhat during recent years, while segmentation between eurozone countries increased slightly.

While we do not uncover a significant role for the euro in driving higher levels of European integration, important questions remain about the very future of the common currency. Indeed, concerns about the fragility of the currency union were expressed in the years prior to the introduction of the euro. Specifically, the requisite institutions (supporting labor mobility, a fiscal and banking union, a binding Stability and Growth Pact, etc.) to facilitate the absorption of asymmetric economic shocks were absent. Rather than fostering greater levels of economic and political integration, Friedman (1997) worried that the euro would "exacerbate political tensions by converting divergent shocks ... into divisive political issues."

Turning to today, political tensions do indeed appear to be particularly elevated among the countries that share the common currency (the British referendum to exit the EU notwithstanding). If the inability to absorb asymmetric shocks has exacerbated these tensions to the point that overall sentiment toward the euro specifically and the European project more generally is souring, the benefits of integration may be at risk. A consequence of a potential euro area breakup is that it might imperil the broader EU too. While the common currency may exhibit certain vulnerabilities in its current form, a breakup that threatens to reverse the many EU initiatives aimed to promote the free flow of trade, labor, finance, and ideas may be economically costly. We consistently find that it is EU membership that is significantly associated with elevated market integration, and this in turn lowers discount rates and enhances economic growth opportunities. This does not need to be a one-way street if dissolution threatens the benefits associated with access to the common market.

Finally, we fully realize that the EU was as much of a political arrangement as an economic agreement. The EU reflects at its very core a shared vision to never again return to the bloodiest half century our world has ever known. Regardless of any other challenges EU or euro membership has created for some countries or constituencies, the peace effort has been a resounding success.

Notes

This chapter is a shortened and updated version of "The European Union, the Euro, and Equity Market Integration," which was published in the *Journal of Financial Economics* 109 (September 2013). A working paper version of the original article is available for free on SSRN: https://ssrn.com/abstract=1573308. Version: April 7, 2017.

1. We also assume that the world real interest rate is constant. It is well known that that real interest rate variation does not account for much variation in valuation ratios.

2. The relative market capitalization of a given industry is calculated as the combined market capitalization of the industry in both countries divided by the combined market capitalization of all industries in both countries. With this weighting scheme, the industry structure of the country with the larger equity market has more influence on the segmentation measure.

3. In particular, we use all US stocks that are covered by the Center for Research in Security Prices and Compustat to form country-industry portfolios by randomly drawing firms from the US data set, mimicking the number of firms found in a given country-industry portfolio in a given year in our European data. We then use these US data-based country-industry portfolios to calculate bilateral segmentation measures as described above. We repeat this process 500 times and thus obtain a distribution of the average level of bilateral segmentation.

4. Specifically, we include the sum of the number of firms from both countries (in natural logs) as well as the average absolute difference in industry leverage, industry earnings growth volatility, and industry return volatility for a given country-pair in a given year. For details, see Bekaert et al. (2013).

5. For the full set of results, see Bekaert et al. (2013).

6. The measure is derived as a nonlinear transformation of the volatility, σ, of a country's exchange rate relative to the deutsche mark and later the euro. Specifically, we transform the volatility into a stability measure on a $[0,1]$ scale by computing $1/\exp(100\sigma)$.

7. We again only include those industries that contain at least five firms in a country and year. Without this requirement, the corresponding EU effect drops to -0.21 *pp*.

8. A second difference is that we use Datastream's precalculated industry indexes instead of industry indexes we constructed from the bottom up. In a few cases, index coverage by Datastream begins after firm-level coverage, so that we are missing 518 observations (1.3% of the expected sample size without missing observations) between 1990 and February 1992. Starting in March 1992, the data set is fully balanced.

References

Adjaouté, K., and J.-P. Danthine. 2004. "Equity Returns and Integration: Is Europe Changing?" *Oxford Review of Economic Policy* 20: 555–570.

Baele, L. 2005. "Volatility Spillover Effects in European Equity Markets." *Journal of Financial and Quantitative Analysis* 40: 373–401.

Beck, T., T. Chen, C. Lin, and F. M. Song. 2016. "Financial Innovation: The Bright and the Dark Sides." *Journal of Banking and Finance* 72: 28–51.

Bekaert, G., C. R. Harvey, C. T. Lundblad, and S. Siegel. 2011. "What Segments Equity Markets?" *Review of Financial Studies* 24: 3841–3890.

Bekaert, G., C. R. Harvey, C. R. Lundblad, and S. Siegel. 2013. "The European Union, the Euro, and Equity Market Integration." *Journal of Financial Economics* 109: 583–603.

Bekaert, G., R. Hodrick, and X. Zhang. 2009. "International Stock Return Comovements." *Journal of Finance* 64: 2591–2626.

Engel, C., and J. H. Rogers. 2004. "European Product Market Integration after the Euro." *Economic Policy* 19: 347–384.

Fratzscher, M. 2002. "Financial Market Integration in Europe: On the Effects of EMU on Stock Markets." *International Journal of Finance and Economics* 7: 165–193.

Friedman, M. 1997. "The Euro: Monetary Unity to Political Disunity?" Project Syndicate, August 28. https://www.project-syndicate.org/commentary/the-euro--monetary-unity-to-political-disunity.

Goldberg, P. K., and F. Verboven. 2005. "Market Integration and Convergence to the Law of One Price: Evidence from the European Car Market." *Journal of International Economics* 65: 49–73.

Goyenko, R., and S. Sarkissian. 2014. "Treasury Bond Illiquidity and Global Equity Returns." *Journal of Financial and Quantitative Analysis* 49: 1227–1253.

Hardouvelis, G., D. Malliaropulos, and R. Priestley. 2006. "EMU and European Stock Market Integration." *Journal of Business* 79: 365–392.

Hardouvelis, G., D. Malliaropulos, and R. Priestley. 2007. "The Impact of EMU on the Equity Cost of Capital." *Journal of International Money and Finance* 26: 305–327.

Discussion: Economic and Financial Integration in Europe

Marco Pagano

In their chapter, Bekaert, Harvey, Lundblad, and Siegel (hereafter BHLS) apply their segmentation measure, which is based on earnings yields, to the European Union (EU) and the euro area. While their findings are interesting, I have two concerns regarding the main lessons to be drawn from the chapter. First, their finding that financial integration stagnated or even decreased in the first seven years after the introduction of the euro is not consistent with the pattern of other indicators of financial integration. These other indicators refer not only to the equity market but also to debt markets, portfolio allocation decisions, and risk sharing. Second, and relatedly, the role of the euro in the financial integration process is arguably more complex than the chapter makes it, as it changed considerably across the three periods of pre-crisis integration (2000–2007), crisis (2008–2011), and post-crisis stabilization (after 2012). Understanding the role of the euro in the process of financial integration in the euro area is also crucial going forward, as it bears on the all-important issue regarding whether integration in the euro area will be more resilient to future systemic shocks or whether it will recede again if faced with such shocks in the future.

The BHLS measure based on earnings yields indicates that in the EU equity market, segmentation rose in the period from 1990 to 2007. This finding accords with the conclusions that can be drawn from other measures of integration. However, the BHLS claim that segmentation rose in 2000–2007—that is, since the inception of the single currency, as shown in figure 4.1 of the chapter—does not match the pattern of other financial integration indicators for equity, bond, and credit markets as well as with measures of portfolio diversification, cross-border lending, and consumption risk sharing.

In particular, the European Central Bank's (ECB) gauge of equity market segmentation did not rise after 2000: the cross-country dispersion in stock returns did not increase relative to their cross-industry dispersion up until 2010 (see ECB 2017, chart 12). And portfolio diversification of corporate and sovereign debt portfolios in the euro area kept increasing until 2006, when euro-area investors' debt portfolios featured the largest share ever of securities from other euro-area countries relative to domestic ones (see ECB 2017, chart 13). Correspondingly, measures of dispersion of government bond yields and other interest rates were close to zero throughout the 1998–2008 decade and started increasing only afterward. Finally, consumption risk sharing in the euro area improved from 2001 to 2007 (see ECB 2017, chart 2): the unsmoothed component of consumption risk declined monotonically, especially owing to the contribution of capital markets (via cross-border ownership of productive assets) and credit markets (via cross-border borrowing and lending).

The overall picture is captured by the composite indicators of financial integration computed by the ECB to summarize the behavior of a host of price-based and quantity-based measures of financial integration. These composite indicators, drawn from chart A of ECB (2017, 3) are shown in figure 4.2. Both indicators kept rising well after the inception of the euro, namely, until 2006. After that date, the quantity-based indicator decreased slightly until 2010 and then dropped more markedly after the inception of the sovereign debt crisis. The price-based synthetic indicator instead decreased more rapidly and substantially during the subprime crisis and especially after the Lehman Brothers default. Both synthetic indicators bottomed out in 2012 and started recovering afterward. Hence, the figure suggests that, after 2000, there were three distinct phases in the pattern of financial integration in Europe: (1) a phase of increasing integration between the introduction of the euro and the inception of the subprime crisis (2000–2006); (2) a phase of dis-integration during the subprime crisis and the sovereign debt crisis (2007–2012); and (3) a phase of (partial) recovery of the integration process since 2012.

This evidence casts some doubt on the view by BHLS that the introduction of the euro did not contribute to financial integration and may even have hindered it. In fact, the opposite may have been true: the euro may have contributed to prompt *too much* financial integration *too early*—before a suitable regulatory and policy framework could be put in place.

With highly integrated markets, capital flowed from the core to the periphery countries of the euro area, attracted by perceived investment opportunities and absence of foreign exchange risk, during the 2003–2006 boom. These capital flows fueled credit expansion in the periphery, raising local asset prices and compressing sovereign bond spreads. This led to real exchange rate appreciation and low productivity growth in the periphery as credit was mainly directed to real estate and nontradable sectors. After 2009, capital flows from the periphery to the core reversed as investors sought safety above all. The flight to safety lowered borrowing costs in core countries and raised them in the periphery above their fundamental level, threatening the solvency of sovereigns,

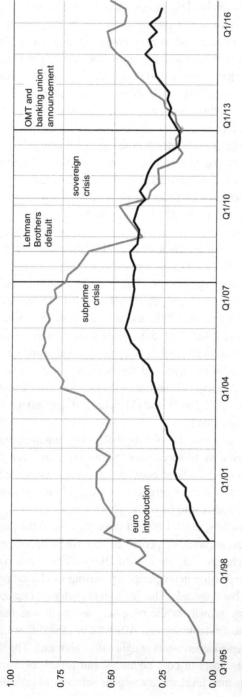

Figure 4.2
Price-based and quantity-based financial integration composite indicators. *Sources:* ECB and ECB calculations.

banks, and firms in the periphery and the survival itself of the euro—until 2012, when the ECB calmed investors' fears first with the announcement of the Outright Monetary Transactions and then with the implementation of the Asset Purchase Program.

The key policy question that this frightening experience leaves open is whether the changes in the euro-area institutional framework that have been introduced in the meantime have made the euro resilient to the financial integration that it tends to elicit. This question is far too vast and complex to be discussed here, especially because a lot has been done on the regulatory front, and therefore the answer would require evaluating many policies and regulations (as well as their interrelationships): bank prudential policies (banking union), bank resolution policies (Bank Recovery and Resolution Directive), structural policies (capital markets union), and several macro-prudential policy interventions, to name only the most important ones. Facing this question would also require discussing the reforms that have *not* been carried out, chiefly the revision of prudential rules regarding banks' sovereign exposures and the introduction of euro-wide deposit insurance. Perhaps a fair judgment is that the reform of euro-area rules and institutions relevant for financial stability has been substantial but is still incomplete. It is hard to say to what extent such residual incompleteness still leaves the financial integration process of the euro area exposed to dramatic setbacks such as those witnessed during the financial crisis.

Note

This discussion was presented at the "Capital Markets Union and Beyond" Conference, London, on January 27, 2018.

Reference

European Central Bank (ECB). 2017. *Financial Integration in Europe*. Frankfurt am Main: ECB, May.

5 The Origins of a Capital Markets Union in the United States

Jeffrey N. Gordon and Kathryn Judge

The free flow of capital was one of the fundamental principles on which the EU was built. Despite the progress that has been made over the past 50 years, Europe's capital markets are still relatively underdeveloped and fragmented.
—EU Commission, 2015 CMU Action Plan

Creation of an European Union (EU)-wide "capital markets union" (CMU) is one of the institutional efforts to advance the economic vitality of the EU in the aftermath of the global financial crisis of 2007–2009 and the eurozone crisis of 2011–2013. The ambition of a CMU is to produce greater growth, greater economic integration across the EU, and greater resiliency within the EU to local economic shocks. The hope is that EU-wide capital markets will help remedy the limitations in the EU's pattern of bank-centered finance. Robust capital markets can enhance resilience by allowing funding to flow around rather than through damaged bank balance sheets after a financial shock. This is critical because, despite the launch of the EU's Banking Union project, banks remain tied to specific member states and thus to local central banks and national governments. A more integrated capital market should also enhance efficiency to provide savers a wider array of investment opportunities and offer firms greater access to financing. Given the present member state–focus of EU banking, cross-border funding will flow more smoothly through securities market issuances than bank debt financings.

The CMU project has unleashed a large regulatory undertaking steered by the Directorate-General for Financial Stability, Financial Services, and Capital Markets Union with the goal of having the regulatory pieces in place by 2019. The nature of this undertaking requires asking whether and how law can bring about the desired end of a more robust and integrated capital market. In the course of writing this chapter, we have come to believe that the "law and finance" literature, with its focus on "investor protection," offers too narrow a frame to understand the interaction between law and the development of a

financial system. Rather, we need a broader understanding of "financial structure law"—the way that the legal choices of repression, substitution, and facilitation shape the environment for the private funding of economic activity. Investor
protection is surely among the key ingredients for a thriving CMU but much
more is required—such as an architecture for a particular sort of financial
system.[1]

Law should have great potency in this undertaking. A financial system is a
product of rules; it is not a "natural" system. As the rules change, the financial
system will inevitably restructure itself. On the other hand, the relationship
among law, financial system design, and financial development is complex
and iterative. Law's greatest impact is often indirect and context dependent;
its repressions can be more important than its explicit permissions. Law
matters, but not necessarily in the ways lawmakers intend.

Forming a "capital markets union" is a project of transnational institution
making and transnational behavioral change. The only way to understand the
myriad mechanisms through which law can help achieve (and try not to hinder)
these ambitions is to dig into the details. For a US observer, there is no better
place to start than the world's largest and most successful CMU, that of the
United States. Despite the initial allocation of power among the several states
of the United States, which included jurisdiction over the state's banks and the
state's securities markets, the United States ended up with a national system
of finance, a CMU from sea to shining sea.

Central to the story is the mismatch between the growing demand for capital
from increasingly large and risky enterprises in the late nineteenth and early
twentieth centuries and banks' limited capacity to provide this funding. Rules
separating banking from commerce, prohibitions on bank branching, and the
absence of a central bank resulted in a stunted US banking system that lacked
capacity to fund large-scale enterprise.[2] The first consequence was the growth
of bond markets that could access both national and international capital
markets; the second was the growth of equity markets. The role of law here
was largely repressive, facilitating the growth of capital markets by limiting
bank capacity.

But the law also came to play an important role in facilitating the ongoing
growth and vibrancy of these markets. Market-based credit intermediation and
public equity markets in the United States were buttressed by Depression-era
securities laws, which greatly strengthened the disclosure regime for the public
issuance of debt and equity securities. Robust disclosure reduced the banks'
advantage in credit assessment and monitoring, and it added depth and liquidity
to equity markets. The federal securities laws also established a single federal
securities regulator, the Securities and Exchange Commission (SEC), which side-

lined potentially inconsistent state regulatory regimes not so much through straightforward preemption but through a broad mandate to facilitate a national system and a large budget.

Subsequent legal changes further diminished the advantages that banks often enjoy. The Trust Indenture Act of 1940 (along with the 1939 Chandler Bankruptcy Act) further reduced the need for bank monitoring by protecting bondholders from expropriation by insiders in debt restructurings. The 1940 Investment Company Act provided a regulatory license for the mutual fund industry, and this eventually made large sums available to buy all grades and maturities of debt issuances in addition to equities. A new vehicle, the open-ended mutual fund, meant that retail investors could acquire a share of diversified credit portfolios while retaining liquidity, reducing yet another advantage of bank-based finance.

Legal developments outside the financial sector also played an important role in the rise of the US CMU. State mandates to pre-fund pension promises of state and local governments and a national similar requirement for private employers (through adoption of the Employee Retirement Security Act of 1974 [ERISA]) produced vast sums to fund credit issuances outside of the banking system. The size and sophistication of these pension fund investors also helped make equity capital a viable source of financing for start-ups and resource-constrained midstream firms.

As even this brief account illustrates, the history of the US CMU is a mixed story for the capacity of lawmakers to create a CMU. The good news is that law matters. The creation of an expert regulatory body with the power to enforce the law, help it to evolve, and suppress state-based efforts that might threaten the union, for example, is core. The less good news is that motivated private actors are also critical. In the United States, the law helped promote the growth of powerful investment banks and institutional investors, but these legal interventions had real costs and were often motivated by distinctly American political concerns.[3]

This chapter addresses three critical elements of the origins of CMU in the United States. Part I provides the requisite background, using history and some figures to develop a stylized account of the difference between capital markets in the United States vs. the EU. Part II sketches the historical basis for the fragmentation of the US banking system and the absence of a central bank. Part III shows how the advent of the railroads and the greater concentration among US industrial firms created credit demand that the fragmented banking system could not provide, especially in the absence of a central bank that could serve as a lender of last resort (LOLR). This led to national securities markets, first for bonds and then, as firms merge using stock as consideration, for equities.

Part IV discusses the importance of the Glass-Steagall Act in the rise of the US CMU. By separating investment banking and commercial banking, Glass-Steagall created a set of financial firms that had strong incentives to develop a securities market–based alternative to bank-based finance. Part IV also discusses how the creation of the SEC and the implementation of far-reaching federal securities laws forestalled and preempted state-based securities regulation that could have resulted in a less unified regime.

Part V reflects on current EU efforts to create a CMU in light of the US experience. One challenge for the EU is to find an appropriate pattern of federal regulation over the EU's capital markets that will facilitate EU-wide issuance of debt and equity securities. A main source of resistance will be "regulatory embeddedness" among the member states and the notable forces of path dependency, both the short-term efficiency based as well as the protectionist rent based. The US experience suggests this can and must be overcome. An important opportunity for the EU's efforts to create a meaningful CMU is to foster the development of asset managers (which include for these purposes the insurers and the pension funds), the funding supply side for CMU. Asset managers can screen potential borrowers and assemble diversified portfolios of credit claims without the help of banks. Moreover, because they engage in far less liquidity transformation, they are less fragile than banks and could function as a "spare tire," helping to provide financing to the real economy when the banking system breaks down.[4] The chapter concludes with specific guidance for ways to promote the growth of EU asset managers.

Part I: Some Introductory Evidence on US vs. EU Differences

The fact of significant differences between capital markets in the United States and the EU is not news, but a graphical display of some of the differences over time is nevertheless revealing. Figure 5.1, drawn from the Goldsmith data over the period from 1850 to 1978, charts the "securities to loan ratio" for the United States vs. Europe. (The US line is the top line throughout most of the period.) This ratio divides the sum of private debt securities and equity by bank loans. The ratio is narrowing by the end of the period but is still significant.

Three comparative measures nicely capture the differences between the United States and the EU and how each evolved over time. The first is a comparative measure of equity funding in capital formation (see figure 5.2). Here the United States and the EU are relatively similar over a period that goes up to the year 2000. Indeed, the equity to gross national product (GNP) ratio for US and European countries is very similar.

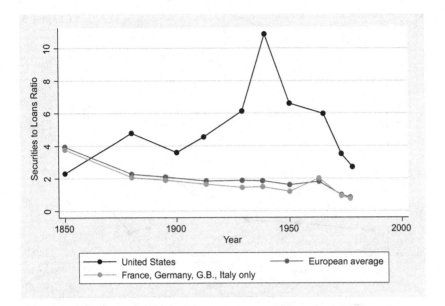

Figure 5.1
Securities to loans ratio for the United States and Europe, 1850–1978. *Source*: Raymond Goldsmith, *Comparative National Balance Sheets: A Study of Twenty Countries, 1688–1978* (Chicago: University of Chicago Press, 1985).

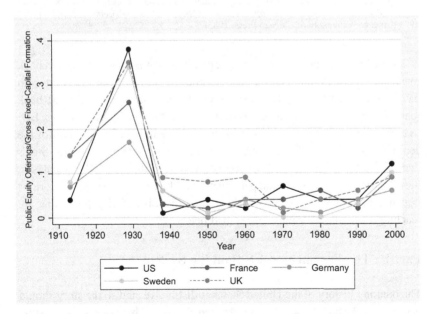

Figure 5.2
Evolution of the fraction of gross fixed-capital formation raised via equity. *Note*: The "fraction of gross fixed-capital formation raised via equity" is the amount of funds raised through initial public offerings and seasoned equity issuances by domestic corporations divided by gross fixed-capital formation (a loose proxy for the total investments of domestic corporations). *Source*: Raghuram Rajan and Luigi Zingales, "The Great Reversals: The Politics of Financial Development in the Twentieth Century," *Journal of Financial Economics* 69 (2003): 5–50.

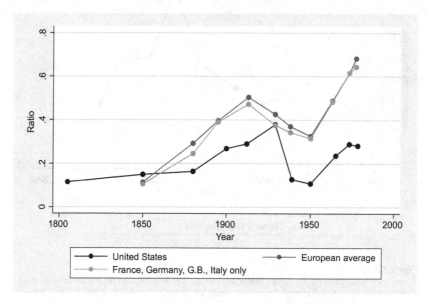

Figure 5.3
Loans by financial institutions/GNP for the United States and Europe, 1805–1978. *Source*:
Raymond Goldsmith, *Comparative National Balance Sheets: A Study of Twenty Countries, 1688–1978* (Chicago: University of Chicago Press, 1985).

The differences show up in the fraction of debt that is financed through bank loans vs. securities markets. Figures 5.3 and 5.4, drawn from the Goldsmith data (which seems to be the most current for comparable data), chart bank loans to GNP and debt securities to GNP comparatively (United States vs. EU) over the 1850–1978 period. A gap opens up beginning before the turn of the century. Bank loans to GNP increase at a much lower rate in the United States than in the EU (figure 5.3). By contrast, debt securities to GNP escalates in the United States (figure 5.4) in part because of the explosion of debt securities issuance in the United States to finance the railroads and enterprises that are reaching for national scale, as described below.

Part II: The Fragmented US Banking System

The banking history of the United States is distinctive, and so the story should begin there. From its founding, the United States has been locked in a battle over the appropriate structure of its banking system, a debate on two distinct axes of state vs. federal power and concentrated vs. small banking institutions.[5] The United States also followed the UK model of seeking to separate banking

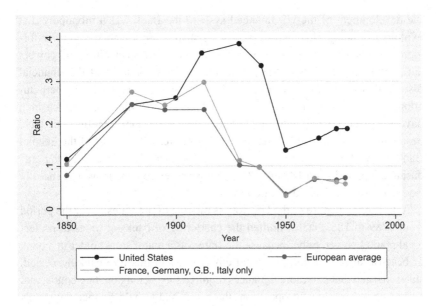

Figure 5.4
Debt securities/GNP for the United States and Europe, 1850–1978. *Source*: Raymond Goldsmith, *Comparative National Balance Sheets: A Study of Twenty Countries, 1688–1978* (Chicago: University of Chicago Press, 1985).

from commerce. Although this barrier has always been imperfect, even its permeable form prevented banks from exercising the kind of control rights commonly enjoyed by their European counterparts.

The first secretary of the treasury, Alexander Hamilton, successfully promoted a Bank of the United States (explicitly modeled on the Bank of England), a private bank with public functions. In light of concerns about the US Congress' constitutional authority to charter such a bank and disagreement over the centralization of banking activities, the Bank was chartered for a limited term—twenty years (1791–1811). Although the Bank successfully fostered economic development and monetary stability, the rechartering legislation failed in part because of the opposition of state-chartered bankers seeking to eliminate a federal competitor.[6]

A general banking panic in the midst of the War of 1812 with the British (in which Washington, DC, was burned) led to a push for the chartering of the Second Bank of the United States for a twenty-year term (1816–1836). As the twenty-year term approached its end, leading the opposition was President Andrew Jackson, who vetoed rechartering legislation. His veto message sounded populist themes that typify the concerns that have long shaped and impeded the development of the US financial system: the Bank was a monopoly that exploited ordinary citizens in favor of its shareholders who were either foreigners or the rich; such a bank was beyond Congress's constitutional powers and was inconsistent with the protection of states' rights; and the financial distress that might come with its unwinding was not a reason for its perpetuation. The core of Jackson's populist message was: "Many of our rich men have not been content with equal protection and equal benefits, but have besought us to make them richer by act of Congress."[7] The end of the Second Bank of the United States ushered in what is known as the "free-banking era" during the period from 1836 to 1863. In this era, entrepreneurs were generally free to charter banks under state law.

A distinctive feature of the US story is the role of the states. Over the period from 1789 to 1863, states limited the chartering of banks at times to protect local market power, either because the state was a major stockholder in a bank or because of rent seeking by local elites. Later in this free-banking period, states insisted that banknote issuances required the backing of state bonds; that is, that as a condition for operation, the banks had to help finance the state's public debt. Although a particular bank's notes might circulate throughout the country (subject to a discount based on an assessment of redeemability), the US Supreme Court sustained state efforts to limit the activities of out-of-state banks if such efforts were explicitly prescribed in state legislation.

The most important part of the US story is "unit banking," meaning that a bank could operate out of one location only. Even in states that permitted banks to open additional branches, branching was limited and underdeveloped. This unit banking/limited branching structure arose from state level decision making, but it persisted even after the National Bank Act of 1863, which permitted the chartering of national banks. National banks were made subject to the restrictions on branching in the state in which they were chartered. The political economy focused on the interests of local elites in protecting rents from their banks and the general populist sentiment against the concentration of bank power.

The consequence was a highly fragmented and decentralized banking system.[8] Although some liberalization of state and federal branching rule occurred in the 1970s and 1980s, it was not until the Riegle-Neal Interstate Banking and Branching Efficiency Act of 1994 that the barriers to interstate branching were comprehensively eliminated.[9] This triggered rapid consolidation in US banking. The relatively high concentration of US banking assets among the global systemically important banks, or "G-SIBs," as of the time of the financial crisis of 2007–2009 is thus a quite late addition to US financial development.

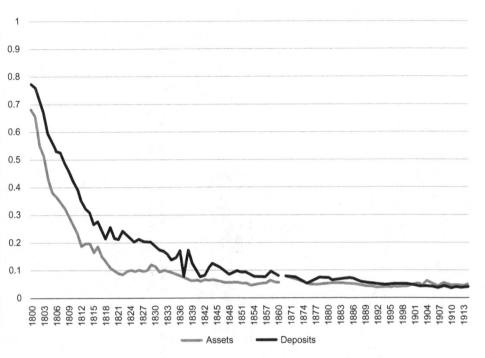

Figure 5.5
Five-firm concentration ratios across the United States, 1800–1914. This figure displays the ratio of either assets or deposits at the five largest banks to the total at all other banks. See Caroline Fohlin and Matthew Jaremski, "Bank Concentration in the United States, 1800–1914" (draft, December 2015, on file with the authors), appendix A for a description of the data sources.

The original fragmentation of the US banking system and the dramatic rise in concentration following Riegle-Neal are illustrated by figures 5.5, 5.6, and 5.7, which show the degree of concentration in the largest firms.[10] The progression goes from highly concentrated in the immediate post-independence period (when there were a handful of banks) to negligible concentration throughout the nineteenth century and into the twentieth century as the number of banks proliferates.[11] Then, relaxation of the interstate branch-banking constraints leads to successive bank merger waves and much higher concentration, rapidly accelerating in the 2000s. Crisis-era mergers accentuated this trend, and the trend has now continued as a result of organic growth following the crisis.[12] A "three-firm" concentration ratio dating back to 1935 shows once again the recency of concentration in the US banking system and underscores the long-standing prior fragmentation.

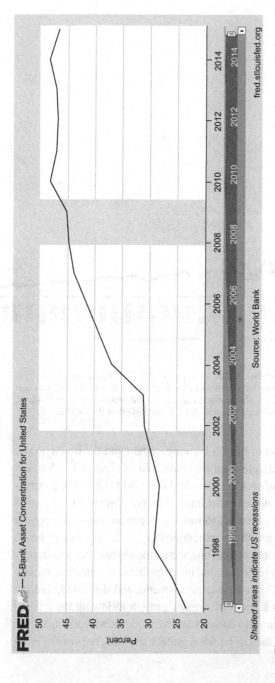

Figure 5.6
Five-bank asset concentration for the United States, 1996–2016. *Note:* Shaded areas indicate US recessions. *Source:* World Bank, "5-Bank Asset Concentration for United States" [DDOI06USA156NWDB], retrieved from FRED, Federal Reserve Bank of St. Louis, https://fred.stlouisfed.org /series/DDOI06USA156NWDB.

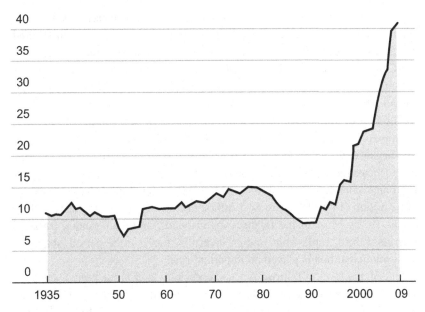

Figure 5.7
Concentration of US banking system. *Note*: Total assets of top three US banks as percent of total commercial banking sector assets. *Source*: Andrew Haldane, Thomas Reuters Datastream, as published in Martin Wolf, "The Challenge of Halting the Financial Doomsday Machine," *Financial Times*, April 20, 2010, https://www.ft.com/content/f2e4dbb0-4caa-11df-9977-00144feab49a.

Part III: The Rise of the Railroads and Large Industrial Companies: The Financing Mismatch between Fragmented Banking and Concentrated Enterprise

The American hostility to large banks meant that until quite recently (the 1990s) individual banks were relatively small, even "money center" banks. Until the early twentieth century, the United States also lacked a central bank. Such fragmentation meant that large-scale single bank loans were not feasible, and this favored conditions for the development of market-based debt finance.[13] Debt finance for large-scale enterprises would require loan syndication, formal or informal; this in turn entailed significant transaction costs. Indeed, part of the populist political economy disfavored out-of-state lending. "In the antebellum decades, a number of states actually passed laws prohibiting bank loans to persons living in other states."[14] By contrast, bond issuance could take advantage of regional, and even national and international, distribution networks to access national credit pools. Moreover, in the absence of an LOLR, US banks were disadvantaged as providers of long-term credit because of the run risk. Credit intermediation through markets could mitigate such problems.[15]

At the same time that banks were proliferating and the banking system was fragmenting, industrial firms were concentrating. Precisely because the United States was constituted as a "single market" in goods and services (fortified by the Commerce Clause in this regard), firms could grow to regional and then national scale to take advantage of scale and scope economies. This led to capital structures that "demanded" national scale to sustain.[16]

The first example was the railroads, the paradigm large industrial firms of the nineteenth century. Railroad development took place in successive waves that began in the 1820s.[17] The level of investment in construction and equipment (measured in 1909 US dollars) rapidly escalated in successive decades from approximately $89 million (1828–1838), to $927 million (1849–1858), to $2 billion (1870–1879), to $4.1 billion (1880–1889), cresting at $5 billion (1900–1909). Most of the finance was in bonds, and a substantial fraction, perhaps a third, came from foreign investors. Early in the period, state and local municipal bonds played an important role.

Indeed, the level of railroad finance, especially later in the period, suggests a separate, complementary theory to the growth of the US CMU. The railroads may have been too risky to finance with bank loans. The high fixed costs and the potential for rate wars meant frequent defaults and frequent railroad reorganizations in which bondholders faced significant haircuts. The high rate of interest in light of these risks was part of the appeal to foreign investors, especially in the United Kingdom, the source of most of the foreign investment. In other words, the railroads issued the original "junk bonds."[18] No US bank at the time was large enough to diversify such risks in its loan portfolio. Especially in the absence of an LOLR, the presence of such risky loans on the balance sheet would unacceptably increase the run risks.

In sum, the fragmented, populist structure of the US banking system gave rise to three separate supply-limitations on railroad finance: The first was the "costly transacting" problem, in which the costs of organizing a large enough syndicate of small banks to provide and then monitor a large-scale loan would have been prohibitive. The second was the "junk debt" problem, in which the risky nature of railroad lending would have required either extreme diversification (extra costly transacting in a fragmented system) or a substantial increase in capital to avoid a risk to bank solvency from a railroad default. The third was the "run risk" problem in the absence of an LOLR. The riskiness of railroad debt (reflected in frequent defaults) could easily produce panic runs against the lending banks because in the absence of an LOLR, they would be unable to borrow against the railroad debt on their balance sheets.

The inability of the banking system to support the burgeoning debt financing needs of railway expansion in the United States was the imperative for the development of an alternative supply side channel in light of the intense demand for finance. Investment bankers of the time arranged for bond issuances that could funnel in financial resources from a national and international catchment area.[19] Eventually the issuance and trading of bonds became centered into a single venue, a national market "centralized and institutionalized" in New York City.[20] The use of national markets rather than local institutions to intermediate debt gave rise to a "capital markets union." The demand for trading in railroad bond and equity issuances is also part of the rise of what became the dominant stock exchange—the New York Stock Exchange (NYSE).[21] One would be remiss to discuss any of these developments without acknowledging the role played by a key financial system entrepreneur, J. P. Morgan, who facilitated the placement of railroad debt, brought about railroad consolidation to reduce the riskiness of that debt, repeated these patterns in other industries, and aided the design changes that enhanced the credibility of securities traded on the NYSE.[22]

The railroads dramatically reduced transportation costs, which in turn transformed the scale economies of production and distribution. This promoted the creation of regional and then national industrial companies, often achieved by roll-ups of smaller firms through holding company transactions and later mergers in which stock was the consideration.[23] The "demand side" for CMU in the United States came from the transformation of the US economy from one characterized chiefly by local manufacturers producing for local markets to one of national manufacturers producing for a national market. The canonical account is provided by Alfred D. Chandler: After the Civil War, "new methods of transportation and communication, by permitting a large and steady flow of raw materials into and finished products out of a factory, made possible unprecedented levels of production. The realization of this potential required, however, the invention of new machinery and processes."[24] These forces led in turn to sharp increases in optimal plant size because they gave large plants substantial cost advantages over smaller ones and led to larger enterprises both to pursue the emerging technologies and also as a result of the accompanying industrial consolidation.

These developments produced a demand for debt markets that could reliably supply large-scale, long-term debt finance. Indeed the mismatch between firm size and US bank fragmentation may have been a persistent feature contributing to a US bond market consistently larger than Europe's and a bank lending market consistently smaller, measuring both as a fraction of GNP, as seen in figures 5.3 and 5.4. These developments also produced the demand for equity markets that not only could provide an avenue for fund-raising through preferred stock issuance as well as common, but also, more importantly, could provide liquidity for the shareholders who had received stock in the industry-consolidating roll-ups.[25]

The "law and finance" scholarship has told a story that implicitly assumes that capital market development is an add-on to bank finance, framed principally in terms of an equity channel. The focus on "investor protection" is a "tell" that public equity issuance is the main object of analysis. A closer look at the US story reveals the importance of public *debt* markets in capital market development. Public debt issuance to finance the railroads and industrial firms created the distribution channels; equity issuances followed. Indeed, the first regulatory protections in the early twentieth century seem to be aimed at speculative and fraudulent debt as much, if not more, than equity.[26]

Part IV: Law Mattered to the US Capital Markets Union

The prior two sections have argued that the origins of the US CMU are to be found in the clash between a long-standing feature of US political economy, suspicion of large financial institutions, and the funding needs of large-scale enterprise. That might have been sufficient to get the capital market going, but a set of New Deal-era laws were critical to its further development. These not only provided better investor protection (the 1933 and 1934 securities acts),[27] but they also created structural conditions for further development of the US CMU. This section discusses two particular instances of law-making that played critical roles. The first was the adoption of the Glass-Steagall Act, which separated commercial from investment banking. The second was the establishment of the SEC and the creation of an extensive structure of federal regulation, which suppressed what otherwise would have become increasingly potent state efforts to regulate securities markets. Thus, the law that mattered to the development and maintenance of a CMU in the United States was not just investor protection law, the usual account of the 1930s "sec-reg" legislation, but "financial structure" law: law that set up the relevant set of competitive institutions and that tamped down the power of local regulatory authorities who would be inclined to focus on local rather than national interests.

The Glass-Steagall Act

The National Bank Act of 1863 articulated a regime of limited powers for a national bank so as to keep it focused on the "business of banking." By historical tradition and law, US banks did not underwrite corporate securities and generally limited their holdings of debt securities to commercial paper. As securities markets became more robust, banks wanted to participate in securities markets activities, especially underwriting. This activity was generally pursued through an affiliate of the bank rather than the bank directly, both for legal and reputation-protecting grounds.[28] In the wake of the Great Depression, various reformers concluded that securities activities by these affiliates in league with the bank itself had been a major contributor to the debacle. (Modern day economists are skeptical of that conclusion.) Part of the reform program was the Glass-Steagall Act, which forbade affiliation between securities firms and banks, thus fully separating banks from the business of underwriting debt or equity securities for private firms or trading securities for its own account.

As Gordon has argued elsewhere, Glass-Steagall insisted on free-standing investment banks, which could make their success only through securities markets and not through commercial banking. These investment banks quickly learned that credit markets were more profitable than equity markets. Firms issue equity only infrequently but are constantly in need of credit, if only to roll over maturing indebtedness. Thus investment banks were powerfully incentivized to develop market-based mechanisms of credit intermediation, which became effective substitutes for bank-based credit. Because investment banks were blocked from conventional commercial banking, they had strong incentives to achieve functionally equivalent credit-provision and to pursue cost advantages relentlessly. By contrast, as European finance demonstrates, a universal bank with a strong commercial lending franchise would be reluctant to cannibalize its existing franchise by developing market-based alternatives.[29] Moreover, such universal banks would have strong incentives to protect their existing franchise by resisting the entry of banking institutions that might specialize in market-based finance.[30] Glass-Steagall cut off that path for US banks.

The arrival of free-standing investment banks interacted with post–World War II decisions in the United States that both privatized retirement provisioning (beyond the social security baseline) and that led to pre-funding of such retirement obligations both by state/local governments as well as private industry.[31] Particularly by the 1950s and 1960s, this fostered the creation of deep capital pools that could fund credit issuances as well as equity.[32] Glass-Steagall had given the investment banks pole-position in deploying these funds. The national reach of the investment banks, including extensive national branching that facilitated retail securities distribution, furthered the development of a CMU in the United States.

A National Regulation and a National Regulator

Another critical element of the New Deal–era regulatory scheme was the suppression of state securities regulation. Central to this development was the creation of a federal securities regulator, the Securities and Exchange Commission, which had a mandate to establish an extensive disclosure system for both initial public offerings and the firm's ongoing financial results. The SEC was also vested with an enforcement mandate to protect markets from fraud.

More broadly, the sweeping adoption of national regulatory systems in the 1930s and 1940 in the United States locked into place a "national" focus for the capital markets that were then developing and under-regulated. This national focus was an essential element in the US CMU.

Before the New Deal legislation, the states had begun to regulate securities activity, the so-called blue sky laws. The first state to adopt the law was Kansas in 1911, and by 1931 all but one of the forty-eight states had adopted a blue sky law. There were two general types—ones that required pre-clearance, either on a "merit" review or a less-stringent "no fraud" test, and others that were aimed at *ex post* fraud. Roughly three-quarters of the states required pre-clearance, though the most stringent review was in the minority.[33] The 1933 Securities Act and the 1934 Securities Exchange Act each preserved the "jurisdiction" of state securities commissions and did not evince the desire to totally occupy the field of securities regulation that might have produced "preemption" of state activity.[34] Why, in the aftermath of the Depression, did states not act more vigorously in the regulatory space? Certainly one reason was the vigor of the SEC, which under the guidance of energetic and knowledgeable leaders rapidly promulgated extensive disclosure requirements and undertook enforcement actions.[35] The national law-making process that culminated in the New Deal securities regulation and the infusion of personnel and funding into the SEC largely froze state regulatory efforts in place.

Various actors recognized the need for federal-state coordination; these efforts were organized through a preexisting quasi-official body that worked to promote coordination among disparate state regimes—the National Conference of Commissioners on Uniform State Laws.[36] Eventually these efforts culminated in the Uniform Securities Act of 1956, which enabled most large corporate issuers to use their federal filings to satisfy state requirements. Nevertheless, significant disparity has persisted among the different state schemes for smaller issuers, leading to ongoing efforts to widen federal preemption of state pre-clearance regimes.[37] The point is that a well-funded national regulator wielding broad authority to impose disclosure standards and to regulate securities markets suppressed what otherwise would have been strong regulatory impulses at the state level, and in that way that has helped to foster and sustain a US capital markets union.

Part V: Conclusion

Are there generalizations from this peculiarly American story? One takeaway is that where a banking system labors under constraints, a capital market channel can robustly support the flow of finance to large-scale enterprise in the real economy. For a certain segment of the financing spectrum, banks and capital markets can be substitutes. This is consistent with the EU experience of strong banks and relatively weak capital markets. A major barrier in the United States to bank finance of national-scale enterprise was a state-based banking system. Capital markets institutions and channels, which are not so heavily reliant on support from the state, can funnel funds around such a barrier. This obvious analogy is a major reason why CMU is so promising and urgent for economic integration in the EU.

Separately, it may be that one reason US banks recovered more quickly from the crisis is that the alternative credit market channels provided a route for selling off troubled assets at a manageable discount. The availability of such channels may empower EU supervisors to insist on such strategies from troubled banks in the EU.

Other key issues are institutional competence, both public and private, and uniformity across member states. The US experience highlights how a powerful federal regulator can help suppress costly diversity by instituting a credible disclosure and enforcement regime and by aiding evolution in the law in the face of new challenges and opportunities. One challenge for the EU is to find its own pattern of federal regulation over the EU's capital market that will facilitate EU-wide issuance of debt and equity securities. This is less a problem of the financial institutional architecture than the regulatory architecture. With the Markets in Financial Instruments Directive II (MiFID II), the European Securities and Markets Authority has been forging ahead in ways that may well lay the groundwork for further harmonization and coordination. Elements of MiFID II, most notably the requirement that research services be charged separately from brokerage services, also suggest that the relatively weaker EU CMU may enable the EU to leapfrog over the United States in areas where entrenched interests may be impeding the efficiency of the US regime.[38] Nonetheless, substantial challenges remain. A main source of resistance will be "regulatory embeddedness" among the member states and the notable forces of path dependency, both the short-term efficiency based as well as the protectionist rent based.

Another approach for the EU is on the "supply" side. The US experience illuminates the importance of private actors who stand to gain from producing robust capital markets. The increasing wealth of EU citizens and the flow into retirement savings is creating capital pools that can, with appropriate facilitation, flow through securities markets for investment throughout the EU. The key actors are asset managers (which include for these purposes the insurers and the pension funds) to fund the supply side. Asset managers can screen potential borrowers and assemble diversified portfolios of credit claims without the aid of banks. Institutions like asset managers may also be particularly important in the EU where language differences may impede cross-border capital flows in ways the United States has never had to confront.

The systemic stability concerns that are among the reasons for the CMU also argue for permitting the growth of asset managers. Asset managers generally do not engage in a high level of liquidity transformation, making them inherently less fragile than banks. Robust capital markets have also long been viewed as potentially enhancing financial system resilience by serving as an alternative source of credit when banking systems face periodic distress. With due regard for systemic stability and the protection of a beneficiary's claims in the case of insurers and pension funds, regulation that permits use of these funds for market-based credit intermediation is a critical element for the CMU in the EU. Thus attention should turn to various directives with this objective in mind, including the Alternative Investment Fund Management Directive, the Solvency II Directive for insurers, and Directive on Institutions for Occupational Retirement Provision. With a sufficiently broad view of the range of actions that may be necessary to cultivate the conditions for a thriving CMU, the EU has the opportunity to write the next chapter in the role of law and regulatory architecture in shaping financial market structure.

Notes

Special thanks to Andres Rovira for excellent help with difficult data problems. Thanks also for comments on a prior draft to Brian Cheffins and Leslie Hannah and for research guidance from Charles Calomiris and Richard Sylla.

1. This is similar to the implicit claim in Mark Roe's work that equity ownership diffusion (and thus managerial empowerment) in the United States followed from politically inspired repression of financial intermediaries rather than from the status of investor protection. See Mark Roe, *Strong Managers, Weak Owners: The Political Roots of American Corporate Finance* (Princeton, NJ: Princeton University Press, 1994).

2. The claim here is that the demand for capital exceeded banks' lending capacities. This does not deny that banks also contributed to industrialization and enterprise growth in the United States during this time, nor does it ignore the role banks played in facilitating debt financing prior to the Glass-Steagall Act. For further insight into the role of banks, see Eric Hilt, "Banks, Insider Connections, and Industrialization in New England: Evidence from the Panic of 1873" (NBER Working Paper No. 24792, National Bureau of Economic Research, Cambridge, MA, 2018); Howard Bodenhorn, *A History of Banking in Antebellum America: Financial Markets and Economic Development in an Era of Nation-Building* (Cambridge: Cambridge University Press, 2000); Vincent P. Carosso, *The Morgans: Private International Bankers, 1854–1913* (Cambridge, MA: Harvard University Press, 1987); Naomi R. Lamoreaux, "Banks, Kinship, and Economic Development: The New England Case," *Journal of Economic History* 46, no. 3 (1986): 647–667.

3. A number of scholars have explored the ways that the limits imposed on banks for much of American history continue to shape today's financial and business landscape. Mark Roe, as noted above, shows how such constraints meant that financial intermediaries could not become powerful corporate stakeholders, thus clearing the path to dispersed owners and powerful managers (Roe,

Strong Managers, Weak Owners). Our colleague Charles Calomiris (with coauthors in several papers) has described how banking fragmentation limited US banks' financing capacity and the synergies that would derive from an alternative universal banking model. Charles Calomiris and Carlos Ramirez, "The Financing of the American Corporation, 1800–1990," in *The American Corporation Today*, ed. C. Kaysen (New York: Oxford University Press, 1996), 126; Charles Calomiris, "The Costs of Rejecting Universal Banking: American Finance in the German Mirror, 1870–1914," in *Coordination and Information*, ed. Naomi Lamoreaux and Daniel Raff (Chicago: University of Chicago Press, 1995), 257; Charles Calomiris and Daniel Raff, "The Evolution of Market Structure, Information, and Spreads in American Investment Banking," in *Anglo-American Finance: Financial Markets and Institutions in 20th-Century North America and the U.K.*, ed. Richard Sylla and Michael Bordo (Cambridge: Cambridge University Press, 1995), 103. Our account builds on these and others to show how repression of the banking system was an important factor in the growth of capital market alternatives.

4. Alan Greenspan popularized the notion that robust capital markets can function like a "spare tire" when a banking system goes into crisis. Alan Greenspan, "Do Efficient Financial Markets Mitigate Financial Crises?" (speech before the Financial Markets Conference of the Federal Reserve Bank of Atlanta, Sea Island, Georgia, 1999). For evidence regarding the recent crisis, see Ross Levine, Chen Lin, and Wensi Xie, "Spare Tire? Stock Markets, Banking Crises, and Economic Recoveries," *Journal of Financial Economics* 120, no. 1 (2016): 81–101.

5. For a useful short history from which this account is drawn see Richard Scott Carnell, Jonathan R. Macey, and Geoffrey P. Miller, *The Law of Financial Institutions*, 5th ed. (New York: Wolters Kluwer Law and Business, 2013), chap. 1; Charles W. Calomiris and Stephen H. Haber, *Fragile by Design* (Princeton, NJ: Princeton University Press, 2014), chap. 6. See also the sources cited in note 4 above.

6. The competition was not just in commercial lending but in the issuance of bank notes that functioned as currency. The state-chartered banks wanted more of the seigniorage.

7. The Jackson Bank Veto speech may be found at https://millercenter.org/the-presidency/presidential-speeches/july-10-1832-bank-veto.

8. For more on this history, see Calomiris and Haber, *Fragile by Design*, chap. 6.

9. Among the drivers for interstate banking was the advent of the automated teller machine, which opened the way to nationwide deposit gathering, and the banking crises of the 1980s, which underscored the fragility of undiversified unit banks.

10. A "five-firm concentration ratio" is the ratio of the assets/deposits of the five largest banks relative to total assets/deposits in the system. The figure on the historical ratio is found in Caroline Fohlin and Matthew Jaremski, "Bank Concentration in the United States, 1800–1914" (draft, December 2015, on file with the authors), figure 1. The figure showing the modern ratio was generated by the FRED system of the Federal Reserve Bank of St. Louis based on the World Bank's government-furnished data (GFD).

11. The following table, from Carnell, Macey, and Miller, *The Law of Financial Institutions*, p. 13, shows the steady increase in the number of banks, which produces the low concentration ratios. The number of banks peaked at more than 30,000 shortly before the Depression, which over a five-year period of closing and consolidation halved the number of banks. US Department of Commerce, "Historical Statistics of the United States, Colonial Times to 1970," Washington, DC.

Year	Number of Banks
1865	1,643
1880	2,696
1890	5,585
1900	8,100
1914	22,030

12. Rachel Louise Ensign, "Biggest Three Banks Gobble Up $2.4 Trillion in New Deposits since Crisis," *Wall Street Journal*, March 22, 1918.

13. Charles Calomiris also observes the ramifications of limiting US bank capacity during this period, but his focus is on the way that the US decision not to allow universal banking increased the cost of financial intermediation across channels. Calomiris, "The Costs of Rejecting Universal Banking," 257.

14. Lance E. Davis, "The Investment Market, 1870–1914," *Journal of Economic History* 25, no. 3 (1969): 372 (with sources).

15. In the interest of space, this chapter does not address the distinct and important role of private placements of debt in facilitating the growth of market-based finance in the United States, particularly in the 1940s. Calomiris and Raff, "The Evolution of Market Structure," 103.

16. Lamoreaux describes the legal and other barriers to bank mergers (including the resistance of incumbent bank managers) that might have produced banks of such larger scale. Naomi R. Lamoreaux, "Bank Mergers in Late Nineteenth-Century New England: The Contingent Nature of Structural Change," *Journal of Economic History* 51, no. 3 (1991): 537–557.

17. Some of the detail in this account is drawn from the *Cambridge Economic History of the United States*, ed. Stanley L. Engerman and Robert E. Gallman, vol. 2 (Cambridge: Cambridge University Press, 2000), especially chapters by Albert Fishlow, "Internal Transportation in the Nineteenth and Early Twentieth Century"; Lance E. Davis and Robert J. Cull, "International Capital Movements, Domestic Capital Markets, and American Economic Growth, 1820–1914"; and Stanley L. Engerman and Kenneth L. Sokoloff, "Technology and Industrialization, 1790–1914." See also Alfred D. Chandler Jr., "Patterns of American Railroad Finance, 1830–50," *Business History Review* 28, no. 3 (1954): 248–263.

18. Snowden reports that the average annual nominal total return on railroad bonds was notably higher for the 1872–1899 period (6.87%) than for the 1900–1925 period (4.06%). Kenneth A. Snowden, "Historical Returns and Security Market Development, 1872–1925," *Explorations in Economic History* 27 (1990): 381, 387, 389.

19. For a thorough history of the rise of investment banks, their evolving role in shaping and maintaining the capital market channel, and theory supporting the same, see Alan D. Morrison and William J. Wilhelm Jr., *Investment Banking: Institutions, Politics, and the Law* (Oxford: Oxford University Press, 2008).

20. See Alfred Chandler, *The Visible Hand: The Managerial Revolution in American Business* (Cambridge, MA: Belknap Press, 1977), 91–92.

21. See Mary O'Sullivan, "The Expansion of the U.S. Stock Market, 1885–1930: Historical Facts and Theoretical Foundations," *Enterprise and Society* 8, no. 3 (2007): 489–542 ("122 out of the 151 stocks traded on the NYSE in 1885 were railroad stocks"). O'Sullivan and Richard Sylla ("Schumpeter Redux: A Review of Raghuram G. Rajan and Luigi Zingales's 'Saving Capitalism from the Capitalists,'" *Journal of Economic Literature* 44, no. 2 [2006]: 391–404) have shown that the US equity markets in the early twentieth century were at least as large as European comparators, contrary to Raghuram G. Rajan and Luigi Zingales, *Saving Capitalism from the Capitalists* (New York: Crown Business, 2003) and "The Great Reversals: The Politics of Financial Development in the Twentieth Century," *Journal of Financial Economics* 69, no. 1 (2003): 5–50. The distinctive element for the United States was the way that banking fragmentation led to a national market in debt securities.

22. Vincent P. Carosso, *The Morgans: Private International Bankers, 1854–1913* (Cambridge, MA: Harvard University Press, 1987); Carlos D. Ramirez, "Did J. P. Morgan's Men Add Liquidity? Corporate Investment, Cash Flow, and Financial Structure at the Turn of the Twentieth Century," *Journal of Finance* 50, no. 2 (1995): 661–678; Thomas K. McCraw, "Thinking about Competition," *Business and Economic History* 17 (1988): 9–30.

23. See Brian R. Cheffins, "Mergers and Corporate Ownership Structure: The United States and Germany at the Turn of the 20th Century," *American Journal of Comparative Law* 51, no. 3 (2003): 473–503; Brian R. Cheffins and Steven Bank, "Is Berle and Means Really a Myth?," *Business History Review* 83, no. 3 (2009): 443, 449–450.

24. Chandler, *The Visible Hand*, p. 240.

25. Thomas R. Navin and Marian Sears, "The Rise of a Market for Industrial Securities, 1887–1902," *Business History Review* 29, no. 2 (1955): 105–138; Cheffins, "Mergers and Corporate Ownership Structure"; and Cheffins and Bank, "Is Berle and Means Really a Myth?" See also Alfred D. Chandler Jr., *Scale and Scope: The Dynamics of Industrial Capitalism* (Cambridge, MA: Belknap Press, 1990), chap. 2. From this perspective, the historiography that asks whether bank financial capacity precedes enterprise (or vice versa) misses the possible development of market-based finance (and financial institutions) that requires less expensive infrastructure for establishment and expansion. Compare, e.g., Bodenhorn, *A History of Banking in Antebellum America*, ch. 1.

26. See Jonathan R. Macey and Geoffrey P. Miller, "Origin of the Blue Sky Laws," *Texas Law Review* 70 (1991): 347, 352–359 ("speculative securities" were commonly bonds), 359–377, and n137 (political economy of Blue Sky Laws; the Investment Bankers Association formed to resist Blue Sky Laws was composed of bond dealers).

27. On the initial rise of US capital markets despite robust investor protection law, see John C. Coffee, "Dispersed Ownership: The Theories, the Evidence, and the Enduring Tension between 'Lumpers' and 'Splitters,'" in *The Oxford Handbook of Capitalism* , ed. Dennis C. Mueller (New York: Oxford University Press, 2012), available at https://ssrn.com/abstract=1532922; John C. Coffee, "The Rise of Dispersed Ownership: The Role of Law and the State in the Separation of Ownership and Control," *Yale Law Journal* 111, no. 1 (2001); O'Sullivan, "The Expansion of the U.S. Stock Market, 1885–1930."

28. For the history, see, e.g., Randall S. Kroszner and Raghuram Rajan, "Is the Glass-Steagall Act Justified? A Study of the U.S. Experience with Universal Banking Before 1933," *American Economic Review* 84, no. 4 (1994): 810–832 (with additional sources).

29. Jeffrey N. Gordon, "The Empty Call for Benefit-Cost Analysis in Financial Regulation," *Journal of Legal Studies* 43, no. S2 (2014): S351–S378; John Armour et al., *Principles of Financial Regulation* (Oxford: Oxford University Press, 2016), 438.

30. Compare, e.g., Rajan and Zingales, "The Great Reversals," 5.

31. See Ronald J. Gilson and Jeffrey N. Gordon, "The Agency Costs of Agency Capitalism: Activist Investors and the Revaluation of Governance Rights," *Columbia Law Review* 113, no. 4 (2013): 878–888; Ronald J. Gilson and Jeffrey N. Gordon, "Agency Capitalism: Further Implications of Equity Intermediation," in *Research Handbook on Shareholder Power*, ed. Jennifer Hill and Randall Thomas (Cheltenham, UK: Edward Elgar, 2015), https://ssrn.com/abstract=2359690.

32. Calomiris and Raff, "The Evolution of Market Structure," 103.

33. See Macey and Miller, "Origin of the Blue Sky Laws"; Paul G. Mahoney, "The Origins of the Blue-Sky Laws: A Test of Competing Hypotheses," *Journal of Law and Economics* 46, no. 1 (2003): 229–251.

34. See Russell A. Smith, "State 'Blue-Sky' Laws and the Federal Securities Acts," *Michigan Law Review* 34, no. 8 (1936): 1135–1166; *Hall v. Geiger-Jones Co.*, 242 U.S. 539 (1917).

35. Joel Seligman, *The Transformation of Wall Street: A History of the Securities and Exchange Commission and Modern Corporate Finance* (Boston: Houghton Mifflin, 1982).

36. See generally Louis Loss and Joel Seligman, *Securities Regulation*, 3rd ed. (Frederick, MD: Aspen Law & Business, 1989), 41–60; Daniel J. Johnedis, "Current Legislation: Blue Sky Laws— Uniform Securities Act," *Boston College Industrial and Commercial Law Review* 3 (1962): 218–220.

37. See, e.g., Rutherford B. Campbell Jr., "The Role of Blue Sky Laws after NSMIA and the JOBS Act," *Duke Law Journal* 66 (2016): 619–631.

38. See Howell E. Jackson, John Rady, and Jeffery Y. Zhang, "Nobody Is Proud of Soft Dollars: A Critical Review of Excess Brokerage Commissions in the United States and the Likely Impact of Pending MiFID II Reforms in the European Union" (working paper, 2018) (on file with authors); Kathryn Judge, "Intermediary Influence," *University of Chicago Law Review* 82 (2015): 625–630.

II THE TARGETS: HOUSEHOLDS AND FIRMS

6 Asset and Debt Participation of Households: Opportunities and Challenges in Eliminating Borders

Michael Haliassos and Alexander Michaelides

Recent literature, aptly termed by Campbell (2006) as "household finance," has studied motives for household saving, borrowing, wealth accumulation, and asset allocation, gaining well-deserved prominence in financial economics (Tufano 2009). This was accompanied by increased awareness of the importance of financial institutions for behavior, building on Allen (2001), who emphasized agency problems and liquidity management functions. The global financial crisis of 2007–2009 focused attention on the "plumbing of the financial system" (Blanchard 2015) with a view to prudent regulation, consumer protection, and financial literacy.

The demographic transition and continuous financial innovation broaden the spectrum and riskiness of choices that households need to make over their lifetime. Increased longevity and the move from defined benefit to defined contribution systems are good examples. In view of unequal financial market and product development across European Union (EU) countries, a capital markets union (CMU) can improve individual and social welfare through a variety of mechanisms. A large single market with harmonized laws and regulation can provide substantial economies of scale and bring costs down through competition and improved financing of innovative activity.

Transparency and technology-aided information dissemination over a large market can help increase awareness, trust, and financial literacy. Nevertheless, a number of obstacles need to be tackled. We analyze some key opportunities and challenges for the different actors (households, firms, regulators, and governments) inspired by household finance research. We conclude that, despite challenges, substantial potential exists, especially if new technologies for information dissemination, product access, transparency and regulation are utilized. Indeed, financial technology (fintech) can more readily be applied to a larger market, rendering CMU viable and beneficial to households around the EU.

International Heterogeneity

The literature has identified different motives for saving and portfolio choice over the life cycle. Precautionary saving that involves smoothing background risks like earnings (Carroll 1997; Deaton 1991) is important at younger ages, while saving for retirement gains prominence later on in life (Attanasio et al. 1999; Gourinchas and Parker 2002). Motives for saving during retirement include bequests (De Nardi 2004) and self-insuring health risks (De Nardi, French, and Jones 2010). These motives vary in intensity across different education and occupation groups but also across countries.

Guiso, Haliassos, and Jappelli (2001) illustrate how such heterogeneity translates into heterogeneity in household portfolios in advanced economies, while more recently Badarinza, Campbell, and Ramadorai (2016) and Christelis, Georgarakos, and Haliassos (2013) document considerable household portfolio heterogeneity across a broad spectrum of economies (see table 6.1). Christelis, Georgarakos, and Haliassos (2013) performed decompositions to show that the economic environment, which includes institutions, economic and regulatory policy and cultural factors, matters greatly for the observed international variation in participation rates and in holdings conditional on participation.

Recent empirical evidence suggests that cultural differences in household financial behavior diminish with exposure to a common set of policies and institutions. Haliassos, Jansson, and Karabulut (2017) study the financial behavior of immigrants to Sweden and find evidence that cultural differences in stockownership and homeownership (figure 6.1), as well as in debt participation, get attenuated with length of exposure to a common economic environment, even for immigrants with great cultural distance and with limited informal contact to the host culture. This last feature suggests that a CMU, offering to households and firms a unified access platform without barriers to competition, high fees or intentional segmentation of financial markets, has the potential to reduce international heterogeneity in portfolios over time.

Potential Benefits from CMU

CMU can provide EU households a common platform for informed financial decisions and generate considerable economies of scale in information provision. Aided by fintech, CMU can reduce fixed costs that limit asset market participation among the less wealthy (Fagereng, Gottlieb, and Guiso 2017; Gomes and Michaelides 2005; Haliassos and Bertaut 1995; Haliassos and Michaelides 2003). CMU can lower costs further by promoting international

Table 6.1
Differences in portfolios across countries.

Country/Region	NET WORTH Quantiles			STOCKS Prevalence (%)	Quantiles among owners			HOME Prevalence (%)	Quantiles among owners			MORTGAGE Prevalence (%)	Quantiles among holders		
	25	50	75		25	50	75		25	50	75		25	50	75
United States	***40.0***	***162.1***	***437.0***	***49.7***	***11.0***	***49.5***	***169.0***	***77.3***	***80.0***	***150.0***	***250.0***	***38.3***	***32.0***	***70.0***	***125.0***
Midwest	52.0	178.2	428.1	54.5	10.0	45.0	150.2	80.9	82.0	132.0	200.0	39.3	30.0	65.0	105.0
Northeast	39.7	193.5	475.9	54.7	11.0	52.0	172.5	70.6	92.0	190.0	340.0	32.5	32.0	70.0	124.0
South	29.9	113.0	326.0	42.6	10.0	43.9	153.0	78.3	63.0	100.0	180.0	36.5	28.5	58.0	102.0
West	53.0	228.5	582.0	52.1	14.0	53.3	182.5	76.9	140.0	250.0	400.0	46.0	50.0	100.0	178.7
Europe	***27.3***	***140.6***	***294.6***	***26.0***	***3.3***	***10.4***	***29.2***	***67.6***	***104.9***	***168.7***	***275.6***	***14.7***	***12.4***	***36.7***	***79.0***
Sweden	21.5	86.4	201.1	70.8	3.8	12.1	34.5	68.9	51.2	92.1	153.5	40.2	15.2	30.7	57.0
Denmark	12.8	100.6	242.6	56.1	2.7	8.2	23.0	69.2	90.8	136.2	204.2	44.3	28.4	56.7	90.8
Germany	11.8	95.4	272.6	25.4	3.1	9.7	26.2	51.2	136.3	209.7	314.6	14.8	12.6	36.7	83.3
Netherlands	9.6	140.4	336.4	24.9	4.0	15.2	42.8	55.2	192.3	253.0	374.4	43.1	23.8	54.6	110.4
Belgium	96.6	199.4	370.0	37.7	5.1	20.3	70.7	80.0	127.4	173.6	254.8	11.9	5.2	14.4	32.7
France	49.4	177.1	348.9	43.0	2.8	8.0	26.6	72.2	124.1	186.2	310.4	11.9	7.9	23.7	51.7
Switzerland	35.5	193.4	414.4	36.3	7.2	25.6	80.5	54.8	229.5	317.4	459.1	45.3	51.0	104.6	201.3
Austria	9.4	112.5	244.5	10.2	3.1	8.1	27.4	56.7	108.0	162.0	270.0	9.2	1.9	10.8	43.2
Italy	46.4	149.5	297.2	10.4	4.7	14.3	32.9	75.1	95.4	168.7	281.2	5.6	9.6	27.0	56.2
Spain	73.2	140.7	254.1	12.8	4.0	11.0	24.6	86.9	84.1	131.3	219.7	9.7	9.5	30.2	58.6
Greece	55.8	111.7	215.6	10.6	1.1	4.3	12.4	84.3	62.0	95.5	148.9	5.5	5.0	18.6	37.2
England	75.7	257.4	443.3	39.4	4.6	15.6	52.1	76.1	191.5	275.7	398.3	16.8	10.7	27.6	63.3

Source: Christelis, Georgarakos, and Haliassos (2013).
Note: Households aged 50+, 000s of 2004 US$, purchasing-power-parity adjusted. Computed from SHARE data.

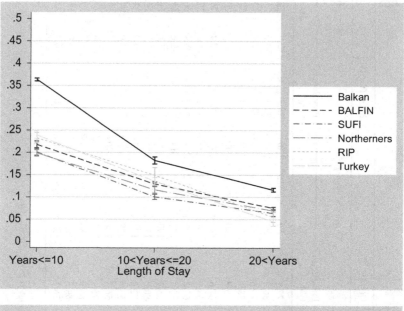

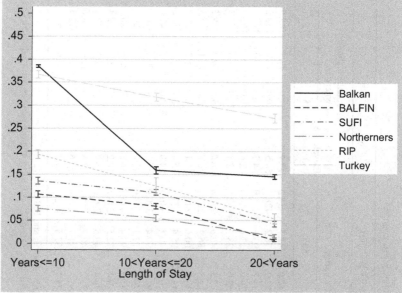

Figure 6.1
Participation differences between Swedes and immigrants, controlling for household characteristics. Difference in stock market participation rates and in homeownership rates, respectively, between native Swedes and members of the cultural group are indicated. Differences control for household characteristics and are plotted against length of stay in Sweden. For corresponding countries of origin, see Haliassos, Jansson, and Karabulut (2017).

competition in financial markets. Enabling households to "shop around" in internet "financial supermarkets" allows greater diversification and consumption risk sharing. Stocks, mutual funds, and also health, life or property insurance, and insurance-linked mortgages can be more widely held.

The same holds for tax-deferred accounts promoting retirement preparedness through large-scale fund management delegation to professionals (Gomes, Michaelides, and Polkovnichenko 2009), possibly coupled with default enrollment. Madrian and Shea (2001) showed that inertia following default enrollment in US 401(k) accounts encouraged participation and maintenance of the default contribution rate and fund allocation. A European pension account allowing contributions from any CMU country can act in a similar way and facilitate labor mobility.

Indirect benefits can be generated through institutional reforms necessitated by CMU. Many European countries, for example, do not have tax deferral incentives for pension accounts despite problematic social security systems. Moreover, international heterogeneity in dividend, interest, capital gains, and property taxation, and in investor protection and personal bankruptcy rules does not foster cross-border asset sales or loans. Positive spillovers from and to the banking union infrastructure are also likely.

Greater international access to a variety of products can promote product awareness and financial literacy among European households. Lusardi and Mitchell (2007) emphasize the role of financial literacy in good financial outcomes, while Lusardi, Michaud, and Mitchell (2017) show how augmentable financial knowledge can be a key predictor of wealth accumulation and inequality. CMU offers stronger incentives for households to invest in financial literacy, since the gains can also be larger. It also exerts greater pressure on governments to introduce financial literacy campaigns early on (in elementary or secondary schools).

Challenges on the Household Side

Challenges will arise in encouraging households to understand the new opportunities and risks posed by CMU, overcome their ignorance, and participate in this brave new world. Awareness of financial products is limited even at the national level (Guiso and Jappelli 2005). Ignorance is amplified at the international level by home bias (Coval and Moskowitz 1999; Feldstein and Horioka 1980). Familiarity bias (Huberman 2001) encourages households to choose the most familiar of a class of financial products. The tendency to prefer national or local products even in violation of portfolio optimization will need to be overcome if CMU is to reach European populations at large.

Financial education facilitates successful implementation of CMU but is a longer-term project. Financial literacy is limited across the world (Lusardi and Mitchell 2014), and it will take time before measures like school courses (Italy) or online programs (Australia and Spain) can be applied to all EU countries and are properly evaluated and fine-tuned. Informative advertising utilizing fintech complements education programs, but reaching broad population segments across CMU members is formidable. CMU will also need to face the limited commitment of governments to financial literacy, as evidenced by the limited country participation in the new financial literacy module of the Programme for International Student Assessment (PISA) tests for teenage students.

Lack of trust can also hinder the take-up of financial products abroad. Guiso, Sapienza, and Zingales (2008) show that trust is already an important determinant of stock market participation within a country. International trust matrices highlight that citizens of one country tend to trust more their compatriots, and there is considerable and variable lack of trust across borders (Guiso, Sapienza, and Zingales 2009).

With a dramatically increased asset menu under CMU, there is an expanded role for financial advisers to guide their clients to EU products and to access potential clients located abroad. Recent literature on (domestic) financial advice has pointed to two key issues: (1) limited knowledge of (many) financial advisers and (2) conflict of interest arising from compensation schemes and lack of separation of advice from sale (Hackethal, Haliassos, and Jappelli 2012; Inderst and Ottaviani 2009). Trust in financial advisers is a double-edged sword. Lack of trust may prevent households from obtaining and following useful advice, but trust can enable advisers to charge higher fees. Gennaioli, Shleifer, and Vishny (2015) show that, with trust in "money doctors," fees do not match costs, and managers on average underperform the market net of fees.

Such problems can be compounded when advisers or products are located abroad. If many financial advisers lack sufficient knowledge of domestic products, how can we expect them to be knowledgeable about products available in the EU? If most EU countries do not feature "fee-only" advice that separates guidance from sale, then how shall we break the conflict of interest that biases advice? If EU households mistrust financial advisers who are compatriots dealing with domestic products, why should they trust them or their foreign counterparts to advise on the international market? Indeed, the enhanced information requirements of CMU may make households even more dependent on (domestic) financial advisers and less sensitive to overcharging and underperformance.

Yet a properly designed CMU would generate economies of scale in the provision of investment and insurance opportunities that is likely to result in some streamlining of available financial products. The size of the market would also justify the emergence of platforms aggregating information and standardizing advice (e.g., robo-advice). Finally, CMU will hopefully exert pressures for harmonization of regulation of financial advice and its compensation, increasing trust across borders.

An alternative way to overcome distrust and to acquire financial information is interaction with knowledgeable peers. Duflo and Saez (2002) and Hong, Kubik, and Stein (2004) show that financial choices of peers and intensive social interactions encourage asset participation. Arrondel et al. (2019) and Haliassos, Jansson, and Karabulut (forthcoming) provide evidence of informative social interactions in stockholding and private retirement accounts.

Which social groups are likely to benefit most from social interactions: the richer and better informed or those currently without market access? The literature shows that the extent and content of peers' knowledge matters for the presence and size of effects. Further, learning is not the only avenue: mindless imitation or social comparisons also influence financial behavior. For example, households that perceive their peers as earning higher income are more likely to borrow and to worsen their indicators for future financial distress (Georgarakos, Haliassos, and Pasini 2014).

Social networks and internet platforms can, in principle, break down some peer group segmentation. Yet they also provide opportunities for manipulation of the least knowledgeable households. CMU will need to find ways to exploit the information potential but harness the threat of exploitation of ignorance so that CMU households can rise over barriers created by limited information or distrust.

Challenges on the Firm Side

Financial firms matter (Allen 2001) and will be instrumental in shaping the future of CMU. They will continue to act as delegated intermediaries in various product classes (mutual funds, pension funds, insurance, mortgages), even in the presence of robo-advisers. Advertising and fee structure are important for the reach of CMU but might also generate conflicts of interest between the sell and buy sides of the market, necessitating financial regulation. Markets in Financial Instruments Directive II (MiFID II) is partly motivated, for example, by the need to have clear rules about who pays for research and how this cost can be made transparent.

The effects of CMU, as a dramatic quasi-natural experiment, will be interesting to study. Provision of financial information across borders is a case in point. Very little is known about the actual cost of information production in the finance industry. The recent literature on information inattention (Sims 2003) and its application to the finance industry (Kacperczyk, van Nieuwerburgh, and Veldkamp 2016) do not have a large empirical counterpart despite the large role of sell-side research in information production. Nevertheless, the hope is that by scaling the market, CMU will reduce such costs and, with greater transparency, help evaluate the cost of cross-border information provision.

CMU can provide an impetus for financial innovation and a symbiotic relationship between academia and business, to the extent that innovation caters to households throughout the EU. An interesting example is target date funds (TDFs) or lifestyle funds that can be marketed at low fees (possibly through robo-advisers) across Europe, just as they are in the United States. TDFs currently ensure that gradual automatic adjustments in portfolio composition over the life cycle are consistent with research-based advice—for example, that the risky share in stocks should optimally decline with age (Cocco, Gomes, and Maenhout 2005)—and that theoretical prediction is consistent with average investor behavior in financially advanced countries such as Norway (Fagereng, Gottlieb, and Guiso 2017). TDFs can be further enhanced by conditioning asset allocation on market information (Michaelides and Zhang 2017) or tailored to specific households (Dahlquist, Setty, and Vestman 2018).

Further research can be spurred by the potential for a competitive price in a much larger market under CMU. Access can be enhanced through trusted financial advice and transparent, rather than complex, product design. Firms, as well as academics, will need to gain the trust of foreigners (Zingales 2015).

Unfortunately, scale and competition under CMU also provide an impetus for product complexity aimed at misleading the less sophisticated market segments. Gabaix and Laibson (2006) show how complex financial products can hide the true cost and pass it directly to the unsuspecting consumer. Celerier and Vallee (2013) show how financial product complexity has risen over time in Europe, especially where competition is tougher. While the profit margins of firms rise with complexity, sale of these products to retail customers need not enhance customers' after-cost returns. Transparent firms, vocal academics, and vigilant regulators need to work together to minimize such downsides of CMU.

Challenges on the Regulatory Side

The extent to which regulations are harmonized across countries and the division of labor across national and supranational authorities will be crucial for effective functioning of CMU. Even within the banking union, which arose partly from the need to deal with cross-border banking regulation, a substantial component of supervision is left to the individual state. This will likely be more pronounced in CMU, where initially small start-ups will need to be regulated at the national level.

A number of relevant examples can be mentioned. The balance between restricting sales of financial products to inexperienced customers (MiFID II) versus regulating producers is important. Fuchs-Schuendeln and Haliassos (2019) show a smooth transition of East German households into products they had never accessed prior to German reunification. CMU will open access to households that never had such access before and will restrict access to those that seem to defeat the main purpose of CMU. A regulatory framework promoting product standardization and simplicity, together with credible investor protection, would seem key to allowing wider access without mis-selling.

The European Securities and Markets Authority (ESMA) is a supranational authority that can provide the necessary leadership but will need to handle potentially complicated negotiations with national authorities and stakeholders. Investor protection becomes especially difficult across borders: Mervyn King famously observed that banks are "international in life and national in death." In the absence of crisis, cross-border selling of financial products is lauded. But at the moment a financial provider faces difficulties, burden sharing largely becomes a national affair.

Clear and supranational rules on delineation of regulatory authority and on a legal framework for investor and consumer protection will be needed for the effective development of CMU. For instance, the sale of complicated contingent convertibles (cocos) to retail investors in Cyprus, Spain, or Italy should probably not have been allowed. Given that cocos were sold by commercial banks, one can argue that consumer protection responsibility lies with the bank regulator. On the other hand, consumer protection typically (but not always) lies with national securities exchange commissions or even with ESMA.

Demands on regulatory authorities extend to regulating financial advice. By expanding the amount of information needed to operate in financial markets and the requirements for trust in financial advisers, CMU may provide a powerful impetus for adopting common requirements in the provision of financial advice. These include minimum financial adviser qualifications, responsibility for continuing education, and authority to test adviser knowledge and ability. Interestingly, what needs to be delineated is not only the responsibilities of supranational versus national competent authorities but also those of regulators versus firms employing financial advisers.

Political Economy Challenges

Design and implementation of CMU will also face political challenges. One will involve harmonization of tax systems. Poterba (2001) points to important implications of heterogeneity in tax structures, as that observed across several EU countries, for household portfolio choices. Capital and corporate taxation is very low in some countries (Cyprus and Ireland, for example), while others have arrived at different national tax structures through a complicated political process that reflects national preferences for redistribution and historical election outcomes. Agreeing on a harmonized tax structure across CMU becomes a non-trivial challenge.

The likely response of national institutional investors to the much wider product access provided by CMU is not obvious. Evidence suggests that such investors invest disproportionately at home, signaling a politically driven home bias (see Bradley, Pantzalis, and Yuan 2015 for evidence from US state pension fund equity holdings). If such bias is observed in a developed and transparent economy like the United States, it is also likely to manifest itself in other countries. Greater transparency, breaking down of borders, or greater international harmonization of institutional investment portfolios might therefore face politically sensitive challenges.

Existence and harmonization of personal bankruptcy rules can also become important for households with access to a much wider, and presumably less familiar, international asset menu. The legal treatment of nonperforming loans, even if those are provided mainly by the banking system, does influence household investment behavior under CMU. Securitization of mortgages is hard to imagine without uniform and effective standards of foreclosure laws. Perhaps more importantly in some instances, the extent of implementation of personal bankruptcy law matters, and uniform implementation standards are not currently in place across the EU. Judicial systems across countries vary in efficiency, as illustrated in the World Bank's "Ease of Doing Business" rankings. Coupled with the possibility that wider access to financial products might materialize mainly for the wealthier and more financially sophisticated households, voter groups feeling left behind might use their vote to end a process that might be perceived to benefit disproportionately politically connected elites. Recent election outcomes not only in the EU but also across the Atlantic suggest that such contingencies should not be downplayed.

Political challenges can also spread across borders if CMU is perceived as a capital drain from weaker economies toward more financially developed ones, further increasing wealth inequality. On the other hand, CMU could provide expanded financing opportunities to periphery firms as well as opportunities for higher returns and greater diversification of mutual funds and real estate funds located in financial centers. Households in the periphery may then become, in part, indirect investors in projects located in their own country. Going a step beyond, the reputation of international fund managers may provide a substitute for national pessimism and an avenue for channeling even local funds to companies operating within the country. Nevertheless, the political challenge of explaining such indirect financing of periphery investments remains in the current environment of limited trust within the EU.

Technological Challenges and Opportunities

The advent of fintech is rapidly transforming the playing field in financial services and can greatly facilitate CMU, as mentioned in various places above. Robo-advisers can reduce the cost of financial advice and asset allocation and are seen as democratizing finance by reducing transaction and advice costs. This optimistic view would have greater credibility if a minimum level of financial sophistication, as well as access to robo-advice, were guaranteed for all households and countries. International comparisons of PISA test performance in the financial literacy module confirm substantial differences even among the limited number of countries participating. Uniform access to robo-advice and robo-investing will also not materialize, at least initially, since internet access and use vary substantially across and even within countries.

A number of further issues with fintech remain largely uncharted territory in the literature but need to be explored. Will fintech platforms make the performance/objectives/menu of products more or less transparent and salient? Will they indeed improve the matching between consumers and products for all demographic groups? Will fintech platforms encourage or reduce herding/social imitation?

Despite the multitude of issues, we are inclined to think that these challenges and risks are more likely to represent "teething problems" rather than longer-term impediments to the huge opportunities of unifying and expanding markets that CMU provides at a fraction of the current cost. It is hard to see how such a reduction in transaction and information costs will not eventually improve individual and societal welfare.

Conclusion

CMU promises to create the largest market in financial products, thus helping to drive financial efficiency, innovation, and welfare. Although discussions typically focus mostly on firms, this chapter has identified numerous opportunities and challenges relating to household access to a unified capital market.

Households need to become more informed and financially literate; firms more open to transparency, simplicity, competition, and responsibility; regulators more astute and sophisticated; and politicians more informed and involved in difficult cross-border harmonization. These challenges will be worthwhile to overcome in the face of the important opportunities that CMU, together with the banking union, provides for household access to financial products.

References

Allen, Franklin. 2001. "Do Financial Institutions Matter?" *Journal of Finance* 56, no. 4: 1165–1175.

Arrondel, Luc, Hector Calvo Pardo, Chryssi Giannitsarou, and Michael Haliassos. 2019. "Informative Social Interactions." Working paper. https://papers.ssrn.com/sol3/papers.cfm?abstract_id =3171564.

Attanasio, Orazio, James Banks, Costas Meghir, and Guglielmo Weber. 1999. "Humps and Bumps in Lifetime Consumption." *Journal of Business & Economic Statistics* 17, no. 1: 22–35.

Badarinza, Cristian, John Y. Campbell, and Tarun Ramadorai. 2016. "International Comparative Household Finance." *Annual Review of Economics* 8: 111–144.

Blanchard, Olivier. 2015. "Looking Forward, Looking Back." Interview, International Monetary Fund, August 31. https://www.imf.org/en/News/Articles/2015/09/28/04/53/sores083115a.

Bradley, Daniel, Christos Pantzalis, and Xiaojing Yuan. 2015. "The Influence of Political Bias in State Pension Funds." *Journal of Financial Economics* 119, no. 1: 69–91.

Campbell, John. 2006. "Household Finance." *Journal of Finance* 61, no. 4: 1553–1604.

Carroll, Christopher. 1997. "Buffer Stock Saving and the Life Cycle/Permanent Income Hypothesis." *Quarterly Journal of Economics* 112, no. 1: 3–55.

Celerier, Claire, and Boris Vallee. 2013. "What Drives Financial Complexity? A Look into the Retail Market for Structured Products." Social Science Research Network, July 1. https://ssrn.com /abstract=2082106.

Christelis, Dimitris, Dimitris Georgarakos, and Michael Haliassos. 2013. "Differences in Portfolios across Countries: Economic Environment versus Household Characteristics." *Review of Economics and Statistics* 95, no. 1: 220–236.

Cocco, Joao, Francisco Gomes, and Pascal Maenhout. 2005. "Consumption and Portfolio Choice over the Life-Cycle." *Review of Financial Studies* 18: 491–533.

Coval, Joshua D., and Tobias J. Moskowitz. 1999. "Home Bias at Home: Local Equity Preference in Domestic Portfolios." *Journal of Finance* 54, no. 6: 2045–2073.

Dahlquist, Magnus, Ofer Setty, and Roine Vestman. 2018. "On the Asset Allocation of a Default Pension Fund." *Journal of Finance* 73, no. 4: 1893–1936.

Deaton, Angus. 1991. "Saving and Liquidity Constraints." *Econometrica* 59: 1221–1248.

De Nardi, Christina. 2004. "Why Do the Elderly Save? The Role of Medical Expenses." *Review of Economic Studies* 71, no. 3: 743–768.

De Nardi, Christina, Eric French, and John Jones. 2010. "Wealth Inequality and Intergenerational Links." *Journal of Political Economy* 118: 39–75.

Duflo, Esther, and Emmanuel Saez. 2002. "Participation and Investment Decisions in a Retirement Plan: The Influence of Colleagues' Choices." *Journal of Public Economics* 85: 121–148.

Fagereng, Andreas, Charles Gottlieb, and Luigi Guiso. 2017. "Asset Market Participation and Portfolio Choice over the Life-Cycle." *Journal of Finance* 72, no. 2: 705–750.

Feldstein, Martin, and Charles Horioka. 1980. "Domestic Saving and International Capital Flows." *Economic Journal* 90, no. 358: 314–329.

Fuchs-Schundeln, Nicola, and Michael Haliassos. 2019. "Does Product Familiarity Matter for Participation?" Social Science Research Network, May 19. https://papers.ssrn.com/sol3/papers.cfm?abstract_id=2384746.

Gabaix, Xavier, and David Laibson. 2006. "Shrouded Attributes, Consumer Myopia, and Information Suppression in Competitive Markets." *Quarterly Journal of Economics* (May): 505–540.

Gennaioli, Nicola, Andrei Shleifer, and Robert Vishny. 2015. "Money Doctors." *Journal of Finance* 70, no. 1: 91–114.

Georgarakos, Dimitris, Michael Haliassos, and Giacomo Pasini. 2014. "Household Debt and Social Interactions." *Review of Financial Studies* 27, no. 5: 1404–1433.

Gomes, Francisco, and Alexander Michaelides. 2005. "Optimal Life-Cycle Asset Allocation: Understanding the Empirical Evidence." *Journal of Finance* 60: 869–904.

Gomes, Francisco, Alexander Michaelides, and Valery Polkovnichenko. 2009. "Optimal Savings with Taxable and Tax-Deferred Accounts." *Review of Economic Dynamics* 12: 718–735.

Gourinchas, Pierre-Olivier, and Jonathan Parker. 2002. "Consumption over the Life Cycle." *Econometrica* 70, no. 1: 47–89.

Guiso, Luigi, Michael Haliassos, and Tullio Jappelli. 2001. *Household Portfolios*. Cambridge, MA: MIT Press.

Guiso, Luigi, and Tullio Jappelli. 2005. "Awareness and Stock Market Participation," *Review of Finance* 9, no. 4: 537–567.

Guiso, Luigi, Paola Sapienza, and Luigi Zingales. 2008. "Trusting the Stock Market." *Journal of Finance* 63, no. 6: 2557–2600.

Guiso, Luigi, Paola Sapienza, and Luigi Zingales. 2009. "Cultural Biases in Economic Exchange?" *Quarterly Journal of Economics* 124, no. 3: 1095–1131.

Hackethal, Andreas, Michael Haliassos, and Tullio Jappelli. 2012. "Financial Advisors: A Case of Babysitters?" *Journal of Banking and Finance* 36, no. 2: 509–524.

Haliassos, Michael, and Carol Bertaut. 1995. "Why Do So Few Hold Stocks?" *Economic Journal* 105: 1110–1129.

Haliassos, Michael, Thomas Jansson, and Yigitcan Karabulut. 2017. "Incompatible European Partners? Cultural Predispositions and Household Financial Behavior." *Management Science* 63, no. 11: 3780–3808.

Haliassos, Michael, Thomas Jansson, and Yigitcan Karabulut. Forthcoming. "Financial Literacy Externalities." *Review of Financial Studies*.

Haliassos, Michael, and Alexander Michaelides. 2003. "Portfolio Choice and Liquidity Constraints." *International Economic Review* 44: 144–177.

Hong, Harrison, Jeffrey Kubik, and Jeremy C. Stein. 2004. "Social Interaction and Stock Market Participation." *Journal of Finance* 59, no. 1: 137–163.

Huberman, Gur. 2001. "Familiarity Breeds Investment." *Review of Financial Studies* 14, no. 3: 659–680.

Inderst, Roman, and Marco Ottaviani. 2009. "Misselling through Agents." *American Economic Review* 99, no. 3: 883–908.

Kacperczyk, Marcin, Stijn van Nieuwerburgh, and Laura Veldkamp. 2016. "A Rational Theory of Mutual Funds' Attention Allocation." *Econometrica* 84, no. 2: 571–626.

Lusardi, Annamaria, Pierre-Carol Michaud, and Olivia Mitchell. 2017. "Optimal Financial Knowledge and Wealth Inequality." *Journal of Political Economy* 125, no. 2: 431–477.

Lusardi, Annamaria, and Olivia Mitchell. 2007. "Baby Boomer Retirement Security: The Roles of Planning, Financial Literacy and Housing Wealth." *Journal of Monetary Economics* 54, no. 1: 205–224.

Lusardi, Annamaria, and Olivia Mitchell. 2014. "The Economic Importance of Financial Literacy: Theory and Evidence." *Journal of Economic Literature* 52, no. 1: 5–44.

Madrian, Brigitte, and Dennis F. Shea. 2001. "The Power of Suggestion: Inertia in 401(k) Participation and Savings Behavior." *Quarterly Journal of Economics* 116, no. 4: 1149–1187.

Michaelides, Alexander, and Yuxin Zhang. 2017. "Stock Market Mean Reversion and Portfolio Choice over the Life Cycle." *Journal of Financial and Quantitative Analysis* 52, no. 3: 1183–1209.

Poterba, James. 2001. "Taxation and Portfolio Structure: Issues and Implications." In *Household Portfolios*, edited by Luigi Guiso, Michael Haliassos, and Tullio Jappelli, 103–142. Cambridge, MA: MIT Press.

Sims, Christopher. 2003. "Implications of Rational Inattention." *Journal of Monetary Economics* 50, no. 3: 665–690.

Tufano, Peter. 2009. "Consumer Finance." *Annual Review of Financial Economics* 1: 227–247.

Zingales, Luigi. 2015. "Does Finance Benefit Society?" *Journal of Finance* 70, no. 4: 1327–1363.

7 Capital Markets Union and Growth Prospects for Small and Medium-Sized Enterprises

Giorgio Barba Navaretti, Giacomo Calzolari, Gianmarco Ottaviano, and Alberto Franco Pozzolo

The capital markets union (CMU) is expected, among other effects, to free financial resources for small and medium-sized enterprises (SMEs), directly and indirectly improving their access to credit and capital markets. It foresees measures specifically targeted to SMEs, like reducing information barriers and developing specialized segments of capital markets. More generally, all areas of intervention envisaged by the Action Plan of the European Commission are expected to reduce the distance between SMEs and capital markets within the European Union (EU).[1] The idea is that an integrated, larger, and pan-European capital market (1) will be more efficient both in terms of better risk allocation and lower operating costs, (2) will be more resilient to shocks, and (3) will allow for deeper and broader European markets, respectively improving the intensive and the extensive margins of financial markets but also of the real economy.

In this chapter, we raise a note of caution. A CMU may deliver integration and efficiency of capital markets, both desirable and well awaited in the European project, but that may create (national) winners and losers not only in financial markets but also, and probably more importantly, in the real economy.

Our key concerns are the market failures, especially related to informational issues, haunting SMEs' access to credit and financial markets. If the CMU is able to address the issues at the root of these market failures, then we will most likely face a further concentration of the financial sector in a European core, still serving the entire EU and its SMEs wherever they are, similarly to the US market.

But if the CMU only addresses the liberalization and integration of financial markets without tackling specific issues concerning SMEs, then it will likely deliver a core-periphery outcome, both for financial markets and for firms and SMEs.

A crucial distinction is between soft and hard information. Soft information requires long-term relationships and proximity. It can thus be seen as a "centripetal force" promoting the geographical concentration of finance and production.

On the other hand, codified hard information can be dealt with at a distance and is thus either a neutral or a "centrifugal force" counterbalancing agglomeration.

Integration of capital markets may drain relationship lending—the first source of funding for SMEs in this scenario. If relationship lending is based on geographical proximity, only the SMEs closest to the core of the financial markets will have access to credit, and periphery countries will lose both financial markets and real activities.

It is therefore crucial to investigate if and how the actions contemplated in the CMU will deliver not only further integration of financial markets but also how they will address the specific issue of information processing of SMEs. In other words, a fully integrated European capital market will be beneficial to SMEs, and the European economy, if it does entice adequate large-scale technologies and actions to solve market failures related to informational issues. We will discuss different channels through which the CMU entices positive outcomes in this respect.

Another crucial distinction concerns the characteristics of the SMEs involved. The information issue is especially relevant as far as global capital, and especially equity capital, aims at financing firms' growth rather than survival. There is a crucial distinction between rapidly growing and efficient SMEs and firms that are small and remain such, either because their business model is inconsistent with growth or because their managers/entrepreneurs are neither capable nor willing to make them grow. Identifying such growing firms requires a large amount of information that is not easily processed into a hard format.

Dealing with SMEs is a highly risky affair anyway. Even if we just consider lending (which has lower information requirements than equity as even stagnant firms can repay their loans), it is still not easy to identify viable firms. Data that we will discuss show how the average share of nonperforming loans (NPLs) is much higher for SMEs than for larger firms. Diversification by lending to large pools of small borrowers does not solve the problem. Even if lending is fully diversified, catering to a fully representative sample of SMEs, average failure rates will be higher than for large firms.

Direct access to an integrated CMU is an affair that should especially matter for fast growing or sufficiently sophisticated and transparent SMEs, particularly if we consider equity capital. Stagnant SMEs remain of course important from a welfare point of view as they provide many jobs. However, it is difficult to see how they could acquire financial resources beyond local boundaries. Even for them, information processing is crucial, and as we will discuss below, this might still happen through local banks.

Summing up, either an integrated capital market favors the development of technologies and actions to discriminate more efficiently than fragmented national ones between viable and non-viable SMEs or, from the standpoint of SMEs, the CMU defeats its purpose, at best.

The organization of the chapter is as follows. The first sction illustrates the importance of SMEs in Europe and benchmarks countries in the world, their dynamics, and their financial structure. The second section discusses the informational issues of SMEs and how they are affected by capital markets integration. The third section looks at the interaction between the CMU and the single market from the specific viewpoint of SMEs. The fourth section concludes with an analysis of specific actions of the CMU.

SMEs Financing in Europe

The Role of SMEs in the Real Economy

SMEs account for a large proportion of aggregate employment in most advanced countries (figure 7.1). However, while very small SMEs (those with fewer than ten employees) account for nearly 40% of aggregate employment in Italy, they only account for less than 12% of employment in the United States. Within European countries, Italy, Spain, and Portugal have the largest share of employment in firms with fewer than fifty employees, while France and the United Kingdom have the smallest.

Even in countries where they account for a smaller share of employment or where a large share of firms is extremely small and not growing, the contribution of young and small SMEs (those up to five years old with fewer than fifty employees) to gross job creation is extremely relevant, and it is only in part balanced by high rates of job destruction (figure 7.2).

The high rates of gross job creation and destruction of SMEs are mainly due to the fact that they are typically young firms, often with risky investment projects, leading to a much higher rate of default than larger corporations. Indeed, a large number of SMEs are new start-ups, which have a relatively high probability of default. In the Netherlands, for example, nearly 40% of start-ups become inactive within three years from foundation, although this share is much smaller in countries such as Belgium and Sweden where it is less than 20%. The share of growing firms is in most countries very small, never above 10% (figure 7.3).

The high probability of default clearly impacts also on job dynamics. Criscuolo, Gal, and Menon (2014) show that start-ups that become inactive within three years from foundation account for nearly 80% of all job destruction in Japan and in the Netherlands, while this share is about 20% in Belgium. Symmetrically, growing and stable firms provide most new jobs.

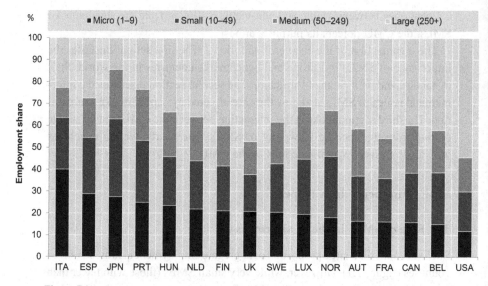

Figure 7.1
Share of employment by firm size and by country, averages between 2001 and 2010 (except a few countries for which data are not available during the whole sample period). *Source*: Criscuolo, Gal, and Menon (2014).

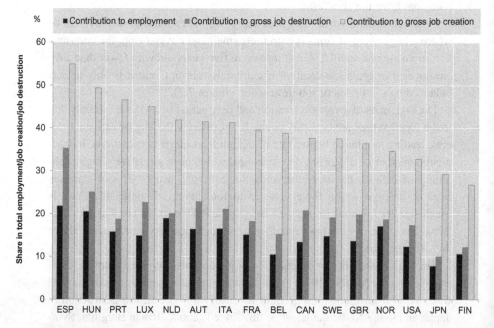

Figure 7.2
Contribution of young and small SMEs to job creation and destruction. *Source*: Criscuolo, Gal, and Menon (2014).

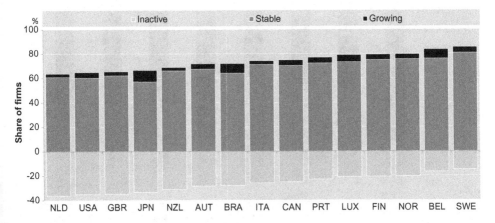

Figure 7.3
Three-year survival and growth performance of micro start-ups. *Source*: Criscuolo, Gal, and Menon (2014).

Although SMEs and especially start-ups account for a significant share of job creation, according to the results of the "Survey on the Access to Finance of Enterprises" (SAFE), conducted by the European Central Bank (ECB) (2018) on a representative sample of about 15,000 European firms, larger and relatively older SMEs have higher rates of employment growth (figure 7.4).

Ownership and Financial Structure of SMEs

The financing needs of SMEs largely depend on the fact that they are young, small, and relatively opaque firms, and in the majority of cases they are family-run businesses. According to SAFE, most SMEs are owned by a family or by a group of entrepreneurs, and an equally significant share is owned by a single owner (figure 7.5). The share of SMEs in which a venture capital firm or a business angel owns the largest stake is negligible in most European countries.

Since they face high fixed costs that hinder their ability to access more sophisticated sources of funding such as public debt and equity, SMEs must resort mainly to bank loans to fulfill their needs of external finance. Figure 7.6 shows that SMEs consider credit lines and bank loans as the most important sources of financing, together with leasing and trade credit. Equity capital is considered a relevant source of funding by about 12% of total SMEs, relatively more so for larger SMEs and those that are two to five years old. Debt securities are considered a relevant source of funding by more than 3% of SMEs. In some countries, trade credit is also a very relevant source of funding.

The high relevance assigned by SMEs to bank financing clearly has relevant implications for their leverage structure. Indeed, SMEs are typically more

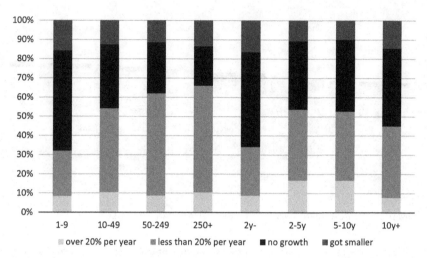

Figure 7.4
Employment growth averages between 2013 and 2015. *Source*: European Central Bank (2018).

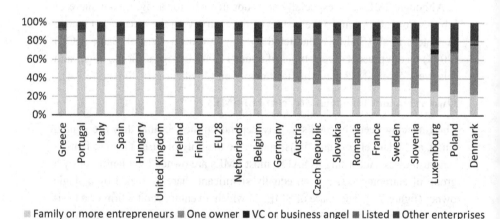

Figure 7.5
Ownership structure of SMEs. Data refer to October 2017. *Source*: European Central Bank (2018).

leveraged than larger firms that have better access to equity financing through initial public offerings. But at the same time, it is also true that very small SMEs may face stronger difficulties in obtaining bank credit and therefore will be forced to employ mainly internal funding. The impact of each country's industrial and financial structure on a firm's funding is therefore the result of many different elements.

On average, firm leverage (measured by the ratio of equity to total liabilities) is very different across European countries, ranging from about 40% in

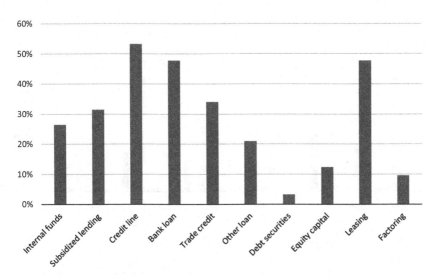

Figure 7.6
Relevance of sources of funding. Share of firms that answered that the specific source of financing
is relevant; that is, that it has been used in the past or has been considered to be used in the future.
Source: European Central Bank (2018).

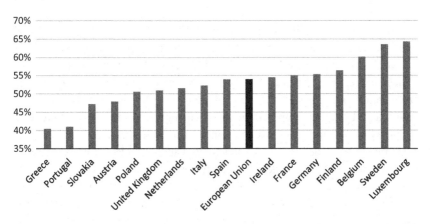

Figure 7.7
Firm leverage. Share of equity to total liabilities in 2016. *Source*: Eurostat (n.d.).

Greece (despite the large incidence of smaller firms) to nearly 65% in Luxembourg (figure 7.7). France, Germany, Italy, Spain, and the United Kingdom,
despite their very different industrial and financial structures, all have leverage
ratios between 51% and 55%.

Focusing on SMEs, the SAFE survey presents again a remarkably diversified
picture. Bank loans and credit lines are considered an important source of funding

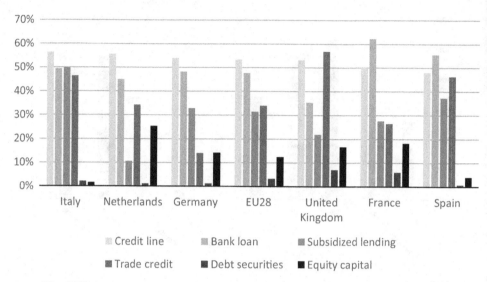

Figure 7.8
Relevance of different sources of financing. Share of firms that answered that the specific source of financing is relevant; that is, that it has been used in the past or has been considered to be used in the future. *Source*: European Central Bank (2018).

by more than half of SMEs in the majority of European countries, although with some variability—the more so in the case of credit lines (figure 7.8).[2]

Loans involving support from public sources in the form of guarantees or reduced interest rates are also considered important in some European countries. Trade credits are a traditional source of funding for SMEs all over the world, as shown also by ample empirical academic literature; among major European countries, values range from over 50% in the United Kingdom to less than 20% in Germany. As to debt securities and equity capital, the low average share of European SMEs that consider them as relevant sources hides sizable cross-country differences. In the case of the Netherlands, about one quarter of SMEs consider equity capital as a relevant source of financing, while in Italy they are less than 2%. In the case of debt securities, values are on average even lower.

When asked to rate possible policy interventions in a range of 0 to 10, SMEs stress the importance of making available measures easier to obtain, for example, through the reduction of administrative burdens and of tax incentives (figure 7.9). Interestingly, facilitating equity investments is not considered a relevant issue, suggesting that the low relevance of equity financing is not due to limits to its supply but rather to a precise choice of SMEs. Export and credit guarantees are considered as the least interesting type of policy intervention, suggesting that export credit is not a relevant issue for European SMEs (as typically they are unlikely to export anyway).

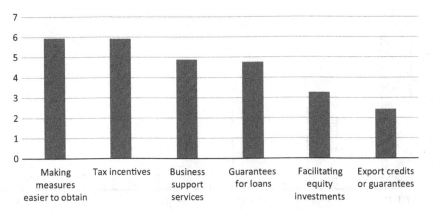

Figure 7.9
Preferred policy interventions. Average score assigned by respondents on a scale from 0 to 10.
Source: European Central Bank (2018).

Guarantees for loans are also considered a relevant policy, and indeed, especially after the crisis, they have become very relevant in some countries, as shown by figure 7.10.

Supplying Funds to SMEs

Having described what SMEs consider their most important sources of funding and how this impacts their equilibrium financial structure, it is now important to understand what are the main suppliers of these funds, what is the incidence of SME financing in their asset portfolios, and what new players might possibly be attracted by a more effective CMU.

As it is clear from the evidence presented above, most of SME financing comes from banks. In the euro area, a bit more than a quarter of total lending to nonfinancial corporations is accounted for by loans of less than €1 million of total value, which are typically used as a proxy for loans to SMEs (figure 7.11). This is indeed a much smaller share than that of employment in smaller firms, as shown in figure 7.1 above. Interestingly, also in this case aggregate data hide large cross-country variability, with values ranging from over 50% in Portugal to about 10% in Ireland and the Netherlands.

SMEs are riskier than larger firms, because they are typically younger and more opaque and are often based on the knowledge and experience of a small number of entrepreneurs (often just one). Loans to SMEs are also charged higher interest rates, the more so during periods of financial distress (figure 7.12).

Being on average riskier, SMEs also have a heavier impact on bank balance sheets despite their smaller granularity that allows in principle for better diversification. Indeed, capital requirements on SME lending can be in some cases

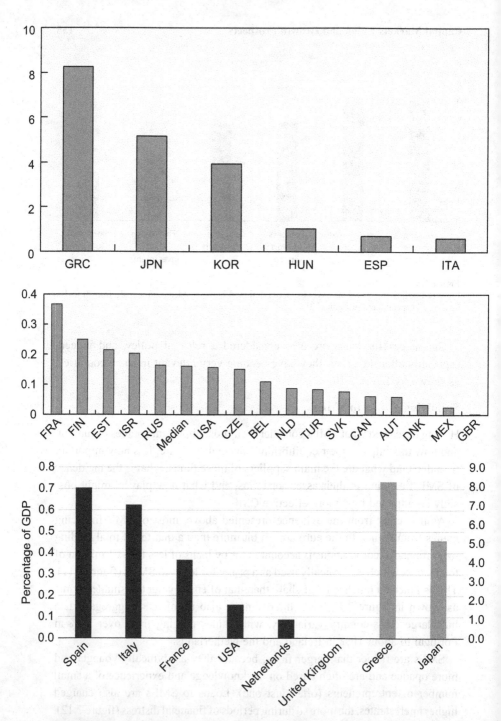

Figure 7.10
Government loan guarantees to SMEs. The scale on the left side of the figure is for Spain, Italy, France, the United States, the Netherlands, and the United Kingdom; the scale on the right side is for Greece and Japan. *Source*: Organisation for Economic Co-operation and Development (2017).

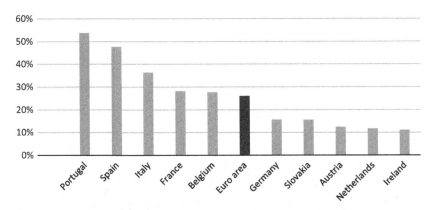

Figure 7.11
Share of lending to SMEs. Loans to SMEs are proxied by loans to of up to €1 million. *Source*: European Central Bank (n.d.).

penalizing. Loans to SMEs are more likely to become nonperforming than average loans to nonfinancial corporations (figure 7.13). However, the impact on bank capital absorption can be different depending on the size of SMEs.

A relevant impact on SME financing could come from the securitization of bank loans. Although the incidence of securitizations is at the moment overstated (because banks securitize their own loans to obtain securities that they then use as collateral for central bank financing), their weight is not negligible (figure 7.14). Simple and transparent securitizations have indeed been advocated by many commentators, including the Bank for International Settlements (BIS).

Apart from banks, institutional investors can be a relevant source of funding for nonfinancial corporations, and facilitating their access to financing SMEs is one of the key policies proposed within the CMU. However, the impact of such policies can be extremely heterogeneous depending on the weight of institutional investors in each country, the more so if their portfolio choices show a significant degree of home bias.

The incidence of the most important institutional investors (investment funds, insurance companies and pension funds) is extremely diversified across most developed countries, ranging from a value of total assets close to three times gross domestic product (GDP) in Denmark to less than 12% in Greece (figure 7.15). Interestingly, also, the composition is rather heterogeneous, with a high incidence of pension funds in some countries and nearly no presence in others.

However, institutional investors are very unlikely to be able to play a significant role in the financing of SMEs by directly lending to them. Indeed, they hold a very limited amount of loans that are typically shares of very large syndicated

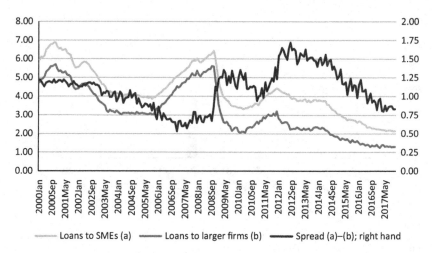

Figure 7.12
Interest rates on new loans to SMEs and larger corporations. Loans to SMEs are proxied by loans of up to €1 million. *Source*: European Central Bank (n.d.).

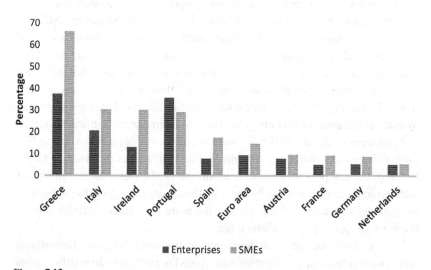

Figure 7.13
Share of nonperforming loans to total loans. Data refer to March 2016. *Source*: European Banking Authority (2016).

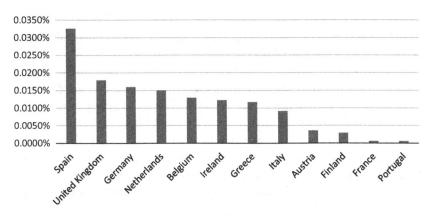

Figure 7.14
Outstanding value of securitizations. Percentages over GDP, by country of origination of collateral.
Source: Association for Financial Markets in Europe (2017).

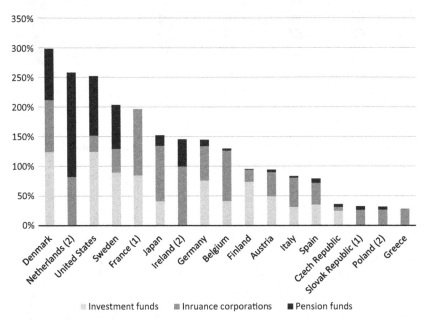

Figure 7.15
Size of institutional investors. Percentages over GDP. (1) Excludes pension funds; (2) excludes
investment funds. *Source*: Organisation for Economic Co-operation and Development (2017).

loans to large corporations, and their portfolio is biased toward equity and invest-ment fund shares (figure 7.16). Purchases of securities obtained from the secu-ritization of bank loans to SMEs could nonetheless play a crucial role.

In addition, institutional investors prefer to invest their assets in their home country as the academic literature has shown to be the case for most financial institutions. The ratio of assets that institutional investors invest domestically is in many countries on the order of 50% (figure 7.17).

Additional sources of funding that have proved to be extremely important especially for innovative and fast-growing SMEs are private equity and angel financing. However, these sources have a very limited incidence compared to the role of banks and institutional investors. The total value of private equity

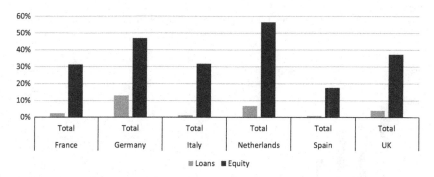

Figure 7.16
Portfolio composition of institutional investors. *Source*: Organisation for Economic Co-operation and Development (2017).

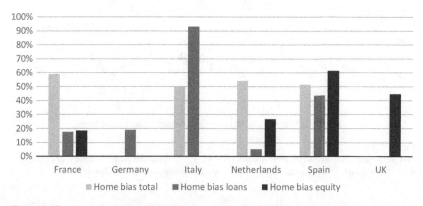

Figure 7.17
Home bias in the portfolio of institutional investors. Share of assets that institutional investors invest domestically. *Source*: Organisation for Economic Co-operation and Development (2017).

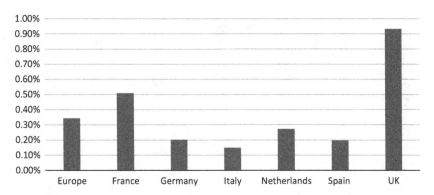

Figure 7.18
Private equity financing over GDP. Data refer to 2016. *Source*: Invest Europe (2017).

investment is at most on the order of 1% of GDP (figure 7.18); that of angel financing is even smaller.

Interestingly, the funding of private equity firms shows a relatively high degree of international diversification, but they tend to finance mainly domestic activities (figure 7.19). With the CMU in place, funds might therefore be attracted by countries with a stronger presence of private equity firms who use them to finance local activities to the benefit of domestic SMEs.

SMEs Financing: Market Failures and Solutions with the CMU

Why do SMEs face more adverse credit conditions than larger firms? Why does size matter in the determination of the availability and the cost of credit? How do market failures affect the provision of funding and generate this wedge between large and small firms?

The initial step requires understanding the technology of financing and how the acquisition of information helps to contain the costs of potential bankruptcies. Let us start with the basic form of financing: lending. Providing loans requires appraising borrowers, monitoring them, and other activities implying considerable per loan fixed costs—that is, costs that are independent of the size of the loan. A simple and immediate consequence of these costs is that banks tend to charge higher interest rates for small loans than for large ones. Figure 7.12 shows clearly that small firms pay 50 to 100 basis points more than large ones for loans in all the main European countries. This difference can rise to up to 250–300 basis points during serious market distress.

The issue is even more severe for equity. In this case investors need not only to assess the financial viability of firms but also their growth prospects.

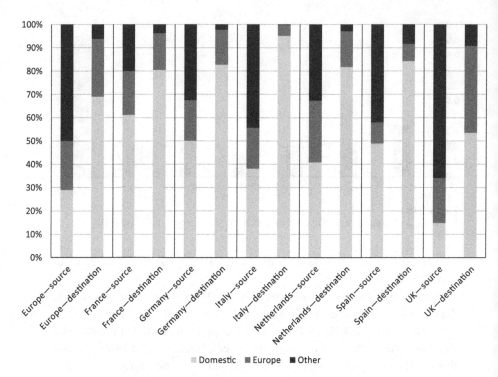

Figure 7.19
Sources and destinations of private equity financing. Data refer to 2016. *Source*: Invest Europe
(2017).

In fact SMEs are typically undercapitalized. This is a serious impediment to
their expansion. In general, entrepreneurs are endowed with different projects
characterized by different levels of risks, the potential of which they know
much better than possible investors. The consequent inability of investors to
carry out an adequate risk assessment of entrepreneurs and their projects
makes them shy away from SMEs.

Undercapitalization has additional effects on the cost of debt, as argued by
Bernanke and Gertler (1989) and the following "static trade-off theory." When
bankruptcy costs faced by a bank dealing with the bankruptcy of a debtor are
high, more leveraged firms that face a higher probability of bankruptcy due
to more severe difficulty in servicing debt (for example, when facing unexpected negative product demand shocks) are charged higher interest rates by
banks. Fixed costs and bankruptcy costs therefore imply that SMEs, especially
those with low equity, will face higher interest rates, ceteris paribus.

The higher level of interest rates generates a typical adverse selection problem. Safer borrowers refrain from borrowing. Higher interest rates apparently

increase banks' profits (when the price effect prevails) but eventually cause their drop because of the growing impairment provisions facing NPLs. As first argued by Stiglitz and Weiss (1981), banks may then prefer to cap interest rates and withhold loans, with the result that entrepreneurs with good and safe projects are left with too little or no borrowing. The higher interest rate required on smaller loans because of the fixed costs of acquiring information also makes adverse selection more frequent among SMEs borrowers than for large firms.

The information asymmetry problem and costly verification imply that banks are often unable to separate good and bad projects. Technically, we may say that the market is unable to reach a "separating equilibrium," in which good and bad projects are kept apart, and is stuck in a "pooling equilibrium," in which all projects are treated alike. As a result, the pool of SMEs that are funded anyway includes "many," possibly too many, risky and inefficient small firms, whereas deserving ones get excluded. In other words, there is not just an issue of insufficient financial capital for SMEs but also an issue of inefficient composition of the pool of *actual* borrowers. This argument is consistent with the evidence reported in the first section that small firms have a much higher rate of NPLs than large ones.

The informational concerns in lending are also compounded by imperfect monitoring and consequent moral hazard. In a highly leveraged firm a small share of the total expected absolute gains or losses goes to the entrepreneur (even though the return on equity will be higher). Thus, because high leverage entrepreneurs exert little of their costly effort, firms are less likely to repay their loans. This moral hazard issue is generated by the absence of observability or verifiability of the entrepreneur's effort by banks that thus react by constraining the credit to small firms with little equity.

On top of this, SMEs are also more opaque than large firms with much less public information available so that the issue of asymmetric information is even more severe. Large firms are subject to more stringent informational requirements that cannot be applied to small firms (again for an issue of scale), which allow investors to better assess and identify their risks. Younger firms, which are smaller for obvious reasons, are even more opaque because signals concerning profitability and riskiness need time to be accumulated, making adverse selection stronger for younger and thus smaller firms.

In a similar vein, since a debtor often has the ability to capture some of the assets in the case of default, the entrepreneur of a highly leveraged firm faces higher incentives to default. Banks then react by restraining credit and requiring larger collateral and equity. Again, small and young firms that are typically less capitalized and have limited collateral to provide suffer more than larger firms from this credit constraint.

Summing up, market failures can generate an inefficient amount of financing for SMEs and also a wrong allocation away from the most deserving firms. Can the CMU help?

Financing Technologies and the Information Problem

Let us reason in terms of a fully integrated capital market as envisaged by the CMU. How can this improve the information problem, compared to fragmented national markets, and therefore reduce or spread more efficiently the risk of financing SMEs?

This can happen in two (mutually nonexclusive) ways. Either the CMU favors the development of efficient information technologies to distinguish between viable and non-viable SMEs, making it more likely to achieve a separating equilibrium. Or, if these technologies are ineffective, it fosters a better diversification and spreading of the risks and costs of financing SMEs, with benefits also in the case of a pooling equilibrium.

A basic common EU framework for providing uniform systems of information and standards would be extremely useful per se toward the achievement of separating equilibriums. Reducing information barriers for SME finance is indeed a crucial objective of the CMU. There are several options here, and the scale of the CMU provides a powerful incentive to reduce such barriers. Possible measures include EU-wide business registers with standardized information, EU-wide comparable rating methodologies, EU-wide credit registers, and a common EU Prospectus Regulation.

These measures have the potential to simplify the comparability of information and thus improve allocative efficiency with a better matching between supply and demand of funding. The implementation of such measures would of course force SMEs to comply with information requirements and procedures. The benefits of accessing a European pool of potential investors would also provide powerful incentives to overcome the costs of adopting such measures. Elements of proportionality will be necessary anyway to sort out the trade-off between transparency and regulatory costly burdens on SMEs.

While rules and standards for transparency would significantly help, financial instruments may in themselves develop technologies for information processes. How does the CMU affect the working of such technologies? We address this issue separately for banking and broader nonbanking capital markets. We will then discuss the potential role of public guarantees and regulation.

Global Banking

Banks are likely to remain dominant in funding SMEs. In particular, because of the opaqueness of SMEs, it is hard to think that new technologies will be able to supplant the collection and processing of soft information through long-term banking relationships. As soft information is intrinsically difficult to standardize, relational banking will still play a crucial role in discriminating between viable and non-viable SMEs. This may appear to be a "back to the future" option, in contrast to the view of fully informed modern markets.

Note that, as discussed above, picking fast-growing SMEs is not necessarily an objective of the lending-based business model of commercial banks. For a lender, what matters is that the borrower is able to pay back its loan, not how fast and how much it will be able to grow. The aim here is to reduce the average default rate of its loans. The information problem faced by banks is therefore simpler than the one faced by equity investors for whom dynamic and fast growth matters a lot.

Yet the CMU may have an important effect on the way in which soft information is used and processed by banks. Consider three possible developments of banking induced by the CMU.

The first one is that the CMU may favor further internationalization of the European banking sector. Foreign or transnational banks may have different lending behavior from national ones, especially from those operating in local markets. On the one hand, they may use different and possibly more selective lending technologies not based on a long-term presence in local markets. On the other hand, they exert competitive pressure on local banks. Petersen and Rajan (1995) have put forward an argument that shows a relative incompatibility between strong competition and relationship lending. The idea is that incomplete contracts between a lender and a borrower are sustained through repeated interactions and expected future rents. When intense competition kicks in, these rents are reduced, if not swiped away, and the relationship breaks down. In this scenario, the sources of credits for SMEs may be negatively affected.

The integration of banking activities within the CMU may consequently force local credit systems to become more selective in their credit allocation toward viable SMEs. Within this logic, there is a shift away from the aim of providing financial support to local communities in a nonselective fashion (eventually lending also to firms that may not be viable as borrowers) toward a logic of cherry-picking, with limited attention to local interests.

As argued as an example by Detragiache, Tressel, and Gupta (2008), this can have important implications for peripheral local markets. As far as the best firms get carried away toward funding from global banks, lending conditions for the other firms will likely worsen. As default rates in the pool of the worse firms is higher, credit for them will become dearer and scarcer. Before integration there was a pooling equilibrium where, because of the adverse selection issue discussed above, the worse borrowers had decent credit conditions. Financial market integration may lead to a separating equilibrium where conditions for good firms improve but for smaller and more opaque SMEs they worsen.

The second and the third developments induced by the CMU on banks may arise also without entry of foreign banks in local markets. The second is that banks may more easily securitize loans in a larger market. After the financial crisis, most of the securities backed by bank loans to SMEs are retained on banks' balance sheets to be used as collateral for central bank refinancing. An integrated European capital market may help banks dispose of such securities, reducing the capital absorption and hence the cost of SMEs' lending (Panetta and Pozzolo 2018). Note that developing a framework for the securitization of SME loans is a key objective of the CMU. A third one is that banks can develop new fee-based lines of business, acting as advisers for SMEs willing to enter capital markets.

In these two latter cases the information technology would be slightly different from above (entry of foreign banks) and perhaps more favorable to weaker firms. Banks are probably the only institutions able to use the soft information they have built through long-term relationships and transform it into hard information and scoring systems. Banks, especially large ones, have long and wide series of data and information on their clients. Global operations provide sufficient scale and benefits to them and to their clients to actually process such data and develop tools to classify and score borrowers. Especially in the case of securitization, local banks would have adequate information to effectively pool the risk of their borrowers and build tranching mechanisms for the securities they issue. Certainly securitization, but possibly also advisory services, would allow local banks to become information brokers and help local firms access indirectly (securitization) and directly (advisory) global markets, thus softening the core-periphery effect of the CMU. This development will take place even if foreign banks do not enter local markets.

Capital Markets
Consider now capital markets at large. Developing a package for SME listing on public capital markets is a key objective of the CMU.

Here information requirements might be more stringent than for banks, especially in the case of equity, where also the growth potential of the companies matters beyond their business viability. Moreover, there is a higher need for hard information because capital markets match investments to investors through decentralized mechanisms and distant geographies. Since it would be too costly for individual investors to carry out adequate assessments of individual investments, information is therefore processed and provided by other agents who act as intermediaries in this process.

These information intermediaries act as such because they have a stake in such information processing. We distinguish two cases. In the first one, information will be processed by agents interested in preserving the functioning of a specific market and of its network externalities. In the second case, the agent has interest in providing accurate information as they are also investors with skin in the game.

The first case applies for example to pan-regional equity platforms where SMEs can list on multiple jurisdictions (e.g., Alternex, Finpoint). These forms of financing are still in their infancy but are essential to achieve a critical mass of listings and liquidity unavailable to national platforms. At present, national differences still hinder the cross-country integration of such platforms (tax, listing and disclosure requirements, antifraud, post-trade, constraints on foreign ownership). Hence the CMU will crucially favor this process of integration and thus improve the matching of demand and supply with deeper and more efficient markets.

Platforms themselves, even though they are unlikely to have direct exposures toward the invested firms, have a strong interest in assessing participants to the market. These being typically two-sided markets, the selection process is crucial so as to attract as many investors as possible on the one side of the market and as many good firms as possible on the other side of the market. There is here of course a critical tension between the need for a low cost of entry into these markets for SMEs and the need of transparency. So, information requirements and assessment procedures (e.g., type of prospectus) will be lighter than in larger established markets, but still, SMEs accessing these platforms would be inevitably subject to much higher scrutiny than if they remained outside capital markets. Entry and assessment procedures will be easier if the standardized common European information and rating procedures discussed above are in place.

Also, as these platforms may function on a crowd funding principle, the behavior of the participants toward the community of the platform will also in itself provide important information on their viability with time. Note that the same principle would apply for lending platforms, even though they would have less stringent information requirements, as discussed for the case of banks.

The second case applies instead when the initial investment assessment is carried out by an agent that also participates in the investment and keeps some skin in the game.[3] This is the case for asset-backed securities if they are retained by the originator (as discussed for banks above) and by venture capital, private equity funds, and all sorts of other funds. Again, all these are measures envisaged within the CMU. Information is therefore directly processed and generated by the initial investor. Note that this process requires geographical proximity to the investment and assessment of soft information. These investors, like local banks in the discussion above, act as information brokers form local to global markets, hence softening the centrifugal forces of integrated financial markets. Here again these types of instruments will benefit enormously from the CMU, as they will be able to tap a much larger mass of financial resources and investment options.

A similar principle could also work to move long-term investors like pension funds and insurance companies toward SMEs. Even though these institutions have the ideal time horizon to undertake such risky but highly diversified investments, they frequently lack the scale and the investments capacity to select viable investments, or they are constrained to do so by regulatory or institutional impediments. Their investment could be intermediated by specialized investors able to process information as discussed above. Once more the CMU will likely lift several barriers against the cross-border investments that face these institutional investors.

Pooling Equilibrium and Public Guarantees
The information processing technologies linked to specific financial instruments likely to expand under a CMU may help the achievement of a separating equilibrium as well as more and cheaper finance for good firms. The allocation of capital will therefore improve across the EU.

Yet it is not obvious how thick the "layer of cream over the milk" will be. A generalized transition toward transparency and standardized information will certainly affect and is already affecting firms' behavior. It is not, however, clear how high the threshold is (or how much milk will evolve into cream) and how many firms will stay below it. If the financial resources pooled by global markets will concentrate only on the most transparent firms and if the lower layer of more opaque firms is deep enough, then a core-periphery pattern in which some viable projects are not financed will likely emerge anyway.

Within this framework markets will not be able to support less transparent firms, which yet provide a large share of employment (see the first section), as their financing will no longer be subsidized by the returns from good firms and even risky start-ups with uncertain futures. We have discussed at length information technologies that may attune such centrifugal forces and hence favor the inclusion of geographical and qualitative peripheries in the CMU. Nevertheless, whether centripetal or centrifugal forces will prevail cannot be assessed ex ante.

It is clear that there is a potential scenario where public intervention might be necessary anyway, with a growing role of instruments like public guarantees. If the separating equilibrium leaves behind a large share of the population of firms, even though the CMU improves allocative efficiency, it may also generate a higher burden on public funding to deal with peripheries. Also in this framework, common European rules for managing guarantee funds will be useful instruments.

Empirical Evidence on Financial Integration and SMEs

We have discussed how, from an analytical point of view, information technologies have a crucial impact on whether the CMU may or may not enhance the access of SMEs to capital markets. Of course, there is no empirical evidence on the impact of the CMU as yet, but many studies have looked at financial integration in general and how this has affected SMEs.

The bottom line of this literature is a differential impact depending on different types of firms and the status of local financial markets. In general, financial markets integration helps larger and more transparent firms comparatively more than small and opaque firms, unless integration installs discipline and increases efficiency of local financial markets.

In general terms, a common theme emerging in the empirical evidence is that small firms are generally at a comparative disadvantage in accessing external finance with respect to large firms (for example, Beck and Demirgüç-Kunt 2009; Beck, Demirgüç-Kunt, and Levine 2003; Beck, Demirgüç-Kunt, and Maksimovic 2008).

If we consider financial integration, Berger, Klapper, and Udell (2001) and Gozzi and Schmukler (2008) are among the many who show that cross-border banks lend relatively less to opaque firms than local domestic banks. Also, Kang and Stulz (1997) confirm that foreign institutional investors hold disproportionately more shares of large firms. Consistently, Mian (2006) finds that larger internal distance (geographical and cultural) between the headquarters of a cross-border bank and its foreign branches makes the latter less likely to finance small firms.

In an assessment of the developments of the EU on access to credit, Muradoglu, Onay, and Phylaktis (2013) study how the mix of equity and credit changes with more financial integration. They show that small firms in the euro area and in joining countries are not able to profit from the lower interest rates, and therefore they are not able to move to longer debt maturity. They also do not increase debt capital and equity financing. These results confirm the relevance of adverse selection in the credit market for these firms which face higher interest rates and worse credit conditions than large firms.

As discussed above, stronger integration in financial markets tends to open the door to cross-border banking. The effect of entry of foreign banks on access to credit for SMEs is complex with mixed evidence. Survey evidence shows

lower reported impediments to access to credit for these firms when more
foreign banks are around (Clarke, Cull, and Martínez Peria 2006). In fact,
international banks may be more efficient in terms of both scale and technologies
and thus able to lend also to less transparent firms, diversifying their portfolio.
Moreover, their entry may force domestic banks to higher efficiency standards
as well. However, Mian (2006) claims that foreign banks may have even less
information on local opaque SMEs and therefore lend less to them than their
domestic counterparts. Claessens and van Horen (2014) and Bruno and Hauswald (2014) go a step further, showing that this mixed evidence could be due
to the combination of local available information and contractual environment.
In countries that have more effective credit information sharing, foreign banks
tend to have a stronger positive impact on SMEs lending. With respect to the
CMU, specific actions designed to improve the transparency of SMEs may turn
out to be a fundamental and necessary ingredient to improve the access to credit
for these firms.

As argued above, more integrated financial markets also imply more intense
competition. The evidence on the impact of competition on SMEs finance is once
more mixed. Consistent with the prediction of the theoretical model of Petersen
and Rajan (1995) discussed above, Cetorelli and Gambera (2001) show that
young firms grow faster in countries with more concentrated banking systems,
and Bonaccorsi di Patti and Dell'Ariccia (2004) show that less transparent firms
have better access to external finance when bank concentration is higher.

An opposing view is provided by Boot (2000), who notes that more intense
competition (not measured as concentration) should reduce a bank's earning
on relationship lending less than transactional lending, as the former is more
protected from competitive pressures. Especially, local banks should then concentrate more on the former, possibly enlarging the options of SMEs that mainly
rely on relationship banking. Degryse and Ongena (2007) provide evidence of
this mechanism in Belgium. Carbo-Valverde, Rodriguez-Fernandez, and Udell
(2009) show that in Spain, more intense competition improved access to credit
for SMEs.

From an empirical point of view, these apparently divergent observations
may be reconciled noting that intensity of competition and concentration are
different concepts. From a theoretical perspective, these two opposing forces
will plausibly coexist, and which one will prevail depends on their relative
strength in the specific environment of the CMU.

It is also conceivable that the effects of competition on SMEs lending depend
on the local environment in terms of the quality and sharing of information about
firms (e.g., a more transparent environment increases the possibility to transfer

collaterals between lenders). Hence, also with respect to the potential effects of competition, the CMU specific actions designed to improve the transparency of SMEs can be fundamental, if not necessary, ingredients for the improved access to credit of these firms.

In this respect, a further twist considered by the literature is the level of development of the financial markets that get integrated in a broader system. The disadvantage of small firms is stronger when financial markets are less developed and the size of the banking sector is smaller (e.g., Beck, Demirgüç-Kunt, and Levine 2003; Beck, Demirgüç-Kunt, and Maksimovic 2008). Lucey and Zhang (2011) show that, in developing countries, with financial integration larger firms obtain more debt (and with longer maturity) and issue more equity than small firms. In their analysis of Eastern Europe, Giannetti and Ongena (2005) show that access to debt increases with the entry of cross-border banks but only for large firms. In particular, these banks tend to concentrate on larger firms more active in the production of tradables (Agènor 2003).

Generally, the benefits of integration in local markets are higher if integration in itself induces an efficient improvement of local financial institutions. Beck, Demirgüç-Kunt, and Maksimovic (2008) find that in this case small firms can benefit more than large ones. On a similar note, Popov and Ongena (2011) have shown that further integration of interbank markets allows small firms to obtain better credit conditions and lower interest rates, the more so if integration generates more competition in the local banking sector.

CMU, SMEs, and the Single Market

An important, specific aspect of the implications of capital market integration for European firms, and in particular for SMEs, is the extent to which the CMU can be expected to complement the single market by fostering firm participation. This is relevant for the development of SMEs with high growth potential, given that in perspective they are the ones more likely to trade their products internationally, and for the everyday operations of all SMEs, no matter whether they are high growth or not. In this respect, a CMU can indeed play an important role not only in complementing the banking union and reinforcing the economic and monetary union but also in promoting the single market for goods and eventually services (ECB 2015).

The single market is an ongoing, ambitious project with the aim of allowing firms to trade their products seamlessly across borders thanks to the dismantling of tariff and, more saliently nowadays, non-tariff barriers (NTBs). These are barriers that "arise from laws, technical regulations and practices, and create obstacles for trade. NTBs can be of a general character, such as problems with the implementation and enforcement of EU law at the national level, missing or differing e-government solutions, or complex value-added tax requirements in intra-EU trade (Szczepański 2017). Broadly speaking, they tend to originate from asymmetries in laws and regulations as well as in the requirements and the collection of information relevant for the implementation of those laws and regulations. These asymmetries create additional costs for firms considering operations in multiple national markets—asymmetries that are particularly penalizing for the cross-border activities of SMEs.

That SMEs are particularly affected can be easily explained relying on recent advances in international trade theory and empirics (Melitz and Redding 2014). All industries are populated by firms with different efficiency, which manifests itself in terms of different turnover and profitability. Only firms that are efficient enough are able to generate the amount of cash needed to pay for the costs of internationalization associated with tariff and NTBs, either directly through internal funds or indirectly through bank loans, equity, and bond markets. That is why such barriers are particularly hard to overcome by SMEs that are typically less efficient or less profitable than bigger firms.

In this respect, a key challenge for the EU is to promote the single market in an inclusive way by making it not only "deeper" but also "broader." On the one hand, "deepening" means that firms that are already active in the single market can get even more involved. For example, bigger firms that already export can export even more, thus further benefiting from European integration. On the other hand, "broadening" means that firms that are currently inactive in the single market can start being involved. For example, smaller firms that do not export can start exporting, thus reaping the benefits they were excluded from. In other words, deepening is about the "intensive margin" of international participation in the single market, and broadening is about its "extensive margin."

The development of the single market has generally followed a straightforward logic bundling intensive and extensive margins: if (tariff and non-tariff) barriers are removed, all firms get more involved in international transactions, and this spreads the gains from trade across the entire firm size distribution. In reality things are more complicated. Sure enough, lower barriers improve participation both at the intensive and the extensive margins. Yet, unless all barriers are erased, less efficient firms at the bottom of the size distributions (which are typically a large fraction of the total number of firms) remain excluded. These firms suffer from competition in their domestic markets by more efficient foreign competitors without gaining access to foreign markets. They are therefore forced to downsize and possibly to shut down altogether. This explains why SMEs often feel that European integration (and, more broadly, globalization) is not good for them. Such feeling is strengthened by the fact that lower NTBs are usually achieved through compulsory adherence to new harmonized rules implying additional costs. It makes sense for bigger firms to pay those costs in order to get access to the single market. Differently, as long as access does not materialize for smaller firms, SMEs feel they end up paying the corresponding costs for nothing. While the Single Market may create a "level playing field" among firms of comparable efficiency, it may not do so among firms with different efficiency: remaining trade barriers tend be biased against SMEs.

More difficult access to finance for SMEs magnifies this pattern of exclusion. The single market can be beneficial to SMEs only if the additional competitive pressures it generates for them in their domestic markets come with enhanced access for them to foreign markets. The costs of internationalization, however, require specific funding. As these costs are already higher for firms in the periphery due to their remoteness, any development in the capital markets that make their funding disproportionately expensive will support the emergence of mutually reinforcing "twin core-peripheries"—one in the real economy and the other in the financial economy.

This offers a word of caution on the impact of the CMU: how much will the CMU contribute not only to the deepening but also to the broadening of the single market? In terms of the latter, three aspects of the CMU we already discussed seem to be crucial (ECB 2015): (1) "enhancing the availability and standardization of information (especially of SME credit information)"; (2) "developing a simplified and harmonized accounting framework for SMEs"; and (3) "developing alternative sources of financing to cater for the specific needs of smaller firms (e.g. further developing alternative investment markets designed for issuance of SME bonds, or peer-to-peer funding)." Both (1) and (2) have to be handled with care to avoid the outcome where they end up creating additional costs for SMEs to no avail, with finance still not flowing to them.

A way to prevent this sort of outcome would be for the CMU to also target the kind of funding that represents the blood of SMEs' everyday activities, beyond any consideration about their growth potential. This funding includes trade finance, factoring, and accounts receivable financing through which firms use their receivables (such as outstanding invoices to domestic and foreign customers) as collateral in a financing agreement. On the one hand, trade and receivables financing represents an important direct source of short-term working capital for SMEs, complementing bank finance especially during recessions. On the other hand, it also allows SMEs to outsource their accounts receivable administration and collection activities, turning the fixed costs of maintaining dedicated in-house departments into variable costs depending on the level of sales realized (Bakker and Gröss 2004). Trade and receivables financing is quite sizable. According to the EU Federation for the Factoring and Commercial Finance Industry (2018), in 2016 the total turnover for the factoring and commercial finance industry across the EU was €1.5 trillion, with the factoring industry turnover representing 10.4% of EU's GDP.

The CMU could foster the efficiency of trade and receivables financing in two main ways. A first problem with this type of financing in the EU today is that the national segmentation of its markets and the resulting home bias of its operations limit its potential contribution to the cause of the single market. Cross-border sales of products would require cross-border trade and receivables financing, but this is largely unavailable. Another problem is that the procedures of trade and receivables financing are still vastly paper based, which makes them unnecessarily cumbersome and unappealing, especially for SMEs. As suggested by ECB (2015), a better functioning and much more efficient trade financing market could be built on the grounds laid down by the Single Euro Payments Area (SEPA) scheme (adopted and adhered to by almost 7000 banks in Europe), in particular when the emerging initiatives to create pan-European scheme(s) for SEPA-based e-invoicing are taken into consideration. In an open and standardized e-invoicing scheme, the acceptance of invoices by debtors as valid claims on themselves could happen in real time; all necessary information could be immediately available to potential bank or non-bank financing parties anywhere in Europe. Furthermore, such a standardized electronic scheme could greatly facilitate the securitization of trade receivables, providing even better financing conditions for SMEs. The Commission's report on achieving greater legal certainty in cases of cross-border transfers of claims for factoring and other means of financing should provide a deeper analysis of the potential barriers to building such a pan-European scheme.

Taking Stock: CMU's Specific Actions and Concluding Remarks

The CMU is expected to free financial resources for high growth and more productive SMEs. The idea is that an integrated, larger, and pan-European capital market (1) will be more efficient in terms of both better risk allocation and lower operating costs, (2) will be more resilient to shocks, and (3) will allow for a deeper and broader European marketplace, improving SMEs' involvement not only in EU financial markets but also in the single market for goods and services.

The European Commission's Action Plan contemplates several activities that are organized in seven areas of intervention:[4]

1. Strengthening supervision and building capital markets capacity in the EU (also contemplating the development of local and regional capital markets);

2. Financing for innovation, start-ups, and unlisted companies;

3. Making it easier for firms to raise money on public markets;

4. Strengthening banking capacity to support the economy;

5. Investing for long-term infrastructure and sustainable investments;

6. Fostering retail investment;

7. Facilitating cross-border investments.

The several activities contemplated in the different areas are more than thirty. We do not intend to systematically review all of them but rather discuss those that directly or indirectly will affect SMEs. First, measures that directly tackle SMEs include:

a. Reducing information barriers for SME finance;

b. Developing European Secured Notes (covered bonds) for SME loans;

c. Developing principles for banks' feedback to declined SME credit applications;

d. Developing a package for SME listing on public capital markets;

e. Developing a framework for the securitization of SME loans.

Second, although not explicitly addressing SMEs, many of the other areas and activities of the Action Plan will have a significant impact on this type of firm. First, at a general level, the elimination of several existing barriers toward the formation of truly integrated European capital markets will reshape the supply side of European finance as well as its demand side. SMEs will be at the center of these changes, both for their disproportionate need of capital and for the options that may open up. Some specific actions will also indirectly affect SMEs, in particular:

f. The development of a secondary market for NPLs benefiting SMEs as originators of risky loans;

g. The reform of the European Venture Capital Funds (EuVECA) Regulation and the steps toward establishing a pan-European Venture Capital Fund-of-Funds;

h. The expansion of innovative forms of financing, such as crowd funding;

i. Harmonization along several dimensions, from legal provisions and the protection of minority investors to insolvency laws, contracts enforcement, and taxation regimes.

This is a very ambitious plan with a wide array of actions. If it is conducted as expected, it will certainly impact the European economy at large, from its capital markets to the real economy of the member states. As the plans contemplate several actions on different dimensions and targets at the same time, the depth of its impact and its several effects will depend on the actual implementation of all these actions. In particular, we can envisage for SMEs very different outcomes, from great new opportunities for fast-growing, young, small firms that can generate a strong impact on European employment and development to less benign scenarios. Since the hype about a CMU is more common than an analysis of its perils in case of its incomplete and disorganized implementation, we will focus more the latter.

As previously discussed, we can expect that SMEs will continue to obtain a significant portion of their credit from banks. A more integrated European banking sector can allow for better matching and deeper risk sharing that together with more intense competition may expand credit supply to SMEs. We have however seen that for this positive effect to effectively materialize, more information about SMEs must become available and shared. It is thus fundamental that the specific actions contemplated in the action plan (points a, c, and i above) are taken to the end, possibly even before other actions.

Related to the possible developments of bank lending, we see a possible reduction of relationship lending to SMEs not necessarily as a negative outcome. The expansion of other sources of funds may better accompany high-tech SMEs with opportunities for fast growth. Actions b, d, and e are thus fundamental pillars for an effective CMU specifically designed for SMEs. The first two respectively refer to fostering the emissions of covered bonds by SMEs and the listing on public capital markets. But in our view, action e on securitization will be a real game changer for SMEs. As we have discussed in the previous pages, securitization could directly address the needs of SMEs without requiring very deep changes in the organization and associated costs for these firms, as for example in the case of receivables. A deep European market of securitized credit to the SMEs has the potential not only to boost their opportunities, but also it can allow one to address the NPL issue plaguing many European national banking sectors (see European Economy, Banks Regulation and the Real Sector 2017). Also in the case of standardization it is imperative that information and standardization of securitized credit is profoundly improved. Only if this were the case, other actions contemplated in the plan could deploy their complementarities. Indeed, action h with the development of European platforms to trade NPL will function and prosper only if they can rely on clear and transparent transactions.

Information will also be the key ingredient for action g on venture capital, although of a different kind. In this respect, the CMU should conceive a policy that at the moment seems less clearly conceived than other actions, as venture capital and private equity will in any case require proximity to conduct effective due diligence and assessment. At the same time, SMEs should be guided in delivering standard financial and economic reporting of their activities and plans. A large European market for venture capital and private equity, possibly organized on pan-European platforms, will very likely ignite this source of funding that is currently lagging behind in Europe. In this context, size matters because the matching will be much more effective the larger the market is, both on the demand and the supply sides.

Notes

This chapter was prepared for the Capital Markets Union and Beyond Volume Conference, Brevan Howard Centre for Financial Analysis, Imperial College Business School, London, England, January 26–27, 2018. Giorgio Barba Navaretti acknowledges funding from The Centro Studi Luca d'Agliano within the project "Is Special Treatment for SMEs Warranted?"

1. See European Commission (2017).

2. In the case of bank loans, the precise amount of the loan and the dates of repayments are fixed, while in the case of a credit line the borrower can draw only part of the money at discretion up to an agreed maximum balance and interest is charged only on money actually withdrawn.

3. Clearly, the skin in the game must be enough to avoid moral hazard as well as originate and distribute syndromes.

4. See European Commission (2017).

References

Ağca, S., G. De Nicolò, and E. Detragiache. 2007. "Financial Reforms, Financial Openness, and Corporate Borrowing: International Evidence." Working paper 07/186, International Monetary Fund, Washington, DC.

Agènor, P. R. 2003. "Benefits and Costs of International Financial Integration: Theory and Facts." *World Economy* 26: 1089–1118.

Association for Financial Markets in Europe (AFME). 2017. *Securitisation Data Report Q3 2017.* London: AFME.

Bakker, M.-R., and A. Gröss. 2004. "Development of Non-bank Financial Institutions and Capital Markets in European Union Accession Countries." World Bank working paper series no. 28, Washington, DC.

Beck, T., and A. Demirgüç-Kunt. 2009. "Financial Institutions and Markets across Countries and over Time—Data and Analysis." Policy Research working paper no. 4943, World Bank, Washington, DC.

Beck, T., A. Demirgüç-Kunt, and R. Levine. 2003. "Law and Finance: Why Does Legal Origin Matter?" *Journal of Comparative Economics* 31: 653–675.

Beck, T., A. Demirgüç-Kunt, and V. Maksimovic. 2008. "Financing Patterns around the World: Are Small Firms Different?" *Journal of Financial Economics* 89: 467–487.

Bekaert, G., and C. R. Harvey. 2000. "Foreign Speculators and Emerging Equity Markets." *Journal of Finance* 55: 565–613.

Berger, A. N., L. F. Klapper, and G. F. Udell. 2001. "The Ability of Banks to Lend to Information-ally Opaque Small Businesses." *Journal of Banking and Finance* 25: 2127–2167.

Berger, N., and F. Udell. 2006. "A More Complete Conceptual Framework for SME Finance." *Journal of Banking and Finance* 30: 2945–2966.

Bernanke, B., and M. Gertler. 1989. "Agency Costs, Net Worth, and Business Fluctuations." *American Economic Review* 79: 14–31.

Bonaccorsi di Patti, E., and G. Dell'Ariccia. 2004. "Bank Competition and Firm Creation." *Journal of Money, Credit, and Banking* 36: 225–251.

Boot, A. W. A. 2000. "Relationship Banking: What Do We Know?" *Journal of Financial Intermediation* 9: 7–25.

Bruno, V., and R. Hauswald. 2014. "The Real Effect of Foreign Banks." *Review of Finance* 18: 1683–1716.

Carbo-Valverde, S., Rodriguez-Fernandez, F., and Udell, G. F. 2009. "Bank Market Power and SME Financing Constraints." *Review of Finance* 13: 309–340.

Cetorelli, N., and M. Gambera. 2001. "Banking Market Structure, Financial Dependence and Growth: International Evidence from Industry Data." *Journal of Finance* 56: 617–648.

Charalambakis, E. C., and D. Psychoyiosa. 2012. "What Do We Know about Capital Structure? Revisiting the Impact of Debt Ratios on Some Firm-Specific Factors." *Applied Financial Economics* 22: 1727–1742.

Claessens, S., A. Demirgüç-Kunt, and H. Huizinga. 2001. "How Does Foreign Entry Affect Domestic Banking Markets?" *Journal of Banking and Finance* 25: 891–911.

Claessens, S., and N. van Horen. 2014. "Foreign Banks: Trends and Impact." *Journal of Money, Credit and Banking* 46: 295–326.

Clarke, G., R. Cull, and M. S. Martínez Pería. 2006. "Foreign Bank Participation and Access to Credit across Firms in Developing Countries." *Journal of Comparative Economics* 34: 774–795.

Criscuolo, C., P. N. Gal, and C. Menon. 2014. "The Dynamics of Employment Growth: New Evidence from 18 Countries." OECD Science, Technology and Industry Policy Papers no. 14, OECD Publishing, Paris. http://dx.doi.org/10.1787/5jz417hj6hg6-en.

Degryse, H., and Ongena, S. 2007. "The Impact of Competition on Bank Orientation." *Journal of Financial Intermediation* 16: 399–424.

Demirgüç-Kunt, A., and V. Maksimovic. 1996. "Stock Market Development and Financing Choices of Firms." *World Bank Economic Review* 10: 341–369.

Demirgüç-Kunt, A., and V. Maksimovic. 1999. "Institutions, Financial Markets, and Firm Debt Maturity." *Journal of Financial Economics* 54: 295–336.

Detragiache, E., T. Tressel, and P. Gupta. 2008. "Foreign Banks in Poor Countries: Theory and Evidence." *Journal of Finance* 63: 2123–2160.

EU Federation, Factoring and Commercial Finance. 2018. "Factoring Turnover in EU." https://euf .eu.com/facts-and-figures/factoring-turnover-in-eu.html.

European Banking Authority. 2016. *EBA Report on the Dynamics and Drivers of Non-performing Exposures in the EU Banking Sector.* July 22. https://eba.europa.eu/documents/10180/1360107 /EBA+Report+on+NPLs.pdf.

European Central Bank (ECB). 2015. "Building a Capital Markets Union—Eurosystem Contribution to the European Commission's Green Paper." https://publications.europa.eu/s/j7rY.

European Central Bank (ECB). 2018. Survey on the Access to Finance of Enterprises. https://www .ecb.europa.eu/stats/ecb_surveys/safe/html/index.en.html.

European Central Bank (ECB). n.d. Statistical Data Warehouse. https://sdw.ecb.europa.eu/home.do.

European Commission. 2017. *Communication from the Commission to the European Parliament, the Council, the European Economic and Social Committee and the Committee of the Regions on the Mid-Term Review of the Capital Markets Union Action Plan.* Brussels: European Union, COM (2017) 292 final, June. https://ec.europa.eu/info/publications/mid-term-review-capital-markets-union -action-plan_en.

European Economy, Banks, Regulation and the Real Sector. 2017. "Non-performing Loans." http://european-economy.eu/book/non-performing-loans/.

Eurostat. n.d. Balance Sheet Statistics, table nasa_10_f_bs. http://ec.europa.eu/eurostat/web/products-datasets/-/nasa_10_f_bs.

Giannetti, M., and S. Ongena. 2005. "Financial Integration and Entrepreneurial Activity: Evidence from Foreign Bank Entry in Emerging Markets." Working Paper 91/2005, European Corporate Governance Institute. https://ecgi.global/working-paper/financial-integration-and-firm-performance-evidence-foreign-bank-entry-emerging.

Gozzi, J. C., and S. Schmukler, 2008. "Internationalization and the Evolution of Corporate Valuation." *Journal of Financial Economics* 88: 607–632.

Invest Europe. 2017. *European Private Equity Activity Report 2017*. https://www.investeurope.eu/media/711867/invest-europe-2017-european-private-equity-activity.pdf.

Kang, J-K., and R. M. Stulz. 1997. "Why Is There a Home Bias? An Analysis of Foreign Portfolio Equity Ownership in Japan." *Journal of Financial Economics* 46: 3–28.

Lucey, B. M., and Q. Zhang. 2011. "Financial Integration and Emerging Markets Capital Structure." *Journal of Banking and Finance* 35: 1228–1238.

Melitz, Marc J., and Stephen J. Redding. 2014. "Heterogeneous Firms and Trade." In *Handbook of International Economics*, vol. 1, edited by G. Gopinath, E. Helpman, and K. Rogoff, 1–54. Amsterdam: Elsevier.

Mian, A. 2006. "Distance Constraints: The Limits of Foreign Lending in Poor Economies." *Journal of Finance* 61: 1465–1505.

Mitton, T. 2006. "Stock Market Liberalization and Operating Performance at the Firm Level." *Journal of Financial Economics* 81: 625–647.

Moscalu, M. 2015. "Financial Integration in the Euro Area and SMEs' Access to Finance: Evidence Based on Aggregate Survey Data." *Financial Studies* 19: 51–66.

Muradoglu, Y., C. Onay, and K. Phylaktis. 2013. "European Integration and Corporate Financing." http://dx.doi.org/10.2139/ssrn.1157868.

Organisation for Economic Co-operation and Development (OECD). 2017. *Financing SMEs and Entrepreneurs 2017: An OECD Scoreboard*. Paris: OECD Publishing.

Panetta, F., and A. F. Pozzolo. 2018. "Why Do Banks Securitise Their Assets? Bank-Level Evidence from over One Hundred Countries in the Pre-crisis period." Bank of Italy, Temi di Discussione (Working Papers) no. 1183.

Petersen, M. A., and R. G. Rajan. 1995. "The Effect of Credit Market Competition on Lending Relationships." *Quarterly Journal of Economics* 110: 407–443.

Popov, A., and S. Ongena. 2011. "Interbank Market Integration, Loan Rates, and Firm Leverage." *Journal of Banking and Finance* 35: 544–559.

Stiglitz, J. E., and A. Weiss. 1981. "Credit Rationing in Markets with Imperfect Information." *American Economic Review* 71: 393–410.

Stulz, R. M. 1999. "Globalization, Corporate Finance, and the Cost of Capital." *Journal of Applied Corporate Finance* 12: 8–25.

Szczepański, M. 2017. "Understanding Non-tariff Barriers in the Single Market." European Parliament Research Service Briefing, October.

8 The Promotion of Small and Medium-Sized Companies Acting as a Catalyst for European Capital Markets Law?

Susanne Kalss

Facts and Terminology

The promotion of small and medium-sized enterprises (SMEs) is a key aspect of the capital markets union's (CMU) agenda. To understand this matter and lead an objective discussion, it is useful to recollect some important numbers and facts.

The European Union (EU) has approximately 511 million inhabitants; this will be reduced to 466 million inhabitants after the implementation of Brexit. The number of SMEs in the EU is 23 million. They represent 99% of all companies in the EU, provide for 67% of jobs, and produce almost 60% of the EU's added value.[1] Looking at this from the other way around, only 1% of all European companies do not qualify as an SME. However, these big companies provide for 33% of jobs and contribute to 42% of the EU's added value. Of course, it is easier and more accurate to adopt regulation targeted at a small group of companies than to focus on a heterogeneous multitude of companies.

When pictured, this means that only a very small slice of a pie chart will be affected by capital markets regulation.

The term SME describes a completely heterogeneous group of companies that can hardly be comprised by its definition. Some of these companies are young start-ups while others are successful and long-established enterprises or companies. These companies operate in different industries, have different legal forms, and are organized in different ways. Most importantly, they have different sizes resulting in varying capital requirements and are embedded in completely different market structures.

Due to this multitude of SMEs, it is no surprise that no uniform and clear definition exists. This, however, is essential in order to determine which type of SME is addressed by the CMU's agenda. Article 2 of the Annex to the Commission Recommendation concerning the Definition of Micro, Small, and

Medium-Sized Enterprises[2] shows that three different categories of companies are defined. The relevant criteria are the number of persons employed, the annual turnover, and the balance sheet total. The majority of SMEs are micro-enterprises that employ fewer than ten persons and have an annual turnover and/or balance sheet total that does not exceed €2 million. In total, this includes more than 20 million companies, which equals 93% of all SMEs. These micro-enterprises do not turn to the capital market, as they do not need it to cover their financing needs. The second largest group of SMEs consists of small companies that employ fewer than fifty persons and have an annual turnover and/or balance sheet total that does not exceed €10 million. These companies, too, do not—or only in exceptional cases—make use of the capital market. Finally, the term SME also comprises medium-sized companies that do not have more than 250 employees and have an annual turnover not exceeding €50 million and/or an annual balance sheet of not more than €43 million. It is precisely this group that could benefit from an increasingly attractive capital market. The remaining microenterprises and small companies are not targeted because of their size and the cost to raise financial means. Thus, in reality the beneficiaries of the CMU's agenda are only medium-sized companies with rather high key figures—a relatively small slice on the previously mentioned pie chart.

On the other hand, other provisions offer a different definition of the term SME. Article 4(1)(13) of the Markets in Financial Instruments Directive (MiFID II)[3] follows an equity instruments approach—that is, a market capitalization not exceeding €200 million—to define the term SME. However, the new Prospectus Regulation[4] considers companies with a market capitalization of not more than €500 million. Where debt capital is concerned, MiFID II refers to the European Commission's definition—relying on a company's key figures. This shows how difficult it is to outline the companies covered by the CMU's agenda. Microenterprises and small companies are definitely not within its scope. On the contrary, the CMU aims to address medium-sized companies and in particular the larger ones among that group. The European Long-term Investment Funds Regulation[5] allows the investment in companies with a market capitalization of €500 million regarding foreign-currency securities. So-called "hidden champions," most of which strikingly seem to originate from either Austria, Germany, or Switzerland,[6] do not always meet the criteria of medium-sized companies. Usually they are not covered since they do not have substantially high turnovers and balance sheet totals. However, in fact those "hidden champions" are the real beneficiaries of the CMU's initiative to promote SMEs.

SME: A Political Catchphrase

The EU has been trying to enact special measures for small and medium-sized companies for over twenty years—an obvious step and a melodious political catchphrase considering the large number of SMEs in the EU. In 1998, the EU started an initiative to promote SMEs in the field of company law. Ten years later in 2008, the European Commission introduced the Small Business Act (SBA),[7] a framework for the EU's SME policy that also established the "think small first" principle. Among other things, the SBA calls for a reduction in red tape for SMEs as well as modernization and simplification of existing EU legislation. In 2012, it was planned to exempt microenterprises from accounting principles and disclosure requirements. In the end, however, only minor promotions could be achieved. Regarding alternative investment funds, management companies are not governed by the firm regime of the Alternative Investment Fund Managers (AIFM) Directive[8] if they invest in SMEs. This is only logical as it would prove a disproportionate effort. In many cases, however, the promotion of SMEs is not more than a political slogan with a negligible effect for its addressees.

The CMU's Action Plan of 2015 again takes up the promotion of small and medium-sized companies. To understand this initiative and its importance for SMEs—or its real beneficiaries—it is necessary to recall the capital market's underlying idea. Regardless of their size, companies develop, produce, and sell goods and services. Identifying, creating, distributing, and advertising goods and services requires money. Thus, companies need money before they are able to generate profits. This simple principle applies to big and small companies equally. Finance, in turn, describes the process of providing a business endeavor with the necessary financial means. Therefore, finance is one of the most important business and managment tasks. An entrepreneur can organize financial funds in different ways. However, apart from equity capital, additional contributions of shareholders, payments by friends and family, and bank loans, the possibilities of receiving money are limited and only suitable for certain groups of SMEs. As a result, a company's need for capital—especially when larger sums are involved—is often not satisfied. Therefore, institutions must exist to facilitate access to additional financial means. Together with the stock exchange as a platform for demand and supply of money and other important intermediaries such as banks, those institutions form the capital market. The financing of companies is the capital market's central task, and it can hence be seen as the backbone of the whole economy.

Money can only be raised when the need for capital is defined. Subsequently the investors' confidence in a company has to be established. One of the capital market's main tasks is to promote and maintain the investors' confidence. This can be achieved by an early and adequate disclosure of information, the prohibition of opportunistic behavior, and the equal treatment of market participants.

Summarizing, this shows that additional payments by shareholders or entrepreneurs or an increase in capital can only mobilize new financial means in a limited number of cases. The same applies to loans by friends and family. Additionally, the conditions for receiving bank loans are more stringent than ever, and the relevant criteria is nearly impossible to accomplish. As a result, companies turn to the capital market; however, there too they have to meet various conditions and requirements that vary from country to country. Another difficulty is the completely different financial structure that exists throughout the member states of the EU. The EU promotions regarding the capital market, therefore, need to consider the member states' different systems.

In general, it seems obvious to reduce information asymmetries and to prevent opportunistic behavior to maintain the investors' confidence in the market. In reality, however, this results in a variety of different regulations that have created an impenetrable jungle of individual provisions for capital seeking companies. In the very last years preceding the launch of the CMU, numerous regulations have been adopted that are particularly burdensome on companies. New and strict regulations were always the reaction to crisis. Accordingly, one year after the enactment of the Market Abuse Regulation (MAR),[9] the EU suddenly awoke and realized that its current regulation is too strict and is no longer feasible for a large number of companies. The MA has increased the burden on companies considerably by confirming and strengthening a one-step concept regarding inside information, extending the scope of the MAR to multilateral trading facilities (MTFs), and finally, significantly aggravating the accompanying sanctions.

The one-step concept regarding inside information means that when inside information exists, three prohibitions apply, according to MAR, Article 14: (1) the prohibition to trade (sell or buy) financial instruments, (2) the prohibition to disclose this information to other persons (unlawful disclosure of inside information), and (3) the prohibition of recommending that another person engages in insider dealing. Additionally, the issuer has to publicly disclose immediately the inside information according to MAR, Article 17. Thus, inside information not only leads to the prohibition of a certain behavior but also leads to the duty to inform the public about the inside information (ad hoc publicity).[10] This results in an enormous burden on companies.

The scope of application of the MAR was extended from regulated markets to MTFs and organized trading facilities (OTFs). Due to this extension new actors are now included;[11] obviously these are exactly the main beneficiaries of the CMU agenda.

The intensification and extension of the scope of the MAR was accompanied by more stringent regulation regarding its enforcement. In a first step, the competence of national and European authorities was extended. Among other things, this led to a significant increase in sanctions, such as fines and other measures like "naming and shaming." Additionally, the civil liability was expanded regarding both the company itself and its leading employees. Consequently, capital markets law can properly bare its teeth.

The Austrian constitutional court has only just confirmed that extremely high administrative fines are permissible and therefore not unconstitutional, as they are based on a European legal basis.[12] Over the past few years, a wave of proceedings was fought by investors against issuers and resulted in very investor-friendly and law-developing case law. This led to extensive civil liabilities in cases of minor errors regarding prospectuses or ad hoc disclosures, even though the decision to invest in a certain company was not based on the false prospectus or the ad hoc disclosure.[13]

Challenges for Medium-Sized Companies

Due to the development of European capital markets law companies are confronted with four challenges:

1. The lack of information and expertise regarding alternative forms of financing.

2. Economies of scale. Raising capital is disproportionally more expensive for medium-sized companies as they tend to need smaller amounts of money than larger companies. Costs for initiating and negotiating a transaction as well as for consultancy do not correlate with the amount borrowed. Hence, when a smaller sum of money is borrowed, these costs make up a larger percentage of the total sum of the loan.

3. Difficulty in complying with regulation. Often it is more difficult for medium-sized companies to comply with regulation regarding the capital market. Larger companies can simply spread the cost for meeting certain regulation evenly over different units.

4. Deterrence and fear. Heavy sanctions can have devastating effects on medium-sized companies. Therefore, it is a huge risk to use the capital market as a source of financing, especially with regard to the ever higher, harsher sanctions and civil liabilities.

This overview shows that capital markets law developments have varying effects depending on each addressee. As a result, standardized and schematized regulation is not adequate, and the idea that "one size fits all" will not work. This focus on big companies is obvious and can apply, for example, to companies such as BP, Royal Shell, Volkswagen, or Siemens. However, this system does not work for medium-sized companies that are not yet present in the capital market or that want to leave the capital market. On the contrary, because of the disproportionately high entry barriers, medium-sized companies are displaced from the capital market.

This deterring effect is backed by the fact that most SMEs are trying to leave the stock exchange. The impact of regulation that addresses big cross-border companies to promote their need for financing and their activities on the capital market is not limited to these big companies. In general, capital markets regulation applies to all companies or, at least, has an indirect effect on all companies. General provisions that also apply to capital markets disproportionately burden SMEs and displace them from the capital markets or prevent them from entering. Specific capital markets provisions go even further. The increase in the standard of care (duty of care) regarding listed companies automatically leads to a higher standard of care regarding nonlisted companies. As a result, SMEs are faced with the burden of capital markets regulation even if they are not listed. This has led to a collective escape from the Frankfurt Stock Exchange at a time of lenient delisting rules (e.g., no takeover bid).[14] This effect could also be observed in Austria, where the possibility of delisting has been introduced on January 3, 2018. Medium-sized companies especially with a low degree of market capitalization left the stock exchange because of the extremely high costs and deterrent effects in spite of the necessary public offer.

The EU's Approach

The European Union did not fail to notice the negative consequences for SMEs that resulted from uniformly addressing companies with capital markets regulation. Thus, the EU launched numerous programs and projects to lead at least medium-sized companies toward the capital market. In 1999, the EU introduced the Financial Services Action Plan, the starting point for a "European Passport" system, to make it easier for medium-sized companies to act internationally and enacted the above-mentioned Small Business Act of 2008 aimed at implementing the "think small first principle." In the field of accounting alone, no major promotions could be achieved. In 2015, the European Commission issued the "Action Plan on Building a Capital Markets Union,"[15] which explicitly addresses the facilitation of SMEs' access to capital markets. The *Mid-Term Review of the Capital Markets Union Action Plan*[16] aims at improving growth markets and SMEs' access thereto. A press release of December 20, 2017, again focuses on these growth markets.[17]

Timeline

When considering the EU's concern to promote SMEs in the field of capital markets law, it is important to discuss the premises. It is important to realize when and at what stage companies can effectively be promoted. And, the beneficiaries of these promotions need to be clearly defined.

The following four stages can be seen on the timeline: first, the stage of starting and expanding an enterprise—a period where the need for capital exceeds the entrepreneur's or the company's funds and has to be met externally. At the second stage, companies reach out toward the capital market for the first time. This marks the "Archimedean point" as capital markets regulation applies for the first time.[18] The third stage concerns the access to a qualified market—specifically growth markets—that offers a permanent source of capital. However, this comes at the price of complying with capital markets regulation such as disclosure obligations. Finally, the last stage includes a possible exit—delisting—from the qualified market.

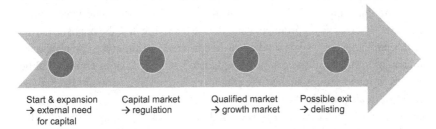

Start & expansion → external need for capital   Capital market → regulation   Qualified market → growth market   Possible exit → delisting

When defining the beneficiaries of capital markets law, the following groups need to be focused on:

- capital-seeking companies,
- investors,
- accompanying service providers, and
- trading and information platforms.

Using this grid, different instruments can be applied depending on the level of development of a company as well as the amount of capital sought and the duration of the financing situation.

Therefore, the EU tries to apply promotions for SMEs using the above-mentioned grid.

Different Instruments

What instruments can be applied? There are four different scenarios:

• information and support,
• the complete elimination of or at least partial relief from existing regulation for SMEs,
• facilitated access to special stock exchanges and markets, and
• the possibility of leaving the capital market (delisting).

Information and Support

Financing deficits largely result from a lack of information regarding different financing alternatives. SMEs usually rely heavily on equity financing and do not have any expertise or experience in gaining external funds. Therefore, it is important to support SMEs and guide them when searching for capital providers for both equity and debt capital.

As a rule, companies from continental Europe prefer bank loans over other types of financing. Eighty percent of all additional funds come from banks, especially a company's principal bank. In the United States, the opposite is true with companies largely depending on securitized instruments. The necessary information and expertise can be passed on to SMEs by various entities. Public bodies or lobby groups such as the chamber of commerce or other associations of SMEs can provide the relevant information. However, service providers such as banks, independent advisers, and other market participants could also assist SMEs to find the ideal financing method. Additionally, special training and networking programs could substantially assist in providing SMEs with a wide variety of financing options. Due to the lack of a central body, SMEs benefit from a range of information of different lengths, often on a case-by-case basis.

Elimination or Relief from Existing Regulation

The MAR applies to all companies that are listed on a regulated market or an MTF. The decision to extend the scope of the MAR to MTFs leads to a massive increase in the range of capital markets regulation. However, the EU promotions for SMEs do not include a discussion about the cardinal rules of capital markets law—namely the prohibition of insider trading and the disclosure of inside information (ad hoc publicity). On the contrary, the EU only exempts SMEs from drawing up insider lists,[19] a rather peripheral rule of capital markets law. However, it is essential to apply a broader picture and question the entirety of capital markets regulation when trying to facilitate SMEs' access to the capital market.

It is true that the exemption from drawing up an insider list brings some relief regarding bureaucracy; however, the basic rule continues to apply and has therefore no relieving effect.

In this respect, the relief regarding different provisions of the MAR might even be a fatal present, as the danger of not complying is even higher. Due to this multitude of obligations, SMEs should carefully reconsider their decision to enter a special growth market because of the strict rules (MAR Articles 7, 13, 14, and 17) regarding the prohibition of insider trading that apply to MTFs. It has to be acknowledged that the Transparency Directive,[20] the Shareholders' Rights Directive,[21] and the Takeover Directive[22] do not apply to MTFs though. The provisions of the Takeover Directive serve a company's current shareholders and therefore benefit not just future shareholders; however, its inapplicability does not lead to a noticeable relief. The publicity of shareholdings and the Shareholders' Rights Directive could in fact impose a burden on companies, and its inapplicability will certainly be a relief for companies listed on MTFs. However, it remains questionable whether this will lead to the desired increase in attractiveness of the capital market. With its attempts to deregulate, the European Commission increasingly aims at ensuring a certain level of business protection—one aspect of the proper functioning of the market—to allocate financing options so that SMEs can benefit from the capital market's supply. In this context, the term business protection should not be understood as to protect smaller companies from all possible risks but rather to fulfill those companies' financing needs. However, this inevitably leads to a lower degree of investor protection. It is the aim of capital markets regulation to find that special balance, thereby at the same time guaranteeing an adequate level of financing for SMEs as well as sufficient investor protection. Therefore, it seems reasonable not only to differentiate among different types of investors (professional, etc.) but also to distinguish among different types of issuers (big, medium, and small companies) and enact legislation accordingly.[23]

Access to Special Markets

As already mentioned, the access to a public capital market can be considered the "Archimedean point." When initially accessing the capital market, companies need to draw up a prospectus. Like books, prospectuses usually consist of 200 pages or more and are written in a rather complicated language containing numerous technical terms. Facilitations for SMEs regarding prospectuses would prove a great relief, especially since hardly any private investor reads the prospectus.[24] Not even financial advisers read the prospectus, making this obligation rather obsolete. Clearly, these observations are also applicable to qualified markets such as growth markets.

As a result, the main instrument aiming to make the capital market more attractive for SMEs is the reduction of existing regulation. This was done by the EU in various cases; however, it only resulted in cosmetic changes with no perceivable facilitations for SMEs. On the contrary, the EU's attempts can only be described as symbolic and merely satisfying political actionism.

Delisting

The European Commission's approach to introduce the possibility of delisting on MTFs is intriguing, especially since currently, no delisting provisions exist on regulated markets.[25] Allowing a market exit without the requirement of a public offer—if a company has only been listed on the MTF for less than three to five years and has referred to that possibility in its prospectus or equivalent document—seems like reasonable concept. If a company uses the capital market for a longer period, an exit can only be conducted if a public offer is made. However, it is clear that these measures will have a promoting effect on SMEs only as a whole.

Summary

Over the past few years, the CMU has exclusively focused on large companies, introducing extensive and heavily sanctioned regulation. As a result, the majority of companies within the EU have been displaced from the capital market. The promotion of SMEs in the course of the CMU is primary a political catchphrase. It should, therefore, be taken as an opportunity to question the existing concept of capital markets regulation and not only as a way to exempt SMEs from certain provisions.

Regulation ensuring investor protection—that increasingly tends toward consumer protection—should especially be reevaluated. Many particular burdensome rules that aim at protecting investors do not achieve their objectives. On the contrary, companies issue numerous statements, reports, and so on that do not satisfy anyone's need for information.

Indeed, existing capital markets regulation should be dismantled where possible and realigned in general. This, however, requires an increase in differentiation and a more flexible system of investor protection. That will be the real endeavor for the coming years.

Notes

1. Annual Report on European SMEs 2016/2017, EASME/COSME/2016/010 of November 2017.

2. European Parliament, "Commission Recommendation of 6 May 2003 concerning the Definition of Micro, Small and Medium-Sized Enterprises," COM (2003) 1422 final.

3. European Parliament, "Directive 2014/65/EU of the European Parliament and of the Council of 15 May 2014 on Markets in Financial Instruments."

4. European Parliament, "Regulation (EU) 2017/1129 of the European Parliament and of the Council of 14 June 2017 on the Prospectus to be Published when Securities Are Offered to the Public or Admitted to Trading on a Regulated Market," Article 2(f).

5. European Parliament, "Regulation 2015/760 of the European Parliament and of the Council of 29 April 2015 on European Long-Term Investment Funds."

6. Hermann Simon, *Hidden Champions des 21. Jahrhunderts* (Frankfurt am Main, Germany: Campus Verlag, 2007).

7. European Parliament, "Guidelines for an Integrated Approach to Maritime Policy: Towards Best Practice in Integrated Maritime Governance and Stakeholder Consultation," COM (2008) 395 final.

8. European Parliament, "Directive 2011/61/EU of the European Parliament and of the Council of 8 June 2011 on Alternative Investment Fund Managers."

9. European Parliament, "Regulation (EU) No. 596/2014 of the European Parliament and of the Council of 16 April 2014 on Market Abuse (Market Abuse Regulation [MAR])."

10. Alain Pietrancosta, "Public Disclosure of Inside Information and Market Abuse," in *Market Abuse Regulation: Commentary and Annotated Guide*, ed. M. Ventoruzzo and S. Mock (Oxford, UK: Oxford University Press, 2017), A.4.18 ff.; Katja Langenbucher, "In Brüssel nichts neues?—'Der verständige Anleger' in der Marktmissbrauchsverordnung," *Die Aktiengesellschaft*, no. 12 (June 2016): 417–422.

11. Alain Pietrancosta and Marco Dell'Erba, "Disclosure Requirements," in *Market Abuse Regulation: Commentary and Annotated Guide*, ed. M. Ventoruzzo and S. Mock (Oxford, UK: Oxford University Press, 2017), B.17.12.

12. VfGH 5.1.2018, G 408/2016, and others.

13. Susanne Kalss, "Civil Law Protection of Investors in Austria—A Situation Report from Amidst a Wave of Investor Lawsuits," *European Business Organization Law Review*, no. 13 (June 2012): 211–236; Susanne Kalss, "Der zivilrechtliche Schutz der Anleger in Österreich—ein Überblick über die große Verfahrenswelle," *Zeitschrift für Bankrecht und Bankwirtschaft*, no. 2 (April 2013): 126–137.

14. Chris Thomale and Andreas Walter, "Delisting als Regulierungsaufgabe," *Zeitschrift für Unternehmens- und Gesellschaftsrecht* 45, no. 5 (October 2016): 679–728; Chris Thomale and Andreas Walter, "Börsennotierung und unternehmerisches Ermessen—Wider die Überregulierung des Delistings," *BOARD—Zeitschrift für Aufsichtsräte*, no. 6 (2016): 231–233.

15. European Commission, *Economic Analysis Accompanying the Document Communication from the Commission to the European Parliament, the Council, the European Economic and Social Committee and the Committee of the Regions Action Plan on Building a Capital Markets Union* (Luxembourg: Publications Office of the European Union, SWD[2015] 183 final, 2015).

16. European Commission, *Economic Analysis Accompanying the Document "Communication from the Commission to the European Parliament, the Council, the European Economic and Social Committee and the Committee of the Regions on the Mid-Term Review of the Capital Markets Union Action Plan,"* Commission Staff Working Document SWD (2017) 224 final, June 8 (Brussels: European Commission, 2017).

17. European Commission, "Capital Markets Union: More Proportionate and Risk-Sensitive Rules for Stronger Investment Firms," press release IP/17/5304, December 20, 2017; Miriam

Parmentier, "Die Entwicklung des europäischen Kapitalmarktrechts in den Jahren 2016–2017," *Europäische Zeitschrift für Wirtschaftsrecht*, no. 2 (January 2018): 53–60.

18. Peter Mülbert, "Anlegerschutz und Finanzmarktregulierung," *Zeitschrift für das gesamte Handels- und Wirtschaftsrecht* 177, no. 2–3 (March 2013): 160–211, 164; Susanne Kalss, *Das Scheitern des Informationsmodells gegenüber privaten Anlegern*, Gutachten I, Verhandlungen ÖJT 2015, II/1 (Vienna: Manz Verlag, 2015), 29.

19. European Parliament, "Regulation (EU) No 596/2014 of the European Parliament and of the Council of 16 April 2014 on Market Abuse (Market Abuse Regulation [MAR])," Article 18(6).

20. European Parliament, "Directive 2004/109 on the Harmonisation of Transparency Requirements in Relation to Information about Issuers Whose Securities Are Admitted to Trading on a Regulated Market," December 15, 2004.

21. European Parliament, "Directive 2017/828 Amending Directive 2007/36/EC as Regards the Encouragement of Long-Term Shareholder Engagement," May 17, 2017.

22. European Parliament, "Directive 2004/25/EC on Takeover Bids," April 21, 2004.

23. Christoph Kumpan, "Die Europäische Kapitalmarktunion und ihr Fokus auf kleinere und mittlere Unternehmen," *Zeitschrift für Unternehmens- und Gesellschaftsrecht* 45, no. 1 (February 2016): 2–35, 13 ff., 35.

24. Kalss, *Das Scheitern des Informationsmodells gegenüber privaten Anlegern*, 24.

25. Susanne Kalss, "Geregelte Märkte dürfen keine Einbahnstraße sein!," *Europäische Zeitschrift für Wirtschaftsrecht*, no. 9 (2016): 321–322.

9 Recent Initiatives in Favor of Listed and Nonlisted Small and Medium-Sized Enterprises: A Legal Perspective

Alain Pietrancosta

Improving the Financing of SMEs: A Core Objective of the CMU Action Plan

The necessity of such an improvement is hardly arguable. It lies at the heart of the capital markets union (CMU) plan, which encompasses a wide-ranging agenda to remove barriers to the free flow of capital in Europe and to increase the role of market-based finance in funding European businesses. Its importance should not be underestimated.

Indeed, some may only see this new plan as a mere reaction to the latest financial crisis and to the wave of financial regulation it prompted in the European Union (EU) to deal with the potential adverse consequences for the real economy. For example, it is often stated that the reduction in access to credit or equity for nonfinancial corporations (in particular for SMEs), induced by banks' and insurance companies' new capital requirements, has to be counterbalanced by measures facilitating the access to capital markets by those same firms. Certainly, the ongoing deleveraging of the banking sector provides a unique impetus for capital markets development in Europe.

In reality, the CMU plan deals with more deeply rooted and structural problems of the overall EU financial system that undermine its efficiency and stability—problems that have simply been exacerbated by the crisis.

These structural problems are twofold. Firstly, the EU financial system is too unbalanced: it suffers from an overreliance on the banking system. The European bank intermediation ratio (ratio of bank financing to total financing) is very high: approximately 70%, compared to 30% in the United States and 50% in Asia. This is especially true for European small and medium-sized enterprises (SMEs), which are said to receive more than 75% of their external finance from bank loans and five times less funding from capital markets than their US counterparts. According to the 2017 ECB Survey on the Access to Finance of Enterprises, market-based sources of finance such as equity and debt securities account only for 10% and 3% of the total funding of SME, respectively.[1] Europe is host to 23 million SMEs, but only 13,000 are represented on the European capital markets. Particular challenges are faced by SMEs seeking to raise less than €100 million through public issuances.

Secondly, the EU financial system remains insufficiently integrated. There exists a strong home bias in the credit or securities markets and a lack of contestability in national markets that undermine the efficient allocation of resources in the EU, especially for SMEs.

Fighting the Attrition of European Public Capital Markets

The Relative Decline of European Capital Markets

Relatively underdeveloped and fragmented as they are, European public capital markets suffer nonetheless from the same long-term downward trends as the other Organisation for Economic Co-operation and Development (OECD) capital markets. They also experience an attrition in their primary and secondary functions.

The European initial public offering (IPO) market faces a long-term decline, with the capital raised in the last ten years being only about half of that raised in the 1990s and an increasing trend for listed SMEs to go private. The size of EU IPO markets is half that of the US markets and only one-third for smaller companies.

To be sure, going public no longer appears as the requisite path for any ambitious SME, as evidenced by the "unicorn" phenomenon. SMEs have been more and more hesitant to go public[2] and to remain public because of the increase in the costs and constraints of listing that often outweigh its benefits relative to other sources of financing. High-tech SMEs with heavy intangible assets have more recently criticized the alleged short-sightedness and conservativeness of stock markets as being unsuitable for their particular needs.

Interestingly for lawyers, the continuous addition of regulatory constraints imposed on listed companies, contrasting with the liberalization of the rules for offering and trading private securities, is often pointed out among the chilling factors. While this accumulation of requirements aimed at improving market transparency and investor protection (Market Abuse Regulation, Prospectus Regulation, International Financial Reporting Standards, Transparency Directive, Multi-Interchange Fee Regulation, Takeover Bid Directive, Shareholder Rights Directive, and so on) may have positive effects, notably in reducing the cost of capital, it has significantly increased the costs and the risks of being listed, created a fatigue on the part of large capitalization (cap) companies, and acted as a deterrent for SMEs.

SMEs consider that their special needs are not taken into consideration and that market operators and lawmakers have a strong bias toward large caps. They see themselves continuously subjected to regulatory requirements that were reserved for large caps at a time when they got listed through a sort of contamination effect, favoring a "one size fits all" approach. This regulatory bias is problematic, as more than 90% of listed companies in Europe are mid or small caps, although they only represent 5% of traded volumes.[3] Since the main actors in the financial markets (stock exchanges, brokers, and investment management companies) all share a common business model based on traded volumes, one can begin to understand the general bias in favor of blue chips.

The Latest Wave of Regulatory Initiatives Designed to Enhance the Public Capital Markets' Appeal to SMEs

Even if Europe has many more listed companies than the United States, for example, the European situation is perceived as critical: without the blood of the newcomers, the European system is deprived of oxygen and inexorably aging. This has led market operators and lawmakers to take measures to enhance the attractiveness of the stock market, particularly for SMEs.

Market operators such as Euronext have showed some determination to act in this direction, notably through the development of alternative markets designed for SMEs (see Euronext's creation of Alternext—now called Euronext Growth—on the London Stock Exchange's Alternative Investment Market [AIM] model); through the creation of EnterNext, designed to develop and promote its stock markets specifically for the 750 companies listed on Euronext with market capitalizations under €1 billion; and through the facilitation of the listing of private placement bonds or of voluntary delistings, a field left out of European legal harmonization.

For their parts, EU lawmakers now seem determined to take greater action.

Previous Regulatory Measures Were Rather Disappointing
At the European level, a few regulatory initiatives have been designed these past years to alleviate the regulatory burden weighing on listed companies, especially on SMEs. Some examples include:

• the establishment in 2010 of a proportionate prospectus regime reserved for SMEs;

• the proposal to create a European Electronic Access Point (EEAP), a web portal intended to ease access to information on listed SMEs for investors; and

- the creation with the Directive 2014/65/EU on Markets in Financial Instruments (MiFID II), Article 33, of a new label called "SME growth markets" (GMs) open to any multilateral trading facilities (MTFs) whose listings are at least 50% SMEs (i.e., companies with a market capitalization of less than €200 million on the basis of end-year quotes for the previous three calendar years[4]), to allow these markets to gain visibility, attract investors, and become more liquid.[5] These GMs and the issuers listed on them are meant to be exempted from complying with some burdensome legal requirements laid down in the MiFID II and Regulation (EU) No. 596/2014 on Market Abuse (MAR).

Unfortunately, most of these measures proved disappointing. The EEAP should have been operational on January 1, 2018, but was deprioritized because of budget constraints. The so-called proportionate prospectus regime has not delivered on its intended effect and is still not widely used as it is perceived as too burdensome by smaller entities. Regarding the MAR, the effects of the provisions designed for SMEs are limited to those whose financial instruments are admitted to trading on an SME GM and look minimal (the exemption from the requirement of drawing up insider lists on an ongoing basis; and the possibility of posting inside information on the trading venue's website instead of on the website of the issuer, where the trading venue chooses to provide this facility).[6] As for SME GMs, the imperfections in their definition, in particular the 200 million threshold (which is perceived as quite low); the alleged inappropriate calibration of the criteria relating to bond issuers; their lack of sufficient liquidity, due to the small number of member states allowing liquidity contracts; and the absence of mandatory float conditions at the time of introduction, all hindered their development. Of the forty European MTFs that meet the criteria, only three have so far registered (AIM [UK], AIM Italy [IT], and NEX [UK]).[7]

Overall, these simplification measures appear insufficient and scattered and are largely outweighed by new cumbersome legal requirements, as recently shown in the MAR and MiFID II.

For example, the market abuse regime now extends its scope to MTFs and is criticized for the administrative burdens imposed on issuers with regard to continuous disclosure or management of privileged information. Regarding market manipulations, the conditions for the recognition of liquidity provision contracts as an accepted market practice have been seriously constrained, which could significantly affect the liquidity of the market for SMEs' securities.

The MiFID II is also accused of carrying the risk of reinforcing the concentration of transactions on large caps to the detriment of SMEs, especially regarding its provisions on product governance and on the remuneration for order execution and research services. This is worrying considering the notoriously unsatisfactory level of research on SMEs: it has been estimated that 50% of listed SMEs have no research coverage.

New Initiatives Are Evidencing a New Awareness

Fortunately, recent initiatives taken in the context of the CMU plan evidence a growing awareness of the importance to address the specific needs of listed SMEs.

The Prospectus Regulation of June 2017 is a good illustration. We know that prospectus costs are an important entry barrier on capital markets: they represent on average 2% to 3% of the issuance amount for large corporations and three times more for SMEs. Bearing this in mind, it was first decided to refrain from extending the prospectus requirement to admission on MTFs. More positively, the Prospectus Regulation creates a simplified prospectus for secondary public issuances for issuers whose securities have been admitted to trading on a regulated market or an SME GM for at least the last 18 months (Article 14) and, more specifically, introduces the concept of an EU growth prospectus with reduced content requirements and a standardized format[8] that may be used by (1) SMEs[9]; (2) issuers other than SMEs, whose securities are traded or are to be traded on an SME GM, provided that their average market capitalization is less than €500 million; or (3) other issuers where the offer of securities to the public is of a total consideration in the European Union that does not exceed €20 million over a period of twelve months, provided that such issuers have no securities traded on an MTF and have an average number of employees of up to 499 during the previous financial year.

Noticeably, SME GM issuers have also been included in the range of eligible undertakings in which European Venture Capital Funds (EuVECA) can invest, in order to accommodate growth stage entities that already have access to other sources of financing and to contribute to the development of the SME growth markets.[10]

Much more important is the European Commission decision to, in its own words, raise its "level of ambition" and "strengthen its focus on capital-raising by SMEs on public markets." This policy inflection was announced in the *Mid-Term Review of the Capital Markets Union Action Plan* of June 2017 (also known as the *CMU Mid-Term Review*) and materialized in a public consultation document named "Building a Proportionate Regulatory Environment to Support SME Listing," running from December 18, 2017, to February 26, 2018.

The consultation is designed to help the European Commission (EC) set in motion several legislative actions, possibly in the form of a "Small Listed Company Act," and nonlegislative actions aiming to revive the public markets for high-growth SMEs. These measures intend to build on the creation by the

MiFID II of the SME GM category, encompassing the British AIM or the French Alternext, opportunistically renamed Euronext Growth. Recent amendments to the MiFID II level 2 provisions reflect this promotional objective. A draft delegated regulation of December 13, 2018, reads thus: (1) "changes the SME criteria regarding issuers that have no equity instruments traded on any trading venues in order to include all issuers whose nominal value of their debt issuances over the previous calendar year, on all trading venues across the Union, do not exceed EUR 50 million"; (2) "offers the possibility for an SME GM to exempt issuers that have no equity instruments traded on the MTF from the requirement to publish half yearly financial reports"; and (3) "introduces the obligation for an issuer seeking first admission of its shares to trading on an SME GM to provide for a minimum float, as set by the market operator."

This first set of measures should be followed by a second, more ambitious one, aiming at alleviating the administrative burden on SME GM issuers. These alleviations, announced by the European Commission on May 24, 2018, and contained in a proposed regulation amending both MAR and the prospectus regulation no. 2017/1129 (Prospectus 3) "as regards the promotion of the use of SME growth markets,"[11] concern the disclosure regime of management's transactions, the insider lists, the justification of the delay in disclosing inside information, the market soundings regime for private placements of bonds with qualified investors, the liquidity provision contracts, and the transfer prospectuses required when an SME GM issuer wants to graduate to a regulated market.[12]

The upside is that it creates an opportunity to reestablish a meaningful distinction between regulated markets and certain nonregulated markets. However, it is still difficult to see how much can be expected from this new policy. There is indeed very little to be found in the consultation about the proper method for adapting capital markets regulation to the particular situation of SMEs. Here, the regulators seem to be trapped in a dilemma: their willingness to soften the regulatory constraints for listed SMEs is often hampered by their core mission to protect investors, which is of paramount importance when involving companies with higher risk profiles. Hence the temptation to introduce new requirements on SME GMs, such as imposing the accompaniment of key advisers, creating a minimum free float, or providing additional delisting conditions.

Reserved to SME GMs , these simplification measures will not reach a large proportion of SMEs since, of the over 13,000 companies with shares publicly traded on European exchanges, only 20% are quoted on the smaller, exchange-regulated (growth) markets. Focused on SME GMs, the European Commission will also have to set the right level of simplification to avoid regulatory arbitrage since only 50% of these GMs listed companies are required to be SMEs while the other half are potentially large caps but also benefit from the alleviations. The very definition of SME GMs[13] risks consequently to curb the ambition of the EU Commission. If these alleviations are significant, they may also create arbitrage issues among stock markets since it would pressure regular MTFs to apply for the SME GM status for fear of paradoxically ending up more regulated than SME GMs and even encourage small- or mid-sized regulated markets to make the same move, as the €200 million cap appears rather high in some EU member states.

As for the regulatory and supervisory arbitrage among member states, it should be reduced by the more frequent use of European regulations (as opposed to directives) and would be reduced if the proposal, presented by the European Commission on September 20, 2017, to make the ESMA the competent authority for the approval of prospectuses drawn up for certain types of issuances or issuers goes through. Among these issuers, the proposal specifically mentions non-EU issuers and EU scientific research-based companies. However, this perspective seems to recede due to disagreements among member states.

Interestingly, a similar movement to ease the life of listed SMEs is ongoing in company law and corporate governance, as evidenced by the OECD report *Flexibility and Proportionality of Corporate Governance Frameworks* (2018). There certainly is an appetite among public company wannabees for corporate governance structures that deviate from traditional standards, as evidenced in the growing use of disproportionate voting shares by emerging growth companies, especially in the tech sector, as a means for insiders to maintain control and insulate against the risk of short-sighted activism, which creates an important competitive pressure on stock markets that do not make enough room for such deviations.

Therefore, one can only regret the limited scope of the current public consultation[14] and the lack of a comprehensive reflection on the listed SMEs' legal ecosystem.

Addressing the Financing Needs of Nonlisted SMEs

For their part, nonlisted SMEs should first benefit from the CMU measures favoring the general development of capital markets since it would facilitate the refinancing of bank loans.

Regarding refinancing, we could also mention the adoption of two European regulations (2017/2401 and 2017/2402), both dated December 12, 2017, that aim at developing a *securitization* market in order to provide an additional source of finance, particularly for SMEs and start-ups, as only 6% of SME finance is currently securitized.

In June 2017, the EC General Services presented a mapping of national and regional best practices designed to tackle *information barriers* in the field of SMEs. SMEs themselves need more information about existing financing sources. In a recent survey, SMEs named "accessing external finance" as their poorest area of expertise. For outside investors, asymmetric information is a serious problem since SMEs often do not produce credible financial information, a situation that therefore creates a competitive advantage for relationship banks.

On the *primary credit market*, some relaxation could be expected from the proposed amendments to review the Solvency II's ("On the Taking-up and Pursuit of the Business of Insurance and Reinsurance") prudential treatment of private equity and privately placed debt.

For the *primary debt market*, the Commission announced in its *CMU Mid-Term Review* a recommendation on private placements designed to broaden the availability of finance for unlisted mid-sized companies.[15]

For the *primary equity market*, the amending Regulation 2017/1991 of October 25, 2017, on European venture capital funds is of note. It aims at boosting the EuVECA funds, a lighter touch regime for venture capital, instituted in the 2013 Alternative Investment Fund Managers Directive (AIFMD), open to professional and nonprofessional investors able to commit a minimum of €100,000 but whose success has been rather limited until now. Significant changes will therefore be introduced from March 2018, allowing larger fund managers (with assets under management of more than €500 million) to market and manage EuVECA funds; to expand the ability of EuVECA funds to invest in small mid-caps and also in SMEs listed on SME GMs; and to facilitate and simplify their cross-border marketing and registration processes. The European Commission is also working on the CMU proposal to establish a pan-European Venture Capital Fund-of-Funds.

Regarding *crowd funding*, the European Commission's report of May 2016 concluded that, as this market, although rapidly growing, remains relatively small and largely local, there was no strong case for an EU framework. However, the feedback the European Commission received last year to its fintech public consultation and its inception impact assessment of October 2017 showed the existence of numerous calls (including from the ESMA) for an EU legislative proposal on crowd and peer-to-peer finance, with the objective to facilitate cross-border activity. Responsively, the European Commission published a report called "Identifying Market and Regulatory Obstacles to Cross-Border Development of Crowdfunding in the EU" (December 2017) and a proposal for regulation in March 2018.[16]

As for *private placements of securities*, the new Prospectus Regulation will increase (as of July 21, 2018) the annual and European threshold that triggers the obligation to draw up a prospectus from €100,000 to €1 million and the upper limit to which member states may elect to exempt public offerings from the prospectus requirement from €5 million to €8 million. However, this remains far from the US$50 million threshold provided in Regulation A as amended in 2015 by the US Securities and Exchange Commission (SEC) pursuant to a mandate included in the 2012 Jumpstart our Business Startups (JOBS) Act. Besides, while raising these limits, the regulation explicitly allows member states to require other disclosure requirements at the national level, if such requirements do not at least constitute a disproportionate or unnecessary burden, which may increase disharmony on the European private placement market.

One should also beware of the important conceptual change brought by this Prospectus Regulation, which openly characterizes offers made to a limited number of persons or to qualified investors as *public offerings*—contrary to the solution prevailing in many member states, such as France, Germany, Italy, Spain, and Portugal.[17] Considering the extremely large positive definition of a public offering, this extension has practically killed the distinction between public and private offerings regarding the prospectus requirement in the EU. More generally, this quasi-limitless notion of public offering will have tremendous side effects on other legal areas, such as company law, where the expression "public offering" is usually referred to. Think, for instance, about the prohibition for a private company to offer its shares to the public if this expression were to be understood as in the Prospectus Regulation, therefore covering all types of offers, including the most private ones! Think also about the legal status of "public" companies, which are often subjected to higher disclosure requirements, if such an extension were to prevail. Here again, the opportunity should be taken to set the right calibration for this sort of requirement. In France, for instance, a drastic decision was made in 2009 to abolish the legal status of public but nonlisted companies (i.e., *sociétés faisant publiquement appel à l'épargne*), which was perceived as putting French companies at an international competitive disadvantage. As such a legal status may make sense from an agency standpoint, but a less radical road could have been taken by having a set of requirements that are incrementally and gradually applicable. This approach is followed in the United States, where there exists a simplified disclosure regime for "smaller reporting companies"—that is, those companies with less than US$75 million in public common equity float (with an SEC amendment proposing to raise the threshold up to US$250 million). It was also amplified by the US JOBS Act that chose to exempt a separate class of issuers named "emerging growth companies" (EGCs) from some of the more onerous accounting and disclosure requirements currently applicable to all public companies. EGCs are generally defined as issuers with annual gross revenues of less than US$1 billion; EGC status can be retained during a period of five years following an IPO. This regulatory relief seems to prove effective as EGCs have represented more than 85% of IPOs since the JOBS Act.

Finally, there is the use of *new financial technologies* to help SMEs, start-ups, and scale-up companies that face difficulties tapping the traditional banking channels and accessing alternative funding sources. The European Commission touched on these technologies in its fintech public consultation of March–June 2017, which recently translated into an action plan published on March 8, 2018.[18] If the consultation raised the issue of blockchain applications to securities markets that had just been reviewed by the ESMA,[19] it barely mentioned the use of tokens and the expansion of "initial coin offerings" (ICOs). The ESMA published two statements on ICOs in November 2017. One statement highlights the speculative nature of ICOs and the risks that some ICOs may pose to investors. The other, more law-oriented one is a warning to firms involved in ICOs that they may be carrying out regulated activities in the EU, especially if the tokens offered can be characterized as financial instruments.

In France, the Financial Markets Authority (AMF) published a discussion paper on ICOs in October 2017 that opened a public consultation until December 22, 2017, and launched a program involving the support and analysis of these transactions, the Universal Node to ICO's Research & Network. The feedback from the eighty-two respondents to the discussion paper (published by the AMF on February 22, 2018) shows a high level of interest in the French marketplace, where twenty-one ICOs have been identified for a total amount of €350 million and a large consensus among the respondents were in favor of the creation of *ad hoc* legislation adapted to ICOs, as most of them would fall outside of the current specific regimes of our financial regulation. This legislation would offer the possibility for token issuers targeting the French public to apply for a visa from the AMF, which would be subject to the satisfaction of several conditions and guarantees for investors—an application that would incidentally facilitate the submission to French law transactions that are inherently global and impose a warning for nonapproved ICOs. Interestingly, some of the responses call for a European legal framework on ICOs.

Concluding Remarks

It is quite telling that, after the overflow of financial regulation sparked by the financial crisis, the last major CMU initiative aims at deregulating. Rather than evidencing a contradiction or an inconsistency, this policy inflection may be analyzed as an effort from the European lawmaker to refine the objectives and differentiate the means of its interventions along with the array of the financial needs that deserve special attention. If one should refrain from taking for granted the adequacy and efficiency of the legal requirements designed for large corporations as well as their everlasting capacity to absorb them, the need to avoid an undue contamination of smaller entities that are less able to support such constraints or willing to accept them is clearly making its way as a new imperative in securities regulation as well as in company law or corporate governance.

For public capital markets, the integration of this imperative will help improve their relative attractiveness and secure their future as a unique vector of capital formation and allocation. Their responsiveness to the expectations of smaller firms, particularly within the tech sector, will be determinative, as clearly evidenced in the United States. This benchmark model of a capital-market oriented economy is referenced in the CMU action plan, where the sharp decline in the overall number of listed companies and of IPOs over the last decades is not equally distributed but is mostly attributed to the reluctance of SMEs to go public. The factors contributing to this evolution are certainly multiple and complex and may call for a policy apprehending the whole SME ecosystem, and the regulatory developments in the last two decades have undoubtedly played their part, particularly in the formidable scissor effect created by the relaxation of the private capital regulation on one side and in the strengthening of the public capital regulation on the other. In light of this, the European authorities seem rightly inspired to reconsider the egalitarian approach that has prevailed so far and would be well advised to staunchly engage in streamlining, simplifying, or at least adapting the regulation applicable to listed SMEs to reduce the costs of listing and compliance without unduly compromising investor protection, thereby going beyond the scope of the current public consultation aimed at "building a proportionate regulatory environment to support SME listing."[20] This effort to tailor these legal requirements and to make them more accessible and intelligible for SMEs should be combined with a differentiation by choice to be materialized by a clearer market segmentation, allowing SMEs to distinguish themselves in terms of commitments toward their investors. The fluidification of the entries into and exits from public capital markets could also be improved in order to espouse the different life cycles of firms and avoid presenting IPOs and listings as one-way streets.

Fighting the attrition of public capital markets will radiate beyond the scope of listed SMEs. It will positively impact on the EU funding escalator. Bridging the finance gaps between the most important stages of a firm's development is certainly a sound objective that deserves to be better served at regulatory level. Filling these gaps, understanding how funding needs evolve for growing companies, avoiding the creation of negative threshold effects through greater use of progressivity in the application of regulatory requirements, and offering diversified corresponding options (both traditional and innovative) as a continuum of financing sources should indeed be fully understood and integrated by regulators. Here, too, the heterogeneity of the SME population makes the case for a higher level of regulatory differentiation.

From a regulatory standpoint, it would certainly be quite useful to devote a higher level of effort in a proper and consistent method to calibrate the scope of legal requirements imposed on companies, according to their legal forms, sizes, businesses, shareholding structures, or listings. Further refinements should be used when appropriate within such categories to account for the risks posed for investors and/or other stakeholders or the desire of such companies to distinguish themselves in terms of governance commitments or investor protection. Such a differentiated approach would help to improve the efficiency of the contemplated legal requirements and prevent the above-mentioned pernicious contamination effect dreaded by SMEs. This differentiation exercise should be systematically carried out and prioritized in all *ex ante* and *ex post* impact assessments.

Notes

1. See also OECD, "Enhancing SME Access to Diversified Financing Instruments: Plenary Session 2," OECD Discussion Paper, Mexico City, February 2018, showing that "only 13% of SMEs surveyed between October 2016 and March 2017 in the EU 28 considered equity financing as relevant for their business."

2. "Europe is producing only half of the SME initial public offerings that it generated before the financial crisis." European Parliament, Committee on Economic and Monetary Affairs, "Promoting SME Growth Markets: Amendments to the Market Abuse Regulation and the Prospectus Regulation, Impact Assessment," May 24, 2018, p. 10.

3. MiddleNext, *The 2017 European Small & Mid Cap Outlook*, 2017 ed. (Paris: La Financière de l'Echiquier and the MiddleNext Research Institute, 2017).

4. Art. 4(1)(13) and Art. 77 of the Commission Delegated Regulation 2017/565 of April 25, 2016, which surprisingly sets different criteria for issuers with no equity instrument traded on any trading venue, relating to the average number of employees (250), the total balance sheet (€43 million), and the annual net turnover (€50 million).

5. See C. Di Noia and R. Veil, "SME Growth Markets," in *Regulation of the EU Financial Markets: MiFID II and MiFIR*, ed. D. Busch and G. Ferrarini (Oxford: Oxford University Press, 2017).

6. See A. Pietrancosta, "Public Disclosure of Inside Information and Market Abuse," in *Market Abuse Regulation: Commentary and Annotated Guide*, ed. M. Ventoruzzo and S. Mock (Oxford: Oxford University Press, 2017), 51.

7. European Parliament, Committee on Economic and Monetary Affairs, "Promoting SME Growth Markets."

8. See European Securities and Markets Authority (ESMA), "Consultation Paper: Draft Technical Advice on Content and Format of the Prospectus" (ESMA 31-62-649, Paris, July 6, 2017); "Draft

Delegated Regulation Supplementing Regulation (EU) 2017/1129 of the European Parliament and of the Council as Regards the Format, Content, Scrutiny and Approval of the Prospectus to be Published When Securities Are Offered to the Public or Admitted to Trading on a Regulated Market, and Repealing Commission Regulation (EC) No 809/2004," Ref. Ares(2018)608 9173-28/11/2018.

9. That is, "(i) companies, which, according to their last annual or consolidated accounts, meet at least two of the following three criteria: an average number of employees during the financial year of less than 250, a total balance sheet not exceeding EUR 43 000 000 and an annual net turnover not exceeding EUR 50 000 000; (ii) small and medium-sized enterprises as defined in point (13) of Article 4(1) of Directive 2014/65/EU," meaning "companies that had an average market capitalisation of less than EUR 200 000 000 on the basis of end-year quotes for the previous three calendar years."

10. Regulation (EU) 2017/1991 of the European Parliament and of the Council of 25 October 2017 amending Regulation (EU) No 345/2013 on European Venture Capital Funds and Regulation (EU) No 346/2013 on European Social Entrepreneurship Funds.

11. EC European Commission, "Communication: Completing the Capital Markets Union by 2019—Time to Accelerate Delivery" (communication, COM [2018] 114 final, Brussels, March 8, 2018).

12. *Adde,* European Parliament, Committee on Economic and Monetary Affairs, *Report on the Proposal* ... (COM [2018] 0331–C8-0212/2018–2018/0165[COD]), A8-0437/2018, 6.12.2018.

13. For a critical view, see L. Enriques, "What Should Qualify as a 'SME Growth Market'?," *Oxford Business Law Blog,* January 26, 2018, https://www.law.ox.ac.uk/business-law-blog/blog /2018/01/what-should-qualify-sme-growth-market.

14. See ESMA Securities and Markets Stakeholder Group, *Access to Public Capital Markets for SMEs* (Paris: ESMA SMSG, ESMA22-106-535, November 8, 2017).

15. See Boston Consulting Group and Linklaters, *Identifying Market and Regulatory Obstacles to the Development of Private Placement of Debt in the EU* (Brussels: European Commission, February 16, 2018).

16. European Commission, "Proposal for a Regulation of the European Parliament and of the Council on European Crowdfunding Service Providers (ECSP) for Business" (Brussels: EC, COM [2018] 113 final and 2018/0048 [COD], March 8, 2018); European Commission, "FinTech: Commission Takes Action for a More Competitive and Innovative Financial Market," press release, March 8, 2018.

17. A. Pietrancosta and A. Marraud des Grottes, "Has the Notion of 'Private Offerings' Been Abolished by the Prospectus Regulation of 14 June 2017?," *Bulletin Joly Bourse* 01/01/2018 no. 1 (February 2018), 60, https://papers.ssrn.com/sol3/papers.cfm?abstract_id=3124225.

18. European Commission, *FinTech Action Plan: For a More Competitive and Innovative European Financial Sector* (Brussels: EC, COM [2018] 109/2, n.d.).

19. European Securities and Markets Authority, *The Distributed Ledger Technology Applied to Securities Markets* (Paris: ESMA, ESMA50-1121423017-285, February 7, 2017). See also ESMA, "ESMA Response to the Commission Consultation Paper on Fintech," ESMA50-158-457, June 7, 2017, mentioning the issuance of securities by SMEs and the record of ownership of unlisted securities.

20. See more generally, International Organization of Securities Commissions, *SME Financing through Capital Markets* (Madrid: IOSCO, July 2015); I. K. Nassr and G. Wehinger, "Opportunities and Limitations of Public Equity Markets for SMEs," *OECD Journal: Financial Market Trends* 2015, no. 1 (2016), http://dx.doi.org/10.1787/fmt-2015-5jrs051fvnjk; World Federation of Exchanges, *SME Financing and Equity Markets* (London: WFE, February 2017).

III THE MARKETS

10 The Role of Fintech for the Capital Markets Union

Ester Faia and Monica Paiella

The creation of capital markets in Europe has been traditionally difficult for two reasons. First, historically most European countries are characterized by bank-centric systems with relationship lending being a crucial function of intermediaries. Second, because of different regulations, bankruptcy laws and investors' protection rights have largely prevented the creation of a single market for trading equities and bonds. The creation of the latter remains difficult today. For this reason much of the buildup of the capital market union relies in fostering niche digital markets whose traded assets are akin to those of private equities or venture capital. There are three reasons why this is an easier implementable route. First, those markets represent unregulated segments which are less dependent on harmonized investors' protection laws. Second, the fast advances in information technology (IT) reduce search and information costs in markets that rely on digital platforms. This facilitates the access of investors from different countries. Third, in the case of services such as peer-to-peer lending or crowd funding, these platforms allow the absorption of loan demands from small and medium-sized enterprises (SMEs), which represent the vast majority of firms in most European countries and which, particularly in times of financial distress, have trouble getting funding from banks or from collateralized debt markets.

The general goal of the capital market union is that of fostering investment across the border by facilitating access to funding for SMEs.[1] The latter includes start-ups, often the most innovative companies. In a segmented capital market like Europe, some of the firms that are located in countries with less developed financial systems have trouble getting funds even in face of innovative investment projects. Besides this, a unified capital market can provide alternative forms of investment for consumers and institutional investors during times when the fragility of the banking system is high and most investors have lost trust in the banking system. Lastly, a unified market whose risks are pretty much delinked from individual country risk can improve risk-sharing possibilities, provided that proper investors' protection regulations are enhanced at the European level.

This chapter examines the universe of fintech. First, we provide a definition that classifies which types of intermediaries or markets fall under this category. Within this taxonomy we also describe and compare specific examples of fintech services. Second, based on the above, we discuss the main positive and negative externalities connected to fintech. Third, we discuss whether fintech represents a threat or an opportunity for the banking system. And last, in light of the third point, we discuss how regulations of markets and intermediaries shall be harmonized at the European level to avoid the shadow-banking phenomena.

Definition and Taxonomy

The term *fintech* is often used in connection with the adoption of IT for storing and handling information in finance and banking. This definition is actually too general to capture the real essence of fintech. In fact, if it were just about advances in IT and their adoption by the intermediation sector, then we could trace the phenomenon back to the 1980s. In contrast, fintech is a newly emerging trend that exhibits two critical features. First, there is substitution of human labor with digital technology. This is most evident when thinking of, for example, robot advisers, which are replacing financial consultants. In this respect fintech is a transforming process, affecting also the traditional intermediation sector, in that digital technologies substitute for rather than complement human labor. This process has already been taking place in manufacturing with the consequence of reducing its labor shares.[2] The second feature concerns the handling of information. In the traditional intermediation sector, investors and firms were disclosing information to their bank, which was delegated to manage the information and to maintain confidentiality. It was primarily this task that justified the intermediation rents. In contrast, within the many emerging and fast-growing fintech services, such as peer-to-peer (P2P) lending, crowd funding, and so on, investors and borrowers voluntarily disclose information to a network represented by the members of a platform. This undermines the mere existence for the delegated intermediary. To sum up, we classify as fintech all traditional intermediation services where robots substitute for human labor and also all services provided by the so-called disintermediation industry, in which information is voluntarily disclosed. Based on this, we can define the following taxonomy.

Within the first category of fintech services—namely the one where automation substitutes for human labor in the traditional intermediation service—we have two main types of activities. The first is automated advice or robo-advice, which is rapidly replacing advice by humans. Robo-advisers provide customized and diversified portfolios and wealth management services previously accessible only to wealthy households. Currently, several of them exist; a popular one is US-based Betterment, which primarily takes a passive strategy of investing in a mix of low-fee stock and bond index funds and provides investors with diversified portfolios based on a risk questionnaire. A similar service is provided by Wealthfront, which has US$7.5 billion assets in management as of October 2017. Other digital platforms offering automated advice and a variety of services include Schwab Intelligent Portfolios, Personal Capital, and SigFig. By making advice on asset management accessible to all, they effectively provide a financial literacy externality. The second type of activity is the automation of loan officer jobs. These services are expanding rapidly, thanks to the advantages that IT offers in terms of document preparation and processing and loan tracking; a particular advancement is in the form of e-mortgages, namely platforms offering basic financial education services, paperwork expedition and loan tracking related to mortgage issuance. Few such examples are Lenda, a home-loan provider also offering digital mortgage solutions; Rocket Mortgage by Quicken Loans; and SoFi, a company specializing in student and personal loan services. The main advantage offered by these types of services is namely a form of convenience good,[3] since they reduce the cost of search and matching for consumers.

The second category of fintech services are actually provided outside of the traditional intermediation sector and include P2P investment services and P2P trading services. The first subcategory includes services like P2P lending and crowd funding. Those consist of digital platforms, where lenders supply funds directly to borrowers. In most cases, debt is uncollateralized, and there is no delegated monitoring from an intermediary. Borrowers voluntarily disclose information about their investment projects and other personal characteristics. Equally, lenders disclose information related to their risk propensity. Lenders and borrowers are matched directly to each other with no intermediary. Two such platforms in the United States are Lending Club and Prosper; in the United Kingdom, the biggest ones are Zopa, Funding Circle, and Rate Setter.[4] In principle, the absence of delegated monitoring of investment projects should raise concerns related to asymmetric information.[5] In practice, default rates on these platforms are very low compared to the traditional banking sector.[6] The reason for this can be traced to the availability of signals in the platforms that reduce the information premium. All platforms offer hard information signals, since machine learning algorithms store large amounts of data on borrowers and can compute and update FICO or other credit scores, all of which are visible on the platform. Some platforms such as Prosper also offer soft information signals, namely recommendations or investment decisions by "friends" of the borrower, or membership to groups of borrowers sharing some characteristic or belonging to a particular social media platform.[7] Signals have a double role.[8] On the one hand, they reduce ambiguity and its premium. On the other, by exposing borrowers to the market discipline, they provide a reputation-like device and, in turn, improve borrowers' selection over time.[9] These platforms are growing steadily, and we see two reasons for this. At their onset, the fragility of the traditional banking systems and the lack of trust in it following the 2007–2008 financial crisis fostered the migration of investors toward these services. These platforms reduce the search and information costs for investors, and the voluntary disclosure from borrowers effectively discards the monopolistic intermediation rents stemming from the handling of confidential information and from relationship lending services. Another option within the disintermediation service industry is crowd funding. The main difference with respect to P2P lending is that crowd funding implies a form of joint liability that provides incentives for lenders and borrowers to bring the project to completion.

The second subcategory of disintermediated services includes all forms of P2P trading. An example of this is eToro, a social media–type of investment platform where investors copy strategies from more expert traders. This form of disintermediated finance effectively makes direct asset management accessible to all, independently from their degree of financial literacy. Besides this, within the P2P trading category, blockchain could provide room for additional forms of secondary markets in asset trading—although this technology has not yet been exploited to its full potential. Blockchain is a technology that was created jointly with the so-called crypto-currencies, such as Bitcoin.[10] To clarify the role of blockchain we can describe the trading taking place in the Bitcoin market. Requests for transactions are sent to a network. Once matched, the sequence of transactions is merged into a block. The block is validated only when "miners" solve a cryptogram, and the solution is verified by other miners through majority voting. Miners as well as traders can freely enter the network. Hence, blockchain provides an alternative validation tool that in traditional payment systems was delegated to banks. The blockchain technology can also be used for validating asset transaction through smart contracts. The latter are digital types of contracts embedding all regulations related to investor protection and best practice in trading. The use of the blockchain for trading smart contracts might foster competition and reduce monopoly fees for validation services.

Externalities

Given the above taxonomy, we can disentangle the positive and negative externalities related to fintech services, also in relation to the type of segmented capital markets characterizing the European landscape.

First, a common element to all those fintech services is a reduction in the cost of search and matching. Whether the fintech service is linked to the traditional banking system, digital platforms facilitate consumer search for investment opportunities. By making information about investment alternatives public and easily accessible, fintech also facilitates matching between investors' tastes and projects' quality. This is particularly important for innovative investment projects as the diversity of investors' opinions, pervasive in markets, increases the probability of funding as opposed to the case of a single intermediary.[11] All of the above can be classified as *search and matching externalities.*

Second, the possibility of storing and managing large amounts of information, a service linked to the use of machine learning technologies, as well as the possibility of making it public and hence verifiable to all, reduces the cost of gathering information and the extent of information asymmetries. Obviously, human labor would be much less efficient in data storing and updating. Besides this, the low cost of gathering information coupled with voluntary disclosure, which is typical of P2P platforms and which renders information publicly verifiable, is effectively discarding the monopoly rents of relationship-type intermediation services. The reduction in the cost of gathering information is particularly evident in platforms like eToro, where investors simply learn from more expert traders. This form of externality for financial literacy, however, can have both positive and negative implications. On the one hand, it reduces asymmetric information among investors, and through this, it facilitates the spread of the "wisdom of the masses" as well as the information aggregation in pricing. On the other hand, it can potentially lead to a herding and contagious cascading phenomena. Indeed, even the expert trader, although more financially literate, might not have full information, and on digital platforms their mistakes are effectively propagated through the "learning from the others" strategy. All of the above can be classified as information externalities.

Third, these types of investment services provide a substitute in times when the banking system is fragile. This function is particularly important in Europe, which has been traditionally a bank-centric system. Banks have provided relationship lending services through the monitoring of loan takers and liquidity services through the matching of consumers, who require demand deposits or other liquid investments, and firms, which instead need stable funding. The 2007–2008 financial crisis as well as the bank runs observed in some countries following the 2009–2012 debt crisis have impaired the ability of the banking sector to continue to offer those services—the more so in countries with weaker financial systems. One of the goals of the capital markets union is to provide alternative means for channeling funds from investors to firms. Those alternative means of funding can provide a backup when the banking system is fragile or when investors have lost trust in it.[12] We can call this a risk-insurance externality. The emergence of markets that substitute for traditional intermediation services might indeed improve risk-sharing possibilities.

The last form of externality that we envision is the one connected to the use of trading technologies such as Bitcoin. They effectively make the market for validation services accessible to all, thereby increasing competition and potentially reducing the rent-extraction externalities. We can label this pro-competitive externality.

Threats to Traditional Banking Systems

Given the positive externalities associated with fintech services (and as discussed above), it is legitimate to ask whether they pose a threat to the survival of the traditional banking sector.[13] Likewise, the automation process had been the main reason for the decline of the labor share in the manufacturing sector.[14] On the one hand, the coexistence of traditional banking and disintermediated digital finance might be justified because historically, in all countries, intermediaries and markets coexisted, albeit to varying degree. Allen and Gale (1999) have argued that markets are more apt to intermediate funds for innovative investment projects where the diversity of opinions facilitate the matching between investors and loan takers. On the other, when there is convergence of priors, intermediated finance is more efficient since delegation is possible to an adviser who holds beliefs similar to those of the investors and therefore has lower costs than direct finance. In this respect, current digital markets, often funding innovative investment projects from start-up companies, respond to the market paradigm of Allen and Gale (1999). However, banks play additional roles, including producing liquidity on both sides of the market and managing maturity mismatch. In systems where risk-averse and low-financial-literacy investors prevail, intermediated finance might be more efficient.

Beyond the traditional arguments on the merits of markets versus intermediated finance, there are additional reasons to believe that fintech might pose a threat to traditional banking. If fintech was only a technology improving information management, facilitating matching, and reducing costs, banks could simply adopt that technology and eliminate the threat of competition. But the biggest risk comes from the forms of disintermediated finance, where large amounts of information are disclosed to the public. In fact, an important component of banks' rent extraction comes from managing confidential information, and as IT facilitates information dissemination, one reason for the banks' existence is undermined.

So far we have highlighted potential threats. However, we shall mention that there might also be complementarities in various forms. First, many digital platforms also provide investment opportunities for banks. Hence they facilitate intermediaries' portfolio diversification. Second, for loan management, banks might benefit from information disclosed through platforms, which often have even more refined data than that available from traditional credit registries. Rather than endanger the banking industry, those forms of complementarity might instead help to shelter banks' margins.

Regulatory Challenges

The emergence of the fintech intermediation services might effectively pose two types of regulatory challenges.

First, an increasing number of intermediation services, ranging from digital mortgage issuance to P2P lending, are not subject to regulatory requirements such as equity capital or liquidity ratios. This might create a parallel intermediation sector, akin to the shadow-banking sector which emerged in the United States during the 2000s, and thereby give raise to a type of dual banking system.[15] This has two implications. First, risks that develop within fintech might spread to the other intermediation sectors. Second, unregulated intermediation sectors such as fintech exploit a competitive advantage vis-à-vis the regulated ones. The competition that would arise would effectively increase fragility in all intermediation segments.

The second important regulatory challenge concerns investors' protection, and this is particularly relevant for P2P consumer investment services and for P2P trading systems such as eToro. While those platforms provide more information regarding investment and, in some cases, also provide some basic financial education (see Betterment), it is possible that many of the investors who are lured by media news to enter the platforms are unequipped to process even the most basic information. Some of those services should then be subject to rules that prevent investors with low levels of financial literacy or with small portfolios from investing in those products or locking their wealth into them. In fact, some investor protection regulation has already been issued, both in the United States and in the United Kingdom. Shortly after the P2P lending industry took off, the US Securities and Exchange Commission (SEC) established that a company that sells loan notes through an internet platform, in combination with that company's undertaking to service the loans and perform certain other services, is in fact issuing a "security." This implies that all regulation related to investors' protection in security issuance is applicable.[16] Moreover, in some instances, the SEC has required P2P lending platforms to retain a certain proportion of the risky loans. This parallels the requirement of retaining the junior tranche in the issuance of asset-backed securities and helps to maintain incentives through the "skin in the game" rule. More recently, in the United Kingdom, the Financial Conduct Authority has also undertaken steps for increasing regulation of the fintech industry. Indeed, concerns were raised during the recent periods of low interest rates, when investors progressively shifted their savings from low returns deposits to more attractive P2P loans. The main fear was that among those investors, a large majority was not aware that P2P loans are not equally guaranteed as deposits. Beside this, in some UK-based platforms it was possible for investors to withdraw money earlier than the project completion date, and this raised concerns of possible runs.

Europe and Fintech

In the design of the capital market union, the European Commission, both in its action plan[17] and in the mid-term review[18] of the process, has emphasized the opportunities provided by the digital technology and the growing fintech industry. Specifically, the *Mid-Term Review of the Capital Markets Union Action Plan* (European Commission 2017) states:

Financial technology (FinTech) is transforming capital markets by bringing new market players and more efficient solutions, increasing competition, and lowering costs for businesses and investors. Examples of financial innovations that can make the EU capital markets broader and deeper include: crowd-funding and other alternative funding tools; supply chain finance; robo-advice; online shareholder voting; and the possible application of block chain technology in post-trading. FinTech can offer solutions in several capital market segments and functions, such as: equity issuance; corporate governance; asset management; investment intermediation; product distribution; and post-trade market infrastructure including securities custody services.

Against this background, fintech development was much faster in the United Kingdom than in the rest of Europe. This trend might change, however, in the post-Brexit scenario. Indeed, with the United Kingdom's departure from the single market, both banks and fintech companies residing there would lose the passport through which they can intermediate funds for European investors, who constitute the vast majority of their portfolio. In continental Europe,

Germany is very active in terms of fintech development. Two very successful Berlin-based platforms are Spotcap, which provides online loans to SMEs, and Lendico, which is a P2P lending platform. Much of the fintech development in Germany has been fostered by the government-sponsored German Accelerator program that includes several initiatives aimed at advancing German start-ups and emerging companies. Besides this, in continental Europe, several innovative services are provided by ING Direct, which has been experimenting on several fronts for many years.

Given the rapid growth of the fintech industry in Europe, the European Banking Authority (EBA) has recently issued a report to map the universe of fintech companies within Europe with the goal of spotting regulatory loopholes. Indeed, the EBA has found that as much as 33% of fintech companies are effectively unregulated because they are subject to national regulatory frameworks; they are calling for a more unified approach to industry regulation.

Conclusions

The successful implementation of a capital markets union in Europe largely depends on the possibility of harmonizing regulations and bankruptcy laws for equity and bond markets. This might actually prove rather difficult. For this reason the European Commission is fostering a complementary approach through which it encourages the development of digital financial services. There are niches that, thanks to the low costs of search, matching, and information, foster participation of investors who not only have different degrees of financial literacy but also come from many countries and that facilitate the channeling of funds to SMEs with innovative projects.

In this chapter, we have reviewed the universe of such services with the main goal of discussing positive and negative externalities. We have also discussed the regulatory approach taken thus far and the future steps that should be undertaken for fintech to be sustainable.

Notes

1. See Organisation for Economic Co-operation and Development (2015).
2. See Karabarbounis and Neimann (2014).
3. See Buchak et al. (2017).
4. A review of the literature can be found in Bachmann et al. (2011).
5. See Freedman and Jin (2016).
6. Faia and Paiella (2017) report that, of all loans issued by Prosper in 2010, the share that was not fully paid back in 2014 amounted to 17%. As a comparison in 2014, US banks charged off

or reported as delinquent 16.6% of all consumer loans (18.5% in 2013) (Board of Governors of the Federal Reserve System 2016).

7. Faia and Paiella (2017), using data from Prosper and Lending Club, have shown that the availability of hard and soft information signals is crucial in reducing the information premium. The specific role of soft information is discussed also in Iyer et al. (2015) and Lin, Prabhala, and Viswanathan (2013).

8. Kawai, Onishi, and Uetake (2016) discuss the role of privately provided signals into peer-to-peer lending platforms.

9. See Liskovich and Shaton (2017).

10. See for description among many others Nakamoto (2009), Velde (2013), and Yermack (2013).

11. See also Allen and Gale (1999).

12. Faia and Paiella (2017) have shown, for instance, that P2P lending tends to substitute for traditional banking services, the more so in times of high fragility of the banking sector, as captured by the probability of bank runs.

13. See also Constancio (2016).

14. See again Karabarbounis and Neimann (2014).

15. See Bayoumi (2017).

16. There is a list of requirements for providing credit that includes: the Truth in Lending Act, the Equal Credit Opportunity Act, the Fair Credit Reporting Act, the Gramm-Leach-Bliley Act, the Electronic Fund Transfer Act, and the Fair Debt Collection Practices Act.

17. See European Commission (2015).

18. See European Commission (2017).

References

Allen, F., and D. Gale. 1999. "Diversity of Opinion and Financing of New Technologies." *Journal of Financial Intermediation* 8: 68–89.

Bachmann, A., A. Becker, D. Buerckner, M. Hilker, F. Kock, M. Lehmann, P. Tiburtius, and B. Funk. 2011. "Online Peer-to-Peer Lending—A Literature Review." *Journal of Internet Banking and Commerce* 16, no. 2. http://www.icommercecentral.com/open-access/online-peertopeer-lending-a-literature-review.php?aid=38238.

Bayoumi, T. 2017. *Unfinished Business: The Unexplored Causes of the Financial Crisis and the Lessons Yet to Be Learned.* New Haven, CT: Yale University Press.

Board of Governors of the Federal Reserve System. 2016. "Charge-Off and Delinquency Rates on Loans and Leases at Commercial Banks." http://www.federalreserve.gov/releases/chargeoff/.

Buchak, G., G. Matvos, T. Piskorski, and A. Seru. 2017. "Fintech, Regulatory Arbitrage, and the Rise of Shadow Banks." Working Paper No. 3511, Stanford University, March.

Constancio, V. 2016. "Challenges for the European Banking Industry." Speech at the Conference on "European Banking Industry: What's Next?," University of Navarra, Madrid, Spain, July 7.

Duarte, J., S. Siegel, and L. Young. 2012. "Trust and Credit: The Role of Appearance in Peer-to-Peer Lending." *Review of Financial Studies* 25, no. 8: 2455–2483.

European Commission. 2015. *Action Plan on Building a Capital Markets Union.* Brussels: European Union, COM/2015/0468 final, September. https://ec.europa.eu/info/publications/action-plan-building-capital-markets-union_en.

European Commission. 2017. *Mid-Term Review of the Capital Markets Union Action Plan.* Brussels: European Union, COM (2017) 292 final, June. https://ec.europa.eu/info/publications/mid-term-review-capital-markets-union-action-plan_en.

Faia, E., and M. Paiella. 2017. "P2P Lending: Information Externalities, Social Networks and Loans' Substitution." CEPR Discussion Paper No. DP12235, Center for Economic and Policy Research, London.

Freedman, S., and G. Jin. 2016. "Learning by Doing with Asymmetric Information: Evidence from Prosper.com." NBER Working Paper No. 16855, National Bureau of Economic Research, Cambridge, MA.

Galloway, I. 2009. "Peer-to-Peer Lending and Community Development Finance." Community Development Investment Center Working Paper No. 2009-06, Federal Reserve Bank of San Francisco. http://ideas.repec.org/p/fip/fedfcw/2009-06.html.

Iyer, R., A. Khwaja, E. Luttmer, and K. Shue. 2015. "Screening Peers Softly: Inferring the Quality of Small Borrowers." *Management Science* 62, no. 6: 1554–1577.

Karabarbounis, L., and B. Neimann. 2014. "The Global Decline of the Labor Share." *Quarterly Journal of Economics* 129, no. 1: 61–103.

Kaufmann, C., M. Weber, and E. Haisley. 2015. "The Role of Experience Sampling and Graphical Displays on One's Investment Risk Appetite." *Management Science* 59: 323–340.

Kawai, K., K. Onishi, and K. Uetake. 2016. "Signaling in Online Credit Markets." Unpublished paper. https://files.webservices.illinois.edu/6981/uetake,_kosuke_-_paper_-_9-21-17.pdf.

Leech, C., and M. Cauvas. 2015. "Direct Lending: Finding Value/Minimizing Risk." Presentation, Liberum, London, October 20. https://slideplayer.com/slide/8938760/.

Lin, M., N. Prabhala, and S. Viswanathan. 2013. "Judging Borrowers by the Company They Keep: Friendship Networks and Information Asymmetry in Online Peer-to-Peer Lending." *Management Science* 59, no. 1: 17–35.

Liskovich, I., and M. Shaton. 2017. "Borrowers in Search of Feedback: Evidence from Consumer Credit Markets." FEDS Working Paper No. 2017-049. https://ssrn.com/abstract=2964440.

Nakamoto, S. 2009. "Bitcoin: A Peer-to-Peer Electronic Cash System." Working paper, the Bitcoin Project. https://bitcoin.org/en/bitcoin-paper.

Organisation for Economic Co-operation and Development (OECD). 2015. *Financing SMEs and Entrepreneurs 2015: An OECD Scoreboard.* Paris: OECD Publishing.

Pope, D., and J. Sydnor. 2011. "What's in a Picture? Evidence of Discrimination from Prosper .com." *Journal of Human Resources* 46, no. 1: 53–92.

Velde, F. 2013. "Bitcoin: A Primer." *Chicago Fed Letter*, no. 317 (December).

Yermack, D. 2013. "Is Bitcoin a Real Currency? An Economic Appraisal." NBER Working Paper No. 19747, National Bureau of Economic Research, Cambridge, MA.

Zopa.com. 2016. "About Us: The FeelGood Money™ Company." https://www.zopa.com/about.

Discussion: The Market for Crowd Funding and Peer-to-Peer Lending

Ugo Albertazzi

Starting from the thoughtful investigation provided in Faia and Paiella's chapter, this discussion offers additional remarks about the prospects for traditional banks and fintech. It does so by considering that banks' role is to minimize the transaction costs related to the different information frictions and by discussing how well fintech can perform this function. It then elaborates on possible financial stability implications of fintech and on the external factors that may limit its expansion.

In a context of adverse selection, fintech intermediaries screen investment projects by relying on traditional credit-scoring techniques as well as by utilizing "soft information" obtained from the Internet (Faia and Paiella 2017; Iyer, Khwaja, Luttmer, and Shue 2015). Some remarks on the quality of fintech's soft information can be made. First, it may be expected that, once decisions are perceived to rely heavily on specific signals, incentives to manipulate them may arise. An example of this is provided by the problem of fake Internet reviews (Forbes 2017). Second, it is not clear whether the information obtained from the internet and Big Data is comparable to the soft information accessible to traditional banks, which, unlike fintech, obtain it in the context of lending relationships (Barba Navaretti, Calzolari, and Pozzolo 2017). Fintech, moreover, may not be suited to such lending relationships.[1]

Concerning moral hazard, the theory says that, in a context of costly state verification, banks arise as delegated monitors that minimize total monitoring costs (Diamond 1984). The interesting remark here is that, thanks to technology, fintech seems to be poised to become an effective and intrusive monitor. Real-life examples are already available in some segments of the financial sector, such as the insurance market. The adoption of telematics devices in the car insurance market is by now an established practice (Verbelen, Antonio, and Claeskens 2016). These technologies detect how much insurees drive, how fast, where (risky versus safe roads), and when (evening versus daytime). They effectively counter frauds related to fake accidents (the costly state verification problem in the car insurance sector). It will be interesting to observe if such innovations will be followed by analogous developments in the fintech credit sector.

Another reason why banks exist is maturity transformation, the issuance of liquid deposits matched with investments in long-term illiquid investment projects (Diamond and Dybvig 1983). As of today, peer-to-peer lending and crowd funding operators do not appear able to exploit this economy of scope because investors in these platforms do not benefit from the liquidity provision available to bank depositors (Barba Navaretti, Calzolari, and Pozzolo 2017).

Concerning financial stability, a preliminary remark is that credit scoring and automation in lending based on (backward-looking) ratings makes loan supply pro-cyclical (Lowe 2002). An important question is then whether fintech represents a technology that relies even more heavily on backward-looking data. This is far from clear: it could be that the data collected from social networks and other Big Data sources incorporates more forward-looking information compared to traditional credit scores. Or, instead, it could be that such information is backward-looking and ultimately exacerbates pro-cyclicality.

A related issue is whether fintech may lead to coordination failures and increase the probability of financial instability episodes. It is well established in the literature that, in a context of strategic complementarities, it pays to follow the crowd, even if this is on aggregate inefficient and destabilizing (see Diamond and Dybvig 1983 for coordination issues among depositors; Chamley 1999 for nonfinancial firms; Bebchuk and Goldstein 2011 for banks; and Albertazzi and Esposito 2017 for banks and firms altogether). If the information that fintech incorporates into decision making de facto reflects the decisions taken by other agents in the economy (e.g., invest if anyone else is investing), then fintech could implement decisions that are optimal from an individual standpoint but detrimental for the whole economy. In a digital technology context other than fintech, a clear example of how difficult it may be to deal with individually optimal decisions that are socially inefficient is provided by the notorious ethical dilemma for self-driving cars (in some instances, the algorithm may need to decide whether to save the car passenger even if this comes at the cost of losing more lives, which is socially undesirable).

Finally, a possible limiting factor for the development of fintech is its opacity. In most cases the algorithm behind a fintech is a black box, often not interpretable by users. But opacity comes with information frictions, meaning that adverse selection and moral hazard problems may not disappear with fintech but just change shape. Another possible challenge for fintech could originate in relation to security and privacy issues, which may lead to a regulatory setback (Gai, Qiu, Sun, and Zhao 2017).

Summing up, as of today fintech seem poised to potentially exert a significant competitive pressure on traditional banks but does not appear to be able to fully displace them. The success of fintech in gaining market shares may vary across different market segments and will depend on the future developments in the technology and the regulatory framework. The latter will have to consider the new financial stability challenges posed by fintech.

Note

1. For these implicit contracts to be viable the losses incurred in the early phases of the relationship, when little is known, need to be compensated by the rents obtained once good quality borrowers are identified. If the information was not soft it could be conveyed to competing lenders who would underbid the incumbent bank and eliminate its ex-post information rents (Sharpe 1990; van Thadden 2004). Fintech could not be compatible with this business strategy as their technology may result in a "hardening" of the soft information obtained from the Internet, making it measurable and verifiable.

References

Albertazzi, U., and L. Esposito. 2017. "Credit Demand and Supply: A Two-Way Feedback Relation." Bank of Italy Working Paper No. 1134.

Barba Navaretti, G., G. Calzolari, and A. F. Pozzolo. 2017. "FinTech and Banks: Friends or Foes?" *European Economy* 3, no. 2. SSRN, https://papers.ssrn.com/sol3/papers.cfm?abstract_id=3099337.

Bebchuk, L., and I. Goldstein. 2011. "Self-Fulfilling Credit Market Freezes." *Review of Financial Studies* 24, no. 11: 3519–3555.

Chamley, C. 1999. "Coordinating Regime Switches." *Quarterly Journal of Economics* 114, no. 3: 869–905.

Diamond, D. W. 1984. "Financial Intermediation and Delegated Monitoring." *Review of Economic Studies* 51, no. 3: 393–414.

Diamond, D. W., and P. H. Dybvig. 1983. "Bank Runs, Deposit Insurance, and Liquidity." *Journal of Political Economy* 91, no. 3: 401–419.

Faia, E., and M. Paiella. 2017. "P2P Lending: Information Externalities, Social Networks and Loans' Substitution." CEPR Working Paper No. 12235.

Forbes. 2017. "Amazon's Fake Review Problem Is Now Worse than Ever, Study Suggests." *Forbes*, September 9.

Gai K., M. Qiu, X. Sun, and H. Zhao. 2017. "Security and Privacy Issues: A Survey on FinTech." In *Smart Computing and Communication*, ed. M. Qiu. SmartCom 2016, Lecture Notes in Computer Science, vol. 10135.

Iyer, R., A. Khwaja, E. Luttmer, and K. Shue. 2015. "Screening Peers Softly: Inferring the Quality of Small Borrowers." *Management Science* 62, no. 6. https://doi.org/10.1287/mnsc.2015.2181.

Lowe, P. W. 2002. "Credit Risk Measurement and Procyclicality." Bank for International Settlements Working Paper No. 116.

Sharpe, S. A. 1990. "Asymmetric Information, Bank Lending, and Implicit Contracts: A Stylized Model of Customer Relationships." *Journal of Finance* 45, no. 4: 1069–1087.

Verbelen, R., K. Antonio, and G. Claeskens. 2016. "Unraveling the Predictive Power of Telematics Data in Car Insurance Pricing." SSRN, https://ssrn.com/abstract=2872112.

von Thadden, E. L. 2004. "Asymmetric Information, Bank Lending and Implicit Contracts: The Winner's Curse." *Finance Research Letters* 1, no. 1: 11–23.

11 Equity Crowd Funding: An Acid Test for Securities Regulation

John Armour and Luca Enriques

Start-up firms—with untried products and often untested founders—frequently find it difficult to obtain financing.[1] Because start-up firms are disproportionately associated with innovation and job creation,[2] the possibility of a "funding gap" for start-up firms is a significant concern for policymakers.[3]

In the last few years, a new source of finance for start-ups, known as "equity crowd funding" (CF), has become widely available. As the name implies, this involves raising equity capital from a large number of individuals, each of whom typically contributes a small sum. The internet has lowered the costs of raising funds in this way by facilitating the dissemination of information about small projects.

While the availability of CF is clearly good news for entrepreneurs, its merits for those providing the funding are less certain. Because funders typically invest only small sums in projects, CF may appeal to consumers—that is, unsophisticated individuals. However, consumers have limited capacity to assess the prospects of a business and are prone to making investment decisions subject to biases and herd behavior. In addition to losses to funders, this can cause finance to be misallocated to inferior business projects. These risks raise important questions for regulators.

In this chapter, we sketch out a normative roadmap for the regulation of CF in relation to start-ups. This is a highly salient enquiry, with the European Commission having recently announced a proposal to allow CF platforms to offer their services throughout the European Union (EU) as part of the Capital Markets Union (CMU) action plan.[4] Meanwhile, in the United Kingdom, the Financial Conduct Authority (FCA) has recently conducted its third review of CF regulation in as many years.[5] And in the United States, the Securities and Exchange Commission (SEC) regulations for retail CF came into force in May 2016 pursuant to the Jumpstart Our Business Startups (JOBS) Act of 2012;[6] their operation is being carefully studied.

We begin by considering the use of CF and the characteristics of the typical CF contract, highlighting the advantages for the fund-raising firms and the perils for the investing crowd. Next, we contrast the largely permissive regulation of CF in the United Kingdom (which largely reflects the implementation of EU law) and the more burdensome US regime.

Then, we assess the two regulatory frameworks by asking whether the traditional tool of securities regulation, namely mandatory disclosure, is effective as an investor protection tool. In our analysis, CF markets are sufficiently different from traditional securities market contexts that the justifications for mandating disclosure in those other market contexts do not carry across.

The structure of the problems of CF are common to many consumer finance transactions. However, evidence-based regulatory solutions in consumer finance tend to be context-specific, and poorly crafted intervention can easily make things worse rather than better. At this early stage of the market's development, we consequently advocate a permissive regulatory regime.

Crowd Funding for Start-Ups

Challenges of Start-Up Financing

Most business start-ups fail, so funding a start-up is a risky endeavor. There is no market for the firm's product—indeed, in most cases there is not even (yet) a product—and so profitability forecasts are at best guesstimates of future production costs and market size. Most founders begin by investing their savings, making use of personal credit facilities, and tapping family and friends for funds.[7] For founders who have exhausted such "personal" finance, raising outside finance can be a considerable challenge. Start-ups generally do not generate steady cash flows to pay interest and lack liquid assets to offer as security. This makes them unattractive candidates for debt financing, constraining the supply of bank lending.[8]

Another well-known source of finance for start-ups is from venture capitalists (VCs) and "business angels," whose investment model is designed to accommodate the particular challenges of start-up financing.[9] These investors manage the high risk of failure by diversifying their investments across a portfolio, being very selective in which firms they invest, and using specialist expertise to assess the quality of the entrepreneurial team and their project. They take control rights—often disproportionate to their investment—and use these to enhance the quality of decision making and mitigate potential opportunism by the entrepreneur.[10] However, such expertise is in short supply, and the investment model requires geographic proximity for the investor to be able to participate actively in decision making.[11] Consequently, VCs tend to be based in areas where there are large "clusters" of new firms, typically near a source of technological innovation such as a university.[12] But for an entrepreneur not living in or unable to relocate to the vicinity of a VC, this source of finance is unlikely to be available.

Against this background of apparent funding constraints for start-ups, CF offers the promise of meeting some part of entrepreneurs' unmet demand for outside finance.

The Perils of Crowd Funding

While CF holds promise for entrepreneurs as a source of financing, it appears perilous for investors. Like VCs, crowd funders invest in nascent businesses, with all the associated uncertainty. But unlike a VC, retail CF investors lack specialist expertise about the prospects of the business projects they back. Nor do CF investors take control rights because the costs of doing so would outweigh the benefits, given their lack of expertise and high coordination costs. This leaves them more exposed than a VC to potential opportunism by the entrepreneur.

At the same time, CF investors also look more exposed than those investing in public equity markets when it comes to price formation and informativeness. In public equity markets, a bevy of mechanisms, including the concurring presence on the market of professional, informed investors, combine to protect retail investors by ensuring that the price swiftly reflects all available information—in other words, that it is "informationally efficient."[13] In particular, secondary market trading allows for the swift aggregation of investors' assessments of the price relevance of publicly available information into the market price. In contrast, there is usually no secondary market for CF investments.

CF then takes place in primary markets, but that does not make them much similar to the initial public offering (IPO) market either. A typical IPO is preceded by a book-building process, in which an investment bank sets the initial price based on informed investors' nonbinding bids for the securities.

In contrast, CF offerings typically lack any kind of book-building process. CF platforms provide access to information about the company's (self-produced) valuation, its business plan, the target amount, and the percentage of equity this represents based on the valuation. The offer is generally made contingent on receiving enough commitments to meet the issuer's funding target.[14] Typically, information is provided about how many investors and how much funding are already committed.

Theory suggests that, rather than serving to aggregate information, sequential arrival of investors is likely to engender herding.[15] In a secondary market, investors assess their own valuation of the security against that reflected in the market price that adjusts depending on demand. With CF, the price neither changes in response to demand nor reflects informed investors' bids. Investors therefore draw inferences about the accuracy of the price from the level of observed demand.

It is well known in the sector that "momentum" is crucial to the success of CF projects.[16] If a significant number of funders can be contracted quickly, then others will join. Conversely, a project that does not attract initial support is likely to languish. This suggests a "bimodal" distribution of funding: that projects should typically either get high levels of support or very little. This prediction is consistent with casual empiricism.[17]

Where herding occurs, funders as a group behave as if they attach great significance to the information possessed by early arrivals and little or no significance to that possessed by later arrivals, even if available information is all of equal quality. This means that the quality of decision making will be lower than a process that makes use of all the information available to the group. Herding consequently results in a misallocation of resources—overinvestment in projects for which the prospects are weak and underinvestment in projects for which the prospects are strong—which will consequently reduce returns to investors.

Regulating Crowd Funding in the United Kingdom and the United States

The United Kingdom

The United Kingdom has implemented in full an optional exemption under the EU's Prospectus Directive for securities offerings amounting to less than €5 million (€8 million since July 2018) by a single firm in a twelve-month period.[18] This facilitates CF offerings by exempting relevant issuers from the obligation to prepare a prospectus—a very significant saving in compliance costs.

Nevertheless, portals offering CF in the United Kingdom must be authorized by the FCA because they carry out financial promotions and arrange deals in investments.[19] The FCA introduced specific investor protection rules for CF platforms in 2014, regularizing what had until then been an *ad hoc* approach to authorization.[20] Pursuant to EU provisions on investment services, these rules subject authorized CF platforms to conduct of business obligations. There is a general requirement that financial promotions offered on the platform, including founders' pitches, be "fair, clear and not misleading."[21] In addition, the platform must assess whether CF securities are appropriate for an investor client by determining whether the investor has the "necessary knowledge and experience to understand the risks involved."[22] In practice, this is met by requiring investors to answer a simple automated test about the characteristics of CF investments, for which guidance is provided.

In addition, the FCA introduced restrictions on the extent to which individuals may invest in CF. CF securities may only be offered to retail investors if they certify they have not invested, and will not invest, more than 10% of their net assets in non-readily realizable securities.[23]

The United States

The starting point for CF regulation in the United States was, in contrast to the United Kingdom, a securities law regime that had no exemption for small offers. Title II of the JOBS Act of 2012 removed obstacles to the setup of CF platforms but only permitted access by accredited investors (high net-worth individuals).[24] Then, under Title III of the JOBS Act,[25] Congress inaugurated a "small offering" regime for firms raising no more than US$1 million over a twelve-month period[26] and directed the SEC to pass associated rules. The SEC did not adopt its final "Regulation Crowdfunding" (Regulation CF) until October 2015, and it came into force in May 2016.

In some respects, the conditions for issuing under Regulation CF echo the regulatory treatment of CF in the United Kingdom. In particular, CF transactions must be conducted through an intermediary registered with the SEC, as either a broker or a new type of regulated entity called a "funding portal" that must take steps to ensure investors understand the risks involved.[27] Intermediaries must have a reasonable basis for believing that issuers on their platform are in compliance with relevant regulations and must deny access to issuers they believe may present potential for fraud.[28] To avoid conflicts of interest, an intermediary's directors, officers, and partners are prohibited from taking any financial interest in issuers using its services.[29]

There are also quantitative restrictions on the exposure of retail investors, although—in contrast to the UK rules—these cap the amount that may be invested *per issuer*,[30] as opposed to in the asset class as a whole. Moreover, CF securities may not be transferred by a purchaser within a year of issue.[31]

Where the US regulatory environment for CF differs most significantly from the United Kingdom is regarding mandatory disclosure. US CF issuers must file an extensive list of disclosures with the SEC and make them available to potential investors via the CF platform.[32] They must also provide a complete set of financial statements, prepared under US GAAP, for the previous two years or the period since formation, whichever is shorter, and provide a narrative discussion of their historical results, liquidity, and capital resources.[33] The degree of required external scrutiny of the financial statements increases with the size of the offering: the smallest issues (up to US$100,000) need only be certified by the issuer's chief executive officer, whereas larger issues (above US$500,000) must be fully audited.[34] Having completed a CF issue, annual reports must be filed with the SEC.[35]

The SEC's own estimates of compliance costs suggest that Regulation CF may be unappealing for issuers seeking to raise smaller amounts. Fixed costs for required filings are estimated at US$6,460, and the charges of intermediaries would be 5% to 15% of the amount raised: for a US$100,000 offering, such costs and fees may be as high as 21.5% of the capital raised.[36] In contrast, a CF offer in the United Kingdom has been estimated to incur platform and payment service provider fees of around 8% to 10% of the funds raised.[37] These higher costs make US CF offerings less attractive to founders. Approximately $12.5 million was estimated to have been raised under Regulation CF in the first six months of its operation.[38] This looks very modest when bearing in mind that approximately US$170 million of CF funding was raised in the United Kingdom, representing a much smaller economy, in the same period.[39]

To summarize, the United States imposes a much more onerous regulatory regime for CF than does the United Kingdom. Raising CF from retail investors was prohibitively costly in the United States until May 2016. Since then, the contrast turns on the application of mandatory disclosure. The more onerous US rules have historically inhibited the development of the CF market and appear to make CF issues more costly going forward.[40]

How Should Crowd Funding Be Regulated?

When Is Mandatory Disclosure Useful?

Mandatory disclosure is a cornerstone regulatory strategy in both securities and consumer laws and is often justified as a means of overcoming information asymmetry.[41] However, a body of recent behavioral research reports that the context of disclosure matters greatly for its efficacy.[42] What matters is not so much whether disclosure is required but rather *what* must be disclosed and *how* it must be conveyed. It is costly for most individuals to make sense of, and process, large bodies of information: "disclosure" does not imply *comprehension* by the recipient. Indeed, the less sophisticated the individual, the greater the cost of comprehension. Simply mandating disclosure of information does little, if anything, to improve consumers' decision making if it is beyond their ability to comprehend. Moreover, because disclosures are costly to produce, Ben-Shahar and Schneider argue that the exercise is often "worse than useless."[43] There are, however, circumstances in which mandating disclosure can demonstrably improve outcomes. We shall consider whether these are relevant for CF.

Securities Markets and Mandatory Disclosure

As we have seen, whether to require CF issuers to make extensive disclosures is a fault line distinguishing the US and UK approaches. Although such information is too extensive to be read or analyzed by the vast majority of retail investors, sophisticated professional investors do process and use it. It is rational for professional investors who have large investments at stake to invest time in analyzing pertinent information. Moreover, such investors are typically selected, trained, and remunerated so as to minimize decisional biases.[44]

In liquid securities markets, the benefits of disclosure go beyond just the (sophisticated) investors who analyze the information. The market price moves in response to their trading activity and thereby comes to reflect all publicly available information.[45] Retail investors are thereby *indirectly* benefited by disclosure: they trade at the same price as if they had read the information.[46]

This makes *mandatory* disclosure easier to justify as a tool to protect retail investors in public markets.[47] Yet, things look different in the case of CF: here, market mechanisms do not operate to aggregate information from sophisticated investors' decisions into prices. As we saw earlier, CF offerings involve investors deciding sequentially about whether to invest at a price that is fixed over the offer period. Subsequent investors receive only a very limited signal: that earlier investors chose to invest. This implies that the earlier investors thought the security was worth the price but gives no indication of how many thought it was worth less than that. A liquid secondary market for the security would, in contrast, capture this sort of information. Crowd funders operate in a primary market with little information input from sophisticated traders. What is worse, herding—which our analysis suggests is likely in CF—implies that subsequent investors may disregard their own assessments in favor of those inferred from earlier investors' decisions.

These features of the CF marketplace imply that disclosed information will provide very little benefit to retail investors, suggesting that US-style extensive mandatory disclosure requirements are likely to generate more costs than benefits.

Protecting Retail CF Investors More Effectively

In this section, we make four observations regarding the sorts of investor protection measures that are effective. First, more appropriately structured disclosure might in principle be beneficial to CF investors. For example, the FCA has considered introducing a mandatory "risk warning" for investors in CF, drawing attention to the high risk of losing their capital.[48] Similarly, the European Commission propose a "key investment information sheet" containing a prominent risk warning and highlighting key facts about the offering.[49] However, the lesson from the experimental literature is that consumer-oriented disclosures cannot be effectively designed in the abstract; this must be done on the basis of evidence of actual consumer behavior. For this reason, the United Kingdom's FCA has embarked on a program of using behavioral economics experiments in the design of information regulation for consumer financial products.[50]

Second, there seems to be little risk that retail investors' mistakes will be *systematically* exploited by issuers. Many consumer protection laws are concerned with an "imbalance" between parties. Yet CF entrepreneurs are unlikely to have significant time for designing financing contracts, and so the risk that they will include exploitative terms seems attenuated. More plausibly, CF portals may have economies of scale in contract design. This implies that the focus of regulatory engagement should be on the portal rather than on the issuer. This is already a component of CF regulation in both the United Kingdom and the United States, and it is a key element of the European Commission's proposed Regulation.[51]

Third, while CF contracts are obviously very risky for retail investors, their overall exposure may be mitigated by "stop loss" limitations on the amount that they are permitted to stake in the asset class.

Fourth, in the presence of a new practice such as CF, there may be much for regulators to gain from monitoring the marketplace but postponing firm decisions about intervention. Repeat players in the market, such as portals, have incentives to introduce safeguards that increase investment returns to the extent that this stimulates demand for offerings. Such incentives can be further sharpened by the implicit threat of regulatory intervention.

Conclusion

Crowd funding has grown rapidly in the recent years, albeit much more so in the United Kingdom than the United States. It seems hard to resist the conclusion that regulation has been one of the factors behind this pattern of development. In the United States, CF for retail investors has until very recently been de facto prohibited. Although they seek to facilitate this form of fundraising, reforms introduced under the JOBS Act still impose onerous disclosure obligations on firms. In contrast, the UK regime, while placing restrictions on the amount individual investors can stake in the asset class, imposes no prospectus requirement on founders but rather requires their promotions to be "fair, clear and not misleading."

A functional approach to regulating CF, focusing on the extent to which particular interventions improve outcomes, highlights the inappropriateness of some of the current tools employed by regulators. There is no basis for assuming that retail funders will benefit, however indirectly, from lengthy mandatory disclosures, given that CF takes place in a primary market with no mechanism to aggregate information from sophisticated investors. Similarly, while there may be a case for more nuanced interventions designed to protect consumers' interests, there is insufficient evidence at this early stage of the market's development to know what such measures should look like. Inappropriate mandatory rules can easily do more harm than good.

Notes

This chapter reproduces parts of John Armour and Luca Enriques, "The Promise and Perils of Crowdfunding: Between Corporate Finance and Consumer Contracts," *Modern Law Review* 81, no. 1 (January 2018): 51–84. It is reproduced with the permission of the editors and publisher, John Wiley & Sons. © 2018 The Authors. The Modern Law Review © 2018 The Modern Law Review Limited. We are grateful for feedback received at presentations at the Brevan Howard Centre Conferences on *Capital Markets Union and Beyond* in October 2016 and January 2018. Martin Bengtzen provided excellent research assistance. The usual disclaimers apply. Unless otherwise indicated, all URLs were last accessed May 29, 2017.

1. See British Business Bank, *Analysis of the UK Smaller Business Growth Loans Market* (Sheffield, UK: British Business Bank, March 2015).

2. See, e.g., B. H. Hall, "Innovation and Productivity" (NBER Working Paper No. 17178, National Bureau of Economic Research, Cambridge, MA, 2011); J. Edler and J. Fagerberg, "Innovation Policy: What, Why, and How," *Oxford Review of Economic Policy* 33, no. 1 (2017): 9–10.

3. For details of recent policy initiatives, see the Department for Business, Innovation, and Skills and HM Treasury, "2010 to 2015 Government Policy: Business Enterprise" (policy paper, Gov.uk, United Kingdom, 2015).

4. See European Commission, "Proposal for a Regulation on European Crowdfunding Service Providers (ECSP) for Business" (Brussels: European Commission, COM [2018] 113 final, March 8, 2018).

5. Financial Conduct Authority (FCA), *Interim Feedback to the Call for Input to the Post-Implementation Review of the FCA's Crowdfunding Rules*, FS16/13 (2016).

6. Securities and Exchange Commission, "Crowdfunding: Final Rule," *Federal Register* 80 (2015): 71387–71615.

7. See, e.g., A. M. Robb and D. T. Robinson, "The Capital Structure Decisions of New Firms," *Review of Financial Studies* 27, no. 1 (2014): 153–179.

8. See, e.g., P. Aghion, S. Bond, A. Klemm, and I. Martinescu, "Technology and Financial Structure: Are Innovative Firms Different?," *Journal of the European Economic Association* 2, nos. 2–3 (May 2004): 277–288.

9. See generally P. A. Gompers and J. Lerner, *The Venture Capital Cycle* (Cambridge, MA: MIT Press, 1999); J. Armour and L. Enriques, "Financing Disruption" (working paper, Oxford University, 2016).

10. S. N. Kaplan and P. Strömberg, "Financial Contracting Theory Meets the Real World: An Empirical Analysis of Venture Capital Contracts," *Review of Economic Studies* 70, no. 2 (2003): 281–315.

11. J. Lerner, "Venture Capitalists and the Oversight of Private Firms," *Journal of Finance* 50, no. 1 (1995): 301–318.

12. See R. Martin, P. Sunley, and D. Turner, "Taking Risks in Regions: The Geographical Anatomy of Europe's Emerging Venture Capital Market," *Journal of Economic Geography* 2, no. 2 (February 2002): 121–150.

13. See generally R. Gilson and R. Kraakman, "The Mechanisms of Market Efficiency," *Virginia Law Review* 70, no. 4 (May 1984): 549–644; J. Armour, D. Awrey, P. Davies, L. Enriques, J. N.

Gordon, C. Mayer, and J. Payne, *Principles of Financial Regulation* (Oxford: Oxford University Press, 2016), ch. 5.

14. That is the case for many UK equity CF platforms, such as Crowdcube, Seedrs, and The Right Crowd.

15. See A. V. Banerjee, "A Simple Model of Herd Behavior," *Quarterly Journal of Economics* 107, no. 3 (August 1992): 797–817.

16. See, e.g., Grant Thornton, "Raising Cornerstone Investment: Kicking Off Your Crowdfunding Campaign," https://www.crowdcube.com/explore/entrepreneur-articles/raising-cornerstone-invest ment-kicking-off-your-crowdfunding-campaign.

17. See J. Armour and L. Enriques, "The Promise and Perils of Crowdfunding: Between Corporate Finance and Consumer Contracts," *Modern Law Review* 81, no. 1 (2018): 51–84.

18. Financial Services and Markets Act 2000 (FSMA), sec. 85(5)(a), Sch. 11A, para. 9.

19. FSMA, secs. 19, 21; Financial Services and Markets Act 2000 (Regulated Activities) Order 2001, SI 2001/554, Article 25.

20. See *The FCA's Regulatory Approach to Crowdfunding over the Internet, and the Promotion of Non-Readily Realisable Securities by Other Media*, PS14/4 (2014).

21. FCA, *Conduct of Business Sourcebook* (COBS) 4.2.1R.

22. COBS 4.7.7(3), 4.7.8(2), 10.2.

23. COBS 4.7.7(2), 4.7.9–4.7.10.

24. Individuals are "accredited investors" if they have net worth (excluding their home) exceeding US$1 million or annual income exceeding US$200,000 (or US$300,000 jointly with their spouse): SEC Regulation D, Rule 501. Such persons are presumed to be able to afford access to financial advice.

25. Jumpstart Our Business Startups Act, P.L. No. 112-106, 126 Stat. 306 (2012) (the JOBS Act).

26. Securities Act of 1933 § 4(a)(6).

27. Securities Act of 1933 §§ 4(a)(6)(C), 4A(a).

28. Securities Act of 1933 § 4A(a)(5).

29. Securities Act of 1933 § 4A(a)(11).

30. Securities Act of 1933 § 4(a)(6)(B).

31. Securities Act of 1933 § 4(a)(3). See also Securities and Exchange Commission, "Crowdfunding: Final Rule," 71475.

32. Securities Act of 1933 § 4A(b)(1)(A)–(H).

33. Securities Act of 1933 § 4A(b)(1)(D).

34. Securities Act of 1933 § 4A(b)(1)(D). Issues of between US$100,000 to US$500,000 must be reviewed by an independent public accountant.

35. Securities Act of 1933 § 4A(b)(4).

36. See Securities and Exchange Commission, "Proposed Rules: Crowdfunding," *Federal Register* 78 (2013): 66436, 66521.

37. See, e.g., for Crowdcube, https://help.crowdcube.com/hc/en-us/articles/206232464-What -fees-does-Crowdcube-charge-for-raising-finance-on-the-platform-.

38. A. Wan, "A Comparison of Reg CF and Reg A-Plus," Law360.com, March 14, 2017, https:// www.law360.com/articles/901763/a-comparison-of-reg-cf-and-reg-a-plus.

39. See Armour and Enriques, "The Promise and Perils of Crowdfunding," 56.

40. The level of equity CF raised is, of course, also a function of many other factors, including the availability of substitutes such as venture capital and angel investment.

41. See, e.g., Armour et al., *Principles of Financial Regulation*, chs. 8 and 10.

42. See O. Ben-Shahar and C.E. Schneider, *More Than You Wanted to Know* (Princeton, NJ: Princeton University Press, 2014), 68–69.

43. Ben-Shahar and Schneider, *More Than You Wanted to Know*, 68–69.

44. See, e.g., Z. Shapira and I. Venezia, "Patterns of Behavior of Professionally Managed and Independent Investors," *Journal of Banking and Finance* 25, no. 8 (2001): 1573–1587.

45. See, e.g., Z. Goshen and G. Parchomovsky, "The Essential Role of Securities Regulation," *Duke Law Journal* 55, no. 4 (February 2006): 711–782.

46. See, e.g., M. B. Fox, L. R. Glosten, and G. V. Rauterberg, "The New Stock Market: Sense and Nonsense," *Duke Law Journal* 65, no. 2 (2015): 221–225.

47. We say "easier" because the justification is not uncontested. See, generally, L. Enriques and S. Gilotta, "Disclosure and Financial Market Regulation," in *The Oxford Handbook on Financial Regulation*, ed. E. Ferran, N. Moloney, and J. Payne (Oxford: Oxford University Press, 2015), 520–525.

48. FCA, *Interim Feedback*, 34.

49. European Commission, "Proposal for a Regulation on European Crowdfunding Service Providers (ECSP) for Business," 28–29 (proposed Article 16).

50. See Armour and Enriques, "The Promise and Perils of Crowdfunding," 75, for references.

51. European Commission, "Proposal for a Regulation on European Crowdfunding Service Providers (ECSP) for Business," 23–31 (proposed Articles 10–20).

12 Capital Markets Union and Virtual Funding: Initial Coin Offerings, Tokens, and Digital Corporations

Katja Langenbucher

When policymakers summarize the challenges the European Union (EU) faces in developing a deep and liquid European capital market, a familiar pattern emerges: "finance" in Europe translates as bank financing, but bank lending has remained at low levels after the financial crisis; investors suffer from home bias sticking with their member states rather than the EU; and financing conditions and many rules and market practices remain different among the member states.[1]

The European Commission has developed a plethora of measures seeking to "strengthen the flow of private capital to growing businesses."[2] Among these we find a modernization of the Prospectus Directive; proposals for simple, transparent, and standardized securitization; and a consumer financial services action plan. Rules on ownership of securities and on covered bonds are in the making, "fintech" has people hoping for better access to finance, and rules enabling "crowd funding" form part of the capital markets union's (CMU) initiatives. From there, it seems a natural step to broaden plans of this genre to encompass funding via virtual currencies. A subcategory of these funding initiatives has become known as "initial coin offering (ICO)," even if the available options are not limited to the development of virtual currencies.

How bright could we paint the future of virtual financing?

The Story of Stacy, Luke, and Frank

Let us imagine a person named Stacy Start-up. She works from an old farmhouse in southern Spain that has excellent internet access but is far away from the next bank. She has plans for an innovative multiplayer online 3D video game and seeks funding to support herself and her partner, who has agreed to do the coding. Browsing the internet, two offers catch her attention. Both expect the capital seeker to accept funding in virtual currency. Stacy is happy to do so, knowing that many online services she uses accept virtual currency and that there is a number of platforms taking care of exchanging virtual currency into fiat money.

First, Stacy finds an online peer-to-peer (P2P) lending platform called "Bitbond." It promises to match Stacy with peers who are looking for an opportunity to lend. It has less complicated scoring and lower interest rates compared to her Spanish bank, so Stacy goes ahead and applies for a virtual credit contract. Luke Lender likes her project and offers her credit.

Second, she gets interested in a "decentralized autonomous organization" (DAO) that offers funding for unspecified projects. Frank Funder is engaged in a DAO of this kind. Along with other investors from many different countries, he holds "tokens" that allow him to vote on projects and to receive a share of anticipated earnings of such projects.[3] Stacy prepares a proposal describing her idea, attaches the relevant coding, proposes a "smart contract" that ensures the funding entity will receive a percentage of her earnings, and hopes to get accepted by the DAO community.

This virtual world of projects, investments, and financing, aimed at replacing legal regulation with "tech," has many dreaming of a new world order by making banks redundant and transcending national borders, currencies, and legal regimes. Bitbond's slogan reminds us to "see no bank, hear no bank, speak no bank" and calls itself "The #Unbank."[4] Ventures of the DAO type are reported to have raised hundreds of millions of US dollars in virtual capital to be invested in projects like Stacy's. Such projects very often focus on the development not of a video game but of a new virtual currency—hence the name initial coin offering, or ICO. Not all "tokens" are like the ones Frank received. Some can be exchanged into a new virtual currency. Others grant permission to use services such as cloud storage data or software program downloads.

It seems impossible to assess today whether we will see many Stacys and Franks in the future and to what extent virtual funding will ever be a viable form of financing. However, many countries have started regulating similar initiatives, hoping these could develop into a "key source of financing for SMEs [small- and medium-sized enterprises] over the long term."[5] Against the background of this dynamic, it seems worthwhile to ponder the role legal regulation could play in funding through virtual currency with its enabling and with its more paternalistic instruments.

Painting with very broad strokes, we will limit these remarks to the story of Stacy, Luke, and Frank, considering only two of the many versions of virtual funding: Bitbond, as an example of a virtual lending market, and the DAO, illustrative of a virtual entity engaged in something resembling equity on a virtual equity market.

Peer-to-Peer Lending

Bitbond is a P2P lending platform. Its business model may remind us of US outfits such as Lending Club or Prosper in that it matches lenders and borrowers via an online platform. However, while lending club has a web bank make the loans to borrowers and then assigns it to the lenders, Bitbond refuses this role.[6] Instead, Bitbond waits for a borrower like Stacy to apply, lists her loan request, suggests an interest rate, and uploads the request.[7] An auction follows, leading to a contract between one or more lenders like Luke and the borrower.[8] Funding and repayment are done via a bitcoin account held at Bitbond.[9] The entire administration of the loan is taken care of by Bitbond,[10] which acts as an agent for the parties.[11]

Why would this approach be more interesting for borrowers rather than using a regular (and regulated) bank for a loan? P2P lending platforms market their activities as often cheaper and quicker than a traditional credit contract. Because they employ a different scoring methodology than most banks, borrowers like Stacy will often get better conditions—or a loan at all—if compared with regular banks, so they claim.

Bitbond prides itself on facilitating global lending via its innovative scoring methodology. Borrowers grant access to their credit history on sites using internationally standardized data, such as Amazon, PayPal, or eBay. From there, Bitbond builds its own database. Using virtual currency makes global lending even more attractive, so Bitbond claims, having an eye on borrowers in developing countries.

And what about lenders like Luke? Bitbond markets attractive interest rates of 13% with a credit default risk approaching 9%, which for some offers an appealing risk/reward ratio. The fact that this investment is in virtual currency may bring its own advantages, ranging from better investment opportunities for countries with capital controls to a more favorable tax regime.

ICOs with Equity Tokens

While Bitbond has served as an example of debt financing, the DAO will fill in as a "sort-of-equity" financing option. Why it is usually *not* equity will become clear when we try to understand the DAO structure in more detail.

A venture called "the DAO" has attracted considerable attention due to its being discussed in a US Securities and Exchange Commission (SEC) investigative report. A German limited company going by the name of "slock.it" had pursued a number of projects aimed at, among other things, developing a new virtual currency. To raise funding, the owners promoted a blockchain-based virtual entity they called "the DAO." One of the DAO's interesting features was its attempt to facilitate corporate governance procedures using blockchain technology. Investors like Frank downloaded DAO software and transferred a certain sum, with denominations in virtual currency, to the digitally adopted platform. A smart contract made sure the investor would immediately receive DAO "tokens." These tokens allowed for two things: (1) the investor would get to vote on projects such as Stacy's and (2) the investor would receive project-related (virtual) payments whenever a funded project yielded earnings. "Smart contracts" were supposed to take care of organizing the voting procedure, ensuring that a project like Stacy's would receive the funding and distribute any consideration among all DAO token holders. In the original DAO case, the plan included a share of the anticipated earnings to be paid in virtual currency. Other ventures promise different types of consideration such as fixed interest rate payments, new virtual coins, or a yet different reward. which might be playing the newly developed video game for free. Lastly, return on the token investment could be a mix of all those things.

Why could this "sort-of-equity" financing be attractive for a start-up like Stacy's? Of course, the broad range of available payback options allows her to tailor the financing to her needs. Also, she might find funding that cannot be found elsewhere via enthusiasts for her product.

Interestingly, a good reason might be that it is *only* a "sort-of-equity" tool:[12] Stacy is not required to set up a corporation. Even if she and her partner decide to do so, there is no reason for her to make the investors shareholders in the start-up. True, in one version of the funding scheme they get a share of her earnings, and these will remind us of dividend payments. But remember that the precise percentage is part of Stacy's project proposal. Irrespective of how Stacy's venture develops, investors like Frank have no say in how high the dividend should be. Depending on the proposal, Stacy may have broad leeway in defining what counts as her earnings. She will also be free to decide whether she wishes to take on "real" equity partners. More generally, DAO investors do not participate in Stacy's governance of her venture.

Why would Frank consider an investment in a DAO entity? He might like how the DAO token allows him to cast his vote on which project will get funded. Possibly, the blockchain technique may offer him better monitoring facilities than traditional investments. Of course, his decision depends on what Stacy offers. If he is very enthusiastic about video games, his main reason for investing might be that he is one of the first users to play the new video game. He might instead bet on selling the reward token to an avid gamer. If Stacy offers only a share of any profit she might make, Frank will look out for an attractive risk/reward ratio.

Stacy and Frank, and How the Law Can Help

Many of the issues involving legal regulation—enabling and protective—have surfaced in our funding story. Stacy doubled as the typical start-up founder hoping for better access to finance. Luke and Frank are investors ready to offer financing when an attractive return was promised. They face a number of the information asymmetries legal regulation addresses: How well will they be informed on Stacy's project? Will Luke understand that Bitbond won't take on the credit default risk? Will Frank factor in the difference between a DAO token and a share in a corporation? Does Frank face liability from third parties when things go wrong with a virtual investment? Lastly, both sides may be worried about the nature of the new virtual products they have invested in— legally speaking, what is a "bitcoin," a "token," or a "DAO"?

While not all of these questions will fall under the scope of the EU's CMU project, we see regulatory initiatives around the globe, addressing private law, banking and securities regulation, and to a lesser extent, corporate law.

Virtual Currencies and Private Law

Let us start with the legal nature of virtual currencies. Most EU member states will understand this as raising problems of private law.[13] Virtual currencies will usually not qualify as a tangible object[14] and will in rare cases only be considered as a legal claim against a legal entity or person. Many legal orders will be open to understanding virtual currency as an intangible object, allowing for contractual and unjust enrichment claims to apply, possibly even for tortious interference.[15] There may be problems such as how to validly transfer "ownership" of a bitcoin. What happens when the transfer goes wrong and whether one may hand over virtual currency to a creditor who wants cash will, however, be outside the CMU's immediate attention.

Many of these questions may trouble Luke and Stacy, too. Who is responsible for ensuring that Luke's bitcoins not only are transferred in the books of bitbond but also have been validated on the blockchain? Imagine if a virtual currency in which a loan has been issued is forced out of business. Would Stacy have to pay back her loan in cash, and if so, what would be the applicable exchange rate? Thinking about enforcement, can bitcoins be seized? The FBI puzzled about this question when shutting down the "Silk Road" website, considering whether Fifth Amendment rights would protect a person from having to hand over passwords.[16]

Virtual Lending and Banking Regulation

Closer to the CMU project will be the problem of regulating Bitbond. We have seen that Bitbond refrains from any involvement in handing out a credit contract—it appears as a pure "platform." *As such*, it would not need a license under German law (but see the paragraph below).[17] Similarly, as long as Bitbond does not take deposits, it does not fall under Article 4, para. 1 of the Capital Requirements Regulation's definition of a "credit institution."[18]

However, should Luke be engaged in a banking business, possibly as a commercial lender, this could impact Bitbond too should they be aiding him in running an unauthorized banking business. While many countries require a banking license only for the combination of taking deposits and handing out loans, German law looks at each activity separately. Hence, Luke may at first glance need a license under sec. 1, para. 1, no. 1, 2 of Kreditwesengesetz due to having granted Stacy a loan. The German banking regulator BaFin will say so if one of the following is true: (1) his total credit volume reaches a minimum of €500,000 and includes 20 loans, (2) he hands out 100 individual loans or more, or (3) he intends to make a commercial business out of his activity.

Does this apply even if Luke's loans are made in bitcoin, not in any national currency? BaFin does not equate virtual currency with fiat currency when applying banking law. Instead of understanding bitcoins as a currency, the German regulator has qualified bitcoins as "financial instruments" under German law, a term that, among other things, catches "units of account."[19] Hence, the rules on requiring a banking license for handing out a loan do not apply. Luke will be understood as lending out objects in kind, an activity outside the scope of banking regulation.

By contrast, with bitcoins qualifying as "financial instruments," under German law Bitbond counts as an intermediary engaged in "*investment services*" under sec. 1, para. 1a, no. 1, 1b of Kreditwesengesetz. This rule addresses "investment services" in the form of transactions with financial instruments.[20] Following up on this assessment, Bitbond has successfully applied for a banking license in Germany.

Virtual Corporations and Corporate Law

As we have seen, enabling virtual debt financing from a legal point of view involves a complicated mix of private law and banking regulation. Similarly, what we addressed as "sort-of-equity" financing combines questions of private law (what is a token?), corporate law (what is a DAO?), and securities regulation (may a token be understood as a security?).

Let us move to corporate law first. Just as we wondered how to conceptualize a virtual coin, we may ask ourselves how to understand a "token" equipped with voting and with dividend rights. How can we transfer a token? More importantly, can we understand the DAO as a corporate entity?

Blockchain Initiatives

So far, some jurisdictions have started facilitating the formation of a corporation using blockchain technology for some steps of the foundational infrastructure,[21] including the issuance of electronic stock. Instead of a "paper-based, slow and error-prone"[22] filing process, plans such as Delaware's "blockchain initiative" for "smart filing" will automate much of this procedure. Yet, as "smart" as filing may become, it still requires registration with a state agency and compliance with its rules and regulations. This is far removed from the "virtual corporation" crypto-enthusiasts are after. A truly "virtual" corporation would not only need to be open to finding its owners globally but also have its coding define the process of joining the company or specify the type of contribution required. Typically, the owners would also wish for their corporate structure to shield them from personal liability. But most jurisdictions will be likely to link their corporate veil to compliance with the distinct registration procedure required by that country's law. This sends us back to the "blockchain initiative" we just mentioned: We are seeing efforts to use technology to make registration quick and efficient and reduce the number of flaws and errors. Unsurprisingly, however, states have so far not displayed any interest in using technology to make registration redundant.

DAO Structures as Partnerships

What does this entail for a DAO-like structure if seen from a corporate law perspective? Without registration, we might understand joining a DAO to be something like a video game without the intent to undertake any legally binding act.

However, as soon as actual funding decisions are taken, many jurisdictions are likely to assume legal relevance of the decision to sign up with a DAO or to transfer money to its platform. Usually, they will conceive of a DAO, such as the one Frank had joined, as a partnership with full personal responsibility.[23] Depending on the applicable law, this will open the DAO up to claims from third parties (e.g., funding problems or of wrongful trading) and to claims from their co-owners (e.g., recourse claims among owners)—evidently not an attractive option for investors like Frank. He would probably be surprised if he learned not only that his investment may be lost but also that, in addition, he may be liable to third parties. On the positive side, understanding a DAO as a partnership will provide for considerably more leeway than a corporate charter can offer (for example, tokens as embodying voting or dividend rights or allowing to transfer ownership).

Virtual Tokens and Securities Law

The most intricate question under EU law seems to be whether we may understand "tokens" as financial securities. If we do, a complicated regulatory registration procedure, prospectus rules, and a harsh liability regime toward investors will apply. This presupposes, however, that the EU law's (so far) conservative view of financial securities encompassing (only) equity, debt, or shares in units for collective investment can be expanded to tokens.

Who Is the Issuer?

Before we address this problem, let us first make sure who would qualify as the "issuer," subject to those rules. Three options spring to mind: In the original DAO case, we had "slock.it" as the entity sponsoring and marketing the DAO in a number of ways and submitting its first project. Under most jurisdictions, this would probably be enough to understand it as an "issuer." In the absence of one such sponsor, there might be "managing owners" of the DAO partnership that we could understand as "issuers." In a more theoretical setting, it may also be conceivable to understand the entire DAO partnership as the issuer of the tokens by which one could join the DAO. More realistically, someone like Stacy, submitting a proposal to a DAO in the understanding that money may be raised to back this proposal, may qualify as an "issuer."

This quick overview on potential issuers highlights the impact regulatory law will have on the success of virtual funding efforts. The higher the risk of a start-up's entrepreneur facing personal liability under securities laws, the lower the probability this form of financing will establish itself as a viable, long-term alternative to more traditional venture capital structures.

Tokens and the Howey Test

The original DAO tokens have been considered a security by the SEC. Applying the US Supreme Court's Howey Test, the SEC focused on understanding whether tokens implied an "investment contract," defined as "an investment of money in a common enterprise with a reasonable expectation of profits to be derived from the entrepreneurial or managerial efforts of others."[24] An investment of "money" does not need to be cash as long as value is contributed, and this allows for virtual currency to be subsumed under the Howey Test. The "common enterprise" and the "reasonable expectation of profit" are clearly present in the DAO case. The "managerial efforts of others" seems somewhat more intricate to show since the beauty of the DAO coding lies in allowing all owners to take their investment decisions together. However, the SEC pointed to the "slock.it" owners who screened proposals, determined their order and frequency, and could halve the default quorum. This was enough for the SEC to understand that the rest of the DAO community expected to profit from the managerial efforts of "slock.it."

Tokens and the EU Definition

For European law, things are much less clear. So far there is no equivalent to the broad and flexible Howey Test under EU securities law. Instead, to qualify as a security, the issued unit will at a minimum need to be "transferable, standardised and negotiable/fungible."[25] "Transferability" and "negotiability" for the EU Commission refer to the security understood "as a class."[26] If we can frame the security in question in this way, and if it could be traded on any type of capital market, it could qualify as a security—even if the individual unit under consideration is not being traded.[27] Hence, tokens that, due to their underlying coding, cannot be transferred do not qualify as a security.[28] Whether it follows *e contrario* that anything which may be traded on a platform can be a security remains to be seen.[29]

Distinguishing a security from other tradable products, EU law asks if it can be likened to shares, bonds, or options.[30] For some scholars, this implies the availability of legal protection of ownership acquired in good faith. Oddly, this requirement sends us back to the private law problems discussed at the outset: What is the legal nature of a token, how will ownership be transferred, and could this be done in good faith? The blockchain may "provide for a perfect substitute,"[31] but certainly not without a legal basis. Today, the qualification of tokens under EU security law remains an open question under review by most regulators in the EU.

Summary

Summing up, virtual funding options raise questions extending from private and banking law to corporate and securities law. Regulatory issues will have to be addressed where investor and creditor protection, disclosure, and contract law are concerned. Focusing on enabling components, a clear framework for virtual coins and tokens might be an attractive option. More importantly, the somewhat vague (if compared to the Howey Test) European concept of what qualifies as a security may be one more sign that European securities law is (still) in need of refinement and maturity. The CMU project would allow for further steps, potentially combining a neat concept of a "security" with clear-cut exemptions to the scope of regulation.

Notes

1. See summary at European Commission 2019b.
2. European Commission 2017a.
3. Securities and Exchange Commission 2017 under Section 21(a) SEA 1934.
4. Bitbond 2016.
5. Delivorias 2017.
6. Bitbond 2019, introduction.
7. Bitbond 2019, § 9, paras. 1–2.
8. Bitbond 2019, § 9, para. 8, § 12.
9. Bitbond 2019, § 10, para. 1.
10. Bitbond 2019, § 15.
11. Bitbond 2019, § 13.
12. Hacker and Thomale 2018, 651.
13. Langenbucher 2018a.
14. But see "Argentina," in Law Library of Congress 2014.
15. Langenbucher 2018a.
16. Gabbatt and Rushe 2013.
17. BaFin 2007; Langenbucher 2018a.
18. Renner 2016, 224, 225.
19. A recent court decision has raised doubts on qualifying bitcoins as a "unit of account," referring, however, only to matters of criminal, not of banking law.
20. BaFin 2017.
21. See European Commission 2019a; Tinianow and Long 2017.
22. Tinianow and Long 2017.
23. Mann 2017.
24. SEC v. W. J. Howey Co., 328 U.S. 293, 301 (1946).
25. Art. 1, para. 1, Prospectus Directive (European Commission 2017b); Art. 4, para. 1, no. 44 MiFiD II (European Commission 2014); for a comparison between the "Howey Test" and EU law, see Langenbucher 2018.
26. European Securities and Markets Authority 2017.
27. European Securities and Markets Authority 2017.
28. Hacker and Thomale 2018, 664.
29. Hacker and Thomale 2018, 662 et seqq.
30. Art. 4, para. 1, no. 44, MiFID II (European Commission 2014).
31. Hacker and Thomale 2018, 666.

References

BaFin. 2007. "Merkblatt zur Erlaubnispflicht von Kreditvermittlungsplattformen." Bundesanstalt für Finanzdienstleistungsaufsicht, May 14. https://www.bafin.de/dok/7852546.

BaFin. 2017. "Merkblatt Anlagevermittlung." Bundesanstalt für Finanzdienstleistungsaufsicht, July 13. https://www.bafin.de/SharedDocs/Veroeffentlichungen/DE/Merkblatt/mb_091204_tatbest and_anlagevermittlung.html.

Bitbond. 2016. Website. *The Internet Archive: Wayback Machine*, February 5. https://web.archive.org/web/20160205042601/https://www.bitbond.com/.

Bitbond. 2019. "Terms of Use." https://www.bitbond.com/terms_of_use.

Delivorias, A. 2017. "Crowdfunding in Europe." European Parliamentary Research Service Briefing No. PE585.882, European Union, January.

European Commission. 2013. "Regulation (EU) No 575/2013 of the European Parliament and of the Council of 26 June 2013 on Prudential Requirements for Credit Institutions." *Official Journal of the European Union* L176/1, June 27.

European Commission. 2014. "Directive 2014/65/EU of the European Parliament and of the Council of 15 May 2014 on Markets in Financial Instruments" (MiFID II). *Official Journal of the European Union* L173/349.

European Commission. 2017a. "Completing the Capital Markets Union: Building on the First Round of Achievements." Press release no. IP/17/1529, June 8. http://europa.eu/rapid/press-release_IP-17-1529_en.htm.

European Commission. 2017b. "Regulation (EU) 2017/1129 of the European Parliament and of the Council of 14 June 2017 on the Prospectus to Be Published when Securities Are Offered to the Public or Admitted to Trading on a Regulated Market." *Official Journal of the European Union* L168/12.

European Commission. 2019a. "Directive (EU) 2019/1151 of the European Parliament and of the Council of 20 June 2019 Amending Directive (EU) 2017/1132 as Regards the Use of Digital Tools and Processes in Company Law." *Official Journal of the European Union*, L 186/80.

European Commission. 2019b. "What Is the Capital Markets Union?" https://ec.europa.eu/info/business-economy-euro/growth-and-investment/capital-markets-union/what-capital-markets-union_en.

European Securities and Markets Authority (ESMA). 2017. "67. Transferable Securities." In *Questions and Answers: Prospectuses*, 27th updated version. Paris: ESMA, ESMA-31-62-780, October, 55–56. https://financedocbox.com/Stocks/68074748-Questions-and-answers-prospectuses-27th-updated-version-october-2017.html.

Gabbatt, A., and D. Rushe. 2013. "Silk Road Shutdown: How Can the FBI Seize Bitcoins?" *The Guardian*, October 3. https://www.theguardian.com/technology/2013/oct/02/bitcoin-silk-road-how-to-seize.

Hacker, P., and C. Thomale. 2018. "Crypto-Securities Regulation: ICOs, Token Sales and Cryptocurrencies under EU Financial Law." *European Company and Financial Law Review* 15, no. 4: 645–696.

Langenbucher, K. 2018a. "Digitales Finanzwesen: Vom Bargeld zu virtuellen Währungen." *Archiv fuer die civilistische Praxis* 218, no. 2: 385–429.

Langenbucher, K. 2018b. "European Securities Law: Are We in Need of a New Definition? A Thought Inspired by Initial Coin Offerings." *Revue Trimestrielle de Droit Financier* 2018, no. 2/3: 40–48.

Law Library of Congress. 2014. "Regulation of Bitcoin in Selected Jurisdictions." Washington, DC: The Law Library of Congress, Global Legal Research Center, January. https://www.loc.gov/law/help/bitcoin-survey/regulation-of-bitcoin.pdf.

Mann, M. 2017. "Die Decentralized Autonomous Organization—Ein neuer Gesellschaftstyp?" *Neue Zeitschrift für Gesellschaftsrecht* 2017, no. 26: 1014–1020.

Renner, M. 2016. "Peer-to-Peer Lending in Germany." *Journal of European Consumer and Market Law* 2016, no. 5: 224–226.

Securities and Exchange Commission (SEC). 2017. *Report of Investigation Pursuant to Section 21(a) of the Securities Exchange Act of 1934: The DAO.* Washington, DC: SEC, Release No. 81207, July 25.

Tinianow, A., and C. Long. 2017. "Delaware Blockchain Initiative: Transforming the Foundational Infrastructure of Corporate Finance." Harvard Law School Forum on Corporate Governance and Financial Regulation, March 16. https://corpgov.law.harvard.edu/2017/03/16/delaware-blockchain-initiative-transforming-the-foundational-infrastructure-of-corporate-finance/.

Zetzsche, D. A., R. P. Buckley, and D. W. Arner. 2018. "The Distributed Liability of Distributed Ledgers: Legal Risks of Blockchain." *University of Illinois Law Review* 2018, no. 4: 1361–1407.

13 Equity Markets

Marina Brogi and Valentina Lagasio

In all official documentation, the capital markets union (CMU) is considered a key pillar in the European Commission's Investment Plan for Europe and an important part of the work on the completion of the European economic and monetary union.

Through the CMU, the European Commission aims to facilitate firms' financial funding by fostering investments and increasing financial integration in European capital markets.

While the banking union refers to the nineteen euro area countries, at its inception the CMU was envisaged for the twenty-eight members of the European Union (EU28).

This chapter offers insight into two key issues in the potential contribution of public stock markets to the financing of the EU economy as set out in the CMU action plan: (1) whether European stock markets over a long period of time have been a source of funding for listed companies and support small and medium-sized enterprise (SME) growth and (2) whether financing choices and listing decisions reflect company profitability, size, financing structure, and taxation by using a sample of listed firms.

Institutional Background and Related Literature

One of the key objectives of the CMU is to ensure that SMEs have diversified sources of funds and especially have access to public markets as a means to raise equity.

The *action plan* presented in September 2015 "set out the building blocks for putting a well-functioning and integrated Capital Markets Union, encompassing all EU28 member states into place *by 2019*" with an assessment of achievements and priorities in 2017. Equity markets are just one of the many different aspects addressed in the CMU action plan. It originally entailed thirty-three actions with an indicative timeline for achievement. A section is dedicated to "Making It Easier for Companies to Enter and Raise Capital on Public Markets" (European Commission n.d.), with three actions aimed at strengthening access to public markets regarding (1) the modernization of the Prospectus Directive (Q4 2015), (2) a review on regulatory barriers to SME admission on public markets and SME growth markets (2017), and (3) a review of EU corporate bond markets (2017). There is one action in the support equity financing work stream aimed at addressing the debt-equity bias, as part of the legislative proposal on Common Consolidated Corporate Tax Base (Q4 2016).

The *CMU Mid-Term Review* (European Commission 2017b), presented in June 2017, showed that twenty of the proposed actions had been achieved. As concerns equity markets, an agreement had been reached in December 2016 regarding the Prospectus Directive, and a proposal on the common consolidated corporate tax base had been adopted in October 2016.

Moreover, as envisioned in the original action plan, the *CMU Mid-Term Review* led to the division of this section into four work streams: (1) prospectuses for public offerings, (2) corporate bond markets, (3) SME listing package, and (4) proportionate listing requirements, and the identification of two further priority actions and two new actions, as noted in table 13.1.

Further progress was made after the *CMU Mid-Term Review*; in December 2017 the European Commission launched a public consultation on building a proportionate regulatory environment to support SME listing to end on February 26, 2018, and published a proposal for more proportionate and risk-sensitive rules for investment firms.

To analyze the contribution of public stock markets to the financing of the EU economy as set out in the CMU action plan, we first adopt an explorative analysis on a large sample of listed firms in the period from 2001 to 2017 and investigate capital markets characteristics throughout the world to assess whether European stock markets, over a long period of time, have been a source of funding for listed companies. Second, we run a logistic regression with the purpose of identifying whether financing choices and listing decisions reflect company profitability, size, financing structure, and taxation.

Methodology

Data

The sources of our data are SDC Platinum Software from Thomson Reuters's Refinitiv (for market data) and Orbis's Bureau Van Dijk (for financial statement and firm-level data).

Table 13.1
CMU legislative progress by the European Commission.

Making it easier for companies to enter and raise capital on public markets

Prospectuses for public offerings	Implementing measures	Follow-up action (L2)	2018–2019
Corporate bond markets	Communication (road map) to propose possible follow-up	Follow-up action (C)	Q4 2017
SME listing package	Explore through an impact assessment whether targeted amendments to relevant EU legislation can deliver a more proportionate regulatory environment to support SME listings on public markets (priority action 2)	Priority action	Q2 2018
	Assessment of the impact of MiFID II level 2 rules on listed SME equity research	New action (NL)	Q1 2019
	Monitor progress on IASB commitment to improve disclosure, usability and accessibility of IFRS	Follow-up action (NL)	Ongoing
	Develop best practices on the use by member states of EU funds to partially finance costs borne by SMEs when seeking admission of their shares on the future SME growth markets	New action (NL)	Q2 2018
Proportionate prudential requirements	Legislative proposal to improve the proportionality of prudential rules for investment firms (priority action 3)	Priority action (L)	Q4 2017

Source: European Commission 2017a.

Note: MiFID II refers to the Markets in Financial Instruments Directive II; IASB refers to the International Accounting Standards Board; and IFRS refers to International Financial Reporting Standards.

Using the SDC Platinum Software, we extracted the entire population of equity offerings data available on the platform from 2001. Data refers to offerings of the following instruments: common shares and saving shares. It includes initial public offerings (IPOs) and follow-ons of both primary offerings (capital increases) and secondary offerings (share sales). The geographic scope includes all stock exchanges in the world.

For each issue, we collect data on the principal amount (sum of all markets in millions of euros) that is the total principal amount of the entire transaction plus the overallotment amount. This figure represents all tranches of the transaction. For common stock issues, this figure is calculated by accumulating shares plus overallotment shares sold multiplied by the offer price for each tranche within the transaction.

Using this type of query, we exclude from the final data set firms that did not issue equity, as defined above, in the period of market data extraction.

Under the covered period (January 1, 2001, to December 15, 2017) we found about 250,000 offerings by 85,286 companies in 159 countries, including certain cases of multiple offerings (more than one category of shares or more than one stock exchange) that raised over €13 trillion within the approximately seventeen-year period.

Data as described above are reported below and broken down by the continent in which the operation was based. Table 13.2 shows the geographic breakdown of capital raised, with indication of the countries in which more than €100,000 million was raised.

In order to identify the type of equity offering, the classification considers two categories: (1) IPOs and (2) follow-ons. IPOs represent on average 45% (median 38%) of total issues in terms of amount raised, ranging from a minimum of 0% of total capital raised (in Anguilla, Aruba, Bolivia, Bosnia, Costa Rica, Guam, Macedonia, Montenegro, Dutch Antilles, and Uruguay) to a maximum of 100% (in Angola, Belarus, Brunei, Burkina Faso, El Salvador, Iran, Kyrgyzstan, Libya, Malaysia, Maldives, Moldova, Mozambique, Namibia, Paraguay, Rwanda, and Somalia). The year 2009 had the lowest amount raised from IPOs. The average IPO size is €23,713 million and the median IPO size is €1,486 million.

Seasoned equity offerings raised just under €10 trillion in the period (with an average size of about €71 billion and a median size of €2 billion) and the year 2009 had the highest amount raised from follow-ons.

The geographical breakdown of the total amount raised during the observation period shows that 27% was raised in the United States, 16% in the EU27 (14% in the euro area), and 7% in the United Kingdom. Companies raised €3.5 trillion in the United States as compared to €2.1 trillion in EU27, with IPOs raising €698 billion euro in the United States, €419 billion in the EU27 (of which €360 million in the euro area), and almost €200 million in the United Kingdom. These numbers suggest the underdevelopment of equity markets in the EU, and especially in the euro area.

We ran the same query on the listed companies of Orbis's Bureau Van Dijk. In order to match market, accounting, and firm level data, we decide to exclude cases with missing International Securities Identification Numbers (ISINs).

In this way, we obtain a database with almost 33,000 observations of market operations by 11,834 listed companies from thirty-nine countries that raised approximately €4 trillion on public markets (see tables 13.3 and table 13.4, which respectively show the amount raised on the market and the number of transactions of the "ISIN sample").

In this sample, IPOs represent on average 30% (median 22%) as a fraction of total issues in terms of amount raised, ranging from a minimum of 0% of

Table 13.2
Amount raised on the market (population).

Continent	Nation	Follow-on Euros (000)	%	IPOs Euros (000)	%	Total Euros (000)	%
North America		3,243,613	33.55	823,106	24.44	4,066,719	31.19
Of which:	United States	2,775,528	28.70	697,645	20.72	3,473,172	26.64
	Canada	411,539	4.26	98,704	2.93	510,244	3.91
Europe		2,763,404	28.58	793,960	23.58	3,557,364	27.29
Of which:	United Kingdom	736,611	7.62	196,816	5.84	933,427	7.16
Of which:	*United Kingdom*	712,605	7.37	173,421	5.15	886,025	6.80
EU19 (Euro area)		1,484,635	15.35	359,732	10.68	1,844,368	14.15
Of which:	*France*	322,834	3.34	74,850	2.22	397,684	3.05
	Germany	312,236	3.23	65,250	1.94	377,486	2.90
	Italy	194,802	2.01	45,933	1.36	240,735	1.85
	Spain	170,456	1.76	66,178	1.97	236,634	1.82
	Netherlands	134,684	1.39	30,951	0.92	165,635	1.27
Other EU27		166,163	1.72	58,664	1.74	224,827	1.72
Non-EU Europe		375,995	3.89	178,747	5.31	554,742	4.26
Of which:	*Russian Federation*	104,471	1.08	74,869	2.22	179,340	1.38
	Switzerland	138,571	1.43	39,380	1.17	177,950	1.36
Asia		2,654,240	27.45	1,478,462	43.91	4,132,702	31.70
Of which:	China	998,907	10.33	713,574	21.19	1,712,480	13.14
	Japan	383,289	3.96	129,801	3.85	513,091	3.94
	India	257,070	2.66	102,718	3.05	359,788	2.76
	Hong Kong	260,213	2.69	82,072	2.44	342,285	2.63
	South Korea	204,097	2.11	64,079	1.90	268,176	2.06
	Taiwan	134,833	1.39	21,540	0.64	156,373	1.20
Oceania		550,405	5.69	122,161	3.63	672,567	5.16
Of which:	Australia	532,430	5.51	112,922	3.35	645,352	4.95
South America		351,297	3.63	114,897	3.41	466,194	3.58
Of which:	Brazil	201,162	2.08	72,828	2.16	273,990	2.10
Africa		106,469	1.10	34,691	1.03	141,160	1.08
Total		9,669,429	100.00	3,367,277	100.00	13,036,705	100.00

Source: Authors' own calculations.

Notes: EU19 = Austria, Belgium, Cyprus, Estonia, Finland, France, Germany, Greece, Ireland, Italy, Latvia, Lithuania, Luxembourg, Malta, the Netherlands, Portugal, Slovakia, Slovenia, and Spain; EU27 = Austria, Belgium, Bulgaria, Croatia, Republic of Cyprus, Czech Republic, Denmark, Estonia, Finland, France, Germany, Greece, Hungary, Ireland, Italy, Latvia, Lithuania, Luxembourg, Malta, the Netherlands, Poland, Portugal, Romania, Slovakia, Slovenia, Spain, and Sweden; *United Kingdom* = United Kingdom excluding the self-governing dependencies of Jersey, Guernsey, the Isle of Man, and the Falkland Islands.

total capital raised in Belize, Malta, Tanzania, and Thailand to a maximum of 100% in Egypt, Mauritius, and Slovakia. Sixty percent of IPO companies were SMEs (defined according to the EU classification).[1]

To investigate the relation between equity issuing, company characteristics, and growth, we gathered from Bureau Van Dijk's accounting data (revenues, number of employees, total shareholders' equity [TSE], total assets [TA], income before tax, taxes, net income, and return on assets [ROA]) and populate a panel data set with more than 100,000 observations.

Model

We considered IPOs as a binary outcome dependent variable and use a logit regression model. Hence, the dependent variable takes on two values: 0 and 1.

$$Y = f(x) = \text{IPO} = \begin{cases} 0, & \text{if no} \\ 1, & \text{if yes} \end{cases}$$

Binary outcome models estimate the probability that $y = 1$ as a function of the independent variables.

$$p = \text{pr}[y = 1 | x] = F(x'\beta)$$

The regression model adopted depends on the functional form of $F(x'\beta)$, where x' is the column vector of the values for the independent variables (see table 13.5) and β is the maximum likelihood estimates of the regression coefficients.

In the logit model, $F(x'\beta)$ is the cumulative distribution function of the logistic distribution. Hence:

$$F(x'\beta) = \wedge (x'\beta) = \frac{e^{x'\beta}}{1 + e^{x'\beta}} = \frac{\exp(x'\beta)}{1 + \exp(x'\beta)},$$

where the model is estimated using the maximum likelihood method and the predicted probabilities are limited between 0 and 1.

Running the analysis, a relevant issue emerges: we are investigating rare events, since the portion of "ones" of the dependent variable IPO is thirty-three times fewer than "zero" (i.e., non-IPO observation). Thus, a logistic regression can sharply underestimate the probability of rare events.

Following King and Zeng (2001), we apply a prior correction to address this issue and obtain a balanced sample (where the portion of ones is equal to 50%). The sampling correction is randomly generated, in order to generate subsamples with the whole population of IPOs = 1 observation—gathered from the initial sample—and an equal number of randomly chosen IPO observations = 0. We check for the robustness of this subsampling method and compare

Table 13.3
Amount raised on the market (ISIN sample).

Continent	Nation	Follow-on Euros (000)	%	IPOs Euros (000)	%	Total Euros (000)	%
North America		1,147,444	35	238,661	34	1,386,105	35
Of which:	United States	1,085,248	33	234,572	33	1,319,820	33
	Canada	62,196	2	4,089	1	66,285	2
Europe		1,575,708	48	359,992	51	1,935,699	49
Of which:	United Kingdom	421,053	13	94,630	13	515,683	13
Of which:	*United Kingdom*	404,026	12	78,499	11	482,525	12
	Jersey	7,389	0	14,184	2	21,573	1
	Guernsey	7,562	0	1,330	0	8,892	0
	Isle of Man	2,074	0	590	0	2,665	0
	Falkland Is	2	0	26	0	28	0
EU19 (EA)		915,584	28	195,248	28	1,110,833	28
Of which:	*France*	231,887	7	42,677	6	274,565	7
	Germany	233,986	7	38,227	5	272,214	7
	Italy	83,148	3	23,076	3	106,224	3
	Spain	107,328	3	27,142	4	134,469	3
	Netherlands	105,731	3	24,406	3	130,137	3
	Belgium	19,906	1	7,521	1	27,427	1
	Finland	20,258	1	4,354	1	24,612	1
	Ireland	30,483	1	7,581	1	38,064	1
	Austria	36,841	1	5,817	1	42,659	1
	Luxembourg	12,864	0	10,993	2	23,857	1
	Greece	15,532	0	258	0	15,790	0
	Portugal	17,055	1	2,409	0	19,464	0
	Estonia	102	0	304	0	406	0
	Slovenia	463	0	460	0	923	0
	Slovakia		0	23	0	23	0
Other EU27		108,895	3	36,470	5	145,365	4
Of which:	*Sweden*	57,217	2	15,096	2	72,313	2
	Poland	20,342	1	13,592	2	33,934	1
	Denmark	28,898	1	6,405	1	35,303	1
	Hungary	710	0	349	0	1,060	0
	Faroe Islands	229	0	331	0	559	0
	Czech Republic	1,499	0	698	0	2,197	0
Non-EU Europe		130,175	4	33,643	5	163,818	4
Of which:	*Norway*	33,751	1	13,763	2	47,514	1
	Turkey	23,760	1	9,335	1	33,096	1
	Switzerland	70,723	2	10,490	1	81,214	2
	Iceland	1,940	0	55	0	1,995	0

(continued)

Table 13.3 (continued)

Continent	Nation	Follow-on Euros (000)	%	IPOs Euros (000)	%	Total Euros (000)	%
Asia		307,278	9	82,704	12	389,982	10
Of which:	Japan	260,983	8	73,421	10	334,404	8
	Korea	36,275	1	5,228	1	41,504	1
	Israel	10,020	0	4,054	1	14,074	0
Oceania		221,934	7	14,399	2	236,333	6
Of which:	Australia	216,465	7	12,157	2	228,622	6
	New Zealand	5,468	0	2,242	0	7,710	0
South America		32,575	1	8,327	1	40,902	1
Of which:	Chile	17,685	1	850	0	18,535	0
	Mexico	13,861	0	7,092	1	20,952	1
	Puerto Rico	1,029	0	386	0	1,414	0
Total		3,284,938	100	704,083	100	3,989,021	100

Source: Authors' own calculations.

Note: *United Kingdom* = United Kingdom excluding the self-governing dependencies (in italics).

descriptive statistics of the generated subsamples, in order to assess the viability of our estimation.

Table 13.6 shows the frequency and percentage of IPOs in the unbalanced sample. IPOs are rare events since the percentage of IPOs in the sample is equal to 3.13% (with 3,466 observations that assume the value of IPO = 1) versus a percentage of non-IPO observations that is 96.87% (106,643).

Tables 13.7 and 13.8 report the output that are respectively the logistic regression coefficients and the average marginal effects[2] (computed with the Delta method). An increase in each independent variable increases/decreases the likelihood that IPO = 1 (makes that outcome more/less likely). In particular, an increase in TA, revenues, employees, and tax makes the outcome of 1 less likely; and vice versa, an increase in TSE and ROA makes the outcome of 1 more likely. This confirms that IPO companies are smaller than those that carry out seasoned equity offerings and that companies that raise capital on public markets subsequently grow.

Lastly, we compute the predict probability for each observation (table 13.9), that is:

$$\hat{p} = \text{pr}\left[y = 1 | x \right] = F(x'\hat{\beta})$$

The table shows the consistency of the results, since the predicted probability (which indicates the likelihood of $y = 1$) of an IPO is on average very close to the one included in our sample (0.032931 is the estimation vs. 0.0313019 that is the original average computed on the sample).

Table 13.4
Amount raised on the market (ISIN sample, number of transactions).

Continent	Nation	Follow-on		IPOs		Total	
		N	%	N	%	N	%
North America		7,905	29	1,236	24	9,141	28
Of which:	United States	7,401	27	1,213	23	8,614	26
	Canada	504	2	23	0	527	2
Europe		11,256	41	2,275	44	13,531	41
Of which:	United Kingdom	4,839	17	749	15	5,588	17
Of which:	United Kingdom	4,641	17	692	13	5,333	16
	Jersey	91	0	32	1	123	0
	Guernsey	67	0	16	0	83	0
	Isle of Man	39	0	8	0	47	0
	Falkland Is	1	0	1	0	2	0
EU19 (Euro Area)		3,631	13	887	17	4,518	14
Of which:	France	1,049	4	315	6	1,364	4
	Germany	920	3	161	3	1,081	3
	Italy	289	1	114	2	403	1
	Spain	302	1	49	1	351	1
	Netherlands	262	1	58	1	320	1
	Belgium	172	1	47	1	219	1
	Finland	162	1	38	1	200	1
	Ireland	162	1	23	0	185	1
	Austria	107	0	21	0	128	0
	Luxembourg	67	0	34	1	101	0
	Greece	72	0	11	0	83	0
	Portugal	58	0	6	0	64	0
	Estonia	4	0	7	0	11	0
	Slovenia	5	0	2	0	7	0
	Slovakia		0	1	0	1	0
Other EU27		1,806	7	398	8	2,204	7
Of which:	Sweden	1,109	4	144	3	1,253	4
	Poland	509	2	209	4	718	2
	Denmark	176	1	33	1	209	1
	Hungary	4	0	5	0	9	0
	Faroe Islands	4	0	4	0	8	0
	Czech Republic	4	0	3	0	7	0
Non-EU Europe		980	4	241	5	1,221	4
Of which:	Norway	500	2	87	2	587	2
	Turkey	259	1	109	2	368	1
	Switzerland	212	1	44	1	256	1
	Iceland	9	0	1	0	10	0

(continued)

Table 13.4 (continued)

Continent	Nation	Follow-on		IPOs		Total	
		N	%	N	%	N	%
Asia		4,013	15	1,428	28	5,441	17
Of which:	Japan	2,621	9	1,205	23	3,826	12
	Korea	1,125	4	167	3	1,292	4
	Israel	267	1	56	1	323	1
Oceania		4,318	16	196	4	4,514	14
Of which:	Australia	4,179	15	180	3	4,359	13
	New Zealand	139	1	16	0	155	0
South America		174	1	29	1	203	1
Of which:	Chile	101	0	7	0	108	0
	Mexico	66	0	21	0	87	0
	Puerto Rico	7	0	1	0	8	0
Total		27,666	100	5,164	100	32,830	100

Source: Authors' own calculations.

Note: *United Kingdom* = United Kingdom excluding the self-governing dependencies (in italics).

Table 13.5
Descriptive statistics of dependent and independent variables.

Variable	Obs	Mean	Standard Deviation	Min	Max
IPO	110,089	.0313019	.1741333	0	1
TA	110,089	6.58e+10	1.01e+12	−1	9.30e+13
Revenues	110,089	5.48e+10	1.04e+12	−373,452	1.21e+14
Employees	110,088	215,4561	1.06e+07	0	9.99e+07
TSE	110,089	1.89e+10	2.41e+11	−4.12e+11	1.81e+13
ROA	110,089	−549,798.4	6,295,996	−1.00e+08	9.17e+07
Tax	110,089	1,210,760	1.87e+07	−1.99e+08	2.14e+09

Source: Authors' own calculations.

Table 13.6
Frequency and percentage of IPOs, unbalanced sample.

IPO	Frequency	Percent	Cumulative Percent
0	106,643	96.87	96.87
1	3,446	3.13	100.00
Total	110,089	100.00	

Source: Authors' own calculations.

Table 13.7
Logistic regression, coefficients.

IPO	Coefficient	Standard Error	z	P > |z|	[95% Conf. Interval]	
TA	−2.50e − 12	7.88e − 13	−3.17	0.002***	−4.05e − 12	−9.55e − 13
Revenues	−5.73e − 13	5.97e − 13	−0.96	0.337	−1.74e − 12	5.97e − 13
Employees	−4.64e − 9	1.86e − 9	−2.50	0.013**	−8.29e − 9	−9.99e − 10
TSE	3.34e − 12	1.19e − 12	2.80	0.005***	1.00e − 12	5.68e − 12
ROA	1.55e − 8	3.55e − 9	4.37	0.000***	8.55e − 9	2.25e − 8
Tax	−2.27e − 8	1.45e − 8	1.56	0.118	−5.10e − 8	5.73e − 9
cons	−3.382125	.017924	−188.69	0.000***	−341.726	−3.346993

Source: Authors' own calculations.
Note: Number of obs = 110,088; LR chi2(3) = 148.22; Prob > chi2 = 0.0000; Log likelihood = −15,251.122; Pseudo R2 = 0.0048.

Table 13.8
Logistic regression, average marginal effects (Delta method).

IPO	dy/dx	Standard Error	z	P > |z|	[95% Conf. Interval]	
TA	−7.57e − 14	2.39e − 14	−3.17	0.002***	−1.23e − 13	−2.89e − 14
Revenues	−1.73e − 14	1.81e − 14	−0.96	0.337	−5.28e − 14	1.81e − 14
Employees	−1.41e − 10	5.63e − 11	−2.50	0.013**	−2.51e − 10	3.02e − 11
TSE	1.01e − 13	3.62e − 14	2.79	0.005***	3.02e − 14	1.72e − 13
ROA	4.70e − 10	1.08e − 10	4.36	0.000***	2.58e − 10	6.81e − 10
TAX	−6.86e − 10	4.39e − 10	−1.56	0.118	−1.55e − 09	1.74e − 10

Source: Authors' own calculations.

Table 13.9 also shows the results in terms of suitability of the analysis. Running this model, we obtain that predicted variables are correct in almost 97% of cases. This very high value is obtained due to the bias that we outlined above.

Hence, we apply a prior correction to our sample and rerun the model (see tables 13.10–13.13). We find in table 13.11 the same relationship signs in the coefficients of the regression as in the balanced sample, but the estimation results are much more reliable since the proportion of IPOs in the sample is equal to 50%—that is, the same as non-IPO observations. Indeed, table 13.13 shows that the estimation of the dependent variable is likewise very close to the original IPO distribution (4.99 vs. 5), and prediction power (with a significance level of 0.5) shows that our estimation can correctly classify the dependent variable in almost the 70% of the cases. These results are consistent with those we obtained using numerous other randomly generated comparison samples.

Table 13.9
Logistic regression, estimation results.

Variable	Observations	Mean	Standard Deviation	Min	Max
IPO	110,089	0.0313019	0.1741333	0	1
plogit	110,088	0.0312931	0.0053605	0	0.123395

Classified	True D	$\sim D$	Total
+	0	0	0
−	3,445	106,643	110,088
Total	3,445	106,643	110,088

Classified + if predicted $\Pr(D) \geq 0.5$
True D defined as IPO $! = 0$

Sensitivity	$\Pr(+ \mid D)$	0.00%
Specificity	$\Pr(- \mid \sim D)$	100.00%
Positive predictive value	$\Pr(D \mid +)$	−%
Negative predictive value	$\Pr(\sim D \mid -)$	96.87%
False + rate for true $\sim D$	−2.50 $\Pr(+ \mid \sim D)$	0.00%
False − rate for true D	$\Pr(- \mid D)$	100.00%
False + rate for classified +	$\Pr(\sim D \mid +)$	−%
False − rate for classified −	$\Pr(D \mid -)$	3.13%
Correctly classified		96.87%

Source: Authors' own calculations.

Table 13.10
Frequency and percentage of IPOs, balanced sample.

IPO	Frequency	%	Cumulative %
0	3,446	50.00	50.00
1	3,446	50.00	100.00
Total	6,892	100.00	

Source: Authors' own calculations.

Table 13.11
Logistic regression in balanced sample, coefficients.

IPO	Coefficient	Standard Error	z	$P > \lvert z \rvert$	[95% Conf. Interval]	
TA	−6.53e−12	3.13e−12	−2.08	0.037**	−1.27e−11	−3.89e−13
Revenues	−1.62e−8	4.05e−9	−4.01	0.000***	−2.42e−0	−8.30e−9
Employees	−3.08e−8	2.48e−9	−12.41	0.000***	−3.57e−8	−2.59e−8
TSE	1.35e−8	7.75e−9	1.74	0.081*	−1.68e−9	2.87e−8
ROA	3.77e−8	8.85e−9	4.25	0.000***	2.03e−8	5.50e−8
Tax	−6.77e−8	6.65e−8	−1.02	0.309	−1.98e−7	6.27e−8
Cons	0.0421498	0.0269886	1.56	0.118	−0.0107468	0.0950464

Source: Authors' own calculations.

Table 13.12
Logistic regression in balanced sample, average marginal effects (Delta method).

IPO	dy/dx	Standard Error	z	$P > |z|$	[95% Conf. Interval]	
TA	$-1.55e-12$	$7.42e-13$	-2.09	$0.037**$	$-3.00e-12$	$-9.41e-14$
Revenues	$-3.85e-9$	$9.58e-10$	-4.02	$0.000***$	$-5.73e-9$	$-1.98e-9$
Employees	$-7.31e-9$	$5.66e-10$	-12.91	$0.000***$	$-8.41e-9$	$-6.20e-9$
TSE	$3.20e-9$	$1.84e-9$	1.74	$0.081*$	$-3.95e-10$	$6.80e-9$
ROA	$8.93e-9$	$2.09e-9$	4.27	$0.000***$	$4.83e-9$	$1.30e-8$
Tax	$-1.61e-8$	$1.58e-8$	-1.02	0.309	$-4.70e-8$	$1.49e-8$

Source: Authors' own calculations.

Table 13.13
Logistic regression in balanced sample, estimation results.

Variable	Observations	Mean	Standard Deviation	Min	Max
IPO	6,892	0.5	0.5000363	0	1
plogit	6,891	0.4999274	0.1128982	0.003984	1

		True		
Classified	D	$\sim D$		Total
+	3,273	2,168		5,441
−	172	1,278		1,450
Total	3,445	3,446		6,891

Classified + if predicted $Pr(D) \geq 0.5$
True D defined as IPO! $= 0$

Sensitivity	$Pr(+ \mid D)$	95.01%
Specificity	$Pr(- \mid \sim D)$	37.09%
Positive predictive value	$Pr(D \mid +)$	60.15%
Negative predictive value	$Pr(\sim D \mid -)$	88.14%
False + rate for true $\sim D$	$-2.50\ Pr(+ \mid \sim D)$	62.91%
False—rate for true D	$Pr(- \mid D)$	4.99%
False + rate for classified +	$Pr(\sim D \mid +)$	39.85%
False—rate for classified −	$Pr(D \mid -)$	11.86%
Correctly classified	66.04%	

Source: Authors' own calculations.

Conclusions

One of the key objectives of the CMU is to ensure that European SMEs have access to public markets to raise equity, which in turn is key to support their growth (Brogi and Lagasio 2017). Our descriptive statistics of IPOs all over the world show considerably lower primary equity offerings on the public markets in the EU27 (and even more so in the euro area) compared to the United States. This confirms the need for a CMU, an even more important imperative considering the exit from the EU of the most active public market in Europe.

Our investigation shows that in IPOs all over the world there is a large portion of SMEs and that, by going public and raising equity on the market, listed SMEs tend to grow.

The results of the logistic regression analysis show that equity and profitability increase the probability of going public, with a high level of significance. This is consistent with Pagano, Panetta, and Zingales (1998), who find that "IPOs ... tend to involve companies that before the IPO grew faster and were more profitable" (p. 29). Conversely, taxation is negatively related to the probability of going public, even though this result is not statistically significant.

More analyses could be conducted on this sample, and in particular, on the growth patterns of SMEs once they are listed. From this standpoint it would be useful to verify if there is a path that starts from a listing on a specialized SME market (a growth multilateral trading facility) and moves on to the full-fledged stock market. If this is not the case, the creation of specialized SME growth markets might represent a further source of fragmentation.

Future research could also investigate the net amount raised on the markets by also considering the flows from the companies to their shareholders (through dividends or buybacks) as in Doidge et al. (2018).

Notes

1. "The category of micro, small and medium-sized enterprises (SMEs) is made up of enterprises which employ fewer than 250 persons and which have an annual turnover not exceeding 50 million euro, and/or an annual balance sheet total not exceeding 43 million euro." Extract of Article 2 of the Annex of Recommendation 2003/361/EC in European Commission (2011).

2. The marginal effects reflect the change of the probability of $y = 1$ given a 1 unit change in an independent variable.

References

Amemiya, T. 1981. "Quantitative Response Models: A Survey." *Journal of Economic Literature* 19: 1483–1536.

Brogi, M., and V. Lagasio. 2017. "SME Sources of Funding: More Capital or More Debt to Sustain Growth? An Empirical Analysis." In *Access to Bank Credit and SME Financing*, edited by S. Rossi, 173–199. Basingstoke, UK: Palgrave Macmillan.

Bureau van Dijk. 2019. Website. https://www.bvdinfo.com/en-us.

Doidge, C., K. M. Kahle, G. A. Karolyi, and R. M. Stulz. 2018. "Eclipse of the Public Corporation or Eclipse of the Public Markets?" NBER Working Paper No. 24265, National Bureau of Economic Research, Cambridge, MA.

European Commission. 2011. *The New SME Definition: User Guide and Model Declaration.* Luxembourg: Publications Office of the European Union.

European Commission. 2015. *Communication from the Commission to the European Parliament, the Council, the European Economic and Social Committee and the Committee of the Regions: Action Plan on Building a Capital Markets Union.* Luxembourg: Publications Office of the European Union, COM (2015) 468.

European Commission. 2016. "Commission Proposes Major Corporate Tax Reform for the EU." Press release, European Commission, Strasbourg, October 25.

European Commission. 2017a. *Communication from the Commission to the European Parliament, the Council, the European Economic and Social Committee and the Committee of the Regions on the Mid-Term Review of the Capital Markets Union Action Plan.* Brussels: European Union, COM (2017) 292 final, June. https://ec.europa.eu/info/publications/mid-term-review-capital-markets -union-action-plan_en.

European Commission. 2017b. *Mid-Term Review of the Capital Markets Union Action Plan.* Brussels: European Union, COM (2017) 292 final, June. https://ec.europa.eu/info/publications /mid-term-review-capital-markets-union-action-plan_en.

European Commission. 2017c. "Regulation (EU) 2017/1129 of the European Parliament and of the Council of 14 June 2017 on the Prospectus to Be Published when Securities Are Offered to the Public or Admitted to Trading on a Regulated Market." *Official Journal of the European Union* L168/12.

European Commission. n.d. "Making It Easier for Companies to Enter and Raise Capital on Public Markets." https://ec.europa.eu/info/business-economy-euro/growth-and-investment/capital-markets -union/capital-markets-union-action-plan/making-it-easier-companies-enter-and-raise-capital -public-markets_en.

Fan, J., S. Titman, and G. Twite. 2012. "An International Comparison of Capital Structure and Debt Maturity Choices." *Journal of Financial and Quantitative Analysis* 47, no. 1: 23–56.

Frank, M. Z., and V. K. Goyal. 2003. "Testing the Pecking Order Theory of Capital Structure." *Journal of Financial Economics* 67, no. 2: 217–248.

Hackbarth, D., C. A. Hennessy, and H. E. Leland. 2007. "Can the Trade-off Theory Explain Debt Structure?" *Review of Financial Studies* 20, no. 5: 1389–1428.

Hurst, E., and B. W. Pugsley. 2011. "What Do Small Businesses Do?" NBER Working Paper No. 17041, National Bureau of Economic Research, Cambridge, MA.

King, G., and L. Zeng. 2001. "Logistic Regression in Rare Events Data." *Political Analysis* 9, no. 2: 137–163.

Lawless, M., B. O'Connell, and C. O'Toole. 2015. "Financial Structure and Diversification of European Firms." *Applied Economics* 47, no. 23: 2379–2398.

Myers, S. C. 1984. "The Capital Structure Puzzle." *Journal of Finance* 39, no. 3: 574–592.

Pagano, M., F. Panetta, and L. Zingales. 1998. "Why Do Companies Go Public? An Empirical Analysis." *Journal of Finance* 53, no. 1: 27–64.

Refinitiv. 2019. "SDC Platinum." Website. https://www.refinitiv.com/en/products/sdc-platinum -financial-securities/.

Strebulaev, I.A. 2007. "Do Tests of Capital Structure Theory Mean What They Say?" *Journal of Finance* 62, no. 4: 1747–1787.

Discussion: Taxation, the Level Playing Field, and Equity Markets

Giovanna Nicodano

Brogi and Lagasio (chapter 13 in this volume) highlight that equity markets remain an important source of funding for smaller companies worldwide. Their chapter also investigates the role of taxation in the listing decision. The European Commission touches upon this role as well, suggesting the spreading of tax incentives for venture capital (VC). It also addresses taxation more generally, proposing a common consolidated corporate tax base (CCCTB) for multinationals while supporting tax neutrality across funding forms (see European Commission 2017).

This discussion emphasizes taxation as a central pillar of the capital markets union (CMU) architecture. The first section highlights tax competition as a threat to the sustainability of the CMU, supporting the quick approval of CCCTB. The second section proceeds to examine tax incentives to equity market development, pointing to the advantages of subsidies to both start-ups and their listings in public markets.

CMU and Tax Competition

The CMU should allow firms and intermediaries to compete in a "level playing field" by homogenizing financial regulation and its enforcement. Unfortunately, tax competition destroys such a field.

Uniform regulation (and a single currency) make "beggar thy neighbor" tax policies more attractive for any individual member state if others react with delay. Aggregate outcomes are, however, undesirable. There may be convergence to zero tax rates with rising inequality and political instability. And legal barriers (see Alotti, Bianchi, and Micossi, chapter 19 in this volume) may emerge as a defensive measure in tax-disadvantaged countries, de facto emptying the CMU architecture. Alternatively, desertification in high-taxation countries can occur, with tensions and breakups within the euro area, due to the regulatory level playing field.

The voting mechanism within the European Union (EU) prevents the quick, necessary progress toward a CCCTB. Meanwhile, a paradoxical way to protect the CMU would be a country-contingent regulatory enforcement, tailored to ensure that the implicit regulatory burden weighs less in tax-disadvantaged states.

Tax Incentives toward Equity Market Development

The European Commission (2015) suggests tax reliefs for venture capital firms (VCs). Three reasons guide this recommendation. First, the decline in bank lending during the global financial crisis disproportionately affected younger firms. Secondly, the VC industry is smaller in the EU than in the United States. Third, members of the community advocate tax reliefs for risk reduction.

Unfortunately, VC investment occurs in waves, hardly playing the counter-cyclical role of distressed equity funds.[1] Moreover, transferring best practices across structurally different systems may have unintended effects. Finally, estimates show that tax reliefs due to leverage already account for 50% of the return to established private equity firms (see Acharya et al. 2013). The share due to their abnormal performance relative to public equity is lower (34%), casting some doubts on the cost-benefit rationale for spreading tax reliefs.

The correction of the tax privilege of debt is underway, usually through caps on interest deductions and notional interest deductions in proportion to equity. It is possible to consider tax incentives to VCs in this perspective, even though they privilege one specific source of equity capital. Direct subsidies to the listing of smaller firms are another alternative and generate positive externalities (Pagano 1989). They also indirectly help VCs exit without being subject to the criticism of ineffectiveness that tax reliefs to VCs may encounter.[2] Such listing subsidies would also nicely complement the European Commission's efforts to simplify listing and regulatory requirements for small issuers in the small- and medium-sized enterprise growth markets.

Another policy may dominate both previous measures by respecting the principle of tax neutrality of funding forms, and this would be tax rebates directly to start-ups, whose entry rates respond to the corporate tax rate (Da Rin, Di Giacomo, and Sembenelli 2011).

Notes

1. The 2016 Directive on Restructuring eases their action, which encountered legal barriers (see Valiante 2016).

2. See the debate (Armour and Cumming 2006 vs. Da Rin, Nicodano, and Sembenelli 2006, 2011; and Inderst 2006 vs. Sannino 2018).

References

Acharya, V., O. Gottschalg, M. Hahn, and C. Kehoe. 2013. "Corporate Governance and Value Creation: Evidence from Private Equity." *Review of Financial Studies* 26: 368–402.

Armour, J., and D. Cumming. 2006. "The Legislative Road to Silicon Valley." *Oxford Economic Papers* 58: 596–635.

Da Rin, M., M. Di Giacomo, and A. Sembenelli. 2011. "Entrepreneurship, Firm Entry and the Taxation of Corporate Income." *Journal of Public Economics* 95: 1048–1066.

Da Rin, M., G. Nicodano, and A. Sembenelli. 2006. "Public Policy and the Creation of Active Venture Capital Markets." *Journal of Public Economics* 90: 1699–1723.

Da Rin, M., G. Nicodano, and A. Sembenelli. 2011. "A Reply to Douglas Cumming's Review Essay: 'Public Policy and the Creation of Active Venture Capital Markets.'" *Venture Capital* 13: 95–98.

European Commission. 2015. *Effectiveness of Tax Incentives for Venture Capital and Business Angels to Foster the Investment of SMEs and Start-ups.* Brussels: European Union, TAXUD/2015/ DE/330.

European Commission. 2017. *Economic Analysis Accompanying the Document "Communication from the Commission to the European Parliament, the Council, the European Economic and Social Committee and the Committee of the Regions on the Mid-Term Review of the Capital Markets Union Action Plan."* Commission Staff Working Document SWD (2017) 224 final, June 8. Brussels: European Commission.

Inderst, R. 2006. "Public Policy, Early Stage Financing and Firm Growth." Working Paper, London School of Economics.

Pagano, M., 1989. "Endogenous Market Thinness and Stock Price Volatility." *Review of Economic Studies* 56: 269–287.

Sannino, F. 2018. "A Theory of Venture Capital Fund Size with Directed Search." Working paper, INSEAD.

Valiante, D. 2016. *Europe's Untapped Capital Market: Rethinking Financial Integration after the Crisis.* London: Rowman & Littlefield International.

14 Efforts to Deepen Capital Markets: Lessons from US Mortgage Defaults in the Global Financial Crisis

Sumit Agarwal, Gene Amromin, Itzhak Ben-David,
Souphala Chomsisengphet, and Douglas D. Evanoff

In 2014, in an attempt to further integrate European economic markets, the European Commission announced plans for a capital markets union (CMU). The goal was to allow households and firms in the European Union (EU) to have "access to markets at equal cost and equal legal treatment" regardless of where they were located. This was thought to have the potential to deepen capital markets, allowing firms to have alternative (nonbank) sources of financing and households to have new investment opportunities. It was also thought to have the potential to create a more robust and resilient financial system.[1] Efforts to revive and deepen the housing finance market was part of that effort—particularly through increasing the role of securitization.[2]

The United States has a lengthy history of efforts to expand housing finance. These include public programs to direct financing toward targeted markets (often low-income markets) and encouragement of public and private sector securitization of mortgage loans to further deepen the mortgage finance market. These efforts are undertaken because home ownership is typically thought to produce positive externalities (e.g., see Rossi-Hansberg, Sarte, and Owens 2010). These potential positive externalities are a reason for the traditionally strong public support for home ownership that are supported via tax subsidies, government guarantees, government-sponsored enterprises (GSEs), even US Federal Reserve System monetary policy activities.

However, the housing sector is also known to be cyclical and to be associated with periodic price bubbles.[3] The bursting of these bubbles can have negative externalities as housing prices are driven down and foreclosures increase. In the first decade of the twenty-first century, the boom and bust of the housing market and the subsequent financial crisis resulted in unprecedented mortgage delinquencies. That produced additional adverse spillover effects that further depressed home prices and increased mortgage defaults (e.g., see Campbell, Giglio, and Pathak 2011).

In this chapter we summarize the findings of a study analyzing the performance of mortgages in the United States during the 2008–2009 financial crisis.[4]

In particular, we study the market-based approaches to stem mounting mortgage losses by focusing on loans that became seriously delinquent in the six calendar quarters starting in the first quarter of 2008. This is before the introduction of public programs aimed at subsidizing struggling mortgage holders and, thus, captures the private market's response to the market disruption. How can the rising delinquencies be best managed? Should lenders and mortgage servicers move on their contractual rights to foreclose on delinquent loans, or might they be better off working with the troubled mortgagees to work out problem loans? How can economic losses best be mitigated? A common theme when discussing the US mortgage crisis in both the academic and popular press has been commentary on the scarcity of loan modifications relative to foreclosures in loss mitigation approaches. Much of the existing research has focused on the conflicts between servicers and lenders/investors to explain low modification rates.[5] For example, Agarwal et al. (2011b) document the role of securitization on loan modifications and show that securitization reduces the modification rate by 30%.[6] In this chapter we take a broader perspective and summarize the results from a study that documents the use, determinants, and success of a variety of loss mitigation practices used in the mortgage market. It may be that the US experience can provide lessons for efforts to more fully develop the mortgage finance markets across Europe.

We first describe the process of loss mitigation in the context of the financial crisis and study the determinants of each of the resolution methods. For the loans that were modified we further study the factors influencing changes in contractual terms. Finally, we evaluate the effect of various modification terms on the performance of the new mortgage contract following modification. For a more thorough description of the empirical tests undertaken and a documentation of the results of the analysis, the reader is referred to Agarwal et al. (2011a). We conclude with some potential policy considerations.

Loss Mitigation Practices

The loss mitigation process begins when a mortgage borrower becomes seriously delinquent or "in trouble." We define troubled mortgages as those that became sixty or more days past due or voluntarily entered a loss mitigation program. To ensure that our analysis correctly captures the timing of loss mitigation actions, we required all mortgages in our universe to be current as of the last quarter of 2007. After removing mortgages insured by the Federal Housing Administration and the US Department of Veterans Affairs, we identified about 1.7 million individual mortgages that became troubled during our sample period.[7]

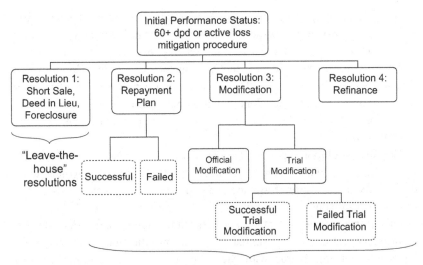

Figure 14.1
Loss mitigation resolutions. *Note*: dpd = days past due.

Figure 14.1 presents a summary chart of different resolution types. Loss mitigation resolutions include four major types of actions that lenders and servicers typically take, some allowing the resident to "stay in the house" and others requiring that they "leave the house."[8] The first class of interventions is liquidation. This includes liquidation of the property in agreement with the borrower through deeds in lieu or short sales, as well as completed foreclosures. Deed in lieu is the process where the borrower transfers the property interest to the lender and thus avoids the legal process of forced foreclosure through the courts. In a short sale, the lender and borrower agree to sell the property (typically at a loss) and transfer the proceeds to the lender who then writes off the balance of the mortgage loan. In foreclosures, the lender takes legal steps to pursue its interest in the property through the courts.

The second type of loss mitigation identified in the data is repayment plans. Under a repayment plan, delinquent borrowers commit to pay back the missing payments over several months (typically three to six months). Once the arrears are paid off, the lender reinstates the borrower status as current. The purpose is to allow the borrower to work through difficult times but to continue to stay in the house. In this type of intervention, the terms of the original loan are maintained.

The next loss mitigation practice depicted in figure 14.1 is loan modifications. The distinguishing feature of loan modifications is the amendment of the original mortgage terms. The usual process has the lender independently offering the borrower a new set of loan terms or negotiating new terms with the borrower. This process can be quite lengthy, as it requires collection of relevant documentary evidence and subsequent negotiations. Modification may also proceed in stages, with a borrower first committing to a trial offer for a certain period of time. Conditional on being able to fulfill the terms of a trial contract, the modification offer can be made permanent. These stages are reflected in the figure.

The final resolution type presented in figure 14.1 is refinancing. Refinancing of distressed loans is similar to the usual refinancing but may need to be done on the basis of more forgiving underwriting criteria, such as higher than typical loan-to-value (LTV) ratios—otherwise the mortgagee could have initiated the refinancing at current market rates without interacting with the lender. In principle, refinancing is similar to a loan modification, as it effectively replaces an existing contract with a new one. However, it may allow the lender greater flexibility in selling off the loan.

Mortgage Modification Determinants and Effectiveness

Table 14.1 presents summary statistics about resolution types offered to troubled mortgages by vintage—that is, the quarter in which mortgages entered the sample. The panel shows three main results: (1) a large share of loans in the troubled sample do not enter any loss mitigation process (over 40% of loans within six months), (2) liquidations play by far the dominant role in observed loss mitigation practices (over 30% within the first six months), and (3) self-cure rates are relatively low (about 11% after six months).

For instance, among loans that enter our sample in the first quarter of 2008, 14.6% are in ongoing foreclosure proceedings within three months (panel A). An additional 6.1% have gotten liquidated through a formal loss mitigation process, and a similar fraction has been modified. Repayment plans and refinancing are very rare, accounting for less than 3% of all troubled loan resolutions. About 11% of borrowers self-cure—that is, resume paying and cover past arrears. More strikingly, nearly 60% of all loans in the sample are not in any resolution process—liquidation or not—within the first three months.

As the horizon for work-out resolutions increases to six months (panel B), the share of completed liquidations through loss mitigation programs rises rapidly to 16%. Other work-out resolutions increase as well, with modifications reaching 9.4% of all loans. Yet, even after six months, nearly a half of all troubled loans (45.8%) are not in loss mitigation or foreclosure proceed-

Table 14.1
Resolution outcomes, by quarter of entry into the sample.

The table presents the resolutions (or no action) of borrowers who became "in trouble" in a particular calendar quarter. Panels A (B, C, D) present the outcomes within 3 (6, 9, and 12) months. The base sample is the universe of residential mortgages serviced by the largest nineteen banks in the United States. The subsample that we study here contains observations of mortgages that became 60+ days past due or entered loss mitigation programs (collectively called "loans in trouble") between January 2008 and May 2009.

Panel A: Resolution within 3 months

	Quarter				
	2008Q1	2008Q2	2008Q3	2008Q4	2009Q1
No. of borrowers in trouble in cohort	309,356	322,498	287,799	341,935	238,475
In foreclosure process	14.6%	13.1%	11.6%	20.2%	23.9%
Liquidation	6.1%	0.6%	0.5%	0.6%	0.9%
Total "leave the house"	20.7%	13.8%	12.1%	20.8%	24.8%
Repayment	1.5%	0.9%	1.1%	1.9%	3.7%
Modification	6.9%	6.4%	4.9%	9.7%	9.2%
Refinance	1.3%	1.3%	1.1%	1.2%	1.7%
Total "stay in the house"	9.7%	8.6%	7.1%	12.8%	14.7%
Self-cure	11.6%	13.3%	14.4%	12.6%	9.5%
No action	58.0%	64.4%	66.4%	53.8%	51.0%

Panel B: Resolution within 6 months

	Quarter				
	2008Q1	2008Q2	2008Q3	2008Q4	Total 2008
No. of borrowers in trouble in cohort	309,356	322,498	287,799	341,935	1,261,588
In foreclosure process	16.4%	19.5%	23.9%	28.4%	22.2%
Liquidation	16.1%	9.1%	5.0%	3.8%	8.4%
Total "leave the house"	32.5%	28.6%	28.9%	32.2%	30.6%
Repayment	2.0%	1.8%	2.6%	3.2%	2.4%
Modification	9.4%	9.7%	9.4%	12.7%	10.4%
Refinance	2.1%	2.5%	1.8%	2.2%	2.2%
Total "stay in the house"	13.5%	14.0%	13.8%	18.1%	15.0%
Self-cure	8.2%	11.9%	12.7%	12.1%	11.2%
No action	45.8%	45.5%	44.6%	37.6%	43.2%

(continued)

Table 14.1 (continued)
Panel C: Resolution within 9 months

	Quarter		
	2008Q1	2008Q2	2008Q3
No. of borrowers in trouble in cohort	309,356	322,498	287,799
In foreclosure process	17.7%	23.0%	30.1%
Liquidation	26.7%	17.3%	10.4%
Total "leave the house"	44.3%	40.3%	40.5%
Repayment	2.9%	2.8%	4.1%
Modification	12.1%	13.5%	12.5%
Refinance	2.8%	3.2%	3.2%
Total "stay in the house"	17.8%	19.5%	19.9%
Self-cure	7.6%	9.5%	10.6%
No action	30.2%	30.7%	29.1%

Panel D: Resolution within 12 months

	Quarter	
	2008Q1	2008Q2
No. of borrowers in trouble in cohort	309,356	322,498
In foreclosure process	18.8%	25.8%
Liquidation	34.8%	22.0%
Total "leave the house"	53.6%	47.7%
Repayment	3.6%	3.7%
Modification	14.7%	15.7%
Refinance	3.2%	4.4%
Total "stay in the house"	21.6%	23.8%
Self-cure	5.3%	7.2%
No action	19.6%	21.3%

ings. At this early date, the servicers appear somewhat overwhelmed at the sheer volume of delinquencies.

Loss mitigation liquidations of the 2008:Q1 vintage troubled loans accelerate further to 35% by the end of the twelve-month window (panel D), and modifications rise to nearly 15%. At that point, nearly three-quarters of all troubled loans are being acted on, with the lion's share of resolutions—71%—coming in the form of loan liquidations.[9] Only 5.3% of this vintage of loans self-cure (which is what the servicers are hoping for) in the year following default.

A qualitatively similar picture emerges for other vintages of troubled loans. One important difference, however, lies in the speed at which foreclosure proceedings become converted into liquidating resolutions. This contrast is illustrated by comparing shares of resolved and unresolved foreclosure proceedings over a six-month window (panel B) for loans that become troubled at the beginning and the end of 2008. Among the 2008:Q1 troubled loans, an equal share (16%) get resolved through liquidation or are in the process of foreclosure. Among the 2008:Q4 vintage, however, 28% of loans are still in foreclosure proceedings, while only 4% reach a liquidating resolution. This is strongly suggestive of a system that has trouble resolving the flood of nonperforming loans through existing loss mitigation channels. Each subsequent vintage brings in more troubled loans over the number that could be addressed in any fashion during the preceding period. The resulting build-up clogs the system even further. Arguably, it may also take away resources from the more labor- and information-intensive loss mitigation approaches that result in keeping troubled borrowers in their homes, such as modifications and repayment plans.

To understand the drivers of high redefault rates and means by which modification success can be improved, we use multivariate[10] analysis to analyze the determinants of redefault and the relationship between modification terms and redefault after controlling for a number of key borrower and loan characteristics. Summarily, we find that redefault rates are higher for low documentation loans. Further, redefault rates decline with FICO scores and increase with LTV ratios. We note, however, that the association of FICO with redefault is 2.5 times larger than the effect of leverage on redefault.

Next, we analyze the determinants of modification terms and their association with post-modification default. While we find some variation in the characteristics of borrowers at loan origination and at the time they enter the loss mitigation process, this variation is dwarfed by differences in servicer modification practices and redefault rates following modification. In fact, servicer fixed effects explain at least as much variation in modification terms as do borrower characteristics. This strongly suggests that servicer loss mitigation choices are driven by institutional factors as well as by variation in their underlying borrower populations. We also document that over the course of the period studied, there is some convergence in modification terms across servicers, which may perhaps be attributed to learning. Interestingly, concessions in modification terms are more generous for borrowers with weaker characteristics (e.g., FICO scores and LTV ratios) at the time of becoming delinquent.

Further, we find a strong relationship between modification terms and subsequent probability of redefault. In particular, greater reductions in loan interest rates (or monthly payments) are associated with sizable declines in redefault rates. As an illustration, a reduction of a 1% point in the interest rate is associated with a 3.9% point drop in the six-month redefault rate. Given that modification terms are more favorable to weaker borrowers, we view this effect as a likely lower bound for the causal effect of affordability on the likelihood of redefault.

Overall, our results suggest that affordability is a prime driver of redefault following modifications. Anything that can be done to resolve this problem and avoid liquidation of the mortgage could be beneficial to both lenders and borrowers; see Pennington-Cross (2006) and Cordell et al. (2008, 2009) who argue that the recovery rates from foreclosed mortgages are so low that significant concessions could be made in a number of work-outs and still be beneficial to both borrowers and lenders. Cordell et al. (2008) argue that 50% or more of the outstanding mortgage balances have been lost in foreclosures during the mortgage crisis period. Pennington-Cross finds that foreclosed properties depreciate on average some 22% relative to the typical, nonforeclosed property. Additionally, Moody's Investor Services suggests that the differences in realized losses and strategies vary significantly across servicers, something that is consistent with our finding of significant heterogeneity across servicers (e.g., see Moody's Investor Services 2008a, 2008b, 2009a, 2009b). Our findings, and the above studies, provide support for the motivation (to help with affordability) behind the Home Affordable Modification Program, initiated in the United States in 2009.

Potential Public Policy Implications

As discussed earlier, it is generally believed that there are positive externalities associated with home ownership. However, housing is a very cyclical industry and is prone to the building up of asset price bubbles, and when they burst, they can have significant adverse spillover effects. Following the financial crisis and the resulting Great Recession, financial regulators realized a need to address sources and causes of systemic risk. The mortgage-backed securities sector, including the servicing of those mortgages, could be one such sector. Just as there are efforts to more fully develop and unify capital markets across Europe, one can argue that the presence of potential negative externalities should encourage efforts to effectively regulate the sector to minimize potential problems from systemic risk.

There are a number of ways to address such risk. As the capital market union is encouraged across Europe, consideration could be given to having servicers display the ability to respond to disruptive markets. One such method would be to require participants to periodically be able to convince regulators that they have a plan in place to address future disruptions in mortgage markets. Similar to the living will requirement in the United States, this would force mortgage servicers to be forward looking and have a plan for operating efficiently during troubled times. These companies would have to satisfy regulators that they are prepared for future crises.[11] The findings from our study, as well as those of Cordell et al. (2008) and Pennington-Cross (2006), suggest that there is a potential for significant benefits from such a policy.

Conclusion

In this chapter we have reviewed a study of loss mitigation practices used by mortgage servicers and lenders prior to the introduction of government programs to provide help to financially struggling homeowners. Our results show that the majority of loans in trouble end up in liquidation, although the importance of liquidation has diminished somewhat over time. We also find that securitized loans are less likely to be modified, consistent with the idea that agency conflicts inhibit aggressive corrective actions. In addition, we document that there is wide variation in the loss mitigation practices of servicers and that this variation converged somewhat over time, possibly due to learning.

An important policy issue is determining the effect of modification terms on redefault rates. We find a statistically significant and economically sizable association between greater reductions in monthly payments and/or loan interest rates and subsequent redefault. These results are consistent with the driving idea behind the Home Affordable Modification Program. In this program, servicers and lenders are incentivized to increase mortgage affordability as much as possible. However, the advantages of this program need to be contrasted with the cost to investors (or lenders) resulting from the lower payment.

While we encourage the expansion and deepening of capital markets in Europe (including that of the mortgage finance markets) by introducing and expanding the CMU, there should also be efforts to ensure that supervisory oversight is adequate. This is particularly true for a sector that is known to have potential negative externalities resulting from potential systemic risk from adverse spillover effects during troubled times—that is, during the housing and financial crises. We offer one means of addressing such concerns.

Notes

The authors thank Gadi Barlevy, Jeff Campbell, Scott Frame, Dennis Glennon, Victoria Ivashina, Bruce Krueger, Mark Levonian, Chris Mayer, Tarun Ramadorai, Nick Souleles, James Wilds, Paul Willen, Steve Zeldes, and participants at the "Capital Markets Union and Beyond" conference sponsored by Imperial College London for constructive comments. Regina Villasmil and Ross Dillard provided excellent research assistance. The views presented in the chapter are those of the authors and do not necessarily reflect those of the Federal Reserve Bank of Chicago, the Federal Reserve System, the Office of the Comptroller of the Currency, or the US Department of the Treasury.

1. For background on the plan and its current status, see Allen and Pástor, chapter 1 in this volume.

2. See Council of the European Union (2017).

3. See Evanoff, Kaufman, and Malliaris (2012); Evanoff and Malliaris (2018); and Posen (2018).

4. For a more detailed discussion of the mortgage default experience during this period, see Agarwal et al. (2011b) and Mayer, Pence, and Sherlund (2009).

5. Gelpern and Levitin (2009) and Stegman et al. (2007) argue that securitization contracts are written in a way that does not allow easy modification. Stegman et al. also find large variation in servicer ability to cure delinquencies, implying that poor servicing quality translated into higher default rates. The theme of conflicting servicer and investor incentives is echoed in Eggert (2007) and Goodman (2009). Magder (2009) goes farthest in claiming that these conflicts of interest are *the* reason for low modification rates.

6. Our work fits well with alternative policy proposals for problems in mortgage markets. Mayer and Hubbard (2010) focus on household inability to refinance their mortgages, which impedes their ability to continue making payments. They consequently propose a streamlined and concerted effort on part of the GSEs to effect refinancing of mortgages guaranteed by the federal government. Posner and Zingales (2009) propose a plan in which the lenders reduce the principal for troubled borrowers and in exchange take an equity position in the home. More broadly, our work is related to the growing literature on explaining the crisis and mortgage foreclosures: see Agarwal and Ben-David (2018); Agarwal, Chang, and Yavas (2012); Agarwal et al. (2011b, 2014, 2017, 2018, 2019, forthcoming); Ben-David (2011); Ben-David et al. (2019); Campbell, Giglio, and Pathak (2011); Keys et al. (2010); Mayer and Hubbard (2010); and Mian and Sufi (2009).

7. For our analysis we use the OCC/OTS Mortgage Metrics data set that includes origination and servicing information for large US mortgage servicers owned by large banks supervised by the Office of the Comptroller of the Currency (OCC), as well as large thrifts overseen by the former Office of Thrift Supervision (OTS). The data consist of monthly observations of over 34 million mortgages totaling US$6 trillion, which make up about 64% of US residential mortgages. Each mortgage record includes its borrower and loan characteristics at the time of origination, the date on which it became in trouble, and updated borrower and loan characteristics. Critically, for modifications, the data contain information about the modified terms and repayment behavior. The ability to observe loan status on a monthly basis also allows us to evaluate post-modification mortgage performance. The data also allow us to differentiate (but not identify) nineteen servicing entities, each of which maintains effective autonomy in making loss mitigation decisions regardless of their ultimate corporate ownership. The study spans the period between October 2007 and May 2009. There is no restriction on origination date.

8. Crews Cutts and Merrill (2008) provide an overview of the different types of interventions.

9. $53.6\% \div (53.6\% + 21.6\%) = 71\%$.

10. Again, the reader is directed to Agarwal et al. (2011a).

11. One criticism of such an approach would be that the regulators and servicers may be attempting to address the last crisis while future problems may be very different than those that occurred previously.

References

Agarwal, Sumit, Gene Amromin, Itzhak Ben-David, Souphala Chomsisengphet, and Douglas D. Evanoff. 2011a. "Market-Based Loss Mitigation Practices for Troubled Mortgages Following the Financial Crisis." Federal Reserve Bank of Chicago Working Paper No. 2011-03, February.

Agarwal, Sumit, Gene Amromin, Itzhak Ben-David, Souphala Chomsisengphet, and Douglas D. Evanoff. 2011b. "Role of Securitization in Mortgage Renegotiation." *Journal of Financial Economics* 102, no. 3: 559–578.

Agarwal, Sumit, Gene Amromin, Itzhak Ben-David, Souphala Chomsisengphet, and Douglas D. Evanoff. 2014. "Predatory Lending and the Subprime Crisis." *Journal of Financial Economics* 113, no. 1: 29–59.

Agarwal, Sumit, Gene Amromin, Itzhak Ben-David, Souphala Chomsisengphet, and Douglas D. Evanoff. Forthcoming. "Financial Education versus Costly Counseling: How to Dissuade Borrowers from Choosing Risky Mortgages?" *American Economic Journal: Economic Policy.*

Agarwal, Sumit, Gene Amromin, Itzhak Ben-David, Souphala Chomsisengphet, Tomasz Piskorski, and Amit Seru. 2017. "Policy Intervention in Debt Renegotiation: Evidence from the Home Affordable Modification Program." *Journal of Political Economy* 125, no. 3: 654–712.

Agarwal, Sumit, Gene Amromin, Itzhak Ben-David, Souphala Chomsisengphet, and Yan Zhang. 2019. "Holdup by Junior Claimholders: Evidence from the Mortgage Market." *Journal of Financial and Quantitative Analysis* 54, no. 1: 247–274.

Agarwal, Sumit, Gene Amromin, Itzhak Ben-David, and Serdar Dinc. 2018. "The Politics of Foreclosures." *Journal of Finance* 73, no. 6: 2677–2717.

Agarwal, Sumit, and Itzhak Ben-David. 2018. "Loan Prospecting and the Loss of Soft Information." *Journal of Financial Economics* 129, no. 3: 608–628.

Agarwal, Sumit, Yan Chang, and Abdullah Yavas. 2012. "Securitization and Adverse Selection in Mortgage Lending." *Journal of Financial Economics* 105, no. 3: 640–660.

Campbell, John Y., Stefano Giglio, and Parag Pathak. 2011. "Forced Sales and House Prices." *American Economic Review* 101, no. 5: 2108–2131.

Ben-David, Itzhak. 2011. "Financial Constraints and Inflated Home Prices during the Real Estate Boom." *American Economic Journal: Applied Economics* 3, no. 3: 55–87.

Ben-David, Itzhak, Pascal Towbin, and Sebastian Weber. 2019. "Expectations during the US Housing Boom: Inferring Beliefs from Vacant Homes." Working Paper, The Ohio State University.

Cordell, Larry, Karen Dynan, Andreas Lehnert, Nellie Liang, and Eileen Mauskopf. 2008. "The Incentives of Mortgage Servicers: Myths and Realities." Finance and Economics Discussion Series 2008-46, Board of Governors of the Federal Reserve System, Washington, DC.

Cordell, Larry, Karen Dynan, Andreas Lehnert, Nellie Liang, and Eileen Mauskopf. 2009. "Designing Loan Modifications to Address the Mortgage Crisis and the Making Home Affordable Program." Finance and Economics Discussion Series 2009-43, Board of Governors of the Federal Reserve System, Washington, DC.

Council of the European Union. 2017. "Capital Markets Union: Council Adopts Securitisation Rules." Press release no. 672/17, November 20, Brussels, Belgium.

Crews Cutts, Amy, and William A. Merrill. 2008. "Interventions in Mortgage Default: Policies and Practices to Prevent Home Loss and Lower Costs." Working Paper UCC08-15, Harvard University, Cambridge, MA, March.

Eggert, Kurt. 2007. "Comment on Michael A. Stegman et al.'s 'Preventive Servicing Is Good for Business and Affordable Homeownership Policy: What Prevents Loan Modifications?'" *Housing Policy Debate* 18, no. 2: 279–297.

Evanoff, Douglas D., George G. Kaufman, and A .G. Malliaris. 2012. "New Perspectives on Asset Price Bubbles: An Overview." In *New Perspectives on Asset Price Bubbles*, edited by Douglas D. Evanoff, George G. Kaufman, and A. G. Malliaris, 3–10. Oxford: Oxford University Press.

Evanoff, Douglas D., and A. G. Malliaris. 2018. "Asset Bubbles and Public Policy." In *Public Policy & Financial Economics*, edited by Douglas D. Evanoff, George G. Kaufman, and A. G. Malliaris, 197–246. Hackensack, NJ: World Scientific Publishing.

Gelpern, Anna, and Adam J. Levitin. 2009. "Rewriting Frankenstein Contracts: Workout Prohibitions in Residential Mortgage-Backed Securities." *Southern California Law Review* 82: 1075–1152.

Goodman, Peter S. 2009. "Lucrative Fees May Deter Efforts to Alter Loans." *New York Times*, July 30.

Keys, Benjamin, Tanmoy Mukherjee, Amit Seru, and Vikrant Vig. 2010. "Did Securitization Lead to Lax Screening? Evidence from Subprime Loans." *Quarterly Journal of Economics* 125: 307–362.

Magder, Dan. 2009. "Mortgage Loan Modifications: Program Incentives and Restructuring Design." Working Paper 09-13, Peterson Institute for International Economics, Washington, DC, November.

Mayer, Christopher, and R. Glenn Hubbard. 2010. "House Prices, Interest Rates, and the Mortgage Market Meltdown." Working Paper, Columbia University, New York.

Mayer, Christopher, Karen Pence, and Shane M. Sherlund. 2009. "The Rise in Mortgage Defaults." *Journal of Economic Perspectives* 23, no. 1: 27–50.

Mian, Atif, and Amir Sufi. 2009. "The Consequences of Mortgage Credit Expansion: Evidence from the U.S. Mortgage Default Crisis." *Quarterly Journal of Economics* 124, no. 4: 1449–1496.

Moody's Investor Services. 2008a. "CitiMortgage Inc. Master Servicing." Servicer report, July 7.

Moody's Investor Services. 2008b. "National City Lending Services, a Division of National City Bank." Servicer report, May 9.

Moody's Investor Services. 2009a. "Bank of America, N.A." Servicer report, October 16.

Moody's Investor Services. 2009b. "HSBC Mortgage Corporation (USA)." Servicer report, August 28.

Pennington-Cross, Anthony. 2006. "The Value of Foreclosed Property." *Journal of Real Estate Research* 28, no. 2: 193–214.

Posen, Adam S. 2018. "A Practical Case for Rules-Based Macroprudential Policy." *In Achieving Financial Stability: Challenges to Prudential Regulation*, edited by Douglas D. Evanoff, George G. Kaufman, Agnese Leonello, and Simone Manganelli, 25–36. Hackensack, NJ: World Scientific Publishing.

Posner, Richard, and Luigi Zingales. 2009. "A Loan Modification Approach to the Housing Crisis." *American Law and Economics Review* 11, no. 2: 575–607.

Rossi-Hansberg, Esteban, Pierre-Daniel Sarte, and Raymond Owens III. 2010. "Housing Externalities." *Journal of Political Economy* 118, no. 3: 409–432.

Stegman, Michael A., Roberto G. Quercia, Janneke Ratcliffe, Lei Ding, and Walter R. Davis. 2007. "Preventive Servicing Is Good for Business and Affordable Homeownership Policy." *Housing Policy Debate* 18, no. 2: 243–278.

IV THE INSTITUTIONS AND GOVERNANCE

15 The EU Response to the Financial Crisis and the Economic Recession: The Juncker Plan, the Capital Markets Union, and the Banking Union

Massimo Marchesi and Mario Nava

This chapter looks at the policies designed and implemented by European Union (EU) authorities to respond to the 2008 financial crisis.[1] In the first section we start from a simple theoretical framework (the safety trap model), which depicts how, in the presence of a shortage of safe assets and very low interest rates, an economic recession might kick in. We suggest that the safety trap mechanism can help in modeling how investors' loss of confidence played a key role in triggering the long-lasting recession of the European economy that followed the 2008 financial crisis, and (in the second section) in determining its specific features, including the important contraction of investments that took place in the EU. We then look at how both demand and supply side EU policies helped the recovery of the European economy. We first turn (in the third section) to the role of the Juncker Plan to fill—at least in part—the investment gap that followed the financial crisis. We show in particular how the Juncker Plan did this via an increase in the supply of safe(r) assets, which is consistent with the safety trap model. In the fourth section we look at the Capital Markets Union (CMU), which was launched to improve, in a context of safe assets shortage, the efficiency of asset allocation mechanisms in the EU. The fifth section analyzes the bank regulatory policy responses progressively developed by the EU—the package on bank capital requirements (CRD4/CRR) and the Bank Recovery and Resolution Directive (BRRD)—and shows how they were broadly appropriate and effective in restoring investors' confidence. In particular, we claim that the CRD4/CRR reform of bank prudential requirements helped the recovery from the economic recession generated by the sovereign crisis and helped to reduce the shortage of safe assets in (some parts of) Europe. Finally, in the sixth section, we show why, now that the EU economic recovery is broad-based and stronger, a prompt completion of the Banking Union is necessary in order to improve the overall ability of Europe to be a better growth-friendly economic environment.

A Simple Model of the Macroeconomic Consequences of the International Financial Crisis: The Safety Trap Mechanism

Over the last three decades, there has been a continuous, slow but steady fall in interest rates, especially in the United States. There are various reasons behind this, but certainly an important contributing factor has been the presence of long periods of expansionary monetary policy in the United States. Since the beginning of the new century, the fall in interest rates has accelerated and definitely spread outside the United States to the entire world, alongside an increasingly expansionary monetary policy, not only in the United States but also in Europe and Asia. Another phenomenon that emerged in parallel was an ever-growing demand for safe assets on the world financial markets, probably as a consequence of the growing globalization of the economy and of the related setting up of global imbalances.[2]

The simple model shown in figure 15.1 presents a possible formalization of the macroeconomic consequences of a growing demand for safe assets in a situation of very low interest rates.[3] Consider either an increase in the demand for

Supply and demand for safe assets as a function of the real interest rate

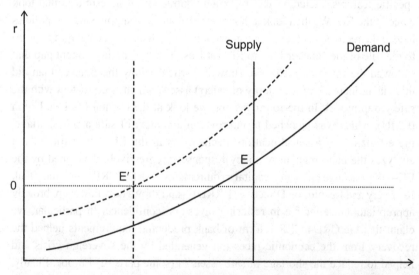

Figure 15.1
A simple model of the safety trap. *Note*: The initial equilibrium is at point E. The dashed lines illustrate how an exogenous reduction in the supply of safe assets pushes the economy against the zero lower bound. Equilibrium is restored at point E′ by an endogenous reduction in the demand for safe assets associated with a recession.

safe assets (captured by a rightward shift in the demand curve of safe assets) or a reduction in their supply (shown via a leftward shift in the supply curve of safe assets). In both cases, equilibrium in the safe asset market is restored by a reduction in interest rates, as with strong price or wage rigidities, this adjustment can only occur through a reduction in interest rates. But when interest rates hit the zero lower bound (due to the existence of growingly expansionary monetary policies), further reductions cannot easily take place. At zero interest rates, there can be an excess demand for safe assets (i.e., a shortage of safe assets) and an excess supply of goods (i.e., an insufficient aggregate demand for goods), generating a recession.

The recession lowers wealth at any given interest rate, endogenously bringing the demand curve for safe assets to the left. Equilibrium in the safe asset market is restored when the reduction in wealth matches either the initial increase in the demand for safe assets or their initial supply reduction. This mechanism is the essence of a safety trap: when the economy falls into it, the equilibrium can only be restored either by reducing the demand for safe assets (via a recession) or by increasing their supply.

In the years before the 2008 international financial crisis, the shortage of risk-free assets on the international financial markets proved a powerful stimulus to US and European securitization markets, which provided large amounts of "privately labeled" risk-free assets as an alternative to government bonds, increasing the supply of safe assets in response to their growing shortage. Later on, these assets made investors lose their confidence and increase their risk-aversion, triggering the financial crisis as summarized below. In figure 15.2 one can see the evolution of Euro Area bank assets and liabilities. In the years preceding the crisis, intrafinancial assets and liabilities grew enormously and at a growing pace while, after the outburst of the crisis, a contraction of these assets led to a very unstable funding condition for banks.[4]

The growth of bank intrafinancial assets and liabilities depended to a large extent on large investment banks (both in the United States and in Europe) buying more and more mortgages from smaller retail banks (especially, but not always, in the United States) and using them as the raw material from which they produced financial assets such as Mortgage-Backed Securities and Collateralized Debt Obligations, which materially increased the size of their balance sheets in the years preceding the financial crisis. As investment banks are to a large extent risk-neutral economic actors, they invested in these financial assets as long as there was a sufficiently high expected return on them and as long as they could find enough funding on the market for this activity.

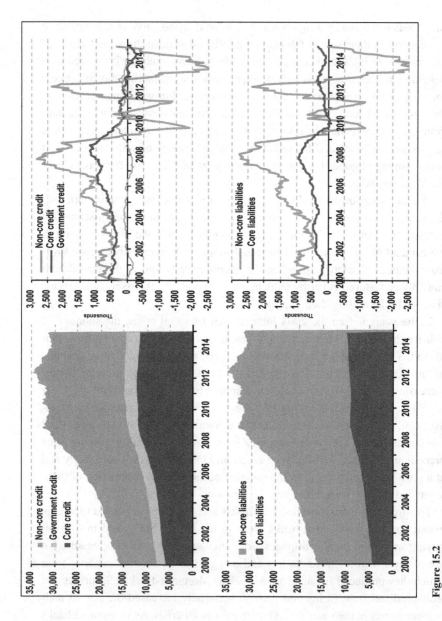

Figure 15.2
Evolution of assets and liabilities of Euro Area Monetary Financial Institutions, 2000–2014 (Euro Area, € billion). *Source:* European Commission 2015a, 67.

Given this scenario, the financial cycle leading to the 2008 crisis began with a rise in asset prices, namely real estate. This strengthened the balance sheet of banks thanks particularly to mark-to-market accounting after the securitization of those assets. As a consequence—and parallel to the role played by collateral in allowing (especially US, but also Spanish, for instance) households to borrow more when the price of their houses went up—both commercial banks and investment banks could borrow more. And the additional assets they could create or buy further increased the size of their balance sheet and pushed the asset prices even higher up.

On the contrary, when the price of the assets and, as a consequence, of the asset-backed securities fell, the balance sheets of both commercial and investment banks suddenly weakened, forcing them to swiftly reduce their indebtedness to keep open their access to funding on the market. Banks started therefore selling more and more (securitized) assets, so that asset prices started falling, and kept on falling as the downswing continued. The banking crisis obviously occurred when for several banks the drop of their assets value was sufficient to wipe out their equity.[5]

Table 15.1 provides an illustration of the investors' perception of the reduction in safe assets that took place during the financial crisis. In the United States, the loss of the safe asset status by government agencies such as Fannie Mae and Freddie Mac were to a large extent promptly offset by an increase of US federal debt held by the public in the first phase of the crisis. At this time, the EU was mainly hit by an important contraction in the funds made available from international investors to large EU banks, as shown also in figure 15.2. EU governments intervened at the time with important bailouts, and this helped to partially reduce the investors' perception of risk in the banking sector, although at the expense of raising the investors' perception of risk for some sovereigns. When this occurred at the same time of the public finance crisis in Greece,[6] safe assets in the EU quickly shrank, mostly in southern EU countries, without yet any compensating measure opposing this trend as swiftly and effectively as the measures taken in the United States, for example, with the Troubled Asset Relief Program (TARP).

Given a context of very low interest rates, this sudden reduction of safe assets could generate a safety trap with all its consequences. The safety trap mechanism can therefore be considered, at least to some extent, as a possible explanation of how the loss of investors' confidence triggered the economic recession that, especially in the EU, followed the international financial crisis.[7]

Table 15.1
Evolution of safe assets in the United States and some EU countries.

	US$ (billions)		% of world GDP	
	2007	2011	2007	2011
US Federal government debt held by the public	5,136	10,692	9.2%	15.8%
Held by the Federal Reserve	736	1,700	1.3%	2.5%
Held by private investors	4,401	8,992	7.9%	13.3%
GSE obligations	2,910	2,023	5.2%	3.0%
Agency- and GSE-backed mortgage pools	4,464	6,283	8.0%	9.3%
Private-issue ABS	3,901	1,277	7.0%	1.9%
German and French government debt	2,492	3,270	4.5%	4.8%
Italian and Spanish government debt	2,380	3,143	4.3%	4.7%
Safe assets	20,548	12,262	36.9%	18.1%

Source: Barclays Capital 2012.
Note: Numbers struck through were perceived by international financial markets to have lost their "safe asset" status after 2007.

Consequences of the Safe Assets Shortage during the European Sovereign Crisis: The Piling up of a Lack-of-Investment-Driven Economic Recession in the EU

Risk-free assets are a cornerstone of the functioning of the financial sector. For this reason, the suddenly perceived scarcity of risk-free assets originated by the sovereign crisis set up unfavorable conditions for economic growth in the EU in several ways, as illustrated below.

Consequences on Bank Liquidity

In the presence of a large set of risk-free assets, the banking system can promptly use them for secured financing transactions, which provide the liquidity banks need. For instance, sovereign debt securities, being highly liquid and relatively risk-free assets, play a central role in the banking system as banks not only invest in these assets but also use them as a liquidity buffer. Moreover, they serve as collateral for refinancing operations, both in the interbank market and in credit operations with the central bank. In fact, government debt represents the single most important type of collateral in these operations. But when the sovereign crisis kicked in and created a scarcity of risk-free assets, much more collateral was suddenly requested by investors, and the EU banking system risked becoming illiquid.

Consequences on Financial Asset Allocation

When managing their portfolios, investors take decisions on how much money to invest in the different asset classes available to them. In this process, the presence of riskless investments allows for a more defined separation between investment decisions and risk profiles. This means that investors with different risk aversions have a wider array of investment opportunities as they can use the risk-free assets to alter the overall risk exposure of their portfolios. The main consequences of not having sufficiently available risk-free assets during the sovereign crisis were less diversified investment portfolios and higher risk premiums.[8] The Capital Asset Pricing Model gives a very clear intuition of it (figure 15.3) as it shows how investors are only able to hold a level of risk that is suboptimal compared to the one they could hold in the presence of a freely available risk-free asset.

In essence, the absence of sufficiently available risk-free investments during the sovereign crisis made risky investments seem even riskier to most investors, who normally are risk-averse economic agents. As a consequence, they invested less in the most risky assets, demanded higher risk premiums (and paid lower prices), and were quicker to flee any assets in the face of danger.

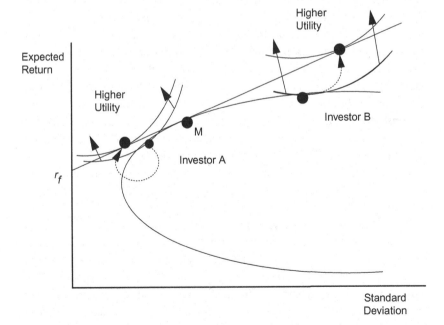

Figure 15.3
Role of the risk-free asset in the Capital Asset Pricing Model

Put another way, not having a safe haven that they could return to made most investors less willing to take risk. As a consequence, we saw lower prices for the most risky assets, higher volatility in prices in financial markets, and abrupt, painful market corrections.[9]

Consequences on Corporate Financial Behavior

Having access to risk-free assets plays an important role in corporate finance decisions—that is, in how firms invest their resources, the mix of debt and equity that they use to fund themselves, as well as the choices they make in how much cash they return to shareholders in the form of dividends and stock buybacks.

In the presence of sufficiently available risk-free assets, cash is a neutral asset, and it does not drive investment choices. When instead there are no risk-free assets or an insufficient amount of them, companies that find better cash-generating investments will be viewed as more valuable than companies that do not. It can therefore be expected that some companies may generate more excess returns on their cash-generating investments than on their business/operating investments. As a result, managers would spend more of their time and resources researching short-term cash-generating investments and less on their long-term (in principle higher-added-value) business/operating investments. This is what happened during the second phase of the crisis, which showed an important reduction in firms' long-term investments.

Mutatis mutandis, the same mechanism applies to dividend policy. In principle, when a firm has a cash surplus from its business operations, after meeting its reinvestment needs and debt obligations it can pay the cash out as a dividend, use it to buy back stock, or retain it as a cash balance. The presence of risk-free assets makes the dividend policy choice in principle neutral for the firm, as demonstrated by Miller and Modigliani in 1961. But when no or insufficient risk-free assets are available, as happened during the sovereign crisis, companies are penalized when they hold back from paying dividends and invest, as the investment would in no or fewer cases be risk-free. Therefore, after 2007 stockholders increased the pressure on firms to have their cash back and valued at a more severe discount companies that would reinvest their cash.

Figure 15.4 shows that it was only well after the beginning of the European sovereign crisis (around the end of 2011) that sovereigns' spreads went back to a convergence path. This happened not only thanks to the European Central Bank's (ECB) monetary interventions, but also to a series of important EU policies and reforms undertaken in those years, including the Juncker Plan, the CRD4/CRR, the BRRD, the strengthening of public finance surveillance tools within the European Semester, and the launch of the CMU.

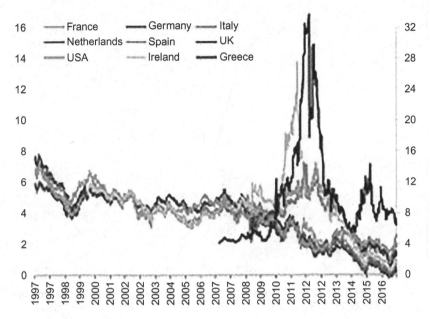

Figure 15.4
Ten-year bond spreads of selected countries, 1997–2016. *Source*: Veron and Zettelmeyer 2017.

The Role of the Juncker Plan: Fostering Investments via the Increase in the Supply of Safe(r) Assets

The financial crisis heavily hit EU investments (see figure 15.5). Annual investments in the EU fell by about €430 billion since their peak in 2007, with reductions concentrated in a few countries. The low level of investments is one of the main reasons why Europe's economic recovery was delayed and remained weak for several years, picking up and becoming more broad-based only from 2014–2015 onwards.

Euro Area investment has notably been much weaker in years following the financial crisis than it would normally be expected in a "typical" recovery. While in previous recessions investment would stop declining after two to three years, in the last recession investments substantially accelerated their slump after two years from the beginning of the crisis (see figure 15.6). This leads many economists to believe that while housing investment certainly played a role in this decline, there must have been more than just developments in housing investment to affect the total investment-to-GDP ratio during the last recession. In particular, recent European Commission analysis shows that the weakness in investment behavior during the last crisis can to a large extent be attributed to

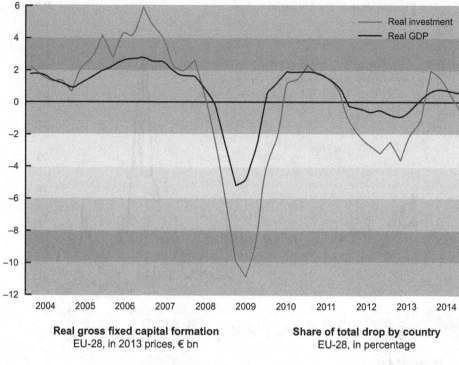

Real gross fixed capital formation
EU-28, in 2013 prices, € bn

Share of total drop by country
EU-28, in percentage

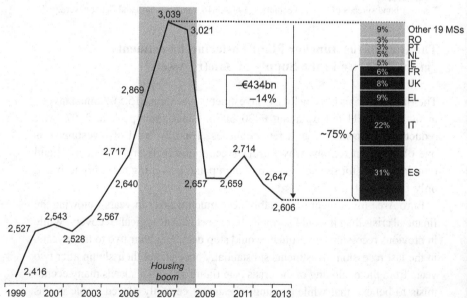

Figure 15.5
Year-on-year EU real GDP and real investment growth rate (*top*) and real investment absolute values (*bottom*). *Sources*: European Commission 2017d; European Commission and European Investment Bank 2015.

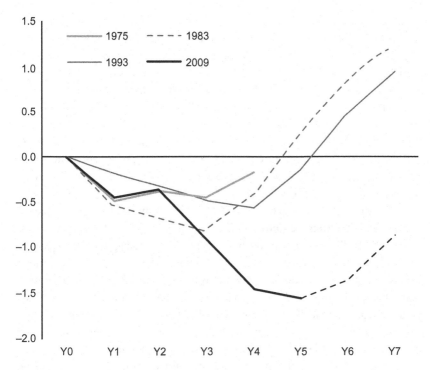

Figure 15.6
Gross fixed capital formation after 2009, percent of GDP, EA12 (BE, DE, IE, EL, ES, FR, IT, LU, NL, AT, PT, FI). *Source*: European Commission 2015b, 36, graph IV.2.

credit factors such as deleveraging in the private sector. This private debt deleveraging has indeed started to play an increasingly more important role over time through the recession, with long-lasting effects on investment dynamics.

Given the protracted effect of private sector deleveraging on investment dynamics, the importance of policies supporting capital formation in the EU—to try and avoid a deeper and longer economic recession—appeared very clearly to the European Commission. After three weeks in office, the Juncker Commission announced an investment plan through the European Fund for Strategic Investments (EFSI) that was aimed at reducing the EU investment gap that originated during the crisis and widened since then. EFSI was therefore designed to generate both additional investment and safe(r) assets, and as a natural complement to the supply side response of repairing the financial system and strengthening bank capitalization levels.

Because the budget of the EU is limited and, in any case, unsuitable for traditional demand policy, unconventional ideas had to be put in place to ensure that investors could directly or indirectly close the investment gap per year of some €300 billion required to boost growth. EFSI built on an important finding linked to the safety trap logic: in the post-crisis market environment, characterized by uncertainty and low investor confidence, investors seeking a safe haven for their funds tend to shy away from the risks associated with infrastructure investments. In response to that, EFSI aimed to tackle the issue of low confidence and limited risk appetite on the part of investors by using public funds to absorb some of the risks (notably the first loss) involved in infrastructure projects, creating new safe (or at least safer) assets by means of a "leveraged demand" policy—that is, a demand policy that uses public money as a lever for private investment.

EFSI was built on a guarantee of €16 billion from the EU budget and €5 billion in capital from the European Investment Bank (EIB). This initial contribution of €21 billion served as the basic risk buffer, enabling the EIB to provide financing to infrastructure projects with a high risk profile, primarily through subordinated debt. This primary risk absorption capacity the EIB could provide being backed by the EFSI guarantees, in turn, allowed to catalyze large-scale additional investments from private investors into the more senior (and therefore low(er) risk) tranches of infrastructure debt. According to European Commission estimates, the EFSI leverage mechanism was designed to reach a blended multiplier effect of up to fifteen. In other words, every €1 of public funds provided as guarantee for risk protection would finally catalyze a total investment of €15 in the real economy (figure 15.7).

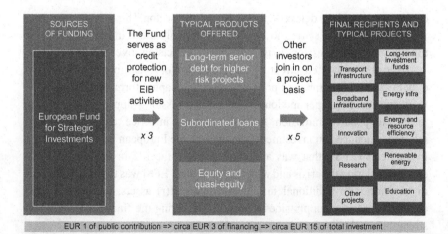

Figure 15.7
EFSI leverage mechanics. *Source*: European Commission 2014, 18.

Based on the leverage ratio of 1:15, the initial €21 billion in public contributions was expected to mobilize a total of €315 billion between 2015 and 2017. Of this overall amount, approximately €240 billion was earmarked for long-term strategic investments of European significance in key areas of infrastructure and innovation. Results of the first years are very encouraging both in terms of aggregate spending (figure 15.8) and in terms of distribution of spending across countries compared to the observed needs (per country output gap) (figure 15.9).[10] In May 2017, following the positive results of the first three years, EU co-legislators agreed to extend EFSI both in size (from €315 billion to €500 billion) and in time (from 2017 to 2020).

Fighting Misallocation of Resources Due to Safe Asset Scarcity: The Role of the European Semester and of the Capital Markets Union

The global scarcity of safe assets, which was to an important extent generated in the first place by the deepening of the globalization process since the turn of the millennium, also generated the emergence of deeper global imbalances. This happened because the countries whose assets foreign investors wish to hold for reserve purposes were demanded to supply the world with an extra supply of their assets, which in turn allowed the safe asset excess world demand to be reduced. In the international monetary system, the United States is the main safe asset provider. There are however also a number of smaller or more regional safe asset providers, such as in Europe, Switzerland, and Germany or, more generally, those Member States sometimes referred to as "core countries" of the Euro Area.

In the peripheral European Monetary Union (EMU) countries, the period preceding the sovereign crisis was marked by massive capital inflows. Up to 2011, banks of core EMU countries like Germany borrowed globally and lent to banks of peripheral euro area countries, earning small but positive excess returns in the process and increasing their external exposure. But when the sovereign crisis materialized, these flows halted[11] and EMU peripheral countries' public-sector balance sheets had to absorb most of the losses emerging from banks' balance sheets, obliging the public sector to either shrink aggressively or to increase taxes. This deeply depressed the economy of EMU peripheral countries and, in particular, it reduced entrepreneurs' confidence in the future and, as a consequence, their investments. Reductions in the interest rates by expansionary monetary policy of the European Central Bank fortunately helped to mitigate, at least partially, these effects.

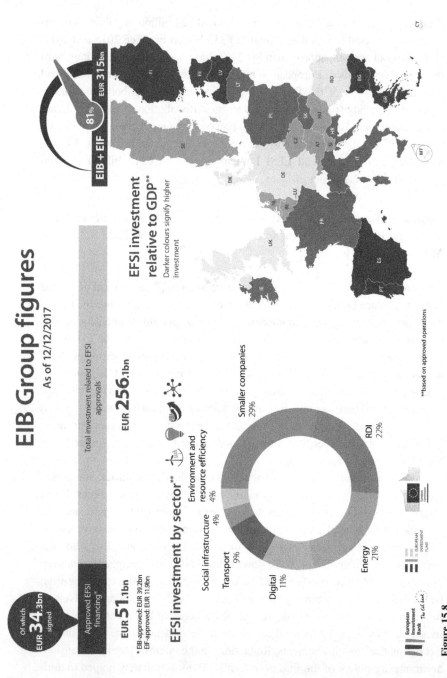

Figure 15.8
EFSI result at December 12, 2017. *Source*: European Investment Bank, http://www.eib.org/efsi/index.htm.

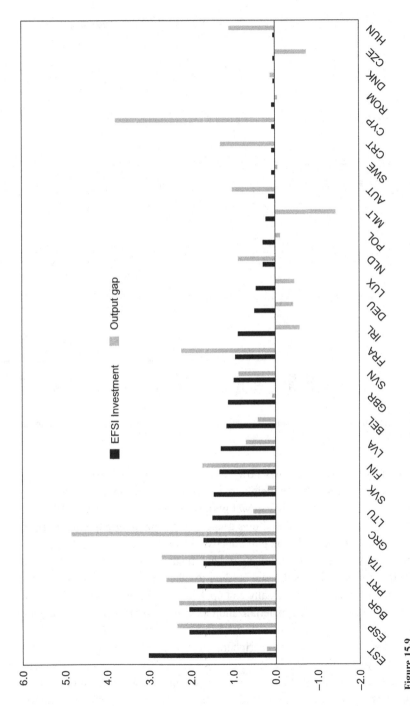

Figure 15.9
EFSI approved funding vs. 2016 output gap per country (in percentage of GDP). *Source*: Gaspar 2017.

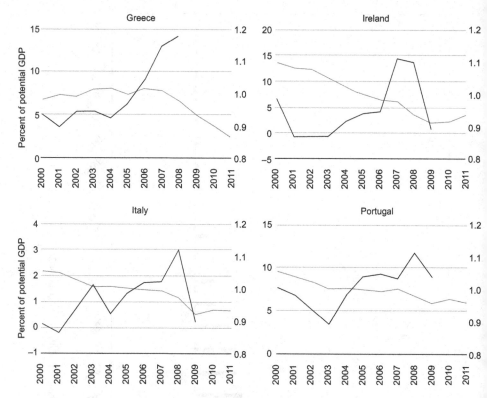

Figure 15.10
Net capital inflows and deterioration of total factor productivity. *Source*: European Investment Bank 2015, 223.

Recent EIB research shows how the massive capital inflows occurring in the period preceding the sovereign crisis might have contributed to deteriorating total factor productivity in EMU peripheral countries (figure 15.10).

Massive cross-border bank flows going through the international interbank market might in fact end up in unproductive sectors abroad. This, as the *de facto* seniority of wholesale (mostly secured) bank financing, can lead to a suboptimal incentive for those banks that are lending to other banks abroad to adequately monitor where their funds actually end up, hence increasing the risk of a misallocation of resources. The materialization of this risk for the European banking system has taken place over time with the emergence of large amounts of nonperforming loans (NPL) in peripheral EMU countries, which were the most affected by the crisis.

These issues highlight the importance of appropriately monitoring and, where necessary, introducing remedies to the consequences of macroeconomic

	Bank restructuring	Indebtedness	Asset quality	Access to finance
BE	●			
BG	●		●	
DE	○●			
IE	○●		○●	○
ES	○		○	○
HR	●		○●	
IT	○●		○●	○
CY	●		●	●
LT				●
HU	○		○	○
MT				○
NL	●	○●		
AT	○			
PT	○	○	○●	○●
RO	●			
SI	○●		○●	●
SE		○●		
UK		○		○
Legend: ○ = 2014; ● = 2016.				

Figure 15.11
Country-Specific Recommendations on the financial and banking sector. *Source*: European Commission 2017b, 168.

imbalances stemming from a global scarcity of safe assets. Within the current EU institutional context, a progressively more important role has been played by the European Semester (managed by the European Commission) and its associated Macroeconomic Imbalances Procedure.[12] In several Country-Specific Recommendations, Member States have been repeatedly asked—for instance—to take all the measures necessary to accelerate the reduction of nonperforming loans, including further improvements to the national framework for insolvency and debt collection (figure 15.11).

In the discussion of the reasons that might lie behind a possible misallocation of resources by the banking and—more generally—the financial system, the term normally used by the economic literature is that of financial frictions. These frictions are rooted in the asymmetric information problems that exist between borrowers and lenders and between entrepreneurs and investors. All these frictions, generally taken, tend to reduce the availability of credit/investment, increasing its cost and possibly giving rise to a not fully efficient allocation of available financial resources, thereby resulting in a lower level of economic activity and lower rates of productivity and economic growth in the medium term.

The consequences determined by these frictions can be appreciated by simply recalling how banking loans have been highly pro-cyclical in the period before and after the crisis (much more than other sources of funding such as equity financing) or by pointing at how large a share of household wealth has been and still is simply being "parked" on bank accounts (risk aversion issue) and sometimes even deposited with central banks instead of being used to finance the real economy.

Within this context, it is possible to see the CMU as a wide-ranging set of initiatives aimed at removing or at least reducing the effect of financial frictions and at improving how efficiently resources are allocated via the financial system in the EU. The CMU is in fact a mix of regulatory and nonregulatory reforms, seeking to better connect savings to investments. It aims at strengthening Europe's financial system by providing alternative sources of financing and more opportunities for consumers and institutional investors. In particular, the CMU Action Plan published in September 2015 set out several actions aimed at increasing funding options for Europe's businesses, increasing investment, and breaking down cross-border barriers to the free movement of capital. The following is a selection of initiatives undertaken so far:

Venture capital: the European Parliament and Council reached an agreement in principle on May 30, 2017, on a revision of the European Venture Capital Funds (EuVECA) and of the European Social Entrepreneurship Funds (EuSEF) that will make it easier for investors to invest in small- and medium-sized innovative companies.

Companies entering and raising capital on public markets: the December 2016 agreement by the European Parliament and Council on a modernized EU Prospectus Regulation will start to apply from mid-2019 onward. The European Commission has also taken steps to address the bias in the tax system in favor of debt over equity as part of its October 2016 proposal for a Common Consolidated Corporate Tax Base (CCCTB).

Bank capacity to lend to the real economy: to free up capacity on banks' balance sheets and, by so doing, generate additional funding for the economy, on December 12, 2017, the European Parliament and the Council approved a new regulation on simple, transparent, and standardized securitization.

Infrastructure investment: the Solvency II delegated act entered into application in April 2016, making it cheaper for EU insurance companies to invest in qualifying infrastructure projects. To encourage private investment by banks in infrastructure projects, in November 2016 the European Commission also proposed to amend the capital requirements legislation.

Preventive restructuring and second chance for entrepreneurs: in November 2016, the European Commission proposed rules on preventive restructuring, to avoid the liquidation of viable companies with financial difficulties and give entrepreneurs a chance to reenter business life after bankruptcy. The proposal also laid down rules to enhance the efficiency of insolvency procedures to make them more predictable, less costly, and speedier.

The CMU has been subject to a mid-term review in June 2017, which set the timeline for new actions and priorities. These include, among others, amendments to the functioning of the European Securities and Markets Authorities (ESMA) and of the other European Supervisory Agencies aimed at promoting the effectiveness and consistency of supervision across the EU, a pan-European personal pension product to help people who have worked in a number of different Member States finance their retirement, a legislative proposal for an EU framework on covered bonds to help banks finance their lending activity, and work on increasing the proportionality of the rules for listed SMEs and investment firms.

The EU Response to the Financial Crisis through Bank Regulation and Its Impact on European Banks and the Overall Economy

The CRD4/CRR package is one of the main elements of the response the EU gave to the financial crisis. The Capital Requirements Regulation (CRR)[13] regulates banks' liquidity, the quantity and quality of banks' minimum capital, banks' leverage, banks' counterparty risks, and the national flexibilities. The Capital Requirements Directive (CRD4)[14] regulates the ability of supervisors to impose prudential buffers, corporate governance rules, harmonized sanctions, and general enhanced supervision rules. CRD4/CRR aimed at making banks safer again, as well as more able to withstand adverse shocks.

CRD4/CRR increased the Minimum Capital Requirements for EU bank best quality capital (CET1) from 2% of Risk-Weighted Assets (RWA) to 7% of RWA, leading to an overall Minimum Capital Requirement of at least 10.5%. The market response to this regulatory change was unambiguous. CET1 ratios quickly attained levels well above the required 7%, with a continuous upward trend confirmed also by most recent data (see figure 15.12).

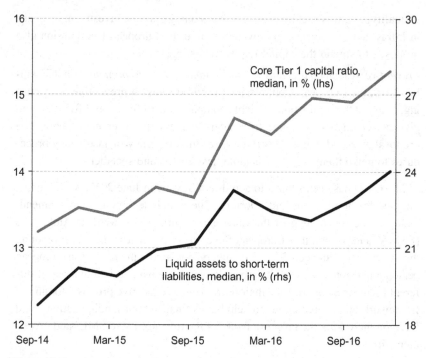

Figure 15.12
Core Tier 1 and Liquid assets ratios in Europe. *Source*: European Commission 2017c, 82.

Along with the regulatory and market-driven increases of bank capital and liquidity, industry soon started claiming that due to the new regulatory capital constraints, banking was no longer a sufficiently profitable business and therefore not a sustainable one in the long run. For instance, in its response to CRD4/CRR consultation dated October 6, 2015, the Institute of International Finance wrote: "In order to form the full picture of the sustainability of banks' businesses, Cost of Equity (COE) must be considered alongside the industry's Return on Equity (ROE). Current levels of cost and returns call this sustainability into question."

However, McKinsey (see figure 15.13) found that, at the global level, the ROE of large banks returned to the long-term average of 8% to 12% after the temporary reduction due to the outburst of the financial crisis in 2008. This is an undeniable fact, even if there are important geographical differences to be acknowledged, with European banks still showing lower ROE than their US or Asian peers.

To analyze the reasons behind these regional differences, one should recall that ROE, as a ratio, is influenced by those elements that affect net income—its

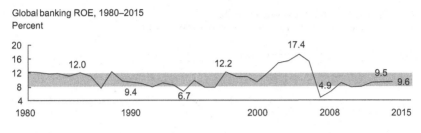

Figure 15.13
EU banks' return on equity, 1990–2015. *Source*: Bugrov, Dietz, and Poppensieker 2017.

numerator (higher net income = higher ROE)—and by those elements that affect the amount of equity banks hold—its denominator (higher equity = lower ROE).

Concerning banks' net income, it should be noted that banks in Europe tend to rely more on interest income and less on fee income compared to non-European banks and that interest rate margins have, over time, come under pressure, also due to the "flattening" of the yield curve in recent years. This is important in explaining European banks' lower profitability, as they can be—generally speaking—more profitable in a steep yield curve environment (as they borrow at low spreads on the short end of the curve and lend at higher spreads on the long end).[15] A second important factor that can influence banks' net income is obviously economic growth. Typically, in periods of low economic growth, banks' balance sheets tend to become less profitable due to the generation of more and more important amounts of NPL and the need to provision them.

Figure 15.14 shows the evolution of NPL in Europe since 2007. In the United States, as problematic loans swiftly emerged to the surface, banks' balance sheets were rapidly cleaned of NPL effects so that US banks' ROE could quickly recover and return to levels comparable to the pre-crisis period. In several EU countries, instead, the cleaning up of banks' balance sheets has been much slower. This struggle in cleaning up EU banks' balance sheets is indeed one important element that has acted as a "pulled handbrake" over recent years on EU banks' ROE, with those banks that are most present in

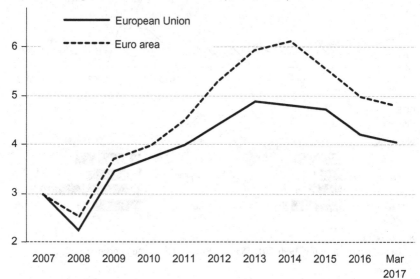

Gross nonperforming debt instruments
(in % of total gross debt instruments, end-of-period values)

Figure 15.14
Evolution of nonperforming loans in the EU and in the Euro Area *Source*: European Commission 2017a, 15.

countries that suffered the most from the crisis being the ones where the gravity of the situation related to NPL emerged most slowly in the books.

A third important factor affecting banks' net income is banks' cost structure. In the last few years a vivid discussion has developed on whether several European banks run too wide a branch network and employ too many people when compared to the amount of revenues they can generate.[16] Across Europe, branch networks have generally decreased more than employees since the crisis, highlighting the difficulty of adjusting workforce to business conditions over time. Effects on cost-efficiency indicators have been mixed.

Going back to the impact of recent bank reforms, it is fair to say that economists are split on the issue of how CRD4/CRR changes to bank regulation relate to the issue of optimal bank capital requirements—that is, the level of bank equity that maximizes sustainable growth in the long term. On the one hand, some economists even recommend capital requirements as high as 30%. On the other hand, other economists support an opposite view that considers as optimal a situation with very low capital requirements and very high leverage by banks.

In recent interventions on this topic, Nataliya Klimenko, in a dynamic model published with Sebastian Pfeil, Jean-Charles Rochet, and Gianni de Nicolo in

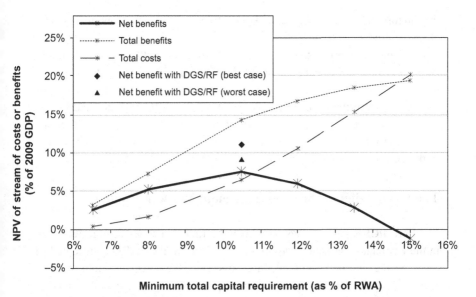

Figure 15.15
Net present value (NPV) of stream of total costs, total benefits and net benefits of CRD4/CRR and BRRD. *Source*: European Commission 2012, appendix 5, 189–199. For methodological details, see Marchesi et al. (2012).

2016, concludes that the short-term impact of higher capital requirements can be very different from the long-term one. Although the two dimensions of stability (supported by higher capital) and growth (supported by lower capital) may be conflicting in the short run, if the capital ratio is not unreasonably high, it is possible to find an optimal equilibrium level in the long run, where the economy is the most stable and it also grows at the highest rate possible.

Figure 15.15 (a graph presented in one of the technical annexes to the Impact Assessment of the BRRD, dated 2012)[17] illustrates this point in a simple way. As one can see, the costs (in terms of short-term reduced growth), the benefits (in terms of long-term increased financial stability), and the net effects in the long term are what European Commission services also tried to evaluate, and they tend to support the calibration achieved in Basel III and translated into CRD4/CRR.[18]

However, it should also not be forgotten that a suboptimal transition path to new capital requirements might have taken place in the recent past. This could partially explain the difficult initial recovery from the crisis. After the outburst of the financial crisis, capital ratios have in fact increased very rapidly due to intense pressure coming from financial markets and in spite of Minimum Capital Requirements being increased very gradually by the new rules. This may have contributed to creating higher funding costs for banks in Europe that, in turn, might have contributed to lowering lending and economic growth, at least in the short term.

In the medium term—that is, from 2014–2015 onwards—growth in the EU consolidated and has become broad based, ensuring recovery to pre-crisis levels. It would be incorrect to attribute this robust recovery to only one of the policies described above (the Juncker Plan, the CMU, and the CRD4/CRR reforms) or to just the ECB monetary policy response to the financial crisis, but certainly the joint impact of all these policies has materially contributed to the current EU solid recovery.

The Completion of the Banking Union: Work in Progress

The CRD4/CRR package has only been the first of a series of improvements in the EU banks' regulatory environment. Later on, the BRRD contributed to breaking the link between banks and sovereign, the so-called doom loop. In particular, the BRRD has provided a triple mechanism of taxpayers' protection based on (1) resolution plans; (2) bail-in of 8% of the liabilities of each bank in need of resolution; and (3) national resolution funds, each equal to 1% of national covered deposits.

Since 2008, the European Commission has been involved in the restructuring or orderly liquidation of more than 100 European banking institutions in more than twenty Member States. More than sixty of these banks have been deeply restructured, and burden-sharing or bail-in rules have been effectively applied in several countries. In relation to the effects of these interventions, it can be acknowledged that the breaking of the link between banks and sovereigns was initially only partial, but it has become more and more effective over time. During 2017 several banks (some also quite significant and important both in their home country and on a European scale) were either privately recapitalized or precautionary recapitalized, resolved, or liquidated without provoking a fraction of the market movements of 2013, when much smaller banks were resolved. This happened as markets trust that the EU environment has improved enough from 2013 to 2017 to take care of several distressed banks without the generation of any material contagion. It is therefore possible to conclude that the CRD4/CRR package and the BRRD—jointly with other important developments such as the introduction of the Single Supervisory Mechanism, of the single rulebook, and of a larger range of bail-inable liabilities—have largely reduced and circumscribed systemic risk in the EU banking system.

The present framework for banking crisis management recently received some criticism for treating distressed banks differently. As shown in figure 15.16,

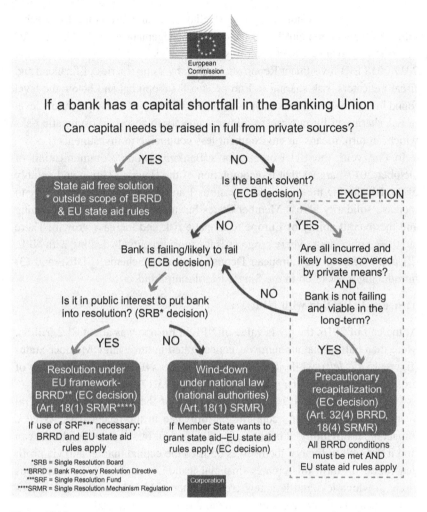

Figure 15.16
EU bank crisis management tools in case of a bank capital shortfall. *Source*: European Commission 2017f.

the system worked, on the contrary, properly and as intended. This, as within the existing framework the various decisions taken by different institutions such as the Single Supervisory Mechanism (SSM), the Single Resolution Board (SRB), and the European Commission determined whether this or that crisis management tool could or had to be used in the specific case at hand. One can therefore conclude that it was completely normal that in different situations, rather different crisis management tools were used for each specific case.

With systemic risk not being a substantial issue anymore in the foreseeable future,[19] what still remains key is the correct management of idiosyncratic risks. The best way to ensure their control is, of course, via risk sharing. However, the 2017/2018 EIB Investment Report shows that, by using a series of financial and fiscal indicators, risk sharing in Europe is still suboptimal and below the level found in mature federations such as the United States or Germany.[20] A low level of risk sharing in Europe means a lower capacity to absorb idiosyncratic risks which, in turn, means an environment less conducive to investments.

In that vein, the EU Commission's Banking Union Communication of October 2017[21] argues that the completion of the Banking Union and notably of its risk-sharing measures (see measures 1 and 2 below) matters not only to increase solidarity across Member States but also to improve its functioning and the overall ability of Europe to manage risk and increase growth. There are three policy areas where progress is the most urgent: (1) dealing with NPL, (2) implementing the European Deposit Insurance Scheme (EDIS), and (3) introducing a backstop to the Single Resolution Fund.

Measure 1: Dealing with NPL

At the end of 2016, the gross value of NPL in Europe was about €1.2 trillion. More than half of that amount was concentrated in three large Member States (figure 15.17, *left*), while in several EU countries NPL constituted a share of gross debt instruments larger than 10% (figure 15.17, *right*).

The presence of NPL is considered as one of the reasons behind several years of weak European economic performance in the recent past. As NPL impact the profitability of banks, jeopardizing their business model, banks can find it difficult to finance themselves both on the capital market and via profit generation. In turn, this creates financial instability and generates a vicious circle in which less and less new credit is supplied by the banks so that economic recovery deteriorates over time and reaches a standstill.

However, the contraction of lending to firms—particularly in EU countries where NPL have increased the most—is the consequence not only of a credit problem on the supply side but also of a lack of credit demand. In fact, in a situation of economic recession, firms lack any clear positive perspective in the near future, so that they normally take the decision to slash their investments and, by doing so, they reduce their demand of credit.

The importance of contrasting the fall in the investments, also by means of a swift and vigorous action tackling NPL, depends on the fact that investments are an important component and even an accelerator of GDP growth. In those countries where it has been possible to attack the (rising) stock of NPL, it has also been possible to better and more quickly contrast the fall in investments, restoring a better and earlier general condition of trust in the perspectives of the national economy. This helped to break the vicious cycle described above: higher NPL, lower trust of the entrepreneurs in the perspectives of the economy, fewer investments, lower economic growth.

For a solution to the NPL issue, it is important to deal both with their existing stock and with their future flows. Typically there is a wide set of possible measures that allow jurisdictions to dispose of large quantities of NPL or to avoid their build-up over time. Some of these measures are normally better taken at the national level (typically those dealing with judicial and national insolvency systems), while others are in principle more effective if developed at the EU level (typically those dealing with legislation and market requirements) (see figure 15.18).

This wide set of possible different measures is sometimes split between "pull" and "push" measures. "Push" measures are essentially all measures aimed at pushing banks to increase NPL provisioning and, by doing so, reducing their net book value. They can be of two natures: Pillar 1 measures valid *erga omnes*, for instance on newly originated loans that become nonperforming, and Pillar 2 measures valid only on a bank specific level and following a careful quality evaluation of the bank assets. On the contrary, "pull" measures typically deal with markets improvement and are named like that as they help to pull the NPL market price up. Today, NPL markets are in fact opaque, oligopsonistic in nature, and unable to ensure an appropriate price discovery, to the detriment of selling banks.

The size and the relative importance of NPL in some countries, coupled with the present NPL market characteristics, make a mixture of push and pull measures inevitable to ensure any rapid progress on NPL. In that vein, in July 2017, the ECOFIN Council published an Action Plan encompassing several types of measures to tackle NPL in Europe.[22] The European Commission is currently working to implement the Council's Action Plan along the four following axes:

1. a blueprint for an Asset Management Company (AMC);

2. measures to develop secondary markets for NPL, possibly through EU legislation;

3. measures to enhance the protection of secured creditors;

4. a report, accompanied (if appropriate) with the necessary proposals to amend the CRR to possibly introduce minimum levels of bank provisions for newly originated loans that turn nonperforming.

Finally, the Commission is also undertaking a benchmarking exercise for loan enforcement regimes.

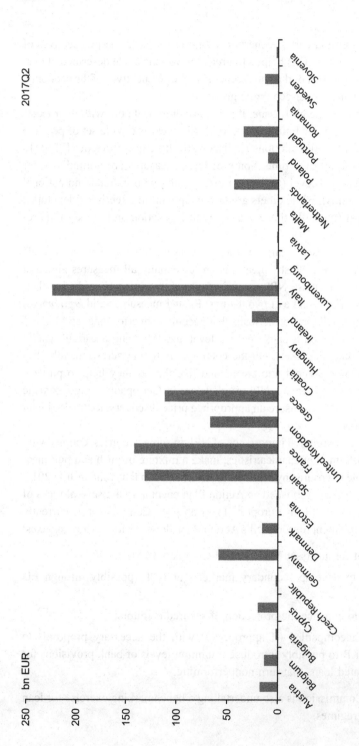

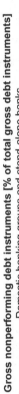
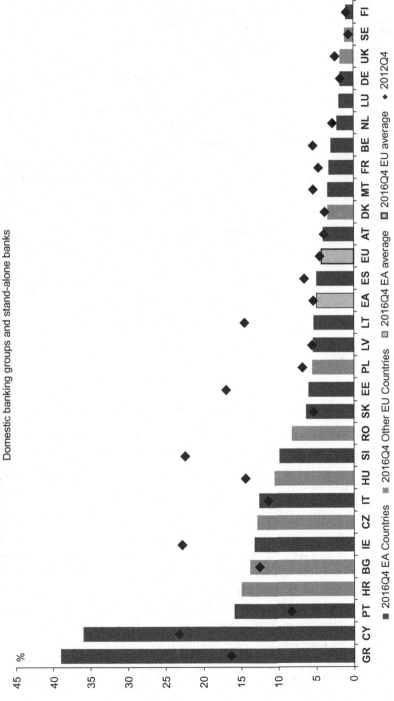

Figure 15.17
Gross book value of NPL (2016) in absolute values (*previous page*) and as percentage of gross debt instruments (*this page*). *Source:* European Commission with ECB data.

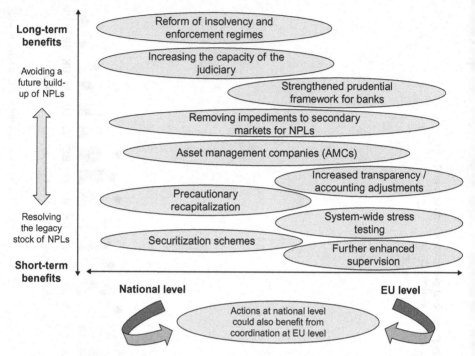

Figure 15.18
Actions at national and EU levels to resolve NPL.

Measure 2: European Deposit Insurance Scheme (EDIS)

EDIS is the third and final pillar of a complete Banking Union. National deposit guarantee schemes are vulnerable to idiosyncratic shocks when they are large at national scale while, by contrast, EDIS can enhance resilience against future national crises, reinforcing depositor confidence and promoting financial stability.

Furthermore, EDIS can reduce the risks of the overall EU banking system as banks' contributions would be risk based according to their risk on a European scale rather than on a national one. This would mean that riskier-than-average EU banks would contribute more, and less-risky-than-average EU banks would contribute less, no matter where they reside in the EU. This comparison with the European average would therefore provide banks with the incentive to further reduce risk in less virtuous countries, with an overall risk reduction expected for the entire European banking sector.

In spite of its good rationale and of the fact that the EDIS proposal was contained in the June 2015 Five Presidents (of the EU Council, EU Commission,

ECB, Eurogroup, and EU Parliament) Report, the November 2015 Commission text that translated that part of the report into a regulation proposal is currently stalled in both the Parliament and Council.[23] The main reason for this blockage is that several countries requested that, before negotiating on a joint deposit insurance scheme, all banking sector legacy risks are eliminated—notwithstanding the fact that the initial Commission proposal foresaw a very progressive risk-sharing mechanism for both liquidity and losses.[24]

The Banking Union Communication of October 2017[25] sets out proposals to help facilitate a compromise on EDIS and allow a political agreement in 2018. Its main innovations (see figure 15.19) are:

1. a reinsurance phase providing only liquidity coverage up to 100% by 2022, where EDIS would not participate in any losses;

2. a targeted Asset Quality Review to address NPL and Level III assets issues, aimed at minimizing any legacy risk before moving to any loss risk sharing;

3. a coinsurance phase providing loss coverage starting at 30% only in 2022 and deepening over time.

As liquidity coverage does not entail by definition legacy risks and as loss coverage would only take place after an Asset Quality Review and validation by the European Commission, this proposal could help to revive negotiations in both the European Parliament and Council.

Measure 3: Backstop to the Single Resolution Fund

At present, the bank resolution framework of the Banking Union relies on the ability of banks to absorb losses (either via sale of assets or via internal bail-in), and only after a sizable loss absorption (8% of total assets), the Single Resolution Fund (SRF), which is progressively built up and which will reach some €55 billion only when fully up to speed, may intervene to avoid financial contagion—that is, the spreading of losses to the rest of the banking system.

A common fiscal backstop would reinforce the overall credibility of such a framework and instill further confidence in the resolution framework. EU Member States agreed in 2013 on the development of a common backstop by 2023 at the latest. The criteria for the backstop have been identified in the *Reflection Paper on the Deepening of the Economic and Monetary Union* (European Commission 2017e). The backstop should be adequately sized, activated in a swift manner, and fiscally neutral—that is, the banking sector would be eventually liable for repayment. The October 2017 Banking Union Communication urges Member States to operationalize the backstop as rapidly as possible. Different options are under discussion even though particular focus is on the

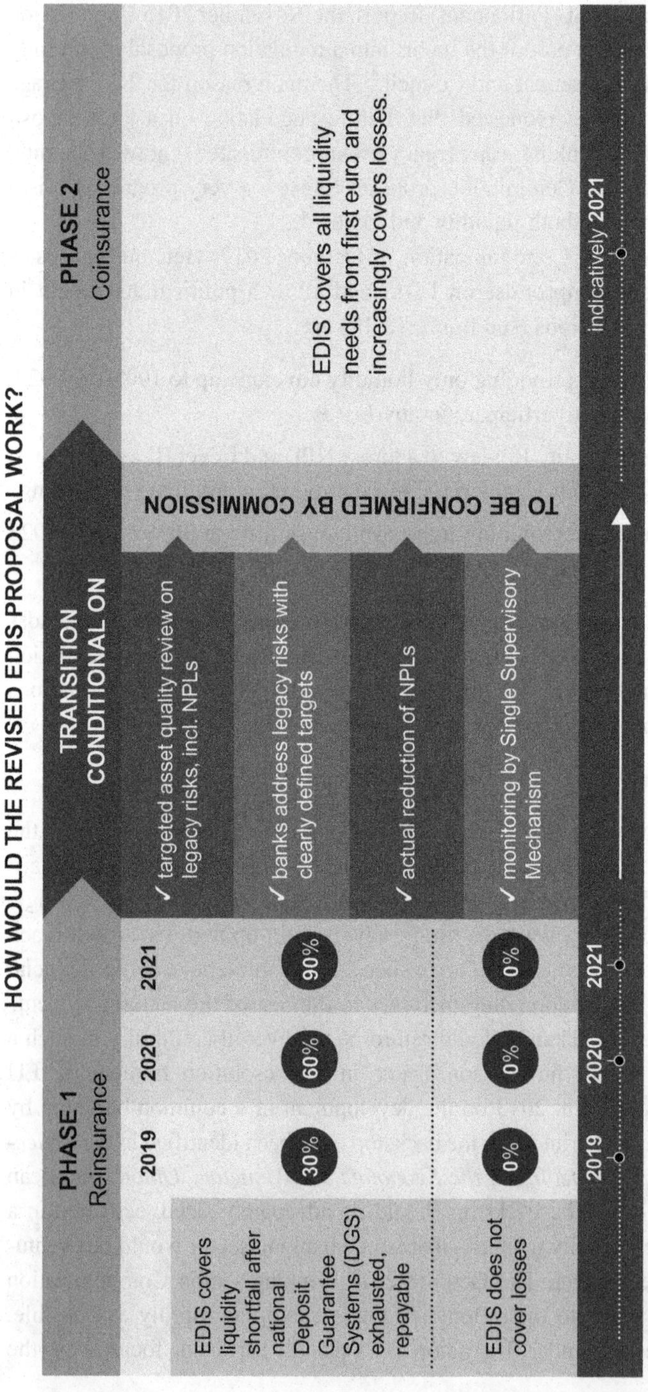

Figure 15.19
Revised EDIS proposal.

possibility of a credit line from the European Stability Mechanism (ESM) to the SRF, which would need to be articulated with the plans for transforming the ESM into a European Monetary Fund.

Conclusion

To investigate the reasons behind the most recent long-lasting EU recession and its very severe reduction in investments, we considered a simple theoretical framework (the safety trap model) which describes how, in the presence of an excess demand for safe assets when interest rates cannot sufficiently decrease, the equilibrium is reestablished via an economic recession. On the basis of this model, we focus on the second phase of the financial crisis, mainly linked to sovereigns, and interpret it as a situation in which safe assets suddenly disappeared, creating the conditions for a loss of investor confidence and for a recession in the EU.

The regulatory response to the financial crisis and the economic recession given by the EU was the CRD4/CRR package, the BRRD, and other measures to create the Banking Union and to make the banking sector safer and stronger. This response was coupled with the Juncker Plan to close the investment gap that emerged after the financial crisis. All these policies, together with the ECB monetary response to the crisis, have helped to take Europe out of the recession. The EU policy response to the financial crisis was therefore broadly appropriate, and it did—generally speaking—work as intended. The increase in the level of bank capital ratios, even if it occurred at a faster speed than foreseen by the regulatory reform due to market pressure on banks, narrowed down systemic risk in the EU banking and financial system and does not appear, all in all, to have made banking in the EU a non-viable business or to have hampered the exit from the recession.

The positive economic data of 2015–2017 showing a robust and broad-based growth are the result of an appropriate combination of mutually supporting initiatives that, on the one hand, have maintained financial stability (namely through the increase in banks' capital requirements, the creation of the Banking Union, and the credible break of the doom loop between banks and sovereigns) and, on the other hand, have ensured an increase in the supply of safe assets and the activation of a sufficient volume of public-private investments, namely thorough the so-called Juncker Plan and the CMU.

In conclusion, Europe is today much better off than it was only three or four years ago—with improved economic prospects, strengthened bank balance sheets, and an effective resolution framework up and running. These elements altogether translated in a substantial reduction and circumscription of systemic risk in the EU financial system. Still, curbing systemic risk does not mean the elimination of all risks. Idiosyncratic risks, which are often legacy risks, still exist and are mostly concentrated in banks' NPL. We therefore argue for swift measures aimed at neutralizing those risks, and we simultaneously argue that their reduction should pave the way for an agreement on EDIS and on the introduction of a backstop to the SRF.

Notes

Directorate-General for Financial Stability, Financial Services and Capital Markets Union of the European Commission. The views expressed in the text are the private views of the authors and may not, under any circumstances, be interpreted as stating an official position of the European Commission.

1. Marchesi and Nava 2016.

2. For the factors lying behind the decline in interest rates since the early 1980s, see Borio et al. 2017. For the reasons behind the growing demand for safe assets, see Caballero, Farhi, and Gourinchas (2008).

3. Caballero and Farhi 2014.

4. See Villar Burke (2013).

5. See Gourinchas and Jeanne (2012).

6. See, for instance, Colasanti (2016).

7. The mechanics of the safety trap model are not universally accepted among economists to explain how, after the outburst of the 2008 financial crisis, an economic recession started in the EU. In particular, the assumptions on investors' risk aversion and the safety trap model reliance on wealth effects to restore the equilibrium of the economy at the zero lower bound have been subject to various forms of criticism. From a financial markets perspective, the main causes of how a shortage of safe assets led to an economic recession in the EU with some of its specific features are discussed in the second section. The arguments of this chapter do not therefore strictly depend on the safety trap mechanics, but we nonetheless consider it a simple model useful in providing an intuitive macroeconomic explanation of how the loss of confidence that hit investors with the outburst of the 2008 financial crisis played a key role in triggering the EU economic recession that followed.

8. See Duarte and Rosa (2015) for a review of models.

9. Bank for International Settlements 2011.

10. European Commission n.d.-b.

11. McCauley et al. 2017.

12. European Commission n.d.-a.

13. European Commission 2013b.

14. European Commission 2013a.

15. Borio, Gambacorta, and Hofmann 2015.

16. The debate on banks' branch network and workforce reduction has emerged in parallel with a more general discussion on the degree of overcapacity in the European banking sector that also encompasses other issues, such as whether the EU banking system intermediates too large a share of the funding to the real economy, and on the (excessive) number of European banks. See for instance European Systemic Risk Board (2014).

17. European Commission 2012.

18. For a macroeconomic cost-benefit analysis of Basel III, see also Fender and Lewrick (2013).

19. In the medium term, efforts to further decrease systemic risk should nonetheless be continued with the objective of reinforcing the resilience of the European banking and financial system. With that aim, after the recent targeted amendments proposed in September 2017 to the functioning of the ESRB, one could for instance consider how to ensure a more targeted and effective use by national macroprudential authorities of the macro-prudential supervisory tools offered by CRD4/CRR.

20. European Investment Bank 2017.

21. European Commission 2017a.

22. Council of the European Union 2017.

23. European Commission 2015b.

24. The initial commission proposal envisaged the following phases: between 2017 and 2020 a reinsurance phase for both liquidity and losses between national deposit guarantee schemes (DGS), between 2021 and 2024 a coinsurance phase deepening over time, and after 2024 all national DGS would have been merged into EDIS.

25. European Commission 2017a.

References

Bank for International Settlements. 2011. "Euro Area Sovereign Crisis Drives Global Financial Markets." *BIS Quarterly Review* (December): 1–14. https://www.bis.org/publ/qtrpdf/r_qt1112a.pdf.

Barclays Capital. 2012. *Equity Gilt Study 2012.* London: Barclays Capital, February 8. https://topforeignstocks.com/wp-content/uploads/2012/10/Barclays-Gilt-Study-2012-Full-Report.pdf.

Borio, C., Piti Disyatat, Mikael Juselius, and Phurichai Rungcharoenkitkul. 2017. "Why So Low for So Long? A Long-Term View of Real Interest Rates." BIS Working Paper 685, Bank for International Settlements, Basel, Switzerland. https://www.bis.org/publ/work685.htm.

Borio, C., L. Gambacorta, and B. Hofmann. 2015. "The Influence of Monetary Policy on Bank Profitability." BIS Working Paper 514, Bank for International Settlements, Basel, Switzerland. https://www.bis.org/publ/work514.pdf.

Bugrov, D., M. Dietz, and T. Poppensieker. 2017. *A Brave New World for Global Banking: McKinsey Global Banking Annual Review 2016.* New York: McKinsey & Company. https://www.mckinsey.com/industries/financial-services/our-insights/a-brave-new-world-for-global-banking.

Caballero, R., and E. Farhi. 2014. "On the Role of Safe Asset Shortages in Secular Stagnation." *VOX: CEPR Policy Portal,* August 11. http://voxeu.org/article/role-safe-asset-shortages-secular-stagnation.

Caballero, R., E. Farhi, and P. Gourinchas. 2008. "An Equilibrium Model of 'Global Imbalances' and Low Interest Rates." *American Economic Review* 98, no. 1: 358–393. https://www.aeaweb.org/articles?id=10.1257/aer.98.1.358.

Colasanti, F. 2016. "Financial Assistance to Greece: Three Programmes." EPC Discussion Paper, European Policy Centre, Brussels, Belgium, February. http://www.epc.eu/documents/uploads/pub_6345_financial_assistance_to_greece.pdf.

Council of the European Union. 2017. "Council Conclusions on Action Plan to Tackle Non-performing Loans in Europe." Press release no. 459/17, July 11. http://www.consilium.europa.eu/en/press/press-releases/2017/07/11/conclusions-non-performing-loans/pdf.

Duarte, F., and C. Rosa. 2015. *The Equity Risk Premium: A Review of Models.* New York: Federal Reserve Bank of New York Staff Report No. 714, February. https://www.newyorkfed.org/medialibrary/media/research/staff_reports/sr714.pdf.

European Commission. 2012. "Impact Assessment Accompanying the Document 'Proposal for a Directive of the European Parliament and of the Council Establishing a Framework for the Recovery and Resolution of Credit Institutions and Investment Firms and Amending Council Directives 77/91/EEC and 82/891/EC, Directives 2001/24/EC, 2002/47/EC, 2004/25/EC, 2005/56/

EC, 2007/36/EC and 2011/35/EC and Regulation (EU) No 1093/2010.'" Commission Staff Working Document, SWD (2012) 166 final, Brussels, Belgium, June 6. https://eur-lex.europa.eu /legal-content/EN/TXT/PDF/?uri=CELEX:52012SC0166&from=fr.

European Commission. 2013a. "Banking Prudential Requirements—Directive 2013/36/EU." EU website, https://ec.europa.eu/info/law/banking-prudential-requirements-directive-2013-36-eu_en.

European Commission. 2013b. "Banking Prudential Requirements—Regulation (EU) No 575/2013." EU website, https://ec.europa.eu/info/law/banking-prudential-requirements-regulation-eu-no-575 -2013_en.

European Commission. 2014. *Communication from the Commission to the European Parliament, the Council, the European Central Bank, the European Economic and Social Committee, the Committee of the Regions and the European Investment Bank: An Investment Plan for Europe.* Brussels: European Commission, COM (2014) 903 final, November. http://eur-lex.europa.eu/legal -content/EN/TXT/PDF/?uri=CELEX:52014DC0903&from=EN.

European Commission. 2015a. "European Financial Stability and Integration Review (EFSIR) 2015." Commission Staff Working Document, SWD (2015) 98 final, Brussels, Belgium, April 27. https://ec.europa.eu/info/system/files/efsir-2014-27042015_en.pdf.

European Commission. 2015b. *Proposal for a Regulation of the European Parliament and of the Council Amending Regulation (EU) 806/2014 in order to Establish a European Deposit Insurance Scheme.* Brussels: European Commission, COM (2015) 586 final, November. http://eur-lex .europa.eu/legal-content/EN/TXT/?uri=CELEX:52015PC0586.

European Commission. 2017a. *Communication to the European Parliament, the Council, the European Central Bank, the European Economic and Social Committee and the Committee of the Regions on Completing the Banking Union.* Brussels: European Commission, COM (2017) 592 final, October. https://ec.europa.eu/info/publications/171011-communication-banking-union_en.

European Commission. 2017b. *Coping with the International Financial Crisis at the National Level in a European Context.* Brussels: European Commission, SWD (2017) 373 final, November. https://ec.europa.eu/info/system/files/eucountries-responses-to-financial-crisis.pdf.

European Commission. 2017c. "European Financial Stability and Integration Review (EFSIR) 2017." Commission Staff Working Document, SWD (2017) 171 final, Brussels, Belgium, May 19. https://ec .europa.eu/info/sites/info/files/european-financial-stability-and-integration-review-2017_en.pdf.

European Commission. 2017d. "Graph of the Week: Why Are Investment Levels in the EU So Weak?" *EC Economic and Financial Affairs,* January 27. http://ec.europa.eu/economy_finance /graphs/2015-03-30_why_investment_low_eu_en.htm.

European Commission. 2017e. *Reflection Paper on the Deepening of the Economic and Monetary Union.* Brussels: European Union. https://ec.europa.eu/commission/sites/beta-political/files/reflection -paper-emu_en.pdf.

European Commission. 2017f. "State Aid: How the EU Rules Apply to Banks with a Capital Shortfall." Factsheet, MEMO/17/1792, Brussels, Belgium, June 25. http://europa.eu/rapid/press -release_MEMO-17-1792_en.htm.

European Commission. n.d.-a. "The European Semester." https://ec.europa.eu/info/business -economy-euro/economic-and-fiscal-policy-coordination/eu-economic-governance-monitoring -prevention-correction/european-semester_en.

European Commission. n.d.-b. "Investment Plan Results." https://ec.europa.eu/commission/prior ities/jobs-growth-and-investment/investment-plan-europe-juncker-plan/investment-plan -results_en.

European Commission and European Investment Bank. 2015. "Factsheet 1: Why Does the EU Need an Investment Plan?" Factsheet. https://ec.europa.eu/commission/sites/beta-political/files/factsheet1 -why_en.pdf.

European Investment Bank (EIB). 2015. *Investment and Investment Finance in Europe.* Luxembourg: EIB. http://www.eib.org/attachments/efs/investment_and_investment_finance_in_europe _2015_en.pdf.

European Investment Bank (EIB). 2017. *EIB Investment Report 2017/2018: From Recovery to Sustainable Growth.* Luxembourg: EIB, November 23. http://www.eib.org/infocentre/publications /all/investment-report-2017.htm.

European Systemic Risk Board (ESRB). 2014. *Is Europe Overbanked?* Frankfurt am Main: ESRB, Reports of the Advisory Scientific Committee No. 4, June. https://www.esrb.europa.eu/pub/pdf /asc/Reports_ASC_4_1406.pdf.

Fender, I., and U. Lewrick. 2013. "Adding It All Up: The Macroeconomic Impact of Basel III and Outstanding Reform Issues." BIS Working Paper No. 591, Bank for International Settlements, Basel, Switzerland. https://www.bis.org/publ/work591.pdf.

Gaspar, V. 2017. "Investment and Investment Finance in Europe: A Policy Perspective." Presentation at the European Investment Bank (EIB) Economics Conference, Luxembourg, November 23. http:// www.eib.org/attachments/general/events/economic-conference-2017-panel1-presentation-vitor -gaspar.pdf.

Gourinchas, P. O., and O. Jeanne. 2012. "Global Safe Assets." BIS Working Paper 399, Bank for International Settlements, Basel, Switzerland. https://www.bis.org/publ/work399.pdf.

Klimenko, N., S. Pfeil, J.-C. Rochet, and G. De Nicolo. 2016. "Aggregate Bank Capital and Credit Dynamics." *Swiss Finance Institute Research Paper No. 16-42,* University of Zurich. https:// papers.ssrn.com/sol3/papers.cfm?abstract_id=2801995##.

Marchesi, M., and M. Nava. 2016. "Bank Regulatory Reform Supporting Growth: The Way out of the Safety Trap." In *Filling the Gaps in Governance: The Case of Europe,* edited by Franklin Allen, Elena Carletti, Joanna Gray, and G. Mitu Gulati. San Domenico di Fiesole, Italy: European University Institute (EUI). http://cadmus.eui.eu/bitstream/handle/1814/41825/Filling_the_gaps _2016.pdf?sequence=3&isAllowed=y.

Marchesi, M., M. Petracco Giudici, J. Cariboni, S. Zedda, and F. Campolongo. 2012. *Macroeconomic Cost-Benefit Analysis of Basel III Minimum Capital Requirements and of Introducing Deposit Guarantee Schemes and Resolution Funds.* Ispra, Italy: Joint Research Centre, European Commission, JRC Scientific and Policy Reports. http://publications.jrc.ec.europa.eu/repository /bitstream/JRC61485/lbna24603enc.pdf.

McCauley, R., A. Benetrix, P. McGuire, and G. von Peter. 2017. "Financial Deglobalisation in Banking?" BIS Working Paper 650, Bank for International Settlements, Basel, Switzerland. https:// www.bis.org/publ/work650.pdf.

Miller, M., and F. Modigliani. 1961. "Dividend Policy, Growth, and the Valuation of Shares." *Journal of Business* 34, no. 4: 411–433. http://www.jstor.org/stable/2351143.

Veron, N., and J. Zettelmeyer. 2017. "A European Perspective on Overindebtedness." Bruegel Policy Contribution No. 25, September. http://bruegel.org/wp-content/uploads/2017/09/PC-25-2017.pdf.

Villar Burke, J. 2013. "The Bonsai and the Gardener: Using Flow Data to Better Assess Financial Sector Leverage." Economic Papers 500, European Commission, Brussels, Belgium, June. http://ec .europa.eu/economy_finance/publications/economic_paper/2013/pdf/ecp500_en.pdf.

Discussion: The EU Response to the Financial Crisis and the Economic Recession

Claudio Borio

This is a broad-ranging and very informative discussion.[1] And I agree with many of the policy conclusions, in particular with the importance of making further progress with the Banking Union (BU) and capital markets union (CMU), as well as fostering a resilient financial system. As a discussant, let me focus on two issues where there may be more disagreement or that I felt had not been stressed enough.

The "Safe Asset Shortage" Narrative

The authors should be congratulated for trying to have a single narrative running throughout the chapter. That said, I feel the one chosen—the safe asset shortage—is not that helpful as an explanation for the global financial crisis and its aftermath, either analytically or empirically.

Analytically, the key result is driven by an unrealistic assumption. The formal model assumes that the choice between safe and risky assets is *not* subject to a marginal portfolio decision (Caballero and Farhi forthcoming). One segment of the population wants to hold only safe assets, regardless of their price. As a result, away from the zero lower bound (ZLB), it is the relative price of safe and risky assets that equilibrates the market for safe assets. But at the ZLB, where the interest rate cannot fall enough, it is the fall in output that does the work: this reduces the wealth of the only agents who will hold the safe assets, reducing the demand so as to meet the smaller supply.

This is odd: one would expect a recession to *worsen* any safe asset shortage. Safe wealth is destroyed as assets become more risky, and people may become more risk averse as they incur losses. The only way a recession helps *in the model* is precisely because nothing changes, except the wealth of the infinitely risk-averse agents who must be invested in the given supply of safe assets.

In a more natural way of modeling behavior, agents would decide how much to spend or save largely based on their income and then adjust their portfolios based on relative yields, both at and away from the ZLB. If so, disequilibria in their portfolios would have first and foremost effects on relative yields and, through those, on the economy.

Empirically, the data are not that consistent with the safe asset shortage hypothesis. Not least, pre-crisis the spread between risky (corporate/household or emerging market) debt and safe government debt was unusually *compressed*, not unusually *wide*. And post-crisis, it has fluctuated, being naturally quite high during the crisis and aftermath but becoming again unusually compressed in recent times. To me this suggests waves of search-for-yield behavior, not a structural excess demand for safe assets.[2]

The BU and CMU Project

The second point concerns the analysis of the implications of the BU and CMU. Here, let me highlight a few aspects that I believe deserve more attention, especially with regard to the need to ensure financial system resilience.

First, while it is of more recent vintage, a CMU relies on a strong BU. There is a tendency in the academic literature to treat markets and banks as alternative financing channels. But complementarities are equally, if not more, important (Borio 2003a): markets rely heavily on banks for their (market and funding) liquidity; banks rely heavily on markets for their own funding and liquidity.

Second, the authors do not stress enough some steps that would support both CMU and BU. These include greater harmonization of insolvency—one could add tax—regimes (Valiante 2016; Walker 2015); reducing the (overt and covert) obstacles to cross-border mergers, from ownership structures to the promotion of "national champions" (Borio 2016; European Commission 2017); and, closely related, the post-crisis "frictions" generated by national supervisors to encircle capital and liquidity within their jurisdictions.

Third, integration supports resilience, but only up to a point. Integration supports resilience mainly by helping to diversify idiosyncratic risks (both funding and credit risks)—a spare tire that supports the economy when banks face stress (e.g., Gambacorta et al. 2014), despite the complementarities I mentioned earlier.

One reason is that integration does not, by itself, reduce systemwide (systematic or systemic) risk, hence the importance of macroprudential frameworks (Borio 2003b; IMF-FSB-BIS 2016). A lot of work has been done in the EU to strengthen this, at least for the banking sector, but more needs to be done for nonbanks.

A second reason is that integration does not, by itself, do much for the balance between debt and equity. In general, there is a need, especially in Europe, to redress that balance. This requires action at many levels, including tax changes.

And it is especially important in the banking sector, through higher bank capital (e.g., Fender and Lewrick 2016). In contrast to some of the rhetoric, higher capital is the basis for more sustainable lending, through thick and thin (e.g., Gambacorta and Shin 2018). It is important to resist the temptation to dilute the standards in the implementation process. And it is important to fully recognize the risks inherent in instruments promoted to develop capital markets and to help finance small and medium-sized enterprises. For instance, simple, transparent, and comparable securitizations are necessarily subject to considerable, and under-appreciated, model risk linked to tranching (Antoniades and Tarashev 2014).

A third reason is that higher bank capital is not enough: the key to resilience is sustainable profitability. Here, the European banking sector is not doing well, as price-to-book ratios indicate. I cannot stress enough the need to address the nonperforming loan problem and to reduce excess capacity (Borio 2016; Enria 2012; ESRB 2014).

Let me conclude by stressing an element that is often underrated but is essential to underpin resilience: national governments' fiscal sustainability. While pruden-tial regulation can help, no financial system can be sound unless the sovereign is. I am concerned that fiscal policy has not as yet properly addressed two closely related issues: the hugely flattering effect that financial booms have on the fiscal accounts and the risk and fiscal cost of banking crises. Recall, for instance, how Spain and Ireland were held up as examples of fiscal probity during the run-up to the global financial crisis. As a result, fiscal policy can be too pro-cyclical and measures of fiscal space overestimated. In some recent research we have been developing ways to address these measurement issues (Borio et al. 2017a, 2017b) but we need more analysis, problem recognition, and remedial action.

This is essential: the sovereign's balance sheet is the ultimate backstop for the financial sector. This, in turn, raises a key question: Will the new arrangements put in place to resolve banks be sufficiently effective and credible? Experience has so far been limited and mixed. When establishing a balance between private sector and public sector involvement in addressing systemic crises, it is essen-tial to bear in mind that public sector support may be necessary (Borio et al. 2010). The risk is that, otherwise, pressures to sweep trouble under the carpet could be overwhelming. If so, the solution could be worse than the problem.

Notes

1. Discussion of the chapter by Massimo Marchesi and Mario Nava for the conference "Capital Markets Union and Beyond," London, January 26–27, 2018. I would like to thank Ingo Fender and Ulf Lewrick for their excellent help in preparing this discussion.

2. By contrast, the evidence regarding the equity premium, used by the authors, is debatable. The equity premium is notoriously difficult to measure: depending on how this is done, one can get very different answers concerning its development (Duarte and Rosa 2015).

References

Antoniades, A., and N. Tarashev. 2014. "Securitisations: Tranching Concentrates Uncertainty." *BIS Quarterly Review* (December): 37–53.

Borio, C. 2003a. "Market Distress and Vanishing Liquidity: Anatomy and Policy Options." In *Liquidity Black Holes: Understanding, Quantifying and Managing Financial Liquidity Risk*, ed. A. Persaud, 213–248. London: Risk Books.

Borio, C. 2003b. "Towards a Macroprudential Framework for Financial Supervision and Regulation?" *CESifo Economic Studies* 49, no. 2: 181–216.

Borio, C. 2016. "The Banking Industry: Struggling to Move On." Keynote speech, Fifth EBA Research Workshop on "Competition in Banking: Implications for Financial Regulation and Supervision," November 28–29.

Borio, C., J. Contreras, and F. Zampolli. 2017a. "The Fiscal Cost of Banking Crises: Implications for Fiscal Sustainability." https://www.cemla.org/red/papers2018/cbrn-23-5.pdf.

Borio, C., M. Lombardi, and F. Zampolli. 2017b. "Fiscal Sustainability and the Financial Cycle." In *Rethinking Fiscal Policy after the Crisis*, ed. L. Odor, 384–413. Cambridge: Cambridge University Press.

Borio, C., B. Vale, and G. von Peter. 2010. "Resolving the Financial Crisis: Are We Heeding the Lessons from the Nordics?" *Moneda y Crédito*, no. 230: 7–47.

Caballero, R., and E. Farhi. Forthcoming. "The Safety Trap." *Review of Economic Studies*.

Duarte, F., and C. Rosa. 2015. "The Equity Risk Premium: A Review of Models." *Federal Reserve Bank of New York Economic Policy Review* 21, no. 2. https://www.newyorkfed.org/research/epr/2015/2015_epr_equity-risk-premium.

Enria, A. 2012. "Supervisory Policies and Bank Deleveraging: A European Perspective." Speech at the 21st Annual Hyman P. Minsky Conference on the State of the US and World Economies: "Debt, Deficits and Financial Instability," April 11.

European Commission. 2017. *Accelerating the Capital Markets Union: Addressing National Barriers to Capital Flows*. Report from the Commission to the Council and the European Parliament, March.

European Systemic Risk Board (ESRB). 2014. *Is Europe Overbanked?* Frankfurt am Main: ESRB, Reports of the Advisory Scientific Committee No. 4, June. https://www.esrb.europa.eu/pub/pdf/asc/Reports_ASC_4_1406.pdf.

Fender, I., and U. Lewrick. 2016. "Adding It All Up: The Macroeconomic Impact of Basel III and Outstanding Reform Issues." BIS Working Paper No. 591, November.

Gambacorta, L., and H. S. Shin. 2018. "Why Bank Capital Matters for Monetary Policy." *Journal of Financial Intermediation* 35, part B: 17–29.

Gambacorta, L., J. Yang, and K. Tsatsaronis. 2014. "Financial Structure and Growth." *BIS Quarterly Review* (March): 21–35.

IMF-FSB-BIS. 2016. *Elements of Effective Macroprudential Policies: Lessons from International Experience*. August.

Valiante, D. 2016. "Harmonising Insolvency Laws in the Euro Area—Rationale, Stocktaking and Challenges." CEPS Special Report No. 153, December.

Walker, M. 2015. "Tax Barriers to Capital Markets Union in the European Union." *International Financial Law Review*, November 2.

16 The Role and Structure of Banks in the Future Capital Markets Union

Lorenzo Bini Smaghi and Michala Marcussen

The sovereign-bank doom loop is well identified as a major contributor to the European debt crisis, and the banking union (BU) initiative in 2012 came as a direct response to it. A consensus further emerged that overreliance on bank-based financing both deepened the crisis and slowed the recovery of the euro area. The capital markets union (CMU) project that was launched in 2015 draws its rationale from this view, placing the emphasis on enhancing nonfinancial businesses' access to market-based finance, notably for small and medium-sized enterprises (SMEs) and long-term investments. The United States, with its large and deep capital market, frequently serves as a benchmark in the CMU debate. Our contribution here is to take a closer look at that model and consider what lessons can be drawn for the future role and structure of banks within CMU.

The first section briefly maps the current financial system in the euro area and identifies three main characteristics: (1) dominance of bank-based intermediation; (2) fragmentation across bank, money, bond, and securities markets; and (3) a large share of debt financing. The US system stands in contrast on all three, but this has not always been the case.

The second section describes the key developments that shaped the shift in the United States from a bank-based system to market-based one. We observe that the emergence of deep and liquid capital markets came hand in hand with the consolidation, greater integration, and further expansion of the banking system. Indeed, the often-used headline numbers on bank assets grossly understate the importance of banks in the United States.

On the asset side of financial intermediation, one of the most significant changes in the United States was mortgage securitization. US banks' financing of SMEs continued in parallel to the expansion of private equity financing. A frequently overlooked point, moreover, is the important role that various government guarantees (implicit and explicit) play for mortgages, student loans, and SME financing. On the liability side, a large pool of long-term and risk-willing savings, which could be invested in capital markets, was a key to disintermediation.

The third section benchmarks the current state of play in the euro area compared to the United States. Several observations emerge. On concentration, the euro area lacks the "genuine" cross-border banks that we consider instrumental to the development of CMU. On the income side, euro area banks have increased their share of noninterest income, but many of the securitized assets are held on the balance sheet and serve as collateral. Markets for securitization need to be developed, but it is important also to consider the demand side, especially in terms of retirement savings.

We also find that the universal banking structure appears best adapted to CMU to ensure both growth and financial stability. Turning to the liability side of financial intermediation, the euro area does not enjoy the same deep pool of long-term and risk-willing savings as the United States, in large part due to the predominance of pay-as-you-go pension systems in the euro area. Finally, with respect to financial centers, we note the strength of London, an asset that the European Union will most likely lose as the result of Brexit.

We conclude with some observations on the policy implications that our vision for the future role and structure of banks in CMU entails. Although CMU is an EU-wide initiative, we focus much of the discussion on the euro area given the single currency and Brexit.

Bank-Biased, Debt-Biased, and Fragmented

The post-crisis recovery in the euro area has taken twice as long as in the United States with euro area gross domestic product (GDP) per capita only just recently returning to the 2007 level, albeit that the situation varies greatly between individual member states (see figure 16.1). One of the reasons for establishing a CMU in Europe is the observation that the US financial system proved more resilient in the face of crisis with a capital market able to substitute for the banking system when the latter went into crisis.

A bird's-eye comparison with the US financial system shows that the euro area has (1) a dominance of bank-based intermediation, (2) a much larger share of debt financing for nonfinancial corporations (NFCs), and (3) a distressful fragmentation across bank, money, bond, and securities markets as illustrated in figures 16.2 and 16.3.

The euro area financial system, moreover, did not enjoy the same benefits of a "single" supervisor and regulator, with a common deposit insurance scheme and an efficient resolution mechanism. The agreement on the BU in 2012 that seeks to remedy many of these shortfalls marked a turning point in the crisis, backed also by European Central Bank (ECB) action in the form of outright monetary transactions. This helped ease financial fragmentation (see figure 16.4).

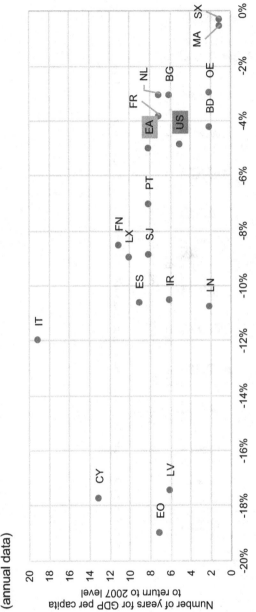

Figure 16.1
Recovery in the euro area has taken twice as long as in the United States. For countries where GDP per capita has not yet returned to the 2007 level, the International Monetary Fund (IMF) forecast has been used, projecting the final available year's forecast growth rate beyond the IMF's forecast horizon. *Sources*: Datastream and IMF.

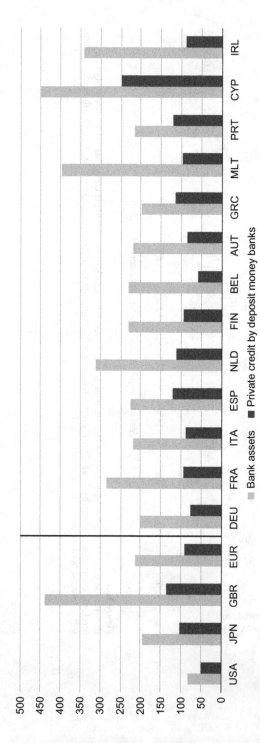

Figure 16.2
Bank assets, percent of GDP in 2015. *Sources:* Datastream, World Bank, Bank for International Settlements (BIS), and authors' own calculations.

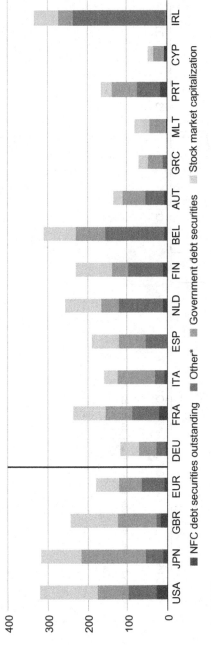

Figure 16.3
Capital markets, percent of GDP in 2015. * Mainly mortgages and commercial paper. *Sources*: Datastream, World Bank, Bank for International Settlements (BIS), and authors' own calculations.

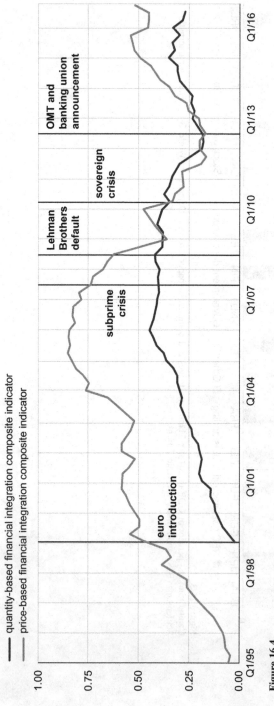

Figure 16.4
European finance remains fragmented. *Source*: European Central Bank.

The absence of a BU, however, was not the only issue. Rigid economic structures, a lack of institutional preparedness, missing fiscal room, and a muddled and slow policy response acted as additional headwinds.

In June 2015, the *Five Presidents' Report* (Juncker et al. 2015) outlined the project for completing the economic and monetary union, with political union, economic union, fiscal union and financial union. Our focus here is on the financing union, which comprises both the BU and CMU. We emphasize, however, that all four unions are interconnected and progress is required on all fronts to ensure that each fully delivers.

The Shift away from a Fragmented Bank-Based System in the United States

The US financial system today stands in sharp contrast to that of the euro area, but this has not always been the case. Back in 1955, the share of private depository institutions (which we will henceforth refer to as banks for ease of language) in the domestic financial sector's assets stood at 45% compared to 20% today (see figure 16.5) and the market was highly fragmented. The shift from a fragmented bank-based system to a single market-based one began in earnest during the 1980s and unfolded over the coming decades. The United States thus offers a reference both for present day comparison and for transition. The vast literature produced during the US transition tackled many of the questions that are debated in Europe today, and we draw on this to identify what lessons the US experience may hold for CMU.

Fewer and More Concentrated US Banks

In the third quarter of 2017, the nine US banks with assets of €250 billion or more[1] held 50% of the total bank assets. In 1960, the ten largest banks held just 21%, and the US Federal Deposit Insurance Corporation (FDIC) reported 13,126 insured institutions as compared to 5,737 today.[2]

Back in 1960, legislation set severe limitations on interstate banking activities. In 1966, the Douglas Amendment allowed interstate banking, but only with the agreement of participating states; it was not used until 1978. The following years saw barriers to cross-state border banks gradually removed, and beginning in 1997, banks could make acquisitions in any state following the Interstate Banking and Branching Efficient Act of 1994—although states could maintain quantitative limits on banking takeovers.[3] Technology and the fading memory of the Great Depression also shaped the banking industry. The predecessor to automated teller machines arrived in bank lobbies back in the 1960s, allowing customers to pay utility bills without queuing.

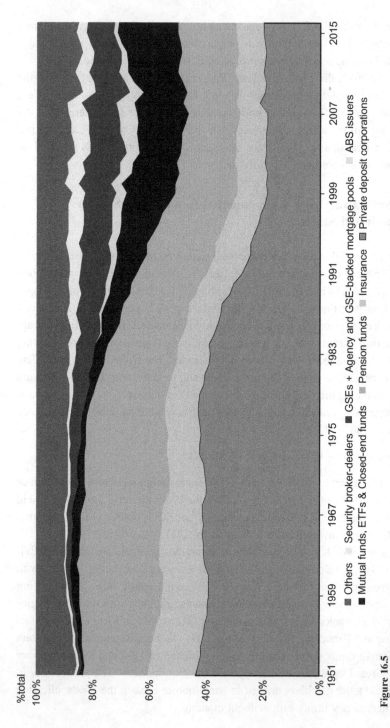

Figure 16.5
A major transformation of the US financial system. *Note*: ABS = asset-backed security; ETFs = exchange-traded funds; GSEs = government-sponsored enterprises.
Sources: US Federal Reserve Board and authors' own calculations.

The Dodd-Frank Act of 2011 allows free interstate banking but does set a concentration limit on large financial companies, prohibiting mergers and acquisitions (M&A) if the resulting company's total consolidated liabilities would exceed 10% of the aggregated consolidated liabilities of all financial companies at the end of the calendar year preceding the transaction. The limit, however, does not apply to organic growth.

The evidence generally supports the idea that free flow of capital across state borders allowed an improvement in the performance of nonfinancial business and of small enterprises. This echoes the principle of free capital movement across the EU.[4]

The deregulation of the US financial system not only focused on cross-state business but also focused on the activities banks could engage in, starting in earnest in 1980 with the Depository Institutions Deregulation and Monetary Control Act and Garn–St. Germain Depository Institutions Act of 1982. In 1999, the US Financial Modernization Act reversed the 1933 Glass-Steagall Act that had forced separation of commercial and investment banks. In 1999, the Gramm-Leach-Bliley Act allowed banks to branch into nonbanking financing activities such as insurance. This was followed by further liberalization in the early 2000s. Deregulation aided the shift to a market-based model. Technology again played an important role, and the early 1980s also saw an internationalization of banking activities as international capital flows were liberalized and domestic markets opened up to foreign competitors.[5] The shift in banks' business composition is visible in the growing share of noninterest income (figure 16.6).

Returning to figure 16.6, it is also very visible when the crisis struck, especially for the US$100 million to US$1 billion asset bracket that saw numerous banks fail. One notable point during the crisis was the speed of US authorities to (relatively) quickly resolve issues. Wheelock (2011) notes that between the end of 2006 and the end of 2010, unassisted mergers of nonfailed banks eliminated 1,002 banks, whereas failures eliminated 324 banks. In turn, this is likely also one of the factors that explain the faster recovery of the US economy post-crisis.

Banks Have a "Hidden" Role in Market-Based Systems

"Are Banks Dead? Or Are Reports Greatly Exaggerated?" is the title of a paper written by Boyd and Gertler back in 1994, and it is a question that pops up in the literature several times over the following decade.

In the early 1990s, several prominent individuals held the view[6] that banks were becoming less central to the US economy, and looking at figure 16.7, it is easy to see why. Here we separated out foreign banks based in the United States, as there was concern at the time that one reason for this view was linked to foreign banks gaining market share.

Number of US banks by asset size

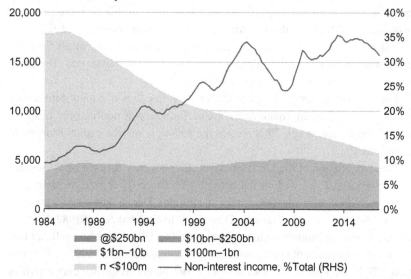

@$250bn $10bn–$250bn
$1bn–10b $100m–1bn
n <$100m   —— Non-interest income, %Total (RHS)

Share of industry asset of US banks by asset size

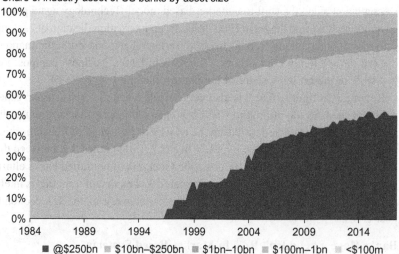

■ @$250bn ■ $10bn–$250bn ■ $1bn–10bn ■ $100m–1bn ■ <$100m

Figure 16.6
US banks: fewer, more concentrated, and a higher share of noninterest income. *Source*: FDIC.

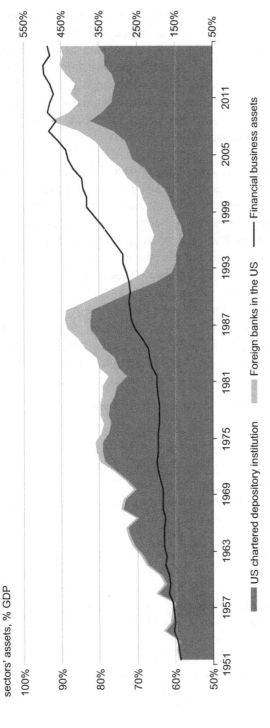

Figure 16.7
US finance expands, but banks shrank in the early 1990s. *Sources*: US Federal Reserve Board and authors' own calculations.

As highlighted by Boyd and Gertler (1994), the widely used bank asset-to-GDP measure of industry size fails to capture off-balance-sheet activities. To capture this, they build a credit equivalent proxy for off-balance-sheet measures and found that much of the decline was indeed attributed to a shift to off-balance-sheet activities. In 2015, the US Federal Reserve introduced a new set of data, the Enhanced Financial Accounts, to capture this. Using these new data, we calculate a proxy for total off-balance-sheet assets[7] (see figure 16.8) and note with interest that this gives similar results to the proxy estimate suggested by Boyd and Gertler.

This is no surprise given that banks play a key role in markets' providing a wide range of interlinked services, such as acting as intermediaries in public offerings and private placements of debt and equity securities; advising on M&A activities, including leveraged buyouts and restructuring of capital; offering structured finance and securitization solutions; providing collateral (unused credit lines, letters of credit, and so on); and offering primary dealer, research, and wealth management services. As illustrated by Song and Thakor (2010), banks and capital markets are clearly integral parts of a coevolving system.

Returning to the concerns on foreign banks, the headline numbers on banks assets again underestimate the true dynamics; this time due to the rise in off-shore activities. McCauley and Rama (1992) point out that foreign banks booked loans offshore to avoid the cost of US regulation, and after the relevant reserve requirement was dropped in 1990, offshore loans declined.

Corporate Bond Markets Offer Welcome Diversification but Not for SMEs

Digging a little deeper, it is worth having a closer look at the instruments financing nonfinancial business. Starting with NFCs, figure 16.9 shows the mix of loans and corporate bonds used to finance them. The growing importance of the corporate bond market is clearly visible, and it also proved more resilient and recovered faster to supply financing even as banks went into crisis; this is one of the motivations for CMU.

Turning to SMEs, we use the nonfinancial noncorporate businesses (NFNCs) category from the flow of funds data as a proxy. This segment is owned by households, and although the segment also contains larger business, around three-quarters of noncorporate employment and receipts comes from SMEs (fewer than 500 employees).[8] In the NFC segment, around 70% of employment is concentrated on large companies. As shown in figure 16.9, the NFNC segment is primarily financed by mortgages and bank loans. Moreover, for this segment, the crisis is very visible. Credit surveys show both weaker supply and weaker demand.

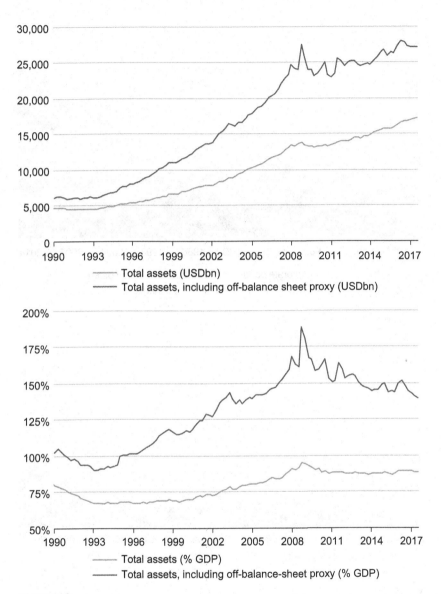

Figure 16.8
US banks expanded with capital markets. *Sources*: US Federal Reserve Board and authors' own calculations.

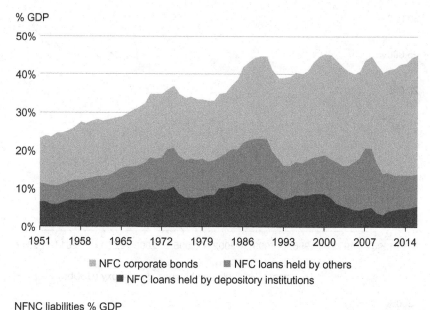

% GDP

■ NFC corporate bonds   ■ NFC loans held by others
■ NFC loans held by depository institutions

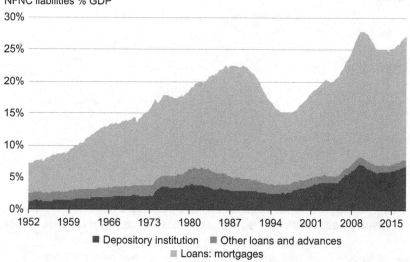

NFNC liabilities % GDP

■ Depository institution   ■ Other loans and advances
■ Loans: mortgages

Figure 16.9
US NFCs shift to corporate bonds; NFNCs remain dependent on mortgages and banks. *Top*: NFC liabilities; *bottom*: NFNC liabilities. *Sources*: US Federal Reserve Board and authors' own calculations.

Corporate bond markets are indeed most readily available for large corporations and when the banks went into crisis, this had a very negative effect on SMEs, and as a result they remained heavily dependent on them. Government sources offered some relief for SMEs during the crisis via the Small Business Administration (SBA), as the SBA supported Small Business Investment Company and the Export-Import Bank.

CMU aims to secure better financing for SMEs through market-based debt and capital. In the United States, securitization has primarily focused on mortgages and consumer credit. These instruments are standardized and transparent. SME securitization requires significant resources and expertise capacity generally held by banks. As such, banks will continue to play a significant role in these markets. It is worth noting that in the United States, the SBA facilitates loans to SMEs by offering partial guarantees, which also supports securitization. The SBA was, moreover, used as a fiscal tool during the crisis; the Recovery Act of 2009 allowed the SBA to support an estimated US$1.8 billion of new lending. The Small Business Jobs Act of 2010 increased the maximum loan size to US$5 million and allowed the SBA to refinance real estate debt. The SBA is the world's largest business loan guarantor and guaranteed 70,000 loans worth US$28.9 billion in 2016, supporting 694,000 jobs.[9]

Significant emphasis has been placed in recent years on the importance of capital for SMEs to grow and expand, and the rapid growth of business angels, venture capital, and private equity in the United States has attracted attention. The evidence suggest that bank lending continues to play a significant role at each of these stages, including the earliest stages.[10] An estimate by the Federal Reserve Bank of San Francisco (FRBSF) found that 22.7% of small business loans came from broad credit markets, compared to 76% for large companies. Nonetheless, banks still issue the bulk of the loans to small businesses, and these loans are, to a large extent based, on real estate collateral.

Small businesses in the United States reported a record tightening in credit standards during the crisis. As highlighted by the FRBSF paper,[11] this was due to a sharp decline in securitization and not a decline in the volume of small business loans. This illustrates the value banks can also offer as a diversification for capital markets. Compared to the euro area, there is little evidence that the US market-based system did a better job of protecting SMEs during the initial stages of the crisis.

The fact that SMEs' employee size (fewer than 250 persons) makes up just over 40% of US employment, compared to around 70% in the euro area, may go a long way toward explaining some of the differences in terms of overall macro-performance together with relatively faster action by US policymakers.

Government-Sponsored Enterprises Play a Major Role in US Mortgages

Digging deeper on mortgages, figures 16.10 and 16.11 illustrate that a declining share of mortgages are held by banks. Note that banks still play an important role in the primary mortgage market in extending mortgage loans.

As discussed above, mortgages have been a major beneficiary of securitization in the United States. When it comes to lender protection, the house being purchased serves as collateral. If a borrower does not have the funds available for a down payment, private mortgage insurance can be purchased. The most important form of insurance, however, comes from the federal government via the Federal Housing Administration (FHA), the Department of Veterans Affairs (VA), and the US Department of Agriculture (USDA). The mortgage lender can either hold the loan on balance, sell it whole, or securitize it. Securitization can take place either via private label securitization (PLS) via the government-sponsored enterprises (GSEs); Freddie Mac and Fannie Mae; or via the government agency, Ginnie Mae. The Federal Home Loan Banks (FHLB) are also classified as GSEs and offer liquidity to their members through secured loans. The FHLBs secure funding in capital markets and are owned by the member financial institutions. Although the GSEs are private companies, they enjoy a special status which means that financial markets perceived an implicit government guarantee; an assumption that essentially proved correct during the crisis.

Note that the marked shift observed in figure 16.11 occurred when the GSEs were required to reclassify these issues on their balance sheets. This was a consequence of the changes implemented after being placed into conservatorship under the Federal Housing Finance Agency. The government support for these entities was a major factor in stabilizing the United States in the wake of the crisis. The recovery has helped the GSEs improve financially, but it is remains unclear what the future status of the institutions will be. It is worth noting that the US government also offers support for student loans.

The United States Has a Large Pool of Savings

While our focus here is on the role of banks, the structure of US household savings deserves mention. Comparing to countries across the Atlantic, several features stand out. First, in aggregate, US households own fewer assets that their euro area counterparts, with total gross assets standing at just over 720% of income compared to just under 840% in the euro area in the third quarter of 2017. This position does, however, vary over time as a function of relative asset prices, including housing. Excluding nonfinancial assets (primarily real estate), things look very different, with US households' financial assets stand-

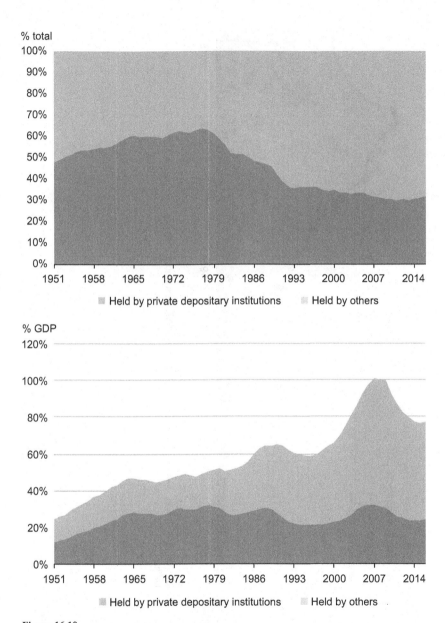

Figure 16.10
A US shift away from mortgages held by banks. *Sources*: US Federal Reserve Board and authors'
own calculations.

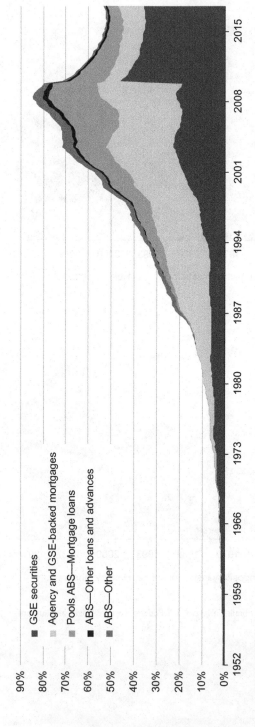

Figure 16.11
US securitization is primarily focused on mortgages. *Notes*: ABS = asset-backed securities; GSE = government-sponsored enterprise. *Sources*: US Federal Reserve Board and authors' own calculations.

ing at 520% of income compared to just 345% in the euro area. One important difference is that US households save for their own retirement, while in the euro area pay-as-you-go systems dominate. Allocation across asset classes also differs greatly, with US households holding a greater share of risky assets and euro area households holding larger bank deposits (cf. figure 16.12).

While retirement systems matter in analyzing these differences, tax incentives, home ownership, mortgage systems (and notably the ability to withdraw home equity), and cultural preferences are also very important factors to take into account. It is also worth noting that substantial differences exist across euro area member states. In preparing for a future CMU, the demand side for assets certainly merits more study.

Benchmarking Europe to the United States

The shift to a market-based system in the United States came with the emergence of a single banking market and deregulation of banking activities that helped to foster the development of a more concentrated banking system with the capacity to support capital market activities. The emergence of corporate bond markets proved a welcome substitute to bank loans when the crisis struck. Turning to securitization, mortgages have been the main beneficiary, and this has happened with government support. US banks continue to play a key role in financing SMEs, and here again, government support plays a role. More importantly, the United States did not suffer the same type of fragmentation shock as the euro area did, including in sovereign bonds.

Benchmarking the United States to the euro area, US banks hold a much higher share of off-balance-sheet items (see figure 16.13), although accounting differences explain part of the difference. US Generally Accepted Accounting Principles allow significantly more netting than the International Financial Reporting Standards when accounting for derivative positions. This accounts for roughly 15% of GDP of the difference in balance sheet assets between the euro area and the United States in 2015. Turning to the share of net interest income, we note that the gap between the United States and the euro area is much smaller. This suggests the euro area banks have also diversified into activities other than traditional bank lending. On the number of credit institutions, the euro area today has 5,587 monetary financial institutions[12] but again with notable differences across member states. Zooming in on the four largest, France has 780, Germany 1,632, Italy 560 and Spain 280 (ECB data).

The special role of the GSEs in the US system also needs to be considered in the comparison. The question on their future structure has yet to be resolved,

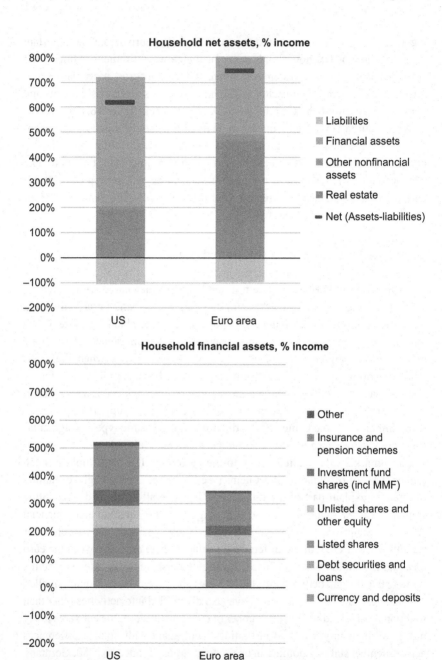

Figure 16.12
More assets and more leverage for US households. *Sources*: US Federal Reserve Board and authors' own calculations.

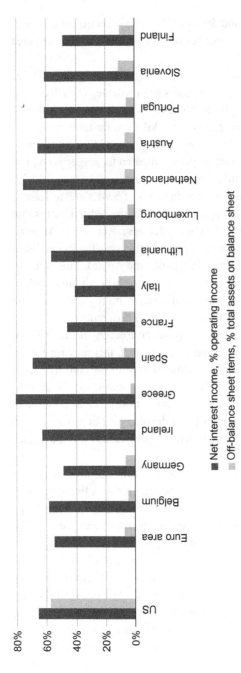

Figure 16.13
A larger share of off-balance sheet items in the United States. *Sources:* US Federal Reserve Board, ECB, and authors' own calculations.

but these securities amount to around 50% of GDP today and go some way to explaining the 130-percentage-point gap between the size of US and euro area banks (see figure 16.2).

Importantly, US banks also continue to play a key role in funding SMEs, and here too the public-sector-backed guarantees are available. The US experience shows that it is much more difficult to develop market-based financing for SMEs than for large corporates. Moreover, SMEs are far more important in the euro area than in the United States, making up around 70% of employment for firms with fewer than 250 employees compared to, respectively, just over 40% of employment in the United States.

One question is whether these differences in terms of SMEs are, at least in part, due to the presence of deeper capital markets in the United States that allow for investor exit (through initial public offerings). Across the Atlantic, there is a significant number of "newer" companies among the major listed stocks (think GAFA—Google, Amazon, Facebook, and Apple). This is a hint that in the United States, SMEs may be growing up to become large and, in some cases, extra-large companies. In a broader sense, more rigid economic structures in the euro area no doubt also explain such differences.

We also note that American companies hold far more equity that their European counterparts, but this is not something new. In part, this may reflect the fact that the US pension system is primarily capitalized while the euro area relies more on pay-as-you-go models, thus also offering a greater supply of risk-willing capital. There is also an interesting question to explore as to whether income distribution matters when it comes to the development of private capital financing. It is worth noting that these structures have gained ground versus more traditional listed equities in recent years.

The discussion on CMU is often focused on the objective of offering greater market access to corporates in terms of debt financing. Euro area firms primarily suffer from a lack of equity capital rather than from a lack of debt (whatever its source), and capital markets are clearly an appropriate channel to provide this. These questions merit more detailed study but lie beyond the scope of this chapter.

In discussing the structure of banks, it is worth keeping in mind that one of the reasons why the Glass-Steagall Act was ultimately repealed was to allow commercial banks more diversified income sources to protect financial stability and to make US banks more globally competitive. It was further argued that conflicts of interest could be prevented by enforcing legislation. Commercial banks made further inroads into investment banking, and this compressed margins and encouraged investment banks to focus on those activities where they held greater expertise. Overall, the system took on greater risks and became increasingly exposed due to greater credit and liquidity risks. With the benefit of hindsight, the error in repealing Glass-Steagall was the failure to ensure not only adequate supervision and regulation but also properly aligned incentives at that time.[13] Even without the repeal of Glass-Steagall, such matters would have required consideration with new financial innovations.

The Dodd-Frank Wall Street Reform and Consumer Protection Act of 2011 sought to remedy this but kept interstate banking and did not re-split investment and commercial banks. A review from the US Treasury Secretary[14] on the depository system highlights the importance of the community financial institutions (bank and credit unions) and calls for protecting the competitiveness of US banks globally. Without wanting to roll back the core ideas of Dodd-Frank, the report concludes that regulation should be efficient and not unnecessarily burdensome or complex and aims to make adjustments to regulation where required.

One of the main ideas behind Glass-Steagall was to manage risks by keeping different liquidity risks in different institutional compartments (commercial and investment banks). There is always a debate on where to place the regulatory cursor between risk and efficiency. The new model, however, is to ensure reduced risks with stronger capital, better liquidity coverage, and lower funding mismatch rather than to return to compartmentalization, even before the repeal of Glass-Steagall had begun showing its shortcomings. Moreover, new resolution mechanisms seek to reduce moral hazard.

On bank structure, a model of concentrated universal banks and the equivalent of community banks would offer the euro area similar benefits to diversification, global competitiveness, and proximity. The US experience also offers a word of warning to ensure proper supervision and regulation, especially crucial when changes to the financial infrastructure occur. This is of importance today with new entrants to banking, including fintechs.

The ambition of CMU is to have capital markets take on a greater role in funding the economy. The initial economic analysis from the European Commission[15] places significant emphasis on addressing the current fragmentation of markets to allow scale effects from origination, access to a broader investor base, better risk sharing, and higher market liquidity. This also requires genuinely European banks that can operate seamlessly across borders.

Conclusion: CMU Needs More Concentrated Euro Area–Wide Banks

Banking fragmentation was the first issue addressed in reforming the US financial system. Reducing fragmentation in the euro area—be it for banks or financial markets—should also be a priority. CMU thus requires a BU, and this must now be completed, especially when it comes to a common deposit insurance scheme. Fragmentation, moreover, should also be addressed in other areas, such as taxation.

The development of US capital markets, moreover, came hand in hand with the emergence of more concentrated banks. Given regulation and information asymmetries, it is challenging to see how the capital market functions performed by banks could readily be conducted by nonbank financial intermediaries. Banks play a key role in supporting capital markets through various interlinked functions, such as facilitating origination and distribution, advising on M&A, providing financing solutions such as hedging, securing market liquidity via market making activities, and providing research.

Fast-track deregulation was a major driver for the development of the US system, although arguably, it went several steps too far. The post-crisis regulatory changes not only are mostly welcome ones but also entail an emergence of a market-based system in Europe that will likely prove to arrive much more slowly than the one in the United States, even abstracting from the fragmentation issues.

The role of corporate bonds in the crisis supported large corporations but were of little support for SMEs. Both bank-based and market-based systems hold merits, offering a strong diversification argument in favor of the CMU initiative—an argument also advanced by the ECB in the policy debate.[16] That it may also help to address fragmentation is a further advantage. Whether it will reduce Europe's debt bias is less self-evident.

Currently, to foster securitization of assets held on European bank balance sheets, further harmonization of legal and institutional frameworks is required. This is not politically contentious but technically complex and will take time. Due to the well-known obstacles to fiscal risk sharing across euro area member states, it is unlikely, however, that a common backstop could be used to enhance the securitization of mortgages on a large-scale basis. When it comes to securitization of SME loans, the European Investment Fund's role could potentially be expanded.

We emphasize, moreover, that finance is a matter of economic security. While the participation of foreign banks is beneficial to competition, dominance entails risks as illustrated by what happened to international claims during the crisis (cf. figure 16.14). The significant inroads made by US banks into European markets post-crisis merits attention.

The crisis offered many important lessons. As seen from the US subprime crisis, CMU may bring unforeseen risks. It should not be overlooked that a flexible and pragmatic approach was an important factor in allowing the US economy to recover more rapidly than the euro area. A fiscal union, economic

BIS reporting banks, total claims on all sectors, 2008:2Q = 100

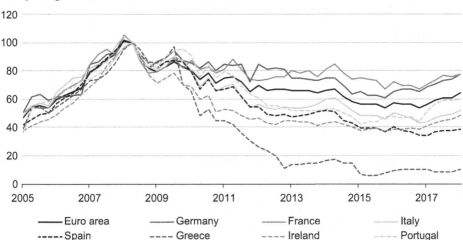

Figure 16.14
Cross-border claims head home in crisis. *Source*: Bank for International Settlements (BIS).

union, and political union are all relevant in this context. The euro area has paid a high price in the past due to bad compromises and incomplete solutions, and advancing quickly on all fronts of the policy agenda holds the key to success.

Brexit provides an additional motivation for CMU, and while it is not our focus in this chapter, we believe that the euro area should aim to develop a few strong financial hubs.

In sum, CMU requires concentrated and truly euro area–wide banks. It is illusory to assume that market-based finance could quickly assume a similar role in the euro area such as in the United States. Moreover, the euro area will not develop an equity culture overnight; SMEs will remain dependent on banks, just as it is the case today in the United States.

Notes

1. Federal Deposit Insurance Corporation (FDIC) insured institutions, FDIC Quarterly Banking Profile time series.

2. Note that in addition, the United States has around 5,800 credit unions that are run as not-for-profit, are largely tax exempt, and are supervised and regulated by the National Credit Union Administration. The credit unions held assets of US$1.32 trillion in the third quarter of 2017. These assets are included in the total assets of private depository institutions and amount to US$18.724 trillion in the third quarter of 2017. The trend for credit unions has also been to one of concentration with a smaller number of institutions, although these on average remain much smaller than banks.

3. Janicki and Prescott 2006; Nieto and Wall 2017.

4. Krishnan, Nandy, and Puri 2014.

5. A full timeline of the key events shaping US banking since the 1700s is available at FDIC (2014).

6. Boyd and Gertler 1994.

7. To calculate our proxy, we sum the total unused commitments, letters of credit, the total fair value of credit derivative swaps sold, the positive fair value of interest rate swaps, and other derivatives.

8. Kobe 2012.

9. Contreras-Sweet 2017.

10. Robb and Robinson 2010.

11. Wilcox 2011.

12. ECB Statistics, December 2017, excluding central banks.

13. Whitehead 2015.

14. Mnuchin and Phillips 2017.

15. European Commission 2015.

16. "Better to have a plurality of channels financing the real economy than to rely on just one" (European Central Bank president Mario Draghi in a speech at the European Parliament, November 2014).

References

Boyd, John H., and Mark Gertler. 1994. "Are Banks Dead? Or Are the Reports Greatly Exaggerated?" *Federal Reserve Bank of Minneapolis Quarterly Review* (Summer): 1–24.

Čihák, Martin, Ash Demirgüç-Kunt, Eric Feyen, and Ross Levine. 2012. "Benchmarking Financial Systems around the World." Policy Research Working Paper No. 6175, World Bank, Washington, DC.

Contreras-Sweet, Maria. 2017. "SBA: Smart, Bold, Accessible." Cabinet Exit Memo, January 5.

European Central Bank (ECB). 2017. *Financial Integration in Europe*. Frankfurt am Main: ECB, May.

European Commission. 2015. "Economic Analysis: Action Plan on Building a Capital Markets Union." Commission Staff Working Document SWD (2015) 183, European Commission, Brussels, Belgium.

European Commission. 2017. *Economic Analysis Accompanying the Document "Communication from the Commission to the European Parliament, the Council, the European Economic and Social Committee and the Committee of the Regions on the Mid-Term Review of the Capital Markets Union Action Plan."* Commission Staff Working Document SWD (2017) 224 final, June 8. Brussels: European Commission.

Federal Deposit Insurance Corporation (FDIC). 2014. "Historical Timeline." FDIC.gov. https://www.fdic.gov/about/history/timeline/1930s.html.

Janicki, Hubert, and Edward Prescott. 2006. "Changes in Size Distribution of US Banks: 1960–2005." Federal Reserve Bank of Richmond, *Economic Quarterly* 92, no. 4 (Fall): 291–316.

Juncker, Jean-Claude et al. 2015. *The Five Presidents' Report: Completing Europe's Economic and Monetary Union*. Brussels: European Commission. https://ec.europa.eu/commission/sites/beta-political/files/5-presidents-report_en.pdf.

Kaousar Nassr, Iota, and Gert Wehinger. 2014. "Unlocking SME Finance through Market-Based Debt: Securitisation, Private Placements and Bonds." *OECD Journal of Financial Market Trends* 2014, no. 2: 89–190.

Kobe, Kathryn. 2012. *Small Business GDP: Update 2002–2012.* Washington, DC: Economic Consulting Services, SBAHQ-10-M-0258, January.

Krishnan, Karthik, Debarshi Nandy, and Manju Puri. 2014. "Does Financing Spur Small Business Productivity? Evidence from a Natural Experiment." NBER Working Paper No. 20149, National Bureau of Economic Research, Cambridge, MA.

Langfield, Sam, and Marco Pagano. 2015. "Bank Bias in Europe: Effect on System Risk and Growth." ECB Working Paper Series 1797, European Central Bank, Frankfurt am Main, Germany.

McCauley, Robert, and Seth Rama. 1992. "Foreign Bank Credit to US Corporations: The Implications of Offshore Loans." *Federal Reserve Bank of New York Quarterly Review* 17 (Spring): 52–65.

McLaughlin, Susan. 1995. "The Impact of Interstate Banking and Branch Reform: Evidence from the States." *Current Issues in Economics and Finance* (Federal Reserve Bank of New York) 1, no. 2.

Mnuchin, Steven T., and Craig S. Philipps. 2017. *A Financial System that Creates Economic Opportunities: Bank and Credit Unions.* Washington, DC: US Department of the Treasury, June.

Nieto, Maria J., and Larry D. Wall. 2017. "Cross-Border Banking on the Two Sides of the Atlantic: Does It Have an Impact on Bank Crisis Management?" Bank of Spain Working Paper No. 1738, Madrid, Spain.

Philippon, Thomas, and Nicolas Veron. 2008. "Financing Europe's Fast Movers." *Bruegel Policy Brief* 2008, no. 1.

Robb, Alicia M., and David T. Robinson. 2010. "The Capital Structure Decisions of New Firms." NBER Working Paper No. 16272, National Bureau of Economic Research, Cambridge, MA.

Song, Fenghua, and Anjan Thakor. 2010. "Financial System Architecture and the Co-Evolution of Banks and Capital Markets." *Economic Journal* 120, no. 547: 1021–1055.

Stiroh, Kevin. 2002. "Diversification in Banking: Is Noninterest Income the Answer?" FRB of New York Report No. 154, Federal Reserve Bank of New York.

Veron, Nicolas, and Guntram B. Wolff. 2016. "Capital Markets Union: A Vision for the Long Term." *Journal of Financial Regulation* 2, no. 1: 130–153.

Wheelock, David C. 2011. "Banking Industry Consolidation and Market Structure: Impact of the Financial Crisis and Recession." *Federal Reserve Bank of St. Louis Review* 93, no. 6: 419–438.

Whitehead, Charles K. 2015. "Size Matters: Commercial Banks and the Capital Markets." *Ohio State Journal of Law* 76, no. 4: 765–811.

Wilcox, James A. 2011. "Securitization and Small Business." FRBSF Economic Letter 2011-22, Federal Reserve Bank of San Francisco.

Discussion: What Type of Banking System Is Needed to Accompany the Capital Markets Union?

Emanuel Moench

Chapter 16, by Lorenzo Bini Smaghi and Michala Marcussen, nicely traces the evolution of the US financial system from a bank-based to a market-based model over the past decades. It analyzes which elements of this evolution may serve as a benchmark for the European Union and which may not. The authors conclude that large cross-border universal banks are instrumental to the completion of the capital markets union (CMU).

This discussion aims to shed some further light on two aspects raised by the authors that are crucial for the understanding of the development of a market-based financial system in the United States: (1) the role of public-sector guarantees in mortgage and small and medium-sized enterprise (SME) lending and (2) changes to the pension system. The discussion concludes by arguing that large universal banks may only be needed for providing some of the services that a more market-based financial system in Europe will require.

Bini Smaghi and Marcussen rightfully point out that mortgage securitization via government-sponsored entities (GSEs) such as Fannie Mae and Freddie Mac played a major role in the transition of the United States from a bank-based toward a market-based financial system. While Fannie and Freddie have undoubtedly served as a catalyst for that evolution, another GSE is often overlooked: the system of Federal Home Loan Banks (FHLBs), which plays an important role in the provision of mortgage credit in the United States. FHLBs provide liquidity support to their member banks in the form of Federal Home Loan Advances. The banks use this support to issue mortgages for their securitization pipeline. FHLB advance lending contributed a nontrivial share to the fast-growing residential mortgage market in the United States in the run-up to the global financial crisis. The FHLBs fund themselves by issuing short-term debt that is mainly held by government money market funds. As discussed in Ashcraft, Bech, and Frame (2010), FHLB debt securities are considered federal agency securities and thus perceived to be implicitly guaranteed by the US government. Explicit and implicit government support of GSE debt thus plays an important role in the provision and securitization of mortgage lending in the United States.

Bini Smaghi and Marcussen highlight another important, albeit little-known fact about government support in the United States. The federal government provides substantial support for bank lending to SMEs via the Small Business Administration (SBA) with the objective to encourage lending to small businesses that face credit constraints. The SBA mainly operates through loan guarantees such as the 7(a) program. The scope of the SBA program has increased sharply in recent years. According to Dilger (2017), the SBA approved about 64,000 7(a) loans in fiscal year 2016, totaling more than US$24 billion.

Combined, these facts show that, when considering the US financial system as a template for Europe, one should keep in mind that explicit and implicit government support plays an important role in the provision of mortgage and SME lending in the United States.

Shifting firm financing from banks to markets requires a sufficiently large investor base for debt and equity securities. While US households keep a substantial amount of their wealth in securities, euro area households hold a larger fraction in bank deposits (Véron and Wolff 2016). Bini Smaghi and Marcussen rightfully point to differences in pension systems as a reason for differential demand for market-based finance in the two economies. The increased use of capital-based private pensions in the United States was triggered in 1978 when Section 401(k) of the Internal Revenue Code established defined contribution plans. From that time onward, US corporations started switching from defined benefit to defined contribution plans, and today the vast majority of these plans are capital based. Without a similar development, capital markets in Europe are likely to remain less deep compared to the United States despite the CMU initiative fostering market-based finance.

What type of banking system is needed to accompany the CMU? Bini Smaghi and Marcussen argue that large cross-border universal banks are key for the completion of the CMU. I agree that increased demand for services related to market-based finance—such as assistance in initial public offerings and private placements, structured finance, dealer services, and market making—will likely be met by large universal banks. That being said, fostering mortgage and SME lending does not necessarily require large banks as highlighted by the US examples discussed above. More market-based finance in the presence of households who continue to prefer short-term deposits suggests an increased role for maturity transformation services. While these services have traditionally been provided by banks, asset management companies are increasingly stepping in. Either way, European regulators need to be cognizant of the changes to the financial system that will come with the completion of the CMU.

Note

The views expressed here are those of the author and do not necessarily reflect the official views of Deutsche Bundesbank or the Eurosystem. I thank, without implicating, Natalya Martynova, Kartik Anand and Philipp Koenig for helpful comments.

References

Ashcraft, Adam, Morten L. Bech, and W. Scott Frame. 2010. "The Federal Home Loan Bank System: The Lender of Next-To-Last Resort?" *Journal of Money, Credit and Banking* 42, no. 4: 551–583.

Dilger, Robert Jay. 2017. *Small Business Administration 7(a) Loan Guaranty Program.* Washington, DC: Congressional Research Service Report R41146, July.

Véron, Nicolas, and Guntram B. Wolff. 2016. "Capital Markets Union: A Vision for the Long Term." *Journal of Financial Regulation* 2016, no. 2: 130–153.

17 Interconnectedness: Shadow Banking and Capital Markets Union

Richard Portes

This chapter discusses interconnectedness among financial institutions (entities) and across financial markets, focusing on the shadow banking system. Even the term "system" here suggests a range of interconnections and interdependencies that are deep and complex. Our data on these entities and activities are still very limited and are often accumulating unprocessed. This chapter deals with the European Union (EU), where the latest collection and analysis of the data are in the *EU Shadow Banking Monitor* (European Systemic Risk Board 2017). Some of the issues are closely related to the EU drive for a capital markets union (CMU) launched with an action plan in 2015 (European Commission 2015).

CMU is nonbank financial integration. Both price and quantity composite indicators of the degree of financial integration in Europe, starting from 1995, show considerable rises to a peak in 2006 and then a disintegration accentuated by the crisis to a trough in 2012 (European Central Bank 2017). Integration has since resumed, but the indexes are still not back to their 2006 levels. Roughly the same is true for individual subindexes for bond and equity markets, except that both show troughs also in 2003. The analysis here, however, will exclude bond and equity markets, with the main attention shown to shadow banking and derivatives markets. Also, we shall not be concerned with individual entities—from a policy viewpoint, we are concerned with macroprudential rather than microprudential oversight.

Definitions are not precise. CMU is the move toward deeper and more integrated capital markets to complement bank financing—a true single market for market-based finance in Europe, with no barriers at national borders. Shadow banking has been defined as "market-based (or non-bank) financial intermediation," but this is much too broad, because taken literally it does include bond and equity markets. The Financial Stability Board (FSB) (2017) regards shadow banking as "credit intermediation involving entities and activities (fully or partly) outside of the regular banking system." Again, this seems very inclusive. The European Systemic Risk Board (ESRB) is considerably less so: "The broad measure of shadow banking in the EU, comprising total assets of investment funds, including money market funds (MMFs) and other financial institutions, amounted to €40 trillion at the end of the third quarter of 2016. This measure includes all entities of the financial sector except banks, insurance corporations and pension funds." Here markets are clearly not entities, if only because they do not have assets as included in the "broad measure." But the exclusion of insurance corporations and pension funds is difficult to justify whether analytically or for policy purposes.

In contrast to the slowdown in shadow banking in the United States, the rapid growth of the sector resumed in Europe after 2007–2009. The demand for its services has come mainly from institutions and corporates seeking "safe" but nonzero yields. The huge growth in managed assets has led to a major expansion of the amounts channeled into shadow banking. On the supply side, much of the activity comes from regulatory arbitrage: developing organizational forms and transaction strategies that avoid regulation. This often involves substitution of shadow banking for "traditional" banks. It poses problems because it is not formally supported by safety nets yet may require bailouts. This creates moral hazard and a form of implicit subsidy.

The first section of this chapter considers interconnectedness and systemic risk. The second section specifies the costs and benefits of interconnectedness (one cost is contagion, explored in the third section). The fourth section details the risks associated with interconnectedness. The chapter concludes with a discussion of available and forthcoming data and their use.

Interconnectedness and Systemic Risk

Interconnectedness is ubiquitous in the financial system, and it is key to systemic risk. The system is endangered if stress in an individual entity or activity is transmitted widely through various forms of interconnection. This is contagion. A fundamental issue in evaluating financial integration is the balance between its benefits—more efficient allocation of capital, risk sharing—and the potential dangers posed by interconnectedness. When we think in systemic terms of the buildup of financial stress and vulnerability, our concerns arise from interconnectedness. With systemic vulnerabilities, shocks may propagate across wholesale funding markets, derivatives markets, and securities financing transactions (SFTs).

Systemic risk is the risk of potential collapse of a financial system resulting from interlinkages such that the failure of individual entities or collapse of a market can cause a cascading failure. Individual shadow banking entities may not seem large relative to major banks (still, recall American International Group's credit default swap market presence before the crisis, or consider BlackRock's balance sheet now). But tremors in the MMF sector, for example, can easily be transmitted.

A recent theoretical analysis (Acemoglu, Ozdaglar, and Tahbaz-Salehi 2015) finds that if negative shocks are small, a more densely connected financial network spreads risk and enhances financial stability. But beyond a certain size of shock, dense interconnections support transmission and propagation of shocks, hence a more fragile financial system. This seems to contrast with Allen and Gale (2000), who find that a network in which all nodes are connected to all others—a "complete" network—will be more stable than an incomplete network. But the complete network is an extreme case, and the earlier paper does not distinguish the size of the shock that is key to the later results. Gai and Kapadia (2010) obtain results similar to Acemoglu, Ozdaglar, and Tahbaz-Salehi.

So dense interconnectedness may be a source of systemic risk if the shocks are large enough. What is "large enough"? Ex post, the failure of Lehman Brothers qualifies. But the "taper tantrum" and "flash crashes" of recent years, nor even the crisis in Cyprus, do not. On the other hand, the discovery of a huge fiscal hole in Greece seemed to threaten the entire euro area financial system to the point where the authorities were convinced of the need for a massive bailout. Suppose there had been at that time a true CMU, at least in the eurozone. Might the risks have been distributed sufficiently widely, or at least less toward banks and more toward nonbank finance, so that the expected impact of a Greek default would have been considerably less threatening? Or would asset managers holding Greek debt have been hit so hard that their European bank parents would have been imperiled? We need data to map the European shadow banking system and its interconnections with the banks.

Direct interconnectedness refers to direct counterparty relationships and the consequent exposures on balance sheets. Indirect interconnectedness may include relationships induced for entities with common exposures, when an action by entity A (e.g., "fire sale") will affect the mark-to-market value of the assets of B. Collateral chains, in which collateral offered by A to B may—through a further transaction by B with C—put this collateral on C's balance sheet, so we now have an indirect connection between A and C, in which A is exposed to the risk that C may not be able to deliver the collateral to B. Reputational risk is when an action by A may harm the reputation of B, who is linked to it not as a counterparty but only by having some perceived common characteristics or ownership link. Step-in risk is if A were to have to support

B, to which it has perceived ties beyond contractual obligations to B that could induce reputational damage to A if B were to fail.

Ownership is a particular form of direct interconnectedness, and this may be a link between banks and asset managers in the shadow banking system. In Europe, banks and insurers have significant ownership stakes in asset managers that are important in the shadow banking system. FSB (2017, section 3) surveys interconnectedness between banks and other financial institutions—mainly asset managers and funds. In the context of CMU, the country aggregate data are of particular interest. Of EU countries, the United Kingdom and Ireland have the highest links between banks and other financial institutions (OFIs)[1] on assets and liabilities; Belgium shows especially high claims of banks on OFIs as a share of the banking sector's assets.

There are also issues regarding the regulatory perimeter. Intermediation has gone from regulated banks to shadow banks without prudential regulation, deposit insurance, or lender of last resort. Using volatile short-term funding (wholesale market) to finance long-maturity assets entails liquidity mismatch and maturity mismatch. Financial innovation (some generated to avoid regulation) may create opaque securities, often held in banks' off-balance-sheet vehicles. So a negative shock will come in a context where there are incentives for lenders to "run," and hence borrowers may face rollover risk. Asset managers like BlackRock and Vanguard hold huge positions in a wide range of assets that are also held by other entities. If redemptions were to force them to liquidate some of these positions, the market impact could be substantial, with effects on other holders of the assets. And we have the substantial exposures of banks to shadow banks explored by Abad et al. (2017). We should also note the particular vulnerabilities discussed in the *ESRB* (European Systemic Risk Board 2017): derivatives markets and synthetic leverage, SFTs, wholesale funding markets, leveraged open-ended funds doing significant maturity or liquidity transformation, and central counterparties (CCPs). There are specific reasons—in terms of liquidity transformation, maturity transformation, and leverage—for concern regarding these areas of the shadow banking system.

Finally, we note that interconnectedness (financial integration) gives rise to the "financial trilemma" discussed by Cecchetti and Schoenholtz (2017) and Berner (2017), following Schoenmaker (2011). They posit the inconsistency of three major objectives: financial integration, financial stability, and national rather than supranational financial regulation. If we believe interconnectedness is not easily reversible except as the consequence of a major crisis (and may indeed be desirable), then the argument suggests that we must choose supranational financial regulation if we wish to minimize financial instability. Since the crisis, the EU has created several new supranational institutions.[2]

But the national regulatory bodies are still very much there, and in most cases the European authorities can only issue recommendations to them rather than binding regulations. So there is considerable "ring fencing" and national policy-making that sometimes even stretches the limits of EU regulations. The national authorities often restrict cross-border financial flows and institutional integration—that is, they directly limit interconnectedness. This is one source of the financial disintegration we saw after 2006 and the slow recovery of financial integration.

Costs and Benefits of Interconnectedness

Financial integration eases the process of financial intermediation, moving funds from savers to investors. It also promotes portfolio diversification, the erosion of home bias, and hence risk sharing across asset holders and across borders. The deeper markets and more extensive network of financial institutions should favor investment and economic growth. But an environment with wider and deeper interconnections in the financial system can be more sensitive to large shocks that might then threaten financial stability. Interconnections can heighten systemic risk. Cross-border capital flows, facilitated by such interconnections, are a particular source of systemic risk. "Capital flow bonanzas" can lead to excessive domestic credit growth, and the home financial system may be unable to intermediate it well. The inflows then go into unproductive uses that do not create the export capacities needed to finance repayment; they may feed the accumulation of vulnerabilities in domestic financial markets that create systemic instability, so a sudden reversal of the inflows can itself lead to a crisis. If the capital inflows go into the nontraded sectors, it will then lead to an appreciation of the real exchange rate (relative price of traded and nontraded goods); real exchange rate appreciation is the single most reliable forward-looking indicator of financial crisis. And they are likely to contribute to asset price inflation and perhaps even bubbles, for example, through foreign investment in commercial real estate and housing.

Greater financial openness, integration, and interconnectedness are likely to have contributed to the development of a global financial cycle where monetary impulses from financial centers (in particular, the United States) are transmitted to the rest of the world (Rey 2016). This is doubtless related to the rising correlations of asset prices across financial markets. Together with the trend to passive investment (in index tracking funds and exchange-traded funds) and a fixation on short-term investment performance, a structural bias toward herd behavior in asset management has been created.

So financial integration comes with costs as well as benefits. Hence the wider acceptance post-crisis of the case for capital flow controls as a potential macroprudential tool that could block some of the interconnections between domestic and foreign markets and the buildup of balance-sheet relationships between domestic and foreign entities. These can create special vulnerabilities if the domestic entities take on unhedged foreign currency liabilities.

Other macroprudential tools, such as limits on mortgage lending, seem to be less effective in financially more open economies and where financial systems are more sophisticated—that is, where interconnections are deeper and more extensive (Cerutti, Claessens, and Laeven 2017). This empirical evidence on the effects of interconnectedness is directly relevant to structural vulnerabilities that might be created by CMU and to efforts to mitigate such vulnerabilities.

Contagion

Direct contagion occurs when, following a negative shock, a counterparty to a transaction does not fulfill its commitments, with a direct impact on the other counterparty. Indirect contagion can propagate through price effects or informational channels. Entities may be vulnerable to the same shocks, may have common exposures, or may be perceived by markets to face related risks. If one must sell assets, others holding the same or related assets will experience a fall in their values that adversely affects their own balance sheets. Bad news about one firm may affect market perceptions of others and trigger hedging behavior (Clerc et al. 2016). All of these instances of both direct and indirect contagion operate through various forms of interconnections.

Informational contagion is of special interest in regard to asset managers. The higher the commonality of their portfolios, the greater the likelihood and extent of informational contagion, and hence the greater the systemic impact of a shock perceived by one that becomes known to others (Allen, Babus, and Carletti 2012). But there are also other systemic dangers posed by contagion that operate through bank ownership of asset managers. Banks derive revenues from asset management fees and sales commissions; even if the entities in question may be off-balance sheet for the bank, it might undertake credit and liquidity risk in respect of the asset manager; market perceptions of problems in the asset management entity might bring reputational risk to the bank.

Conventional bank stress tests miss these contagion effects, direct as well as indirect. But there is evidence that the second-round or feedback effects of a shock to an entity, operating through contagion, are considerably greater than those of the initial shock. In an agent-based model, Bookstaber, Padrik, and Tivnan (2014) find that it is the "reaction to initial losses rather than the losses themselves that determine the extent of the crisis." And because shadow banks are typically not individually as important systemically as large banks, their systemic importance derives from their interconnectedness and the contagion they can create.

Where Are the Risks?

Different risky shadow banking activities concentrate in different segments of the shadow banking sector (European Systemic Risk Board 2017). We find liquidity transformation mainly in real estate funds and bond funds. Maturity transformation is particularly great in bond funds. Leverage is highest in real estate funds and hedge funds. And since asset managers have corporate bond funds and increasingly do direct lending to nonfinancial corporations, they undertake classic risks associated with credit intermediation.

One particularly opaque form of interconnectedness is the synthetic leverage created by the use of derivatives. We now have the data to trace the interconnections, but the true extent of leverage created in this way is very hard to quantify in a form that gives comparability to conventional leverage. We do not even have a common definition of synthetic leverage at a global level. The European Systemic Risk Board (2017) clarifies it somewhat: "Synthetic leverage is a specific form of leverage which differs from financial leverage in so far as it does not involve outright borrowings. Leverage can be created synthetically by generating unfunded exposures through derivative instruments which do not fully show up on the balance sheet, thus allowing a financial institution to control a larger amount of exposures with a smaller amount of invested capital." The risks are the same as with conventional leverage created through borrowing.

Another growing risk in asset management, particularly important for real estate and bond funds, is the rising share of assets in "redeemable funds" coupled with a trend decline in their liquid assets and portfolio shifts toward longer maturities ("search for yield"). Many now have redemption gates, but they have seldom been tested on a wide scale. Again, interconnectedness might amplify the effects of doing so.

Two important examples of interconnections in the shadow banking sector are the repurchase agreement (repo) markets and the central counterparty (CCP) set of entities. Much of the activity in the repo markets is transactions between shadow banks and banks. Seizures in the repo markets were a key factor in the contagion observed after the failure of Lehman Brothers. The stated objective of CCPs is to reduce the likelihood of systemic risk arising from the failure of one counterparty and from resulting chains of failure because of interconnectedness.

But the size and complexity of the CCP sector and some of its individual
entities—the inherent concentration risk—give cause for concern. Hence the
authorities have rightly put considerable effort into designing rescue and resolution procedures for CCPs.

Stress tests have not yet been applied in the shadow banking sector. We
might think this a glaring omission, but the weaknesses of stress testing in the
conventional banking sector suggest that it will be difficult.

Even the most sophisticated stress tests applied to banks do not take account
of direct contagion through exposures or of indirect contagion through deleveraging and fire-sale externalities. In the stress tests, the banks are passive,
so the proxy for feedbacks is to increase the severity of the shocks (adverse
scenario). This can be taken to the point of apparent absurdity. Cross-border
effects are typically ignored. There is no attempt to incorporate the shadow
banking system into bank stress tests, much less to stress test the shadow banks.
Stress tests as currently carried out are not useful in assessing system-wide
vulnerabilities.

Data

We have granular data on bank exposure to shadow banks (used in Abad et al.
2017). As yet, however, we do not have such data on the exposure of shadow
banks to banks. Data generated in response to the Alternative Investment Funds
Directive are in the hands of the national regulators, of which several have been
dilatory in transferring them to the European Securities and Markets Authority.
So there is as yet no such unified database that could be used by EU-level
regulators or academic researchers.

The role of academics here for "big data" is important. Manipulating the data
and bringing out patterns, formulating appropriate models for empirical work
and deriving results—all require the time and skills of experienced researchers.
They may also be commercially sensitive, so it would not be possible to open
them up to the private sector. The possibilities have been illustrated by collabora-
tions between academics and staff from the European Central Bank and national
authorities that have given rise to several papers recently published in the ESRB
Working Paper Series. These use data generated by the European Market Infrastructure Regulation reporting requirements. The research issues addressed
include: "How is interest rate risk allocated within the banking sector and
across other sectors?"; analysis of counterparty networks (interconnections!)
in the centrally cleared interest rate derivatives markets in the EU; and measuring the systemic impact of a global adoption of multilateral portfolio com-

pression in the EU over-the-counter derivatives markets (interconnectedness, often explicitly in networks). The more recent Securities Financing Transactions Regulation will also generate data on the interconnections among banks and shadow banks in securities lending and repos.

This will enable us to map the shadow banking sector—that is, to document and analyze interconnectedness. This work is essential to advance our understanding not only of shadow banking but also of the overall environment within which CMU is to progress.

Notes

1. Other financial institutions (OFIs) here include all nonbank financial intermediation except pension funds and insurers, so we mean trust companies, money market funds, hedge funds, equity funds, bond funds, and mixed funds.

2. The European Systemic Risk Board (ESRB), the European Stability Mechanism (ESM), the European Banking Authority (EBA), the European Securities Markets Authority (ESMA),the European Insurance and Occupational Pensions Authority (EIOPA), the Single Supervisory Mechanism (SSM), and the Single Resolution Board (SRB).

References

Abad, J., M. D'Errico, N. Killeen, V. Luz, T. Peltonen, R. Portes, and T. Urbano. 2017. "Mapping the Interconnectedness between EU Banks and Shadow Banking Entities." ESRB Working Paper Series No. 40, European Systemic Risk Board, March.

Acemoglu, D., A. Ozdaglar, and A. Tahbaz-Salehi. 2015. "Systemic Risk and Stability in Financial Networks." *American Economic Review* 105, no. 2 (February): 564–608.

Allen, F., A. Babus, and E. Carletti. 2012. "Asset Commonality, Debt Maturity and Systemic Risk." *Journal of Financial Economics* 104, no. 3: 519–534.

Allen, F., and D. Gale. 2000. "Financial Contagion." *Journal of Political Economy* 108, no. 1 (February): 1–33.

Berner, R. 2017. "Globalization and Financial Stability." Remarks delivered at the IMF Eighteenth Jacques Polak Annual Research Conference, Washington, DC, November 2.

Bookstaber R., M. Padrik, and B. Tivnan. 2014. "An Agent-Based Model for Financial Vulnerability." Office of Financial Research Working Paper No. 14-05, Washington, DC.

Cecchetti, S., and K. Schoenholtz. 2017. "The Other Trilemma: Governing Global Finance." *Money and Banking* (blog), July 24. https://www.moneyandbanking.com/commentary/2017/7/23/the-other-trilemma-governing-global-finance.

Cerutti, E., S. Claessens, and L. Laeven. 2017. "The Use and Effectiveness of Macroprudential Policies: New Evidence." *Journal of Financial Stability* 28 (Issue C): 203–224.

Clerc, L., A. Giovannini, S. Langfield, T. Peltonen, R. Portes, and M. Scheicher. 2016. "Indirect Contagion: The Policy Problem." ESRB Occasional Paper Series No. 9, European Systemic Risk Board, January.

European Central Bank. 2017. *Financial Integration in Europe.* Frankfurt am Main: European Central Bank, May.

European Commission. 2015. *Action Plan on Building a Capital Markets Union. Luxembourg: Publications Office of the European Union.* https://ec.europa.eu/info/publications/action-plan-building-capital-markets-union_en.

European Systemic Risk Board (ESRB). 2017. *EU Shadow Banking Monitor* No. 2. Frankfurt am Main: ESRB, May.

Financial Stability Board. 2017. *Global Shadow Banking Monitoring Report 2016*. Basel, Switzerland: Financial Stability Board, May.

Gai, P., and S. Kapadia. 2010. "Contagion in Financial Networks." Bank of England Working Paper No. 383, March.

Rey, H. 2016. "International Channels of Transmission of Monetary Policy and the Mundellian Trilemma." *IMF Economic Review* 64, no. 6 (May): 6–35.

Schoenmaker, D. 2011. "The Financial Trilemma." *Economics Letters* 111: 57–59.

18 The Politics of Capital Markets Union: From Brexit to Eurozone

Wolf-Georg Ringe

European Union (EU) policymakers are currently implementing the capital markets union (CMU) agenda—a collection of individual steps that, taken together, should strengthen cross-border market integration in EU capital markets. However, the imminent departure of the United Kingdom from the EU reshuffles the cards in this project, since the absence of the United Kingdom as the continent's most developed capital market jeopardizes the objective of creating a truly Europe-wide deep and liquid market that merits its name.

This chapter argues that the purpose of the CMU project can and should be redefined. The initial thrust behind the project in 2014–2015 seems to have been to court the British public in a bid to influence the Brexit referendum. After the United Kingdom's vote to leave, that objective no longer provides the glue that holds the CMU agenda together. Instead, I show that CMU can helpfully be redefined and reexplained in an entirely new context. Specifically, the CMU agenda provides a sensible set of measures to strengthen the architecture of the eurozone: cross-border integration of national financial markets holds the promise of promoting so-called "private risk sharing" that can serve as an important boost to reinforce the fragile framework of the common currency.

This chapter makes two points. First, it explores the initial motivation behind launching the CMU agenda. The chapter argues that the initial purpose was—among other things—a political bid to influence the growing anti-EU attitude and to win over the City of London. Since this strategy was ultimately unsuccessful—at least, it did not suffice to secure a majority voting for a UK-wide "remain" vote—the entirety of the CMU project was put into question. In a second step, the chapter shows that the CMU agenda currently on the table—if sufficiently reinforced and expanded—may find a new purpose in strengthening the eurozone architecture. The latter point comes amid the ongoing policy debate on the future of the euro.

The CMU's Original Goal: To Avoid Brexit

Even before he was even elected president of the European Commission, Jean-Claude Juncker announced that the creation of a CMU would be one of the key priorities for his time in office.[1] The idea was to strengthen the integration of the divergent national capital markets across the EU. The reasons for this initiative were twofold. First, strengthening the integration of national capital markets across the EU promised a more efficient allocation of resources across the continent and more diversified investment possibilities for European firms. Secondly, as banks and financial institutions had been blamed for large parts of the 2008–2009 global financial crisis, policymakers sought to find ways of making alternative means for firms' access to finance more attractive.

In February 2015, then-commissioner Jonathan Hill launched a green paper outlining intermediate steps and long-term goals of the CMU agenda.[2] This included a revival of ("high quality") securitizations, strengthening of credit information on small and medium-sized enterprises (SMEs), bolstering of a private placement regime, and a revision of the prospectus directive. The long-term goals of CMU were to improve access to finance for SMEs and mid-sized firms, to increase and diversify the sources of funding from international investors, and to ensure that markets work more efficiently. To these ends, the European Commission sketched a number of vague policies. Among them were the development of an integrated market for covered bonds and more support for alternative financing measures such as venture capital, private equity, and also environmentally conscious bond instruments. Further, the Commission proposed to lower the costs for setting up and investing in investment funds and to reform rules on occupational pensions. Among the broader initiatives were plans to address obstacles to cross-border capital flows, such as insolvency, corporate, taxation and securities laws. Finally, the Green Paper sought views on how EU markets can be made more attractive to international investors from outside Europe. The menu of initiatives that are united under the roof of CMU represents a motley collection of policies united by a common desire: to better integrate capital markets across the EU as an alternative to bank financing. The reasons for this are not only sound economic objectives but also—and possibly equally as important—political goals.

The *economic* underpinnings of this initiative are clear: A deeper and more liquid capital market should contribute to a more efficient allocation of capital within the single market. As a complementary consideration, traditional portfolio theory has long established that an efficiently diversified international portfolio carries a higher rate of return for a given level of risk tolerance;[3] a segmented capital market, therefore, does not allow investors to gain the full benefits from diversification. Finally, the global financial crisis drastically demonstrated that bank financing, traditionally strong in Europe, may collapse and thus fail to fulfill its purpose. Banks provide about 70% of business finance in Europe compared to just 20% in the United States, a state of affairs that some have said helped the United States recover from the recession more quickly. Critics may argue that all of these points are nothing new. Indeed, the reasons for the CMU project echo the economic rationale underpinning the principle of free movement of capital already enshrined in the European Treaties since the 1950s.[4]

There was, however, an equally strong *political* case for promoting the CMU agenda, above all concerning the difficult relationship between the EU and the United Kingdom. In fact, the initial thrust of the CMU project can be understood as an attempt to repair the strained bond between London and Brussels. Amid a growing alienation between the United Kingdom and the EU and rising approval rates for the UK Independence Party, then–British prime minister David Cameron announced in 2013 that if the Conservatives won the next general election, they would seek to renegotiate the United Kingdom's relationship with the EU and then give the British people the opportunity to vote in a referendum on whether to leave or to stay in the EU.[5] From the outset, the reaction of EU policymakers has been conciliatory, seeking to do everything to keep the United Kingdom in the club. It is in this context that the CMU agenda was launched by the incoming Juncker administration in 2014–2015. The political contribution of the plan is along two lines.

First, the launch of the CMU agenda was a political signal to strengthen the single market as a project of all twenty-eight member states instead of just the eurozone countries. While some projects—like the creation of the banking union—during the crisis response years had been largely confined to the eurozone (plus participating member states), this had raised fears of a growing bifurcation of the EU single market and, most importantly, leaving out the United Kingdom. In contrast, by early 2015 the CMU project sent a strong signal to the United Kingdom to remain an active part of the EU and represented a commitment to the overall single market idea. This point is illustrated by the fact that the European Commission portfolios were reshuffled to form a new "Directorate-General for Financial Stability, Financial Services and Capital Markets Union," which Juncker eventually awarded to a British national.[6]

Secondly, the CMU is a project that found political support in the United Kingdom and thus was a possibility to help to further its rapprochement to the EU. Against the growing frustration in British politics and the looming threat of an anti-EU referendum as promised by Prime Minister Cameron, the prospect of a deeper market for capital was an attempt to appease the heated atmosphere in London. The City of London stood to benefit from a continent-spanning market, which would have facilitated transactions and promised economies of scale. It was therefore no surprise that the CMU initiative was welcomed by British business groups and politicians, including then-chancellor George Osborne.[7] The House of Lords even hailed the initiative as a "a golden opportunity for the UK" and "a means to demonstrate afresh that the City of London, and the financial sector which is centered there, is an asset not only to the UK economy but to the EU as a whole."[8] Seen from this perspective, proposing a united capital market was a smart move to win back the trust of the United Kingdom (at least the City of London) and to overcome the various confrontations between Europe and Britain that were not just limited to political disagreement concerning financial regulation but increasingly included courtroom battles over financial laws.[9]

Beyond being an offer to Britain, CMU was also to be understood as a promise of a better future for all other EU countries, mostly at the periphery, who were weary, at that time, of their long post-crisis experience of austerity. By putting the proposal in the context of "jobs" and "growth," the CMU idea served as a beacon of hope for light at the end of the tunnel. Finally, and maybe most importantly, CMU was a step that signaled a return to a more traditional EU activity of "market building." In the long history of EU efforts to promote a single market for capital, the EU has always been strong at playing the role at which it is most effective: to facilitate the exchange of capital flows across borders by removing obstacles to cross-border investment. This was the leitmotif of most EU activity throughout the 1980s and 1990s, until the financial crisis caused a sharp turn toward a more market-shaping, regulatory approach.[10] Lord Hill's predecessor, Michel Barnier, had produced a flood of initiatives to regulate and contain financial institutions' excessive risk taking and restore stability to financial markets. His time in office had thus been characterized by a more market-curbing or regulatory type of activity. Hill, in contrast, returned to the classic style of EU lawmaking, ensuring continuity, promising greater effectiveness, and avoiding the legal pitfalls of a more sanctions-oriented EU legal framework.

In conclusion, the main contribution of the CMU agenda was its political symbolism—return to the single market, deepening capital markets, more jobs, and growth.[11] Some support for this interpretation can be found in the fact that a number of the initiatives bundled under the label "capital markets union" had already been pursued or discussed by the European Commission way before the CMU agenda was even initiated. For example, preparations for a revision of the Prospectus Directive had already started as early as 2011 when the Commission charged the European Securities and Markets Authority (ESMA) with exploring options for reform.[12] The ongoing reform efforts could thus readily be inserted into the new CMU agenda to give it some further substance.[13] As the European Commission in all honesty stated: "It is true that many of the issues at stake—insolvency and securities laws, tax treatments—have been discussed for many years."[14]

CMU and Brexit

If Brexit had been the target, the CMU initiative was unsuccessful. As is well known, to the surprise of many, the British public in June 2016 voted to leave the EU. Maybe wooing the City of London turned out to have the opposite effect for the United Kingdom as a whole, and the EU's move of proposing CMU bet on the wrong horse.[15] It is well known that the public mood informing the Brexit vote was highly anti-establishment,[16] and the financial industry in the City of London is typically seen as part of the national elite. Consequently, proposing an agenda that would have been City-friendly may have created a backlash among the broader UK public.

In any case, the political and legal calamities of the referendum outcome are legend and should not be recounted here.[17] Instead, a somewhat underexplored question concerns the implications of the referendum outcome for the CMU project. The obvious question to ask is whether the CMU action plan still remains realistic if London, Europe's financial heart, no longer participates.[18]

Opinions on this question were deeply divided. Many clearly believed that CMU without the United Kingdom would be an exercise without purpose and, at the very least, that Brexit would have "negative implications" for the CMU project[19]—especially since Britain had been the main driving force behind the initiative. Accordingly, British commissioner for financial services Jonathan Hill, who had been a major promoter of CMU, immediately after the referendum tendered his resignation.[20]

The European Commission took the opposite view. After some hesitation, EU policymakers began to understand Brexit as an opportunity toward deeper integration.[21] In a communication of September 2016 entitled "Capital Markets Union—Accelerating Reform," they concluded that the CMU agenda was now even "more important than ever" and that "the implementation of actions in the plan should be accelerated."[22]

There is no doubt that the UK departure changes the dynamics of policy-making in EU financial regulation. Since the 2008 financial crisis, there have been new informal political alliances influencing the EU agenda. France, Italy, and other member states are said to be part of a "market shaping" alliance, supporting stricter regulation of financial institutions. This contrasted with a UK-led club of countries in favor of "market making," championing competition, and market efficiency.[23] For the latter group of countries that typically already have rather developed capital markets, such as Ireland, the Netherlands, or Sweden, the palpable risk was that their coalition, having lost its natural leader, would lose out in the battle for substance in implementing CMU. Put differently, the UK departure meant that the future direction of CMU would change—away from market liberalization toward a more restrictive attitude.

After some period of agonizing, the "market shaping" coalition saw an opportunity to utilize the crippled CMU agenda for their own purposes. Three objectives seem to have been mainly relevant.

First, the UK departure allowed other EU member states to change the character of CMU from a modest, "incrementalist" approach to a more ambitious vision of "institutional change" and of developing "centralized institutions."[24] That approach had suddenly become more achievable as Brexit meant that the United Kingdom would no longer block the creation of new institutions and veto any further reaching centralization.[25] The second opportunity was for the remaining EU countries of the (EU27) to build a deeper capital market "on their own." In other words, the departure of the United Kingdom and prospect of a deregulated City of London at their doorsteps left the rest of the EU no other choice than to stand together and hope that their twenty-seven economies combined could represent an alternative capital market. That vision included the imperative to act quickly, since first successful steps were ideally needed to be already in place before the United Kingdom had even left. Finally, as a third hope, in particular the large member states, such as France and Germany, saw the opportunity of enticing parts of London's financial industry away to bolster their own financial centers. London had long been the envy in particular of French policymakers, and Brexit provided the opportunity to end London's hegemony in Europe. Accordingly, Paris and Frankfurt initiated an unprecedented charm offensive and marketing campaign to woo London-based firms.[26]

All three dreams suffer from one major flaw. They disregard the idiosyncratic nature of the financial market—in particular, they ignore what is called the "agglomeration effect" of finance as one of the fundamental laws of financial centers. Financial market activities are known to benefit from agglomeration and concentration: the assimilation of financial services in a single hub allows for economies of scale and a depth of capital market activity that cannot be easily replicated elsewhere. Moving parts of the industry to the continent will, therefore, reduce the size of the overall pie. Put differently, it would be to the EU's advantage to leave the formidable ecosystem of the City of London intact.[27]

There is, however, a different justification of why it makes sense to further pursue the CMU agenda in a diminished EU27. A redefined objective of CMU lies in the possibility of reinforcing the architecture of the eurozone as a common currency through private risk sharing. The next section will explore this rationale in more detail.

A Reinvented CMU for the Eurozone

Capital Markets Union is essentially an agenda to deepen cross-border financial integration. Such integration leads to so-called private risk sharing. It has long been understood by economists that private risk sharing has the potential to strengthen a common currency area, and this insight is now also slowly arriving in legal and policy circles. Thus, different from the original plans, the *CMU Mid-Term Review* for the first time mentioned that the CMU initiative could also "strengthen ... Economic and Monetary Union (EMU) by supporting economic and social convergence and helping absorb economic shocks in the euro area."[28] The same idea was floated in the famous 2015 *Five Presidents Report*.[29]

The basic concept is simple. Financial markets are the natural place where private risk sharing takes place. They can function as an insurance structure smoothing asymmetric shocks via cross-country ownership of assets.[30] Consider the example of a simple monetary union composed of two countries, A and B. Assume an asymmetric economic shock which leads country A into a crisis, while the economy of country B is booming. If they are not financially integrated, the consumption level should rise in country B and decrease in country A, leading to social tensions and an increase in discontentment with the union. However, if they are fully financially integrated, their consumption should co-move.[31] For instance, considering the equity market, residents of country A would own shares of companies in country B, thus receiving the gains from the boom. On the other hand, residents of country B would own shares in country A, thus share the losses of its companies. On the top of smoothing idiosyncratic shocks, financial integration can also foster economic growth by increasing the allocative efficiency of capital. Resources would be allocated to where they are higher valued. In the context of the eurozone, for instance, countries that have a shortage of capital (thus a higher value) would profit from an influx of resources coming from members with abundance (thus lower value). This would promote growth both in the first region and in the second region since a higher international diversification might allow companies to invest in higher return domestic investments.[32] The same phenomenon can be demonstrated for a fully integrated bond market and for the cross-border integration of banking.

Crucially, greater financial integration would reduce the need for any form of formal fiscal union in Europe.[33]

For countries in a monetary union such as the eurozone, such private risk sharing is particularly important because the common monetary policy steered by the European Central Bank (ECB) is unable to address asymmetric shocks that affect only one country or region within Europe. With disjointed business cycles across countries, idiosyncratic shocks to individual EMU member states need to be insured through a robust and integrated financial market. Reducing the volatility of aggregate consumption through various risk-sharing mechanisms can provide significant welfare gains for countries hit by specific shocks. Moreover, by reducing internal divergences and facilitating macroeconomic adjustment, risk sharing can be beneficial for the monetary union as a whole: a truly integrated financial market is a meaningful component of a monetary union, as without it, monetary policy decisions will not be transmitted equally well across all participating member states.[34]

A number of studies have demonstrated the importance of private risk sharing. For example, when considering the United States, empirical evidence shows that more than 39% of the shocks sustained by individual American states are smoothed by federal capital markets, 23% by the credit markets, and only 13% by the federal budget, while 25% remained unsmoothed.[35] Consequently, even in a full federation, public risk sharing only responds for slightly more than 10% of the shocks. The main responsibility for smoothing the shocks faced by the American states is the financial market (smoothing more than 60% of the shocks). Similar results were found in other studies applying different methodologies or analyzing different federations.[36]

In the euro area, the ECB found that more than 75.7% of the shocks to member states presently are not smoothed at all, 18.2% are smoothed by the credit markets, 5.4% by capital markets, and 0% by cross-border fiscal transfers.[37] In other words, more than three-quarters of the shocks received by the eurozone are not smoothed; the small part that is insured is only insured by the financial market.[38] These numbers are not only consistent with the restrictions on public risk sharing in the EU treaties (since fiscal transfers are basically inherent) but also might give a foundation for understanding the discontentment with the euro in the countries most affected by the last crisis (since they faced more than three-quarters of the pain alone). The situation of financial integration with limited risk sharing exposed the eurozone to a significant capital reversal from the beginning of the sovereign crisis onward.[39]

Why would private risk sharing be necessary at all? The eurozone was originally designed, in great controversy, as a monetary union of sovereign countries. It received substantial criticism from leading economists at the time who pointed out the difficulties associated with such an approach, as Europe was not considered as an optimal currency area.[40] It did not face symmetric economic shocks and did not have a high mobility of factors or mechanisms to absorb any idiosyncratic shocks. Under this framework, the currency union was clearly fragile. Yet the prevailing hope was that the economic momentum created by the EMU would almost certainly provide the ground for subsequent political integration. However, the virtual convergence of interest rates of sovereign bonds issued by EU member states in the years after the introduction of the euro made policymakers numb, slowing the adoption of the reforms necessary to strengthen the delicate currency framework. In particular, policymakers hoped that the adoption of the euro would lead to economic convergence between EU member states.

This fragility of the eurozone has essentially not changed over time. The 2008–2009 global financial crisis saw an almost collapse of the common currency, and it was only ECB president Mario Draghi's courageous crisis management that rescued the euro. More recently, at least since Emanuel Macron's 2017 intervention, a public debate has started on how to secure and improve the eurozone. A number of reform proposals have been made, and reports are circulating.[41] This is not the place to discuss the relative merits of the different concepts and perspectives. The point here is simple: pursuing the CMU project, probably even expanding it, can find a sensible objective in strengthening the common currency.

This idea of strengthening the EMU through private risk sharing has a number of key advantages. The first is of a political nature. In the EU context, attempts at promoting *public* risk-sharing initiatives have proven unpopular in both the main contributing member state (with a more resilient economy) and the main beneficiary member state (with a less resilient economy). The taxpayers of the former are typically reluctant to support a foreign government without seeing the direct benefits of it. On the other hand, such public financing support is usually conditioned on the adoption of austerity measures that are not only highly unpopular in the latter but might also foster a nationalist populist backlash (on the idea that these measures were "imposed" by foreign nations). Secondly, as international experience shows,[42] private risk sharing may also be more functional. First, cross-border holdings of productive or financial assets can provide members of a currency union with insurance against idiosyncratic shocks. Second, well-functioning credit markets can contribute to smoothing consumption against relative income fluctuations, especially if most cross-border lending takes the form of direct lending to households and firms rather than of wholesale lending and borrowing in interbank markets.[43] The conclusion is that greater progress in risk sharing in the euro area would require significantly more developed and integrated capital markets as well as more banks operating at a pan-European level. Finally, private risk sharing would be advantageous from a legal perspective. As explained above, public risk sharing would require arduous renegotiations of the EU treaties and be fraught with uncertainty and subject to high political resistance. The deepening of financial integration, by contrast, can be achieved within the present legal framework as it corresponds much better to the traditional EU mission of market making.

It is safe to assume that, in the foreseeable future, a number of alternative mechanisms that would have the potential to improve risk sharing across countries will not progress quickly in the EU. For example, labor mobility will likely remain below levels achieved in common-language federations such as the United States or Germany. Similarly, building a European supranational system of taxes and transfers is, at present, not a realistic prospect. Finally, the rules on fiscal deficits imposed by the Stability and Growth Pact will continue to set limits on national governments for smoothing large shocks. Private risk sharing and continuing with CMU, therefore, becomes an even more pressing imperative.

Conclusion

In sum, the economic and political motivations for pursuing a genuine "capital markets union" are evident. Until now, the driving force has been a political one, namely to sway the UK referendum toward "remain." Consistent with this, the substance of the 2015 CMU agenda was modest, and many aspects had a largely symbolic value. The British departure now offers the possibility of reinterpreting CMU as a toolbox to reinforce the euro architecture and so move CMU from a political agenda to an economically sensible instrument. To achieve that, policymakers need to be more ambitious in substance. The goal should be steps on the path toward a fully unified European capital market, probably under the remit of a single market supervisor. As a silver lining, decision making on these issues should become easier after Brexit, as the United Kingdom has regularly vetoed important steps toward integration in the past. Where the political center in an EU27 lies is, however, very much uncertain.

Notes

1. Jean-Claude Juncker, "A New Start for Europe," opening statement, European Parliament plenary session, July 15, 2014, http://europa.eu/rapid/press-release_SPEECH-14-567_en.htm.

2. European Commission, *Green Paper: Building a Capital Markets Union* (Brussels: European Commission, COM [2015] 63 final, February 18, 2015).

3. H. G. Grubel, "Internationally Diversified Portfolios," *American Economic Review* 58, no. 5 (1968): 1299–1314; H. Levy and M. Sarnat, "International Diversification of Investment Portfolios," *American Economic Review* 60, no. 4 (1970): 668–675.

4. See European Commission, "Consolidated Version of the Treaty on the Functioning of the European Union," *Official Journal of the European Union* C326/47, October 26, 2012, Articles 63–66.

5. BBC News, "David Cameron Promises in/out Referendum on EU," BBC interview, January 23, 2013, http://www.bbc.com/news/uk-politics-21148282.

6. European Commission, "The Juncker Commission: A Strong and Experienced Team Standing for Change," press release, September 10, 2014, http://europa.eu/rapid/press-release_IP-14-984 _en.htm.

7. M. Dakers, "Europe Launches Blueprint for Capital Markets Union," *The Telegraph*, February 19, 2015.

8. Authority of the House of Lords, *The Post-Crisis EU Financial Regulatory Framework: Do the Pieces Fit?* (London: The Stationery Office Ltd., 5th Report of Session 2014–15, February 12, 2015), 16.

9. Among the many disputes over the last years, consider the recent decisions in cases C-270/12, *UK v Council and Parliament*, ECLI:EU:C:2014:18 (regarding ESMA's powers on short selling regulation); C-209/13, *UK v Council*, ECLI:EU:C:2014:283 (concerning enhanced cooperation for a Financial Transaction Tax); T-496/11, *UK v European Central Bank*, ECLI:EU:T:2015:133 (concerning the location of CCPs). A further case was eventually withdrawn: C-507/13, *UK v Council and Parliament* (concerning CRD IV).

10. Lucia Quaglia, *Governing Financial Services in the European Union: Banking, Securities and Post-Trading* (London: Routledge 2010).

11. See in more detail W.-G. Ringe, "Capital Markets Union for Europe: A Commitment to the Single Market of 28," *Law and Financial Markets Review* 9, no. 1 (2015): 5.

12. See Niamh Moloney, *EU Securities and Financial Markets Regulation*, 3rd ed. (Oxford: Oxford University Press, 2014), 122.

13. See also European Commission, *An Investment Plan for Europe* (Brussels: European Commission, COM [2014] 903 final, 2014), 15.

14. European Commission, *Green Paper*, 2.

15. As is well known, Londoners overwhelmingly voted in favor or remaining in the EU. See BBC, "EU Referendum: Most London Boroughs Vote to Remain," June 24, 2016, https://www .bbc.com/news/uk-politics-eu-referendum-36612916.

16. See, e.g., Evgeniia Iakhnis, Brian Rathbun, Jason Reifler and Thomas J. Scotto, "Populist Referendum: Was 'Brexit' an Expression of Nativist and Anti-elitist Sentiment?," *Research & Politics*, April–June 2018, 1–7.

17. See for my perspective on Brexit and financial services: W.-G. Ringe, "The Irrelevance of Brexit for the European Financial Market," *European Business Organization Law Review* 19, no. 1 (2018): 1–34.

18. See Danny Busch, "A Capital Markets Union for a Divided Europe," *Journal of Financial Regulation* 3, no. 2 (2017): 262.

19. David Howarth and Lucia Quaglia, "Brexit and the Single European Financial Market," *Journal of Common Market Studies* 55, no. S1 (2017): 149, 153.

20. Jim Brunsden, "UK's EU Commissioner Lord Hill Quits as British Departures Begin," *Financial Times*, June 26, 2016.

21. Jim Brunsden and Alex Barker, "City to Be Sidelined by Capital Markets Union Plan," *Financial Times*, June 30, 2016.

22. European Commission, *Capital Markets Union—Accelerating Reform* (Brussels: European Commission, COM [2016] 601 final, September 14, 2016), 7.

23. Lucia Quaglia, *Governing Financial Services in the European Union: Banking, Securities and Post-Trading* (London: Routledge, 2010). See also Sérgio Coimbra Henriques, "Capital

Markets Union: Towards Regulatory Harmonisation and Supervisory Convergence" (working paper, SSRN, 2017), https://ssrn.com/abstract=2983809.

24. Philipp Ständer, "What Will Happen with the Capital Markets Union after Brexit?" (Policy Paper 181, Jacques Delors Institute, Berlin, December 2016), 11.

25. Dirk Schoenmaker, "Stealing London's Financial Crown Would Bring Both Benefits and Responsibilities," *Bruegel* (blog), November 17, 2016, http://bruegel.org/2016/11/stealing-londons -financial-crown-would-bring-both-benefits-and-responsibilities/.

26. "France Turns Anglophone to Woo UK Businesses," *Financial Times*, September 28, 2016.

27. House of Lords European Union Committee, *Brexit: Financial Services* (London: Authority of the House of Lords, 9th report of session 2016–2017, HL Paper 81, December 15, 2016), para 37.

28. European Commission, *Communication on the Mid-Term Review of the Capital Markets Union Action Plan* (Brussels: European Commission, COM [2017] 292 final, June 2017), 2.

29. Jean-Claude Juncker et al., *The Five Presidents' Report: Completing Europe's Economic and Monetary Union* (Brussels: European Commission, 2015), https://ec.europa.eu/commission/sites /beta-political/files/5-presidents-report_en.pdf.

30. Paul de Grauwe, *Economics of Monetary Union*, 11th ed. (Oxford: Oxford University Press, 2016).

31. John H. Cochrane, "A Simple Test of Consumption Insurance," *Journal of Political Economy* 99, no. 5 (1991): 957.

32. Sebnem Kalemli-Ozcan, Bent E Sørensen, and Vadym Volosovych, "Deep Financial Integration and Volatility," *Journal of the European Economic Association* 12, no. 6 (2014): 1558–1585.

33. Mathias Hoffmann and Bent E Sørensen, "Don't Expect Too Much from EZ Fiscal Union— and Complete the Unfinished Integration of European Capital Markets!," *VoxEU* (CEPR Policy Portal), November 9, 2012.

34. Mario Draghi, "Rationale and Principles for Financial Union," speech, Twenty-Second Frankfurt European Banking Congress, Frankfurt am Main, November 23, 2012, https://www.ecb .europa.eu/press/key/date/2012/html/sp121123.en.html.

35. Pierfederico Asdrubali, Bent E Sørensen, and Oved Yosha, "Channels of Interstate Risk Sharing: United States 1963–1990," *Quarterly Journal of Economics* 111, no. 4 (1996): 1081–1110.

36. Stefano G Athanasoulis and Eric van Wincoop, "Risk Sharing within the United States: What Do Financial Markets and Fiscal Federalism Accomplish?," *Review of Economics and Statistics* 83, no. 4 (2001): 688–698; Faruk Balli, Syed Abul Basher, and Rosmy Jean Louis, "Channels of Risk-Sharing among Canadian Provinces: 1961–2006," *Empirical Economics* 43, no. 2 (2012): 763–787; Ralf Hepp and Jürgen von Hagen, "Interstate Risk Sharing in Germany: 1970–2006," *Oxford Economic Papers* 65, no. 1 (2013): 1–24.

37. Plamen Nikolov, "Cross-Border Risk Sharing after Asymmetric Shocks: Evidence from the Euro Area and the United States," *Quarterly Report on the Euro Area* 15, no. 2 (2016): 7–18.

38. The remaining 0.2% is related to cross-border labor compensation.

39. Diego Valiante, *Europe's Untapped Capital Market—Rethinking Financial Integration after the Crisis* (London: Rowman and Littlefield International, 2016).

40. Barry Eichengreen, "Is Europe an Optimum Currency Area?" (CEPR Discussion Paper No. 478, Center for Economic and Policy Research, Washington, DC, 1990); Milton Friedman, "The Euro: Monetary Unity to Political Disunity?" (Project Syndicate, 1997), https://www.project -syndicate.org/commentary/the-euro--monetary-unity-to-political-disunity.

41. In particular, the famous "5 Presidents Report": Juncker et al., *The Five Presidents' Report*.

42. See references in House of Lords European Union Committee, *Brexit*.

43. Falko Fecht, Hans Peter Grüner, and Philipp Hartmann, "Welfare Effects of Financial Integration" (Discussion Paper No. 11/2007, Deutsche Bundesbank, Frankfurt am Main, Germany, 2007).

Discussion: Keep Calm and Carry on ... with Small Steps!

Chris Thomale

In chapter 18, author Wolf-Georg Ringe's first main proposition intends to paint the capital markets union (CMU) as a mere Brexit avoidance device. This seems somewhat counterintuitive. Since when do financial politics "sell" well with the electorate? The average voter, one would assume, cares more about social politics such as immigration, social welfare, and the like, topics that have been very prominent during the Brexit vote. Having said that, Ringe highlights an important cognitive dissonance with regard to the CMU. If it were truly about financial integration, borne by the recital 5 of the Prospectus Regulation that "even small divergencies ... could result in significant impediments," why does the CMU not live up to this ambition rather than virtually carving out such important topics like civil prospectus liability, for which only a skeleton framework is provided without any substantive or choice of law rule to show? Hence, while the projected answer seems to merit further study, this question is even more justified: What is the CMU project really about? That is, what is its underlying political ambition, and is this ambition going to outlast Brexit? As of now, this feels hard to tell.

This takes us to the second main proposition, namely, that even in a post-Brexit European Union (EU) the CMU should move forward. Ringe even asks for a more ambitious version of institutional change and centralized institutions. A different view would be that, if the CMU was about Brexit avoidance, not only has it lost its original purpose but also it seems unapt to support the objective of political integration more generally. This is because the threat of current member states using their exit right under the Treaty on European Union, Article 50, is by no means over. Today's Brexit may become tomorrow's NLexit or SWexit. One of the centrifugal forces menacing the EU is precisely the stubbornness by which EU administration seems to cling to integration *sans frontières*, seemingly never giving up or even adapting an integrating project even in the face of public outrage. From this perspective, it may be unwise, even fatal, to follow through with or even deepen the CMU despite having failed its—alleged—political purpose.

As its third main proposition, the chapter argues that the CMU should serve as a reinforcement of the euro through cross-border redistribution. Admittedly, the reciprocal repercussions that common financial markets have on a common currency and vice versa seem rather straightforward. However, on a political level, one would object that such "rewiring" of the CMU to an economic monetary union (EMU) flies in the face of EU member states outside the EMU. Quite unfortunately, it is these countries, notably in the east, where anti-Brussels resentment is the highest. In fact, the fixation of the EU on an EMU may also have been the most pressing long-term factor isolating the United Kingdom inside the EU, eventually leading to Brexit. One should not take this problem lightly: Even if CMU+ is good for the euro, it may be bad for the EU. Another disadvantage of a hyperintegrated EU capital market lies in its regulatory latency. Effectively, harmonization drives out virtually any regulatory competition from EU capital markets. This would be less of a problem if such competition had come to an end and substantive convergence were afoot, leaving nothing but formal heterogeneities to overcome. To the contrary, however, the regulatory "market of markets" is just about to pick up steam—national regulators comparing their solutions for delisting, private vs. public enforcement of listing duties, and so on. Shutting down this dynamic would come at a significant "epistemological cost" that we cannot yet measure. So, even if it is desirable in the long run, full integration of capital markets may at least be premature.

19 The Institutions of Europe's Capital Markets Union

Valentina Allotti, Marcello Bianchi, and Stefano Micossi

The capital markets union (CMU) is a complex project entailing a host of markets, financial instruments, and legal and institutional dimensions. From the European Commission perspective, a single market for capital would contribute to two overarching objectives: (1) greater support to private and public investments through the development of a capital market architecture that supports all European countries and (2) a sustainable financial integration process able to stabilize and improve Europe's financial system (European Commission 2017a).

While Article 63 of the Treaty on the Functioning of the European Union (TFEU) provides for the full freedom of capital movements between member states, and between member states and third countries, we will show that in practice this freedom is ensured more for portfolio investments and much less for real direct investment. Indeed, the rationale underlying company law harmonization directives was fear that freedom of establishment could unleash an undesirable race to the bottom in corporate law and business arrangements. In this regard, most member states hang on to a "real seat" legal doctrine entailing that the applicable corporate law would be that of the main center of the company's commercial and financial operations. Under this doctrine, the legal seat and the main operations of a company must coincide, potentially limiting company mobility and freedom of establishment.

Two themes blend and intermingle in the CMU action plan. One is capital market reform, with the development of nonbank market segments that appear largely underdeveloped; the other is cross-border capital market integration. In this regard, most of the initiatives undertaken to date have been aimed more at improving national markets and much less at fostering cross-border transactions. Thus, the new prospectus regulation has distinctly failed to allow issuers to choose where to list their equities—a decision reflecting national resistances to fuller capital market integration.

It is important to keep in mind that the European Union (EU) does not have general regulatory powers but normally acts, with the specific legal bases provided for by the treaties, to remove specific barriers to cross-border transactions in the internal market.

As we shall see, over time the Court of Justice of the European Union (ECJ) has opened ever-broader breaches into the closed walls of the real seat doctrine, de facto turning the European company law system into an "incorporation" system whereby the applicable company law is determined by the place of legal incorporation. However, the tension between the two legal systems has not abated, reflecting continuing member states' resistance to real integration of capital markets.

In this chapter we concentrate on key capital market institutions hindering effective integration of "real" capital markets—that is, the cross-border flows of direct investment going well beyond the sheer freedom of portfolio investment. To this end, after a brief review of the evidence on the functioning of the EU market for corporate control, we will analyze the takeover directive; golden shares, or public powers to limit private autonomy in the public interest; the rules for cross-border company mobility; the European Company Statute; and the obstacles to supervisory convergence that continue to hinder the establishment of a level playing field in European capital markets. Our conclusions follow.

The European Market for Corporate Control

Although in principle the member states normally cannot legally block any transactions based on the acquirers' nationality, governments in continental Europe have used various legal and de facto powers to create obstacles to foreign-driven transactions while supporting domestic transactions aimed at creating so-called national champions.

A study by Dinc and Erel (2013) analyzes large corporate merger attempts in the EU between 1997 and 2006, and finds that supporting actions are often undertaken by national governments for domestically driven transactions, while opposing actions are undertaken to counter foreign acquisitions. The study also finds that the widespread nationalistic approach in continental Europe has had a general depressing effect on the European market for merger and acquisition.

A counterbalancing role may be played by European institutions, and notably the European Commission, which have powers to sanction discriminatory measures in contrast with the European legal framework. The study reports that when the Commission challenges individual countries initiatives that impede the free flow of capital, the foreign-driven transactions are more likely to succeed. The problem is that such interventions by the European Commission are not systematic, especially due to the highly charged political nature of the operations.

The Takeover Directive

A missed opportunity to change this scenario was the adoption of the Takeover Directive in 2004.[1] The proposal for a harmonized legal framework for takeovers in the EU aimed at facilitating hostile bids while ensuring transparency and adequate protection of minority shareholders.

To facilitate the bid, the directive included two key provisions: the board neutrality rule, which reserves the decision on the bid, including any defensive measure, to the shareholders; and the breakthrough rule, which provides that any restrictions—statutory or contractual—to the transfer of shares be lifted after the bid.

As to the potential impact of the breakthrough rule, at the time of the directive, negotiations about 1,000 European listed companies out of 5,000 had in place dual-class shares (Bennedsen and Nielsen 2002).

Strong opposition by some member states (especially Germany) eventually led to a watered-down directive through provisions that, while maintaining the board neutrality and breakthrough rules as the default rules, allow the member states and the companies the option not to abide by them. The framework was made even more complicated by linking such system of options to a principle of "reciprocity" whereby the two rules do not apply to the target company when they are not respected by the bidding company. The principle of reciprocity represents a blatant violation of internal market rules and, in addition, may give rise to considerable uncertainty of application in individual cases, as it is open to political interpretations. In practice, the directive offered the member states the opportunity to maintain preexisting national rules (in fifteen out of twenty-eight states representing two-thirds of the total market capitalization), and in seven states (representing some 30% of total market capitalization) it led to the introduction of reciprocity rules.

Thus, it is not surprising that several European cross-border bids have been opposed, often successfully, by the governments of the target company (Powell, Prendergast, and Sharma 2017).[2] More generally, several studies found that the share of European cross-border deals slightly decreased in the post-directive period, notably for hostile bids (Drobetz and Momtaz 2016).

Article 20 of the directive provides that, five years after the transposition deadline, the European Commission should examine the directive "in the light of the experience acquired in applying it and, if necessary, propose its revision." The Commission published its report in June 2012 (European Commission 2012); the European Parliament reacted with its resolution in March 2013 (European Parliament 2013). Both institutions concluded, against the evidence, that the regime created by the directive was working satisfactorily, and to date no legislative procedure has been initiated to amend the legislation.

Golden Shares

In the 1980s and 1990s many governments accompanied the privatization of state-owned companies with legal and statutory rules leaving them special rights—so-called golden shares—to block certain decisions and share transactions deemed in contrast with the public interest.

These special rights can take different forms: caps on shareholdings, including limits on the maximum number of shares that may be held by foreigners; need for approval by a public authority of share purchases beyond a certain threshold; right to appoint members of the company's board outside the general meeting; right to approve or veto certain management decisions such as mergers and acquisitions or the disposal of strategically important assets; and limitations of private investors' voting rights.

The ECJ addressed the issue of the compatibility of golden shares and the privatization laws of different member states with the freedom of capital movement in several decisions adopted in the early 2000s.[3]

Accordingly, the compliance of golden shares with European law should be assessed on the basis of a four-step test, whereby golden shares must (1) be justified by overriding consideration in general interest; (2) be nondiscriminatory on the basis of nationality; (3) be exercised on the basis of publicly known criteria established in advance; and (4) be proportionate—that is, the objective that they pursue could not be attained by less restrictive measures. Economic justifications are in general not recognized as legitimate.[4] In subsequent decisions, the ECJ also clarified that even the special powers adopted through private legal instruments (e.g., the articles of association of the company) or under the general company law are not compatible with the TFEU when the member state has introduced them in his capacity as a public authority.[5] Many special rights have been abolished or modified to ensure their compatibility with EU rules.

In a decision in 2013 (the *Essent* case),[6] the ECJ also stated that the neutrality principle set forth in Article 345 of the TFEU—whereby the treaties shall in no way prejudice the rules in member states "governing the system of property ownership"—also protects the prohibition of privatization.[7] It follows from this decision that member states may legitimately establish or maintain a body of rules mandating the public ownership of certain undertakings. At the same time, the ECJ indicated that member states cannot act in disregard of the free movement of capital. Accordingly, the prohibition of privatization falls within the scope of Article 63 of the TFEU and must be examined in the light of that article.

The application of these legal principles, however, has been undermined by various decisions by member states limiting the freedom of capital flows and the right of establishment based on ill-defined grounds of public and strategic interest that continue to give rise to legal controversies that are settled by ECJ decisions, only with long delays.

Cross-Border Company Mobility

Cross-border company mobility—which rests on the freedom of establishment—is a key element for overcoming market fragmentation and economic nationalism. It can be achieved either through the transfer of the legal seat in a different member state or via a cross-border merger. The latter has been the object of an EU directive that was adopted in 2005 and took effect in 2007 (European Commission 2005) that set up a harmonized procedure addressing also the issue of workers' involvement. According to a study commissioned by the European Commission (Bech-Bruun and Lexidale 2013), the directive elicited a wave of cross-border mergers: between 2008 and 2012, cross-border mergers increased by 173%, from 132 in 2008 to 361 in 2012. And yet the study identifies many obstacles to the full operation of the directive, such as the incomplete harmonization of national rules on cross-border mergers, uneven safeguards for stakeholders, and lack of fast-track procedures for intragroup operations.

A clear legal framework for the transfer of the legal seat is still missing. Originally, the TFEU did not intervene to settle potential conflicts between national corporate laws but encouraged member states to enter negotiations with each other with a view to securing the mutual recognition of companies, the retention of legal personality in the event of transfer of their seat from one country to another, and the possibility of mergers between companies governed by laws of different countries. Accordingly, in 1968 the member states signed a "Convention on the Mutual Recognition of Companies and Bodies Corporate" that, however, did not enter into force as the Netherlands did not ratify it (Gelter 2017). In the ensuing years, the attempts at creating a general legal framework for company law was not pursued any further while few harmonization directives (e.g., on the disclosure of company documents, capital requirements, domestic mergers and divisions, accounting, and so on) improved matters marginally.

Starting in 1999, with the landmark decision in the *Centros* case,[8] the ECJ decisions on the freedom of establishment have progressively liberalized the choice of the place of incorporation of companies, thus fostering company mobility. In *Centros*, the ECJ affirmed that companies can be incorporated in any member state, even if their sole establishment—where their whole activity is carried out—is in another member state. The *Centros* doctrine was lately confirmed by the *Uberseering*[9] and *Inspire Art* decisions.[10] With *Cartesio* (2008)[11] and *VALE* (2012),[12] the ECJ acknowledged that freedom of establishment encompasses the right of a company to convert into a company governed by the law of another member state (i.e., to transfer the legal seat with a change of the applicable law), provided that the conditions laid down by the host state are satisfied, including the test adopted to determine the connecting factor with its national legal order. In its most recent decision of October 25, 2017, in the *Polbud* case,[13] the ECJ upheld the legitimacy of a cross-border "conversion" by way of a mere transfer of the registered office without any activity in the country of arrival. In all cases, the ECJ found national restrictions on these firms' operations to be in violation of the freedom of establishment (Mucciarelli 2017).

According to Gerner-Beuerle et al. (2017), the decisions of the ECJ on the freedom of establishment have had relatively limited effect and have not led to a "race to the bottom."

While the ECJ decisions have gone a long way in undermining the real seat doctrine, this has not reduced the need for a general EU legal framework. Significant legal uncertainty continues to surround cross-border conversions, and the definition of the connecting factor that determines the national law applicable to a company remains in the hands of member states.

True, a transfer of the legal seat may be achieved following the cross-border merger directive by merging the company to be transferred with a shell company in the host member state that then performs all the activities of the old company. However, this operation is less efficient and more onerous than a cross-border conversion, requiring as it does the formation of a new company in the host member state. Therefore, the possibility to implement a de facto cross-border conversion through an alternative instrument provides yet another reason to adopt legislation directly covering the transfer of the legal seat (European Parliament 2016; Gerner-Beuerle et al. 2016; Hopt 2015; Mucciarelli 2017).

In April 2018, the European Commission presented a comprehensive Company Law Package that also includes the transfer of legal seat via cross-border conversion. The procedure appears very cumbersome and seems based on a strong prejudice against conversion, which is described as a mere artificial arrangement aimed at obtaining undue tax advantages or at unduly prejudicing the legal or contractual rights of employees, creditors, or minority members. As a result, stringent requirements are introduced to ensure that the company is validly established in the destination member state.

The European Company Statute

The adoption of a uniform legal structure for companies carrying out their business cross-border, based on a European regulation directly applicable in all member states, was long considered a valuable tool to support the integration and mobility of companies.

The European Company Statute, also referred to as an SE after its Latin name *Societas Europaea*, was approved by the European Council and Parliament in 2001, after more than thirty years of negotiations. The long negotiations and the solution eventually agreed upon provide clear testimony of the paramount role played by labor market arrangements in limiting the cross-border integration of company operations. The SE was originally conceived to allow companies to operate cross-border throughout the EU with common accounting and taxation rules; the former was eventually adopted for the consolidated accounts of listed companies—that is, the International Financial Reporting Standards—and the latter is still the subject of negotiations.

An SE cannot be set up from scratch but may only be created by transformation, merger, acquisition, or creation of a common subsidiary, of existing companies previously established in different EU countries. The regulation provides common rules for minimum capital, the option between a dual and a monistic governing board, and the transfer of legal seat; all other aspects of corporate governance are left to national rules under a general regime of mutual recognition. The legal seat must be placed in the location of the central administration or of the main operations of the companies involved. Two models of workers' involvement in company administration are envisioned. In no case could the creation of an SE lead to a diminution of existing workers' rights within one of the companies involved.

After a slow start, the number of SEs has grown buoyantly: the European Trade Union Institute's[14] European Company Database shows 121 SEs at the end of 2007, 633 at the end of 2010, and 2,757 at the end of the first quarter of 2017. Most SEs (over 80%) were created with a subsidiary; merger and transformations of two separate companies have been few. Most SEs were established in the Czech Republic (1898, or some 69% of the total), with 411 in Germany and 123 in Slovakia. The numbers are much smaller in the rest of the EU (42 in the United Kingdom and typically below 40 in the other main countries). The transfer of legal seats has been rare, owing also to the fact that the legal seat must coincide with the main center of activity. All in all, the highly skewed geographical concentration of SEs seems to point to a context-specific usefulness. The SE can hardly be considered as a success.

An attempt was also made to adopt a regulation for the creation of a European Private Limited Company with a proposal published in 2008 (European

Commission 2008). This proposal was intended to offer small and medium-sized enterprises an instrument facilitating their cross-border activities that would be simple, flexible, and uniform in all member states. Despite strong support from the business community, so far it has proved impossible to find a compromise allowing for the unanimous adoption of the statute by the member states.

Fragmented Supervisory Powers

A fundamental pillar of the European strategy for the integration of capital markets is the convergence of supervisory approaches. These play a paramount role in ensuring that the common rules are uniformly applied and that there is little room for an opportunistic use of discretionary powers by national authorities to protect national interests.

The convergence of supervisory practices entails a gradual buildup of institutional procedures and cultural attitudes under the constraints imposed by the EU Treaties on delegated powers, as interpreted by the ECJ with its *Meroni* and *Romano* judgments.[15]

The first step in this process was the creation in 2001 of the Committee of European Securities Regulators (CESR)[16] as part of the Lamfalussy financial regulatory framework (Lamfalussy et al. 2001). CESR was essentially a network of the national supervisory authorities, with little legal and functional autonomy.

An improved convergence of regulatory standards was expected to come from the transformation of CESR into the European Securities and Market Authority (ESMA), which was set up as an EU body with legal personality and was entrusted with binding powers to develop common implementing standards of the single rulebook for capital markets. Furthermore, ESMA was also identified as a single supervisor for a small set of market participants (credit rating agencies and trade repositories)—a potential harbinger of further transfers of powers.

However, these changes in practice have not changed the very nature of ESMA as a network of national supervisory authorities due to the composition of its governing bodies and its decision-making procedures, still based on the principle of national representation. A useful model for reform is provided by the European Central Bank, where a "management board" independent of national authorities and composed of independent and highly qualified individuals acts as an executive board, setting the agenda and preparing substantive decisions, while the representative of national central banks only intervenes in a broader "governing council" that is called upon to ratify the proposals of the management board. Moreover, the reform in decision making should also address the other relevant threat to supervisory neutrality in respect of national interests—that is, the discretion national authority can exercise in case of large cross-border transactions. A recent proposal by the European Commission for a review of the Regulation on European Supervisory Authorities offers the opportunity to move forward on this front (European Commission 2017b).

Conclusions

We have shown in this chapter that, despite significant legislative and jurisprudential advancements, we are still far away from the creation of an integrated capital market in the EU. Market fragmentation has not been overcome due to persistent strong resistance by the member states. Existing legal arrangements continue to hinder a functioning market for corporate control and an efficient company mobility cross-border.

The CMU project, launched by the European Commission to accelerate the creation of a single pan-European capital market, has failed so far to attack the key impediments to market integration. Most of the initiatives of the CMU turn around the negotiation of ever more complex harmonizing rules while sidelining the measures capable of opening the way to cross-border transactions—that is, the freedom to choose where to place an IPO.

A fundamental step in that direction could be the establishment of a single authorization and supervisory mechanism managed by ESMA for market transactions with transnational dimension or for the intention of appealing to a pan-European investors base.

Notes

1. European Commission 2004. The directive was approved after some fourteen years of discussion since the initial proposal by the European Commission.

2. The study, covering the main cross-border bids in Europe from 1990 to 2013 that have been opposed by the government of the target company's country, finds that more than half of those bids failed.

3. Case Commission v. Italy (C-58–99; EU:C: 2000:280), May 23, 2000; Case Commission v. France (C-483/99; EU:C:2002:327), June 4, 2002; Case Commission v. Belgium (Case C-503/99; EU: C: 2002: 328), June 4, 2002; Case Commission v. Portugal (C-367/98; EU: C: 2002: 326), June 4, 2002.

4. The Belgian legislation on special powers—which was cleared in a decision of 2002—was found to meet this test and be compatible with the free movement of capital. C-503/99, Commission/Belgium—Judgment of the Court, June 4, 2002.

5. Case Commission v. United Kingdom (C-98/01; EU: C: 2003: 273), May 13, 2003; see also Case Commission v. Germany (C-112/05; EU: C: 2007: 323), October 23, 2007; Case Federcon-

sumatori and Others (C-463/04) and Associazione Azionariato Diffuso dell'AEM SpA and Others (C-464/04) v. Comune di Milano (C-463/04 and C-464/04; EU: C: 2007: 752), December 6, 2007.

6. Case Staat der Nederlanden v. Essent NV (C-105/12), Essent Nederland BV (C-105/12), Eneco Holding NV (C-106/12), and Delta NV (C-107/12) (C-105/12, C-106/12, C-107/12; EU: C: 2013: 677), October 22, 2013.

7. A law of the Netherlands requires that shares held in an electricity or gas distribution system operator must be held, directly or indirectly, by the public authorities identified by the national legislation.

8. Case Centros (C-212/97; EU:C:1999:126), March 9, 1999.

9. Case Uberseering (C-208/00; EU:C: 2002:632), November 5, 2002.

10. Case Inspire Art (C-167/01; EU:C: 2003:512), September 30, 2003.

11. Case Cartesio (C-210/06; EU:C: 2008:723), December 16, 2008.

12. Case VALE (C-378/10; EU:C: 2012:440), July 12, 2012.

13. Case Polbud (C-106/16; EU:C: 2017:804), October 25, 2017.

14. European Trade Union Institute independent research and training centre of the European Trade Union Confederation (ETUC).

15. Case Meroni (C-9/56; EU:C: 1958:7), June 13, 1958; Case Romano (C-98/80; EU:C:1981:104), May 14, 1981.

16. European Commission 2001 (repealed by Commission Decision 2009/71/EC).

References

Bech-Bruun and Lexidale. 2013. *Study on the Application of the Cross-Border Mergers Directive for the European Commission, Directorate General for the Internal Market and Services.* Luxembourg: Publications of the European Union, September.

Bennedsen, M., and K. M. Nielsen. 2002. "The Impact of a Break-Through Rule on European Firms." Center for Economic and Business Discussion Paper, September 4.

Dinc, S. I., and I. Erel. 2013. "Economic Nationalism in Mergers and Acquisitions." *Journal of Finance* 68, no. 6 (December).

Drobetz, W., and P. P. Momtaz. 2016. "Corporate Governance Convergence in the European M&A Market." HFRC Working Paper Series No. 17, Hamburg Financial Research Center, January.

European Commission. 1997. "Communication on Certain Legal Aspects concerning Intra-EU Investment (97/C220/06)." *Official Journal* C220, 19/07/1997, 15–18.

European Commission. 2001. "Commission Decision of 6 June 2001 Establishing the Committee of European Securities Regulators." *Official Journal of the European Communities* L191/43, July 13.

European Commission. 2004. "Directive 2004/25/EC of the European Parliament and of the Council of 21 April 2004 on Takeover Bids." *Official Journal of the European Union* L142/12, April 30.

European Commission. 2005. "Directive 2005/56/EC of the European Parliament and of the Council of 26 October 2005 on Cross-Border Mergers of Limited Liability Companies." *Official Journal of the European Union* L310/1, November 25.

European Commission. 2008. *Proposal for a Regulation on the Statute of a European Private Company.* Brussels: European Commission, COM (2008) 396 final, June 25.

European Commission. 2012. *Report to the European Parliament, the Council, the European Economic and Social Committee and the Committee of the Regions on the Application of Directive 2004/25/EC on Takeover Bids.* Brussels: European Commission, COM (2012) 347 final, June 28.

European Commission. 2017a. *Economic Analysis Accompanying the Document "Communication from the Commission to the European Parliament, the Council, the European Economic and*

Social Committee and the Committee of the Regions on the Mid-Term Review of the Capital Markets Union Action Plan." Commission Staff Working Document SWD (2017) 224 final, June 8. Brussels: European Commission.

European Commission. 2017b. *Proposal for a Regulation Amending the European Supervisory Authorities.* Brussels: European Commission, COM (2017) 536 final (2017/0230/COD), September 20.

European Parliament. 2013. *Report on the Application of Directive 2004/25/EC on Takeover Bids (2012/2262(INI)).* Brussels: European Parliament, March 25.

European Parliament. 2016. "Cross-Border Mergers and Divisions, Transfers of Seat: Is There a Need to Legislate?" Brussels: European Parliament, Study for the JURI Committee, June.

Gelter, M. 2017. "EU Company Harmonization between Convergence and Varieties of Capitalism." ECGI Law Working Paper No. 355/2017, European Corporate Governance Institute, June.

Gerner-Beuerle, C., F. M. Mucciarelli, E. Schuster, and M. M. Siems. 2017. "Why Do Businesses Incorporate in Other EU Member States? An Empirical Analysis on the Role of Conflict of Laws Rules." ECGI Law Working Paper No. 361/2017, European Corporate Governance Institute, June.

Gerner-Beuerle, C., F. M. Mucciarelli, E. Schuster, M. M. Siems, and LSE Enterprise. 2016. *Study on the Law Applicable to Companies.* Luxembourg: Publications of the European Union, June.

Hopt, K. J. 2015. "Corporate Governance in Europe: A Critical Review of the European Commission's Initiatives on Corporate Law and Corporate Governance." ECGI Law Working Paper No. 296/2015, European Corporate Governance Institute, August.

Juncker, J. C., D. Tusk, J. Dijsselbloem, M. Draghi, and M. Schulz. 2015. *Completing Europe's Economic and Monetary Union.* Luxembourg: European Commission, June 22.

Lamfalussy, A., C. Herkströter, L. A. Rojo, B. Ryden, L. Spaventa, N. Walter, and N. Wicks. 2001. *Final Report of the Committee of the Wise Men on the Regulation of European Securities Markets.* Brussels: European Commission, February 15.

Mucciarelli, F.M. 2017. "The Last Word on Cross-Border Re-incorporations? EU Freedom of Establishment after the CJEU's Judgment in Polbud." *Oxford Business Law Blog.* University of Oxford, November 20. https://www.law.ox.ac.uk/business-law-blog/blog/2017/11/last-word-cross-border-reincorporations-eu-freedom-establishment.

Powell, R., S. Prendergast, and R. Sharma. 2017. "The Impact of Economic Nationalism in Europe on the Returns to Rivals of Cross-Border M&A Bids." Paper presented at the Thirtieth Australian Finance and Banking Conference, October 10.

Contributors

Sumit Agarwal
Georgetown University

Ugo Albertazzi
European Central Bank

Franklin Allen
Imperial College London

Valentina Allotti
Assonime

Gene Amromin
Federal Reserve Bank of Chicago

John Armour
University of Oxford

Geert Bekaert
Columbia University

Itzhak Ben-David
Ohio State University

Marcello Bianchi
Assonime

Lorenzo Bini Smaghi
Société Générale

Claudio Borio
Bank for International Settlements

Franziska Bremus
German Institute for Economic Research (DIW Berlin)

Marina Brogi
Sapienza University of Rome

Claudia M. Buch
Deutsche Bundesbank

Giacomo Calzolari
University of Bologna, European University Institute, and Centro Studi Luca d'Agliano

Souphala Chomsisengphet
US Office of the Comptroller of the Currency

Luca Enriques
University of Oxford

Douglas D. Evanoff
Federal Reserve Bank of Chicago

Ester Faia
Goethe University Frankfurt

Eilis Ferran
University of Cambridge

Jeffrey N. Gordon
Columbia Law School

Michael Haliassos
Goethe University Frankfurt

Campbell R. Harvey
Duke University

Kathryn Judge
Columbia Law School

Susanne Kalss
Vienna University of Economics and Business

Valentina Lagasio
Sapienza University of Rome

Katja Langenbucher
Goethe University Frankfurt

Christian T. Lundblad
University of North Carolina, Chapel Hill

Massimo Marchesi
European Commission

Michala Marcussen
Société Générale

Alexander Michaelides
Imperial College London

Stefano Micossi
Assonime

Emanuel Moench
Deutsche Bundesbank and Goethe University Frankfurt

Mario Nava
European Commission

Giorgio Barba Navaretti
University of Milan and Centro Studi Luca d'Agliano

Giovanna Nicodano
University of Toronto

Gianmarco Ottaviano
Bocconi University and Centro Studi Luca d'Agliano

Marco Pagano
University of Naples Federico II

Monica Paiella
University of Naples Parthenope

Ľuboš Pástor
University of Chicago Booth School of Business

Alain Pietrancosta
Sorbonne Law School, University of Paris

Richard Portes
London Business School

Alberto Franco Pozzolo
University of Molise and Centro Studi Luca d'Agliano

Wolf-Georg Ringe
University of Hamburg

Stephan Siegel
University of Washington, Seattle

Chris Thomale
Heidelberg University

Diego Valiante
European Commission

Index

Printed in the United States
by Baker & Taylor Publisher Services